HOWE·LIBRARY
HANOVER
NEW HAMPSHIRE

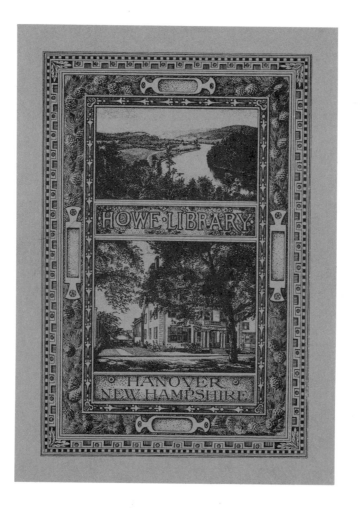

American Widow

American

Widow

Alissa Torres

Illustrated by Sungyoon Choi

Villard V New York

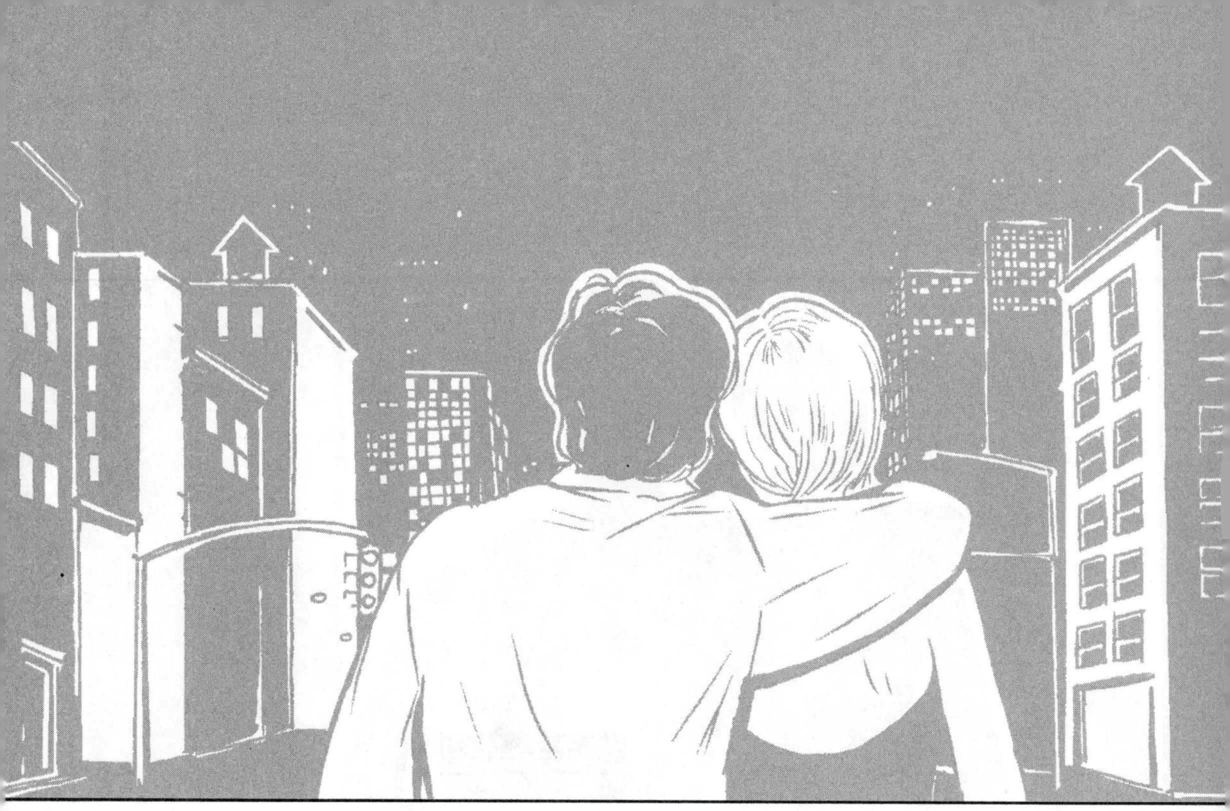

American Widow is a work of nonfiction. Some names and identifying details have been changed.

Published in the United States by Villard Books, an imprint of The Random House Publishing Group, a division of Random House, Inc., New York.

VILLARD and "V" CIRCLED Design are registered trademarks of Random House, Inc.

Library of Congress-in-Publication Date

Torres, Alissa.
American widow / Alissa Torres ; illustrated by Sungyoon Choi.
p. cm.
ISBN 978-0-345-50069-4 (hardcover)
1. Torres, Alissa. 2. Widows—New York (State)—New York—Biography—Comic books, strips, etc. 3. September 11 Terrorist Attacks, 2001— Biography—Comic books, strips, etc. I. Choi, Sungyoon, illustrator.
II. Title
HV6432.7.T67 2008
974.7'1044092—dc22
[B]

2008008396

Printed in the United States of America on acid-free paper

www.villard.com

9 8 7 6 5 4 3 2 1

First Edition

Everything the people of Beslan thought they knew about living, his aunt said, had changed. She rubbed bits of the filament of eggshell onto the boy's blisters and burns, and said the lesson was indelible: "We never knew how happy we were."

"52 Hours of Horror and Death for Captives at Russian School," by C. J. Chivers, *The New York Times*, September 4, 2004.

American Widow

Chapter One

SEPTEMBER 11, 2001

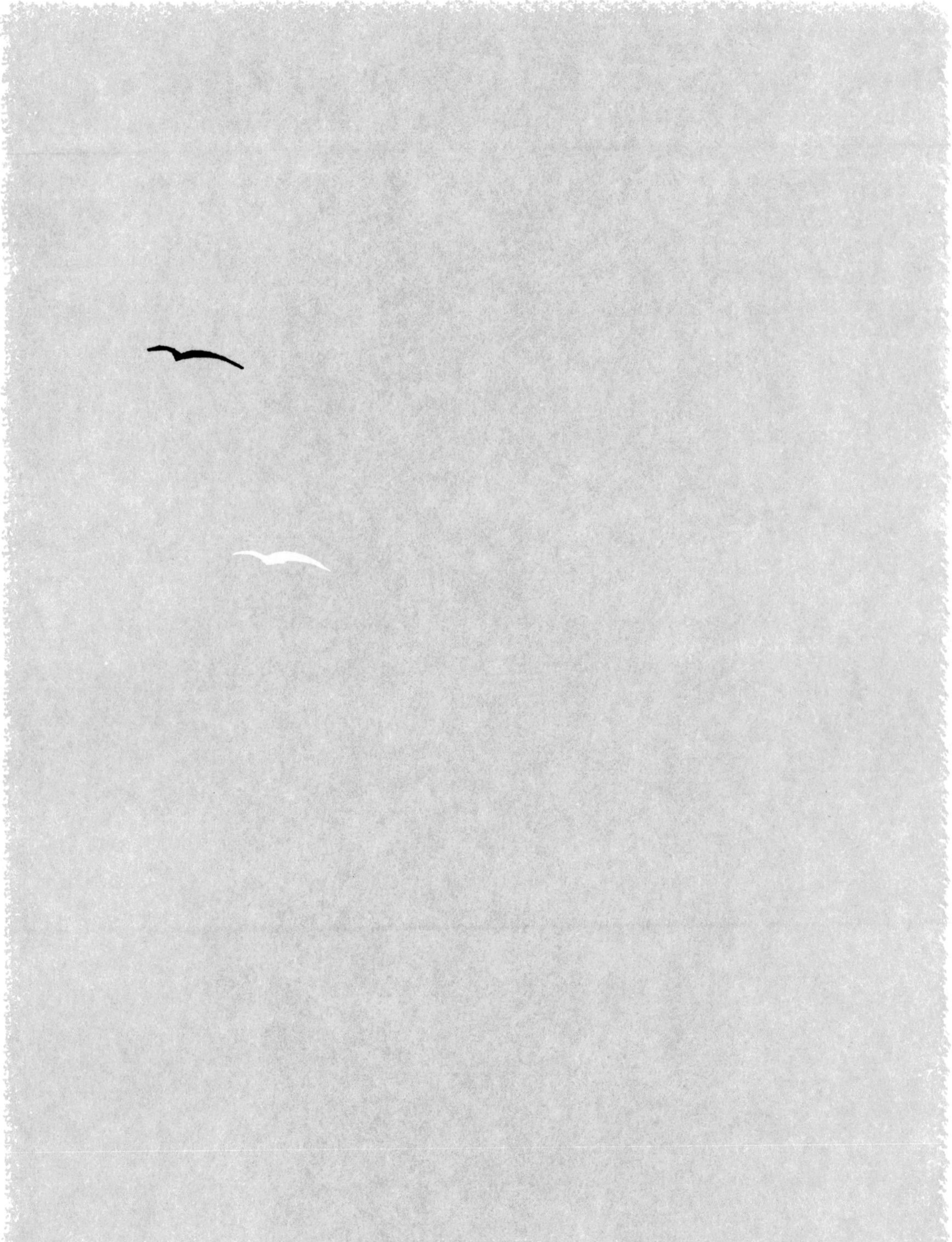

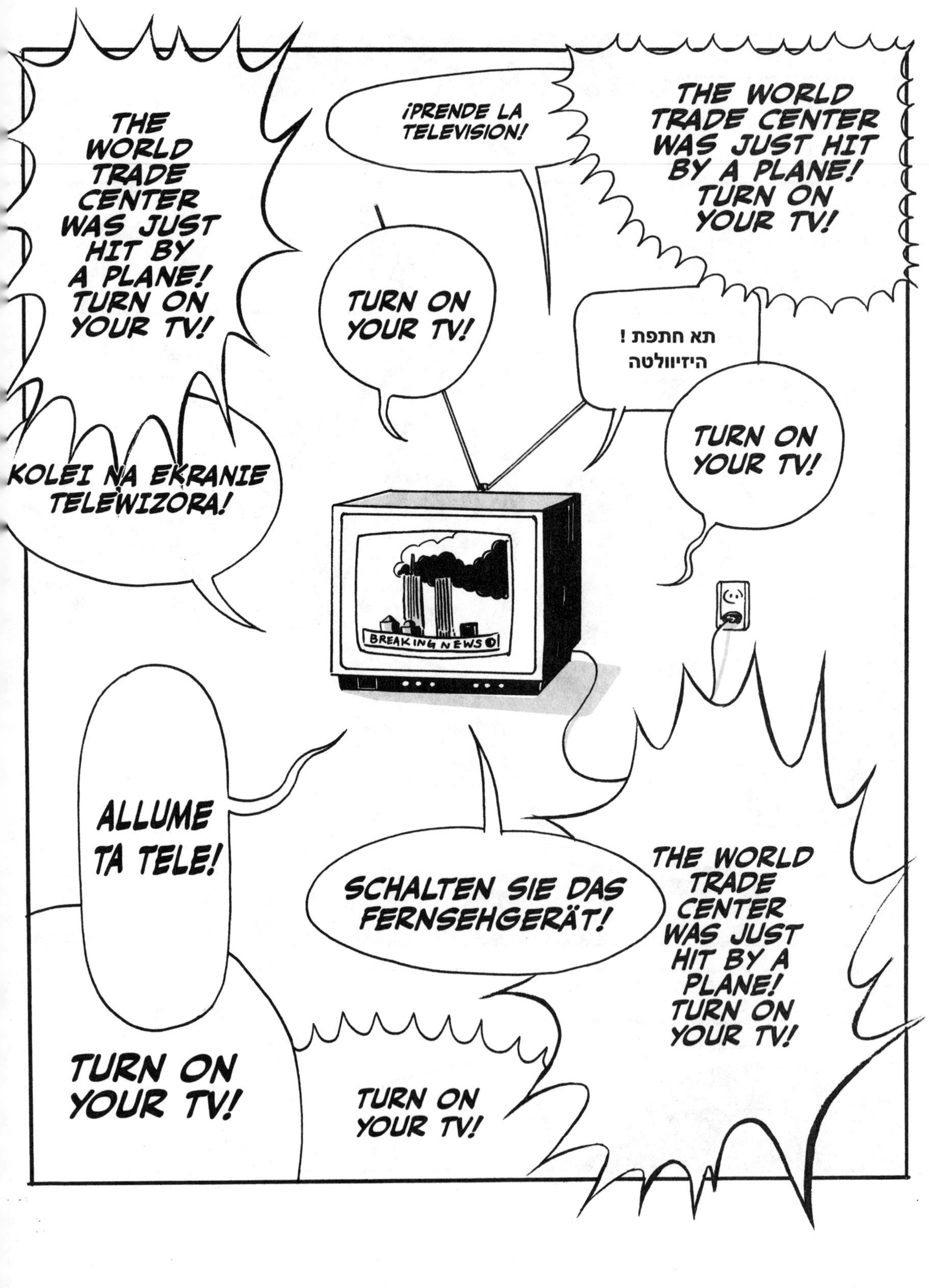
THE WORLD TRADE CENTER WAS JUST HIT BY A PLANE! TURN ON YOUR TV!
¡PRENDE LA TELEVISION!
THE WORLD TRADE CENTER WAS JUST HIT BY A PLANE! TURN ON YOUR TV!
TURN ON YOUR TV!
תא חתפת ! היזיוולטה
TURN ON YOUR TV!
KOLEI NA EKRANIE TELEWIZORA!
BREAKING NEWS
ALLUME TA TELE!
SCHALTEN SIE DAS FERNSEHGERÄT!
THE WORLD TRADE CENTER WAS JUST HIT BY A PLANE! TURN ON YOUR TV!
TURN ON YOUR TV!
TURN ON YOUR TV!

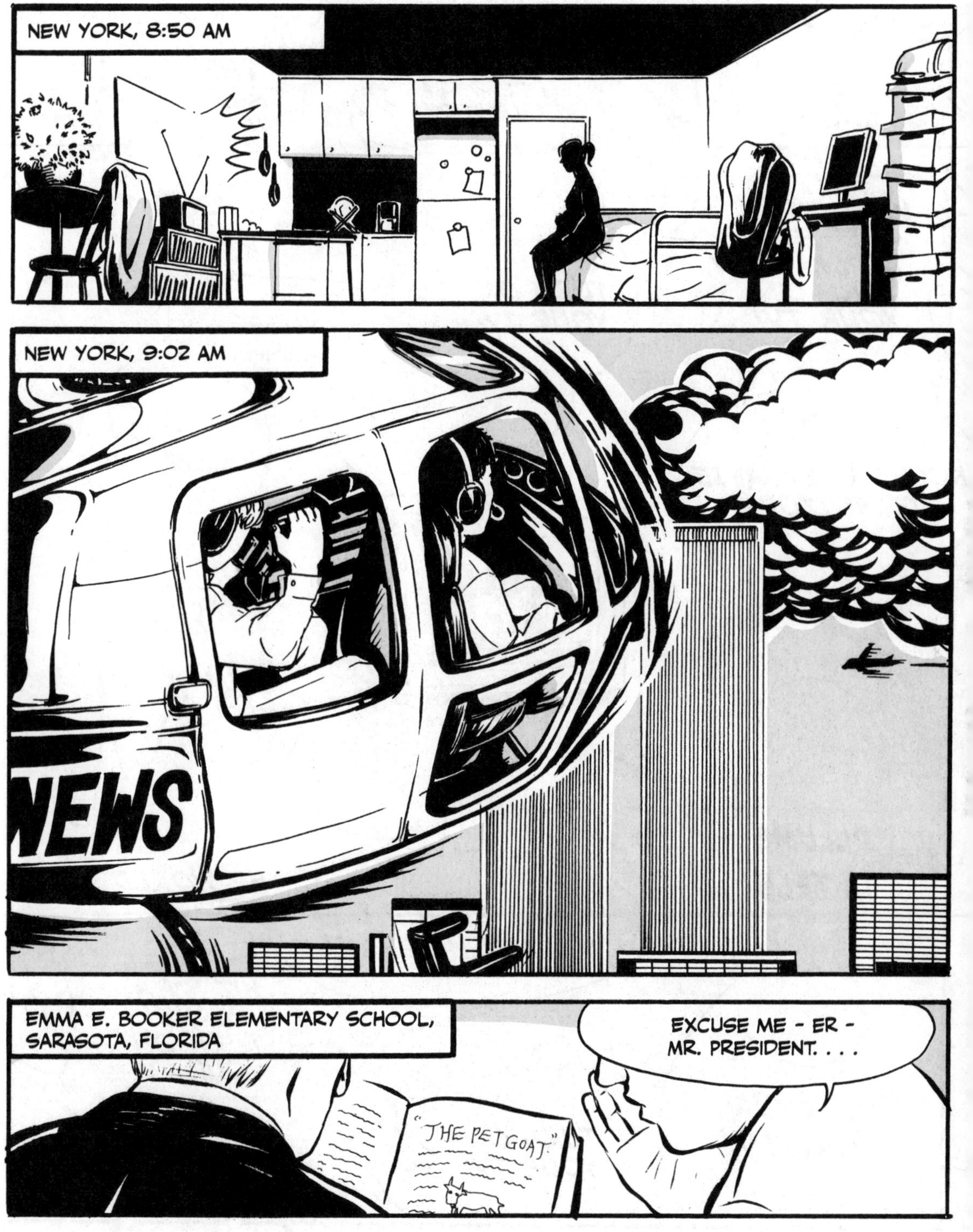
NEW YORK, 8:50 AM
NEW YORK, 9:02 AM
NEWS
EMMA E. BOOKER ELEMENTARY SCHOOL, SARASOTA, FLORIDA
EXCUSE ME - ER - MR. PRESIDENT. . . .
"THE PET GOAT"

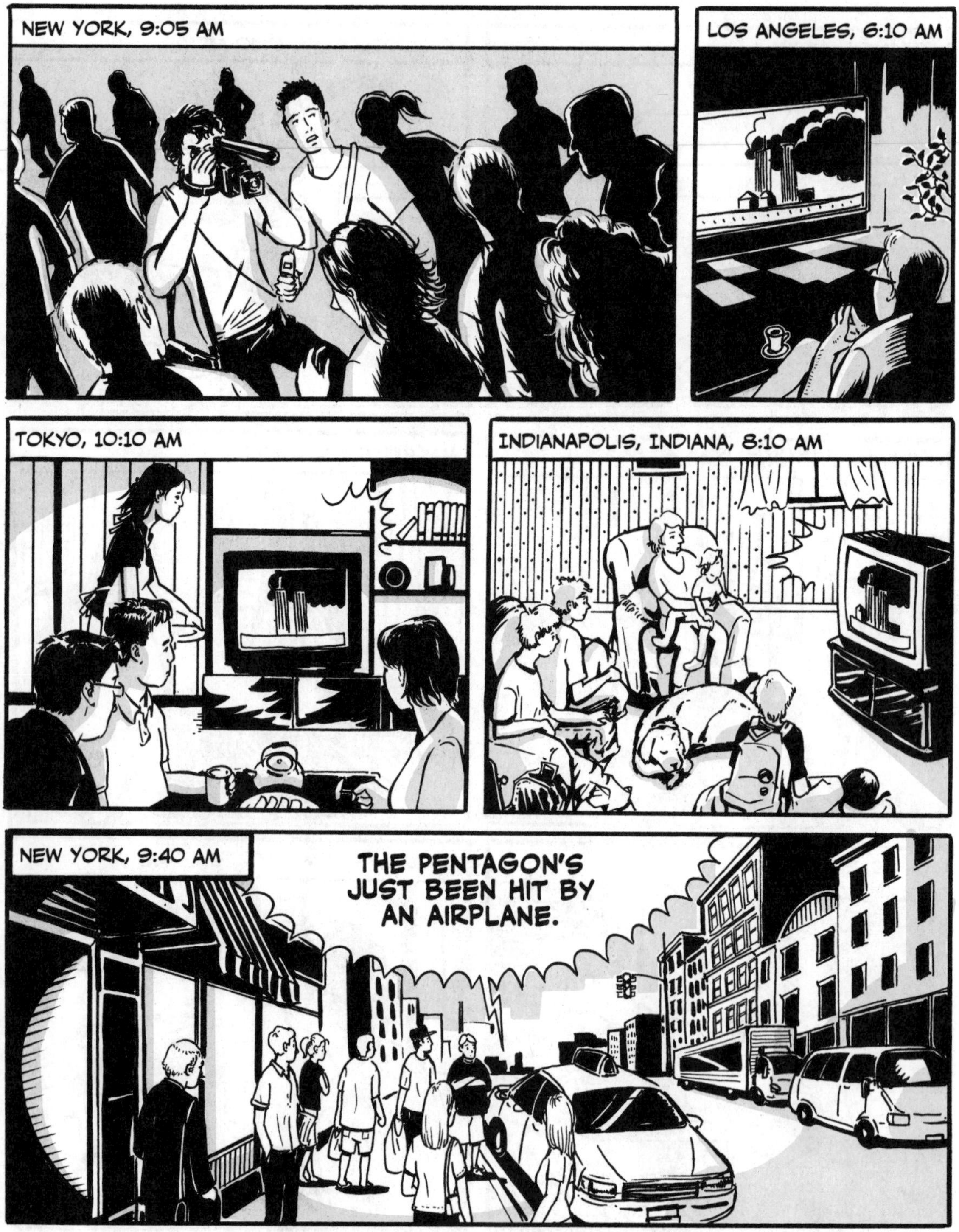
NEW YORK, 9:05 AM
LOS ANGELES, 6:10 AM
TOKYO, 10:10 AM
INDIANAPOLIS, INDIANA, 8:10 AM
NEW YORK, 9:40 AM
THE PENTAGON'S JUST BEEN HIT BY AN AIRPLANE.

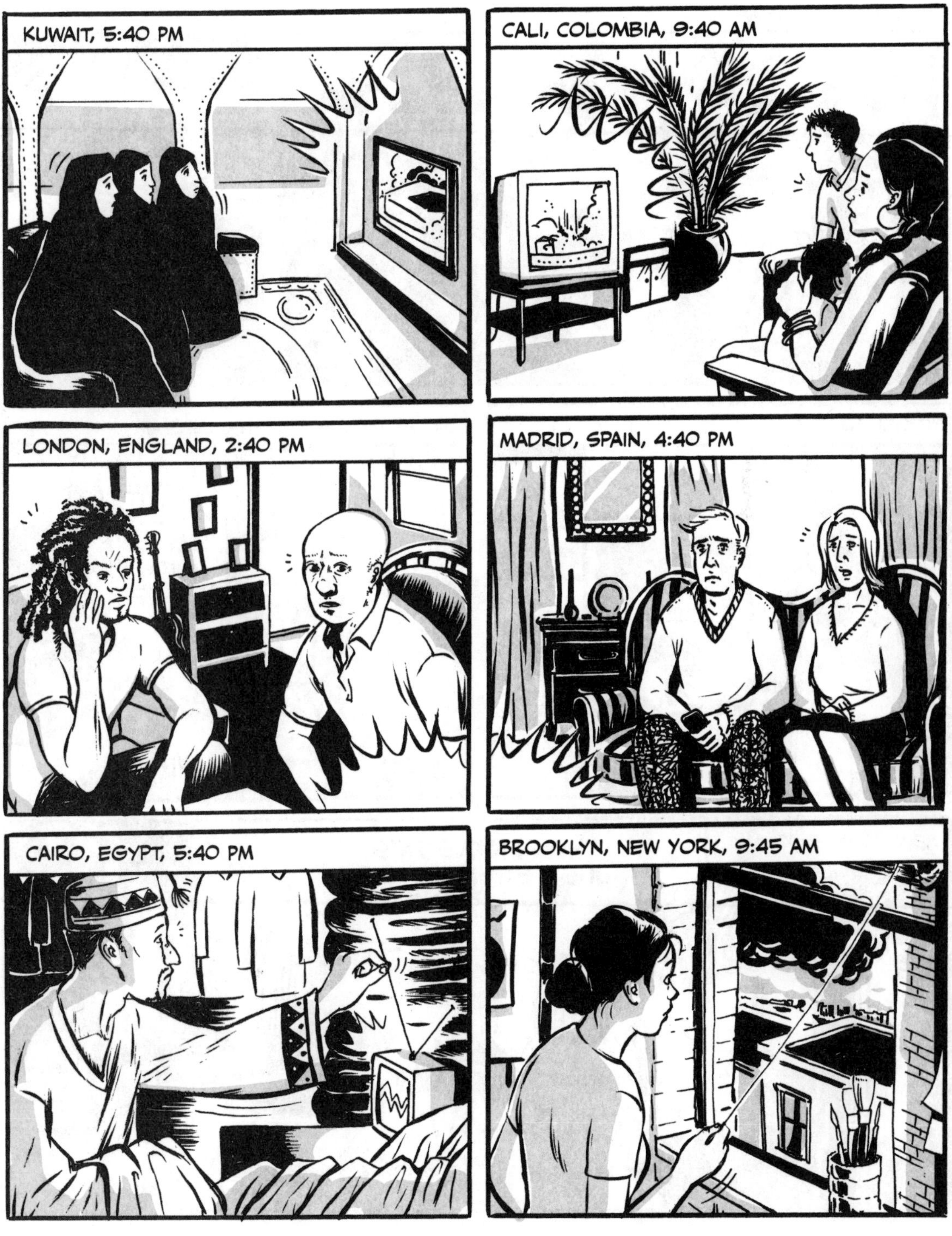
KUWAIT, 5:40 PM
CALI, COLOMBIA, 9:40 AM
LONDON, ENGLAND, 2:40 PM
MADRID, SPAIN, 4:40 PM
CAIRO, EGYPT, 5:40 PM
BROOKLYN, NEW YORK, 9:45 AM

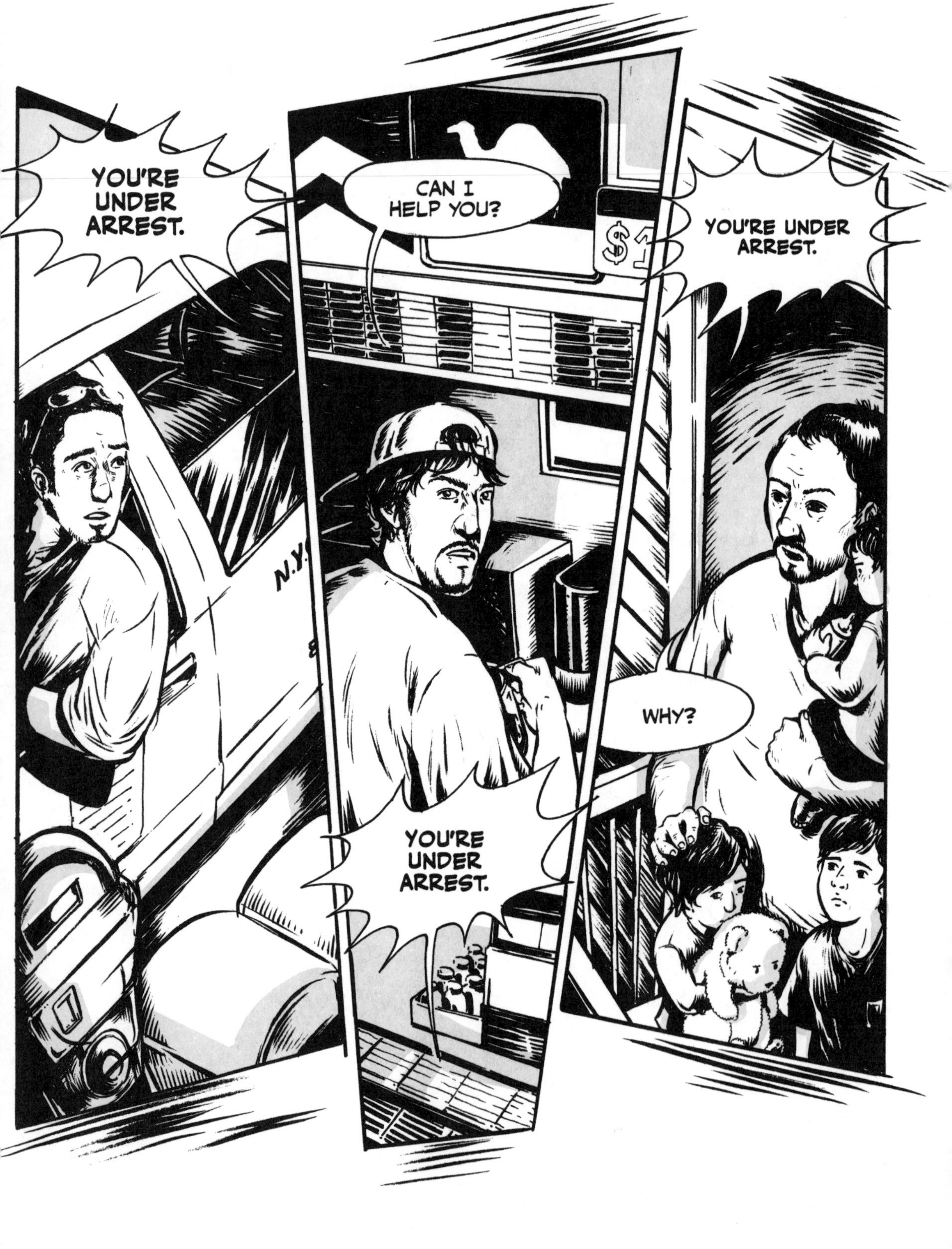
YOU'RE UNDER ARREST.
CAN I HELP YOU?
YOU'RE UNDER ARREST.
YOU'RE UNDER ARREST.
WHY?

Chapter Two

August 1998

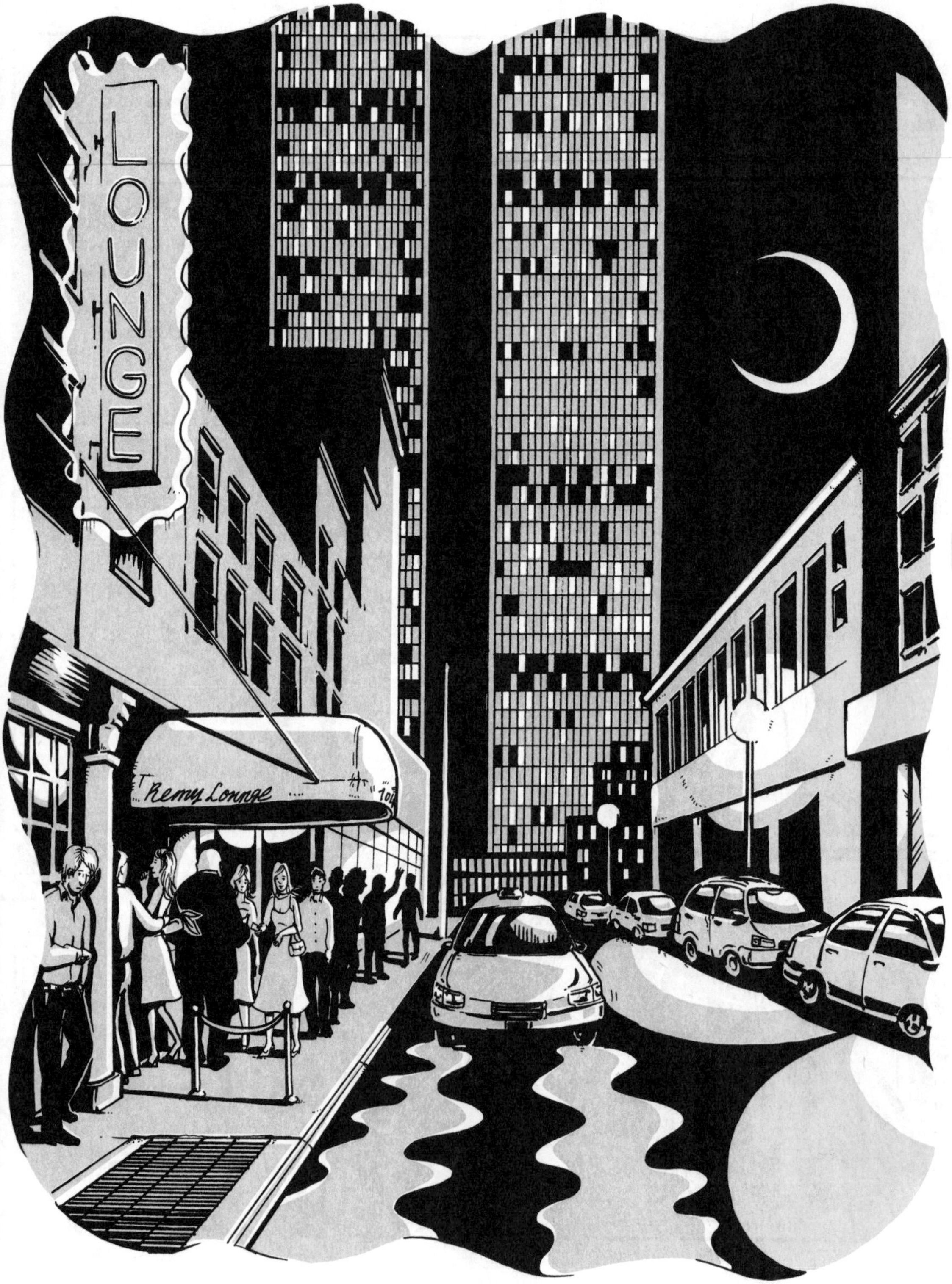
LOUNGE
Remy Lounge

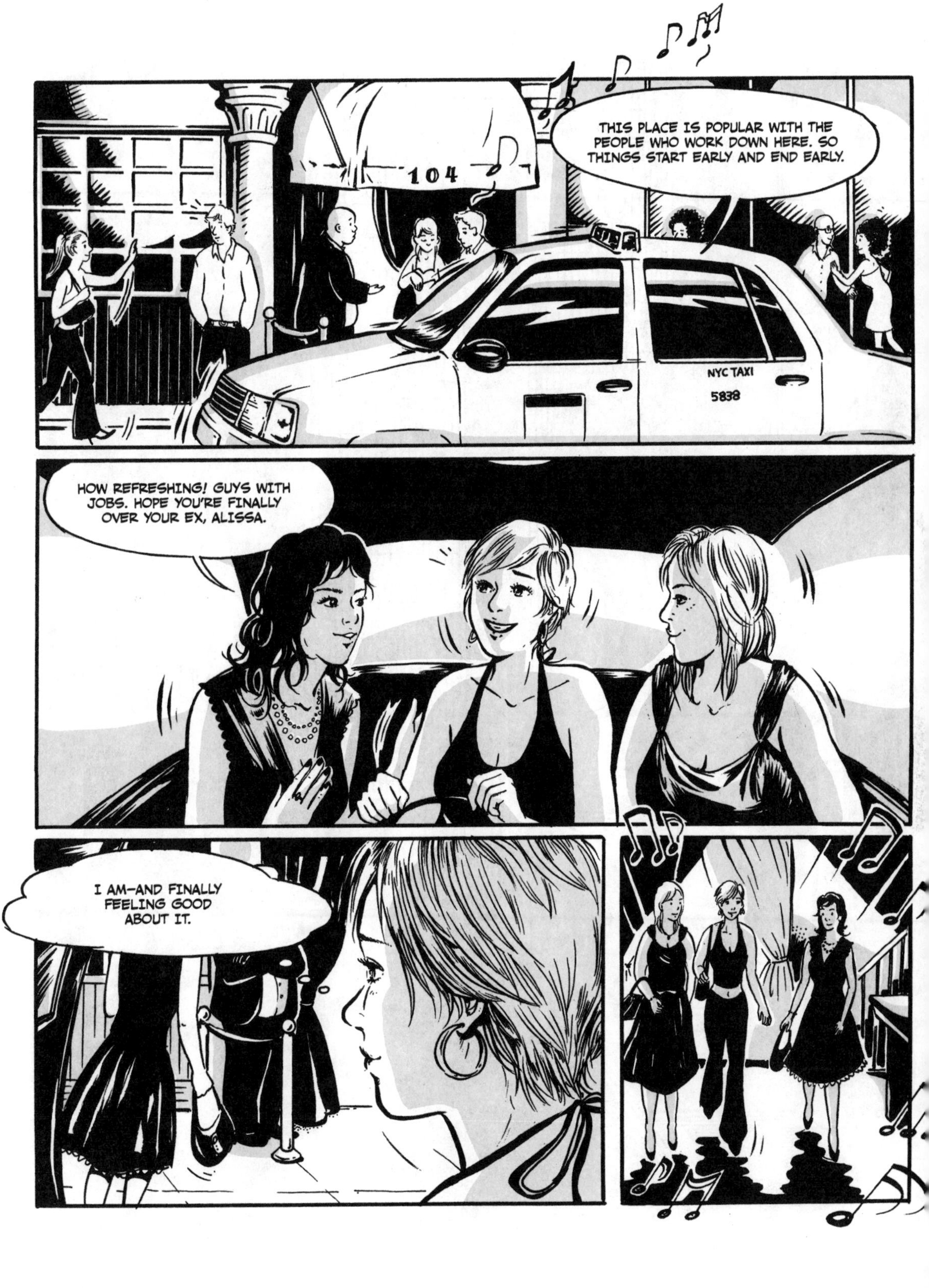

104
THIS PLACE IS POPULAR WITH THE PEOPLE WHO WORK DOWN HERE. SO THINGS START EARLY AND END EARLY.
NYC TAXI
5838
HOW REFRESHING! GUYS WITH JOBS. HOPE YOU'RE FINALLY OVER YOUR EX, ALISSA.
I AM—AND FINALLY FEELING GOOD ABOUT IT.

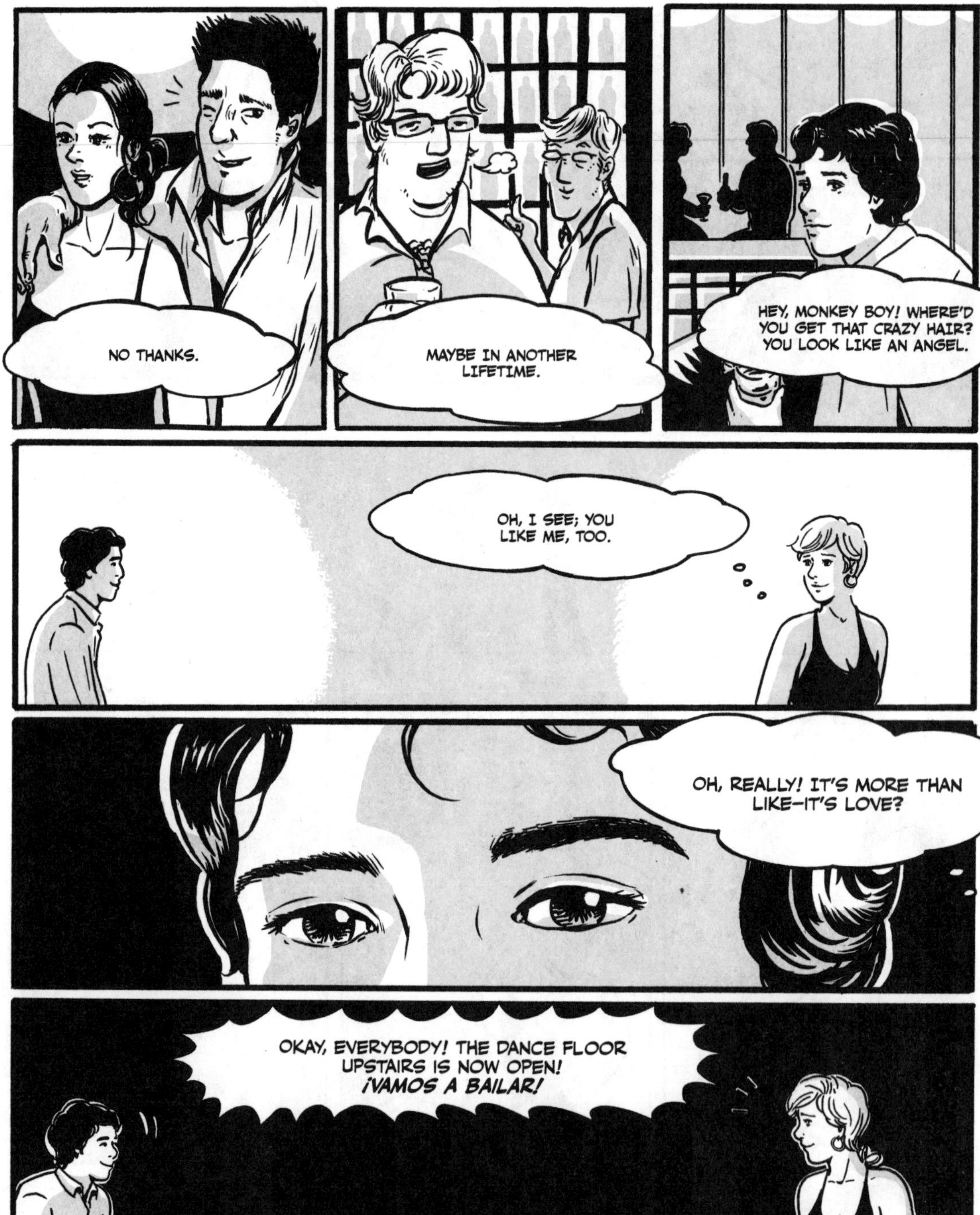
NO THANKS.
MAYBE IN ANOTHER LIFETIME.
HEY, MONKEY BOY! WHERE'D YOU GET THAT CRAZY HAIR? YOU LOOK LIKE AN ANGEL.
OH, I SEE; YOU LIKE ME, TOO.
OH, REALLY! IT'S MORE THAN LIKE—IT'S LOVE?
OKAY, EVERYBODY! THE DANCE FLOOR UPSTAIRS IS NOW OPEN! *¡VAMOS A BAILAR!*

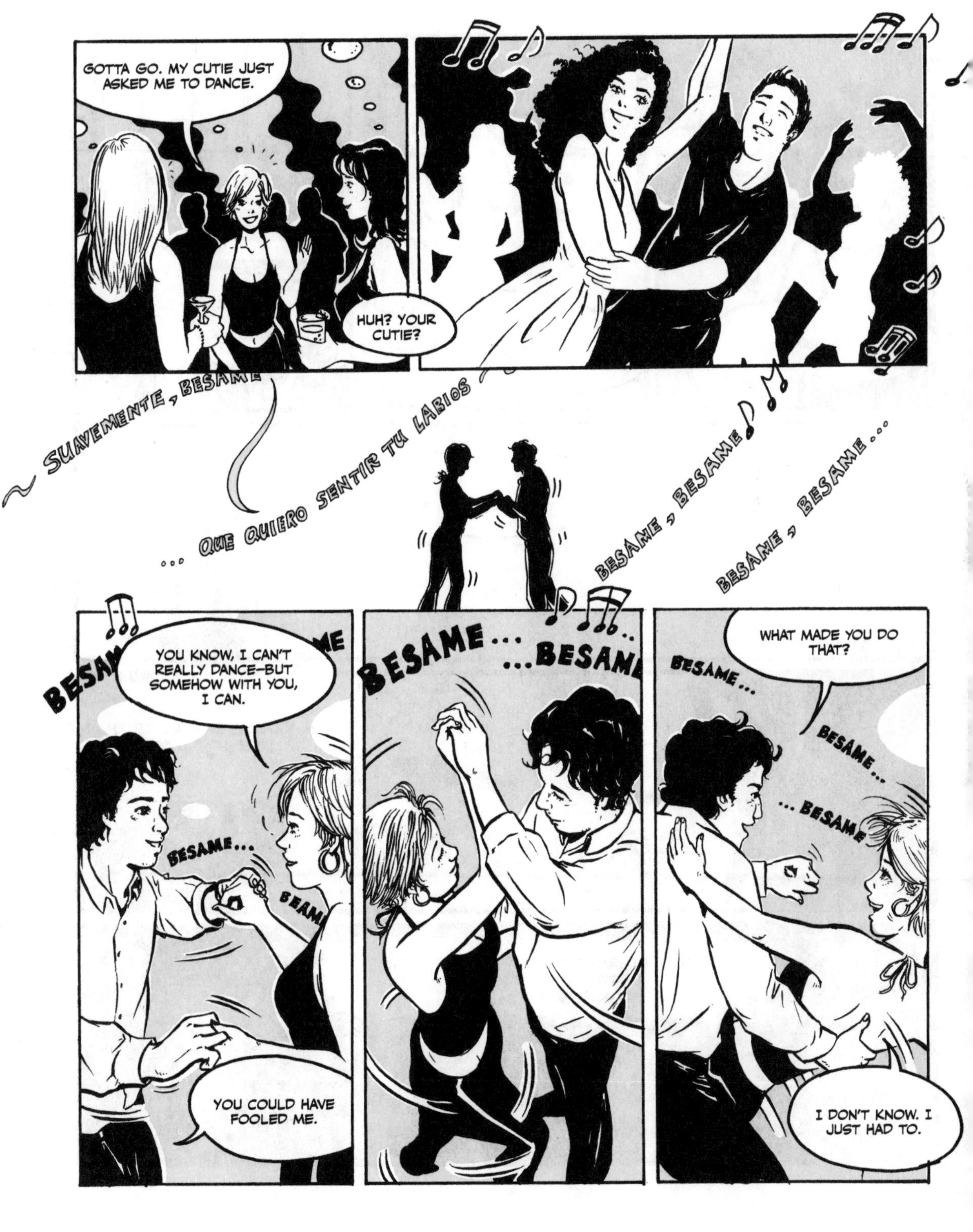
GOTTA GO. MY CUTIE JUST ASKED ME TO DANCE.
HUH? YOUR CUTIE?
~ SUAVEMENTE, BESAME
... QUE QUIERO SENTIR TU LABIOS
BESAME, BESAME
BESAME, BESAME...
BESAME
YOU KNOW, I CAN'T REALLY DANCE—BUT SOMEHOW WITH YOU, I CAN.
BESAME...
BESAME
YOU COULD HAVE FOOLED ME.
BESAME...
...BESAME
WHAT MADE YOU DO THAT?
BESAME...
BESAME...
... BESAME
I DON'T KNOW. I JUST HAD TO.

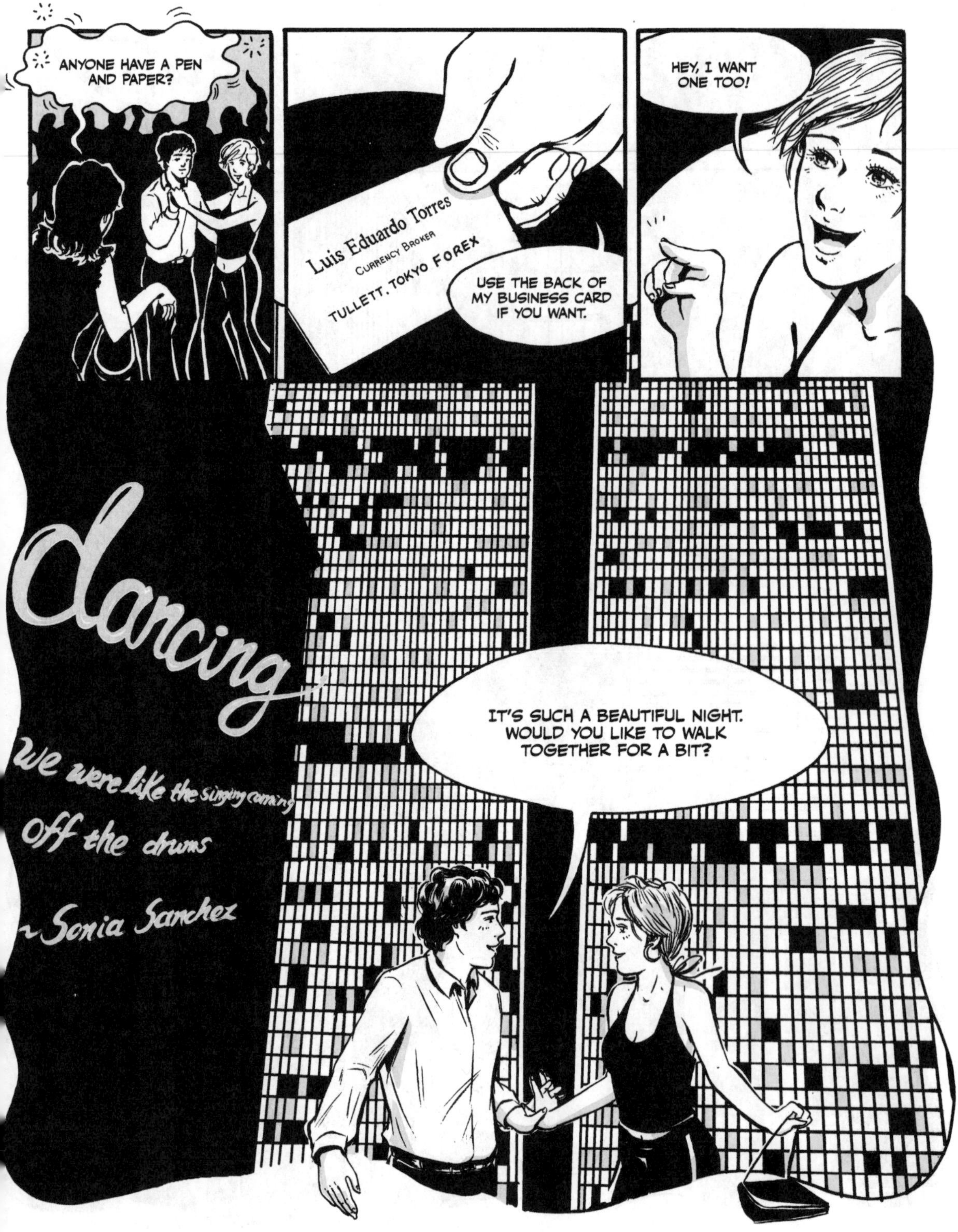
ANYONE HAVE A PEN AND PAPER?
Luis Eduardo Torres
CURRENCY BROKER
TULLETT, TOKYO FOREX
USE THE BACK OF MY BUSINESS CARD IF YOU WANT.
HEY, I WANT ONE TOO!
dancing
we were like the singing coming off the drums
~Sonia Sanchez
IT'S SUCH A BEAUTIFUL NIGHT. WOULD YOU LIKE TO WALK TOGETHER FOR A BIT?

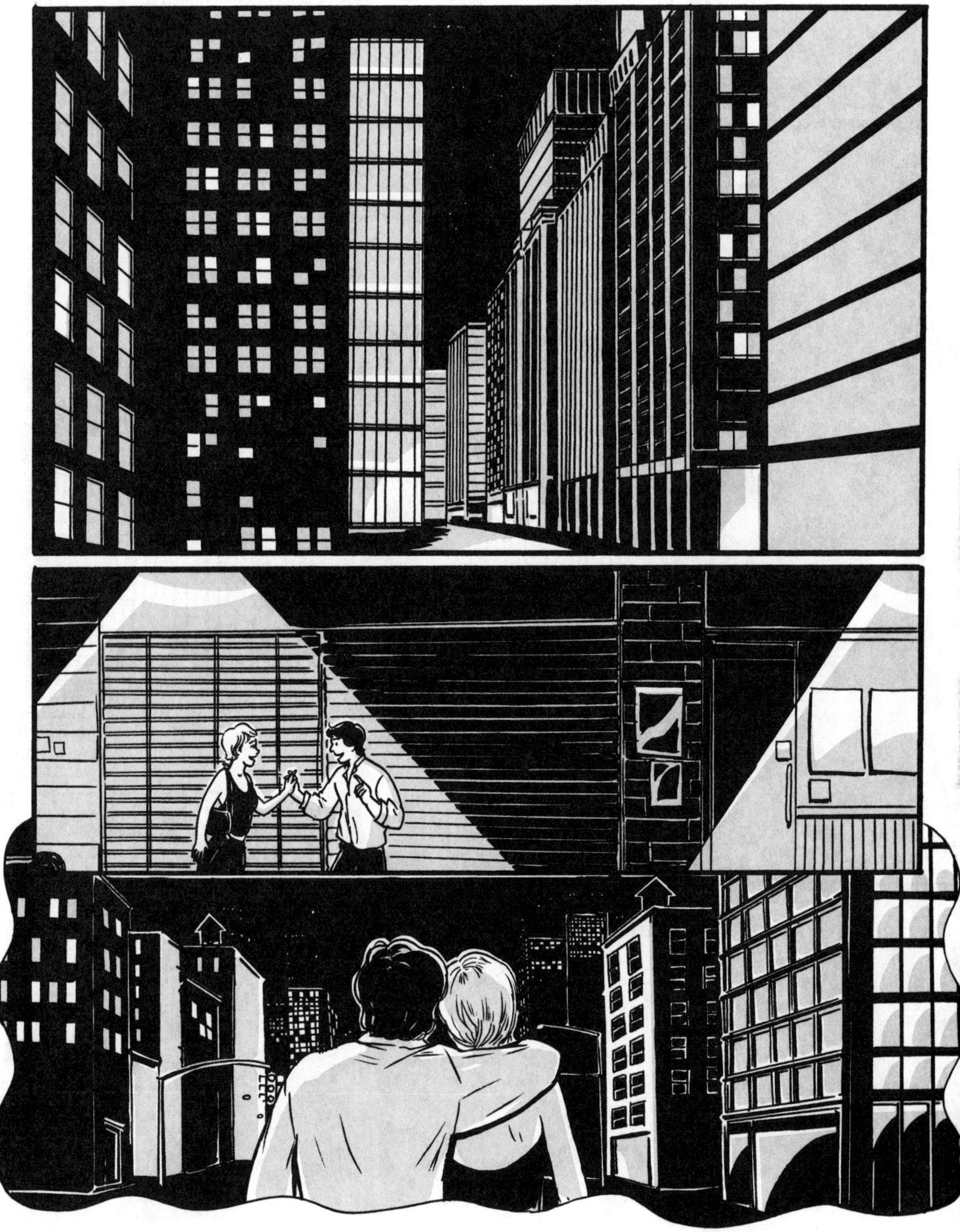

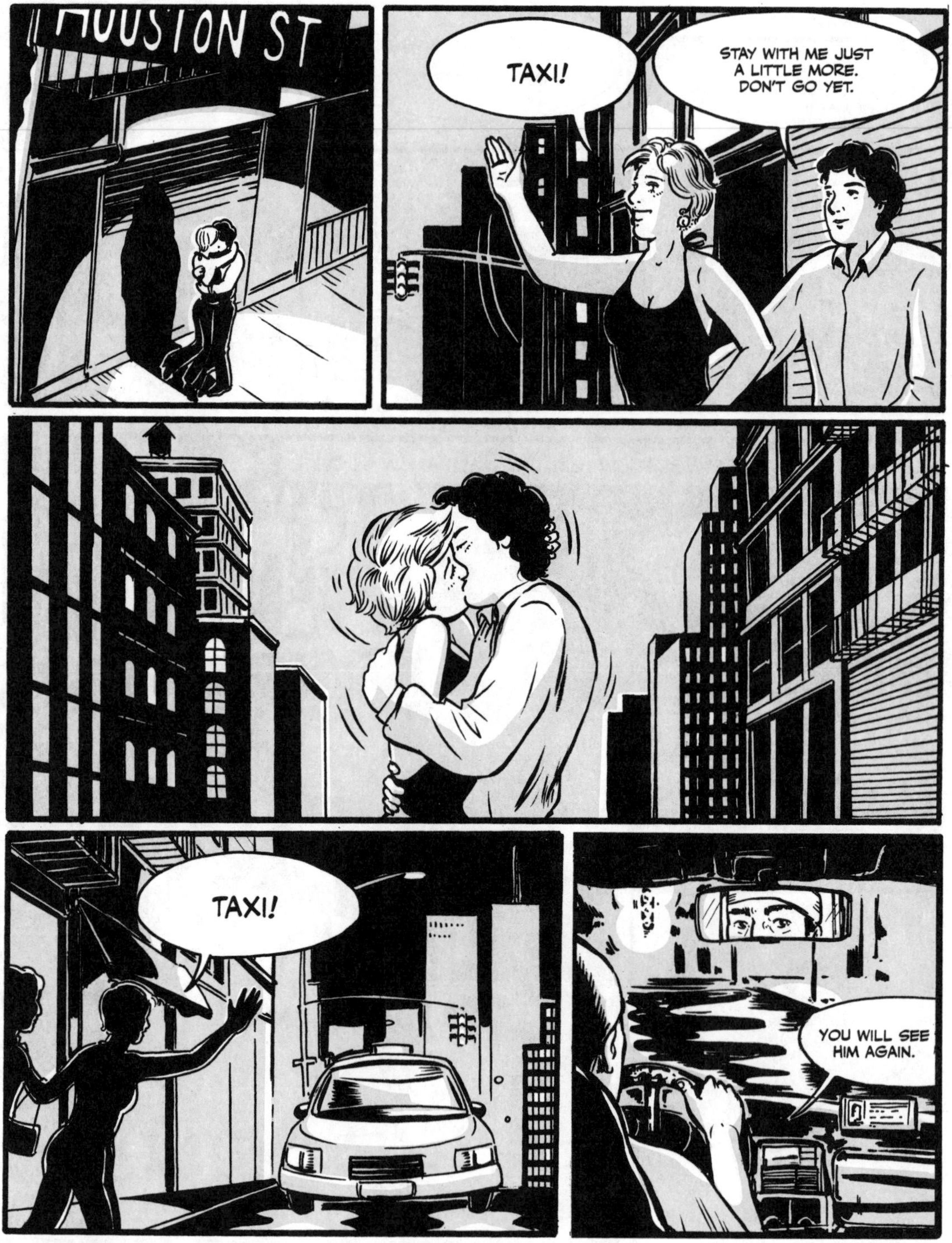
HOUSTON ST
TAXI!
STAY WITH ME JUST A LITTLE MORE. DON'T GO YET.
TAXI!
YOU WILL SEE HIM AGAIN.

ONE WEEK LATER.

I WANT TO BE STRAIGHT WITH YOU: I MAY HAVE TO LEAVE THE COUNTRY . . .

MY WORK PERMIT EXPIRED. IF THEY DON'T RENEW IT, MAYBE I MIGHT BE DEPORTED.

I'D GO WITH YOU— ANYWHERE—IF YOU'D LET ME . . . WOW, WOULD I REALLY GO WITH HIM? YES, I REALLY WOULD.

THE NEXT DAY, 9 AM, IMMIGRATION AND NATURALIZATION SERVICE

GLAD I CAME. IF THEY TAKE YOU, AT LEAST THERE'LL BE A WITNESS.

12 PM

EMPLOYMENT AUTHORIZATION
NAME TORRES, LUIS
INS A # 000-000-000
BIRTHDATE CATEGORY SEX
00/00/00
COUNTRY OF B
COLOMBIA
CARD EXPIRES
RESIDENT SIN
TORRES<<LUIS<<

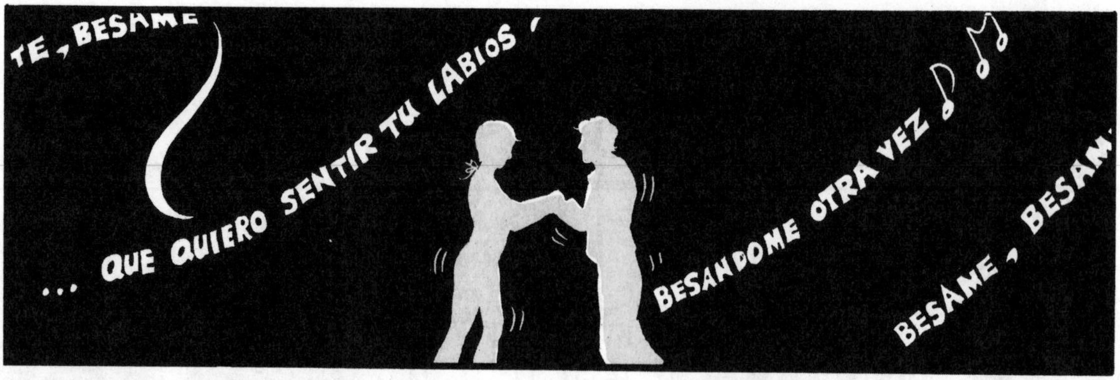
TE, BESAME
... QUE QUIERO SENTIR TU LABIOS,
BESANDOME OTRA VEZ
BESAME, BESAM

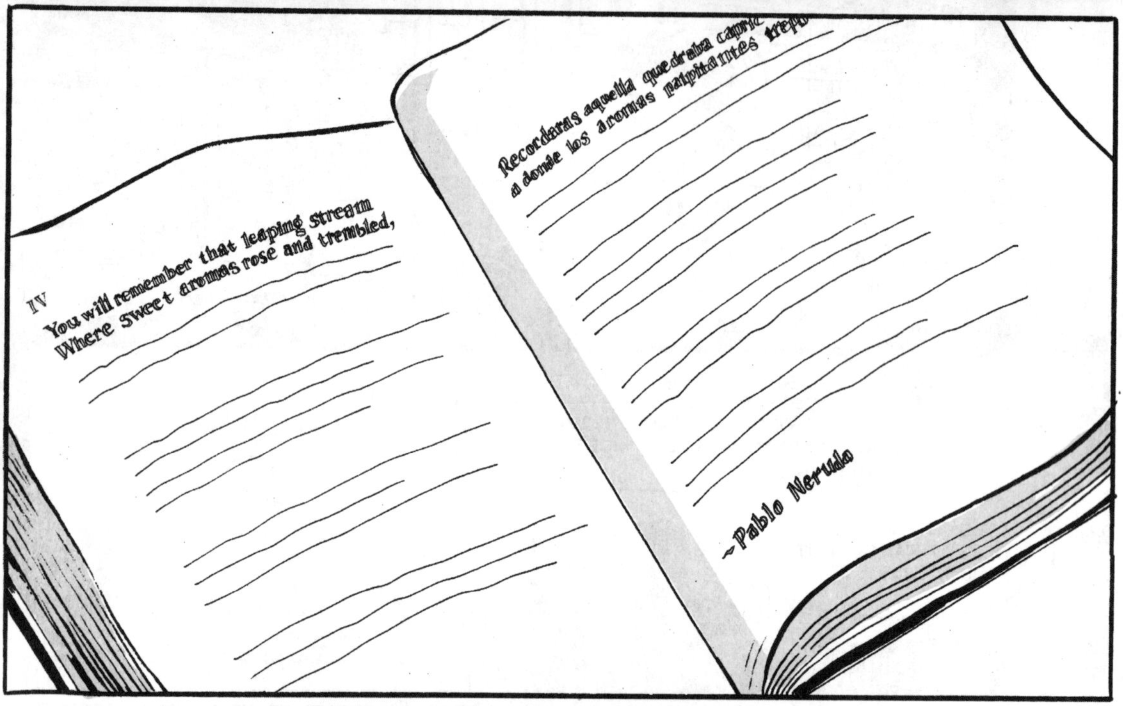
IV
You will remember that leaping stream
Where sweet aromas rose and trembled,
Recordarás aquella quebrada capric
a donde los aromas palpitantes trep
~Pablo Neruda

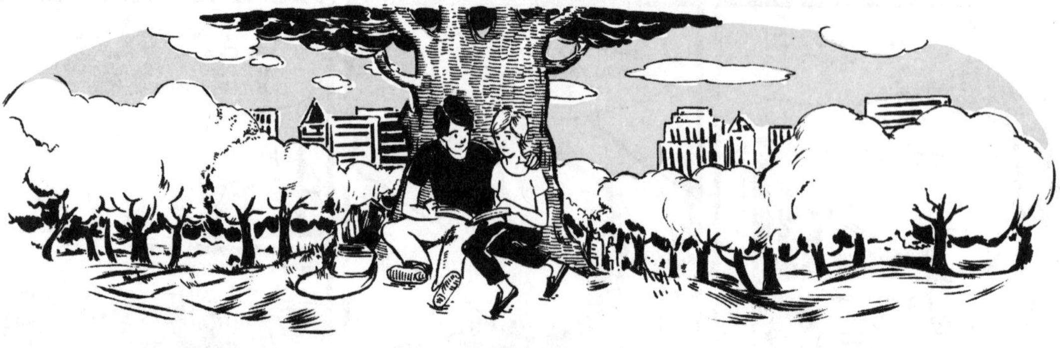

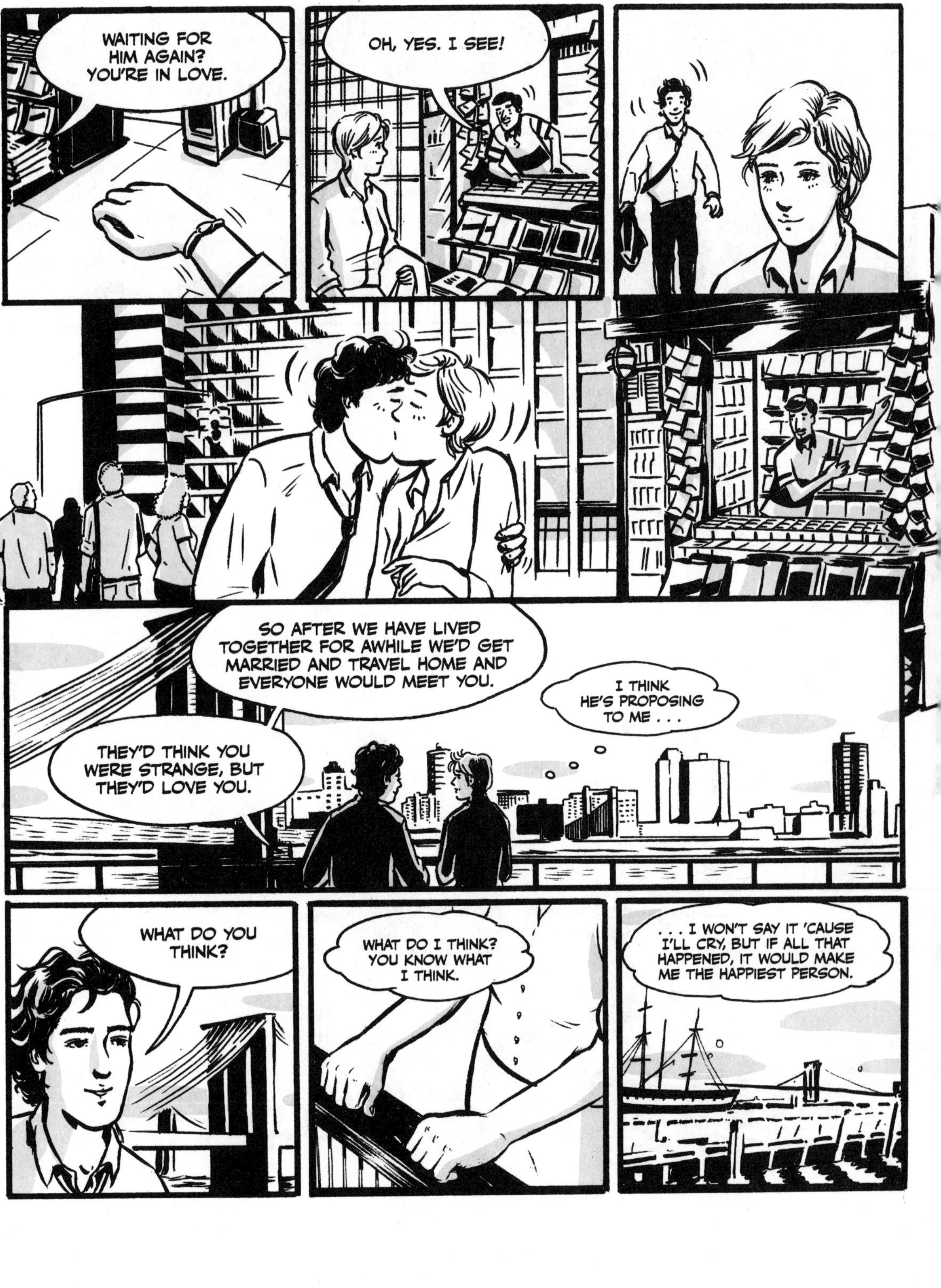
WAITING FOR HIM AGAIN? YOU'RE IN LOVE.
OH, YES. I SEE!
SO AFTER WE HAVE LIVED TOGETHER FOR AWHILE WE'D GET MARRIED AND TRAVEL HOME AND EVERYONE WOULD MEET YOU.
THEY'D THINK YOU WERE STRANGE, BUT THEY'D LOVE YOU.
I THINK HE'S PROPOSING TO ME . . .
WHAT DO YOU THINK?
WHAT DO I THINK? YOU KNOW WHAT I THINK.
. . . I WON'T SAY IT 'CAUSE I'LL CRY, BUT IF ALL THAT HAPPENED, IT WOULD MAKE ME THE HAPPIEST PERSON.

7 MONTHS AFTER THAT— MANHATTAN

WE'RE GETTING MARRIED THIS THURSDAY! WANT TO COME?

. . . YEAH, YOU KNOW HOW IT IS.

ONE YEAR AFTER THAT—QUEENS, NY

WE'LL FIX IT UP NICE, AND THEN WE'LL GIVE UP THE STUDIO.

SOLD

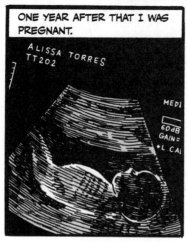

ONE YEAR AFTER THAT I WAS PREGNANT.

ALISSA TORRES
TT 202

MEDI
60dB
GAIN
•L CAI

Chapter Three

August–September 2001

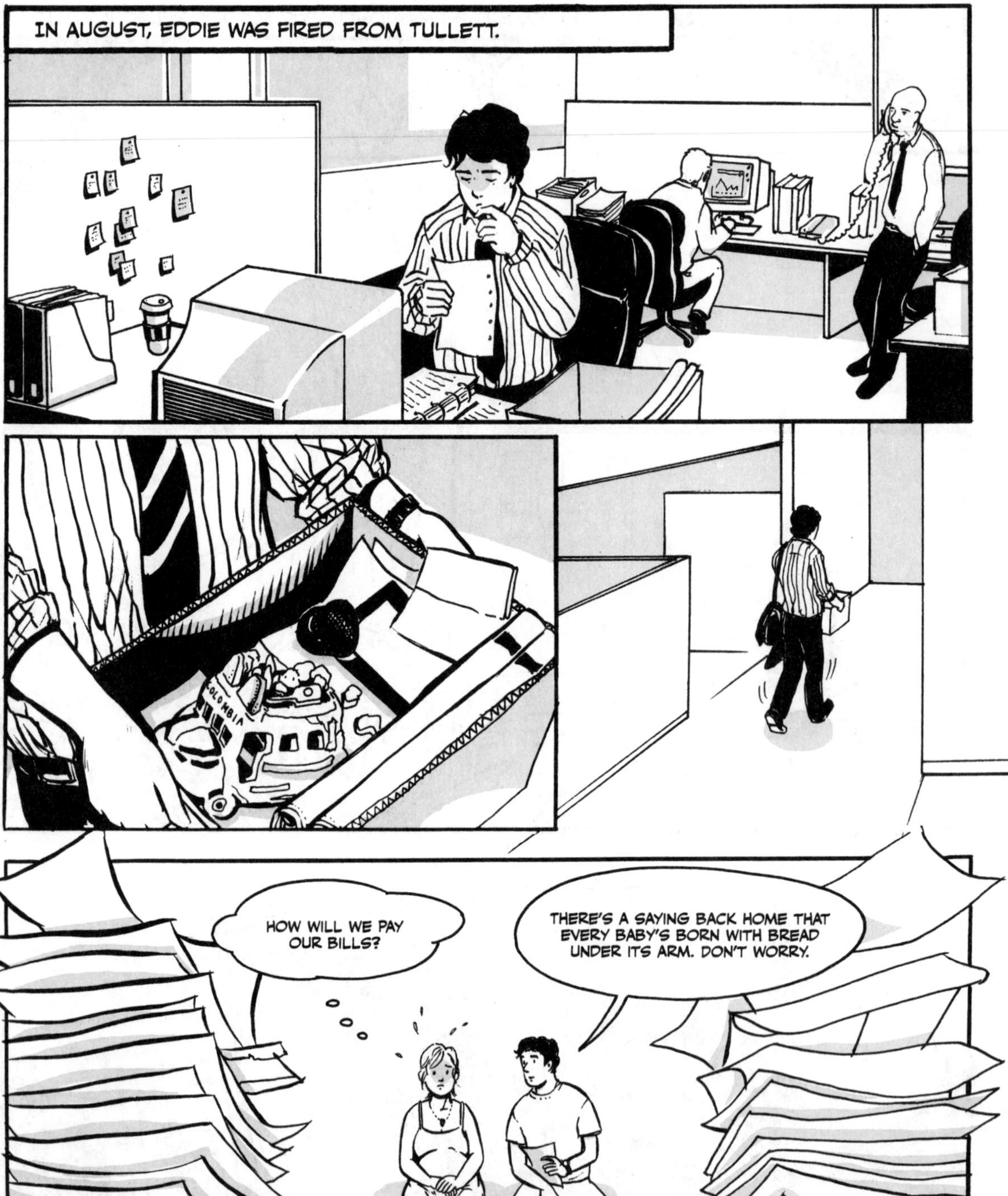
IN AUGUST, EDDIE WAS FIRED FROM TULLETT.
COLOMBIA
HOW WILL WE PAY OUR BILLS?
THERE'S A SAYING BACK HOME THAT EVERY BABY'S BORN WITH BREAD UNDER ITS ARM. DON'T WORRY.

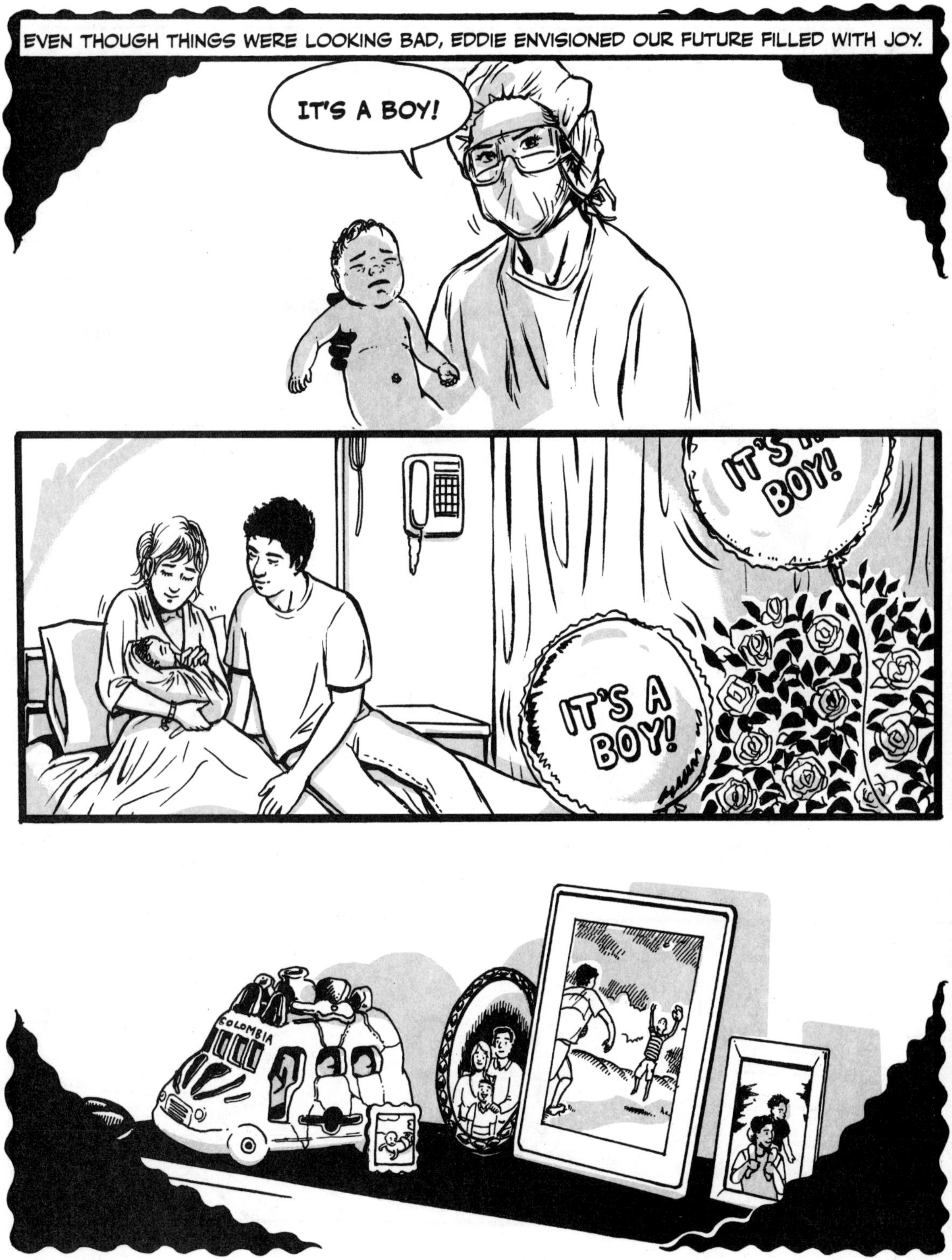
EVEN THOUGH THINGS WERE LOOKING BAD, EDDIE ENVISIONED OUR FUTURE FILLED WITH JOY.
IT'S A BOY!
IT'S A BOY!
COLOMBIA

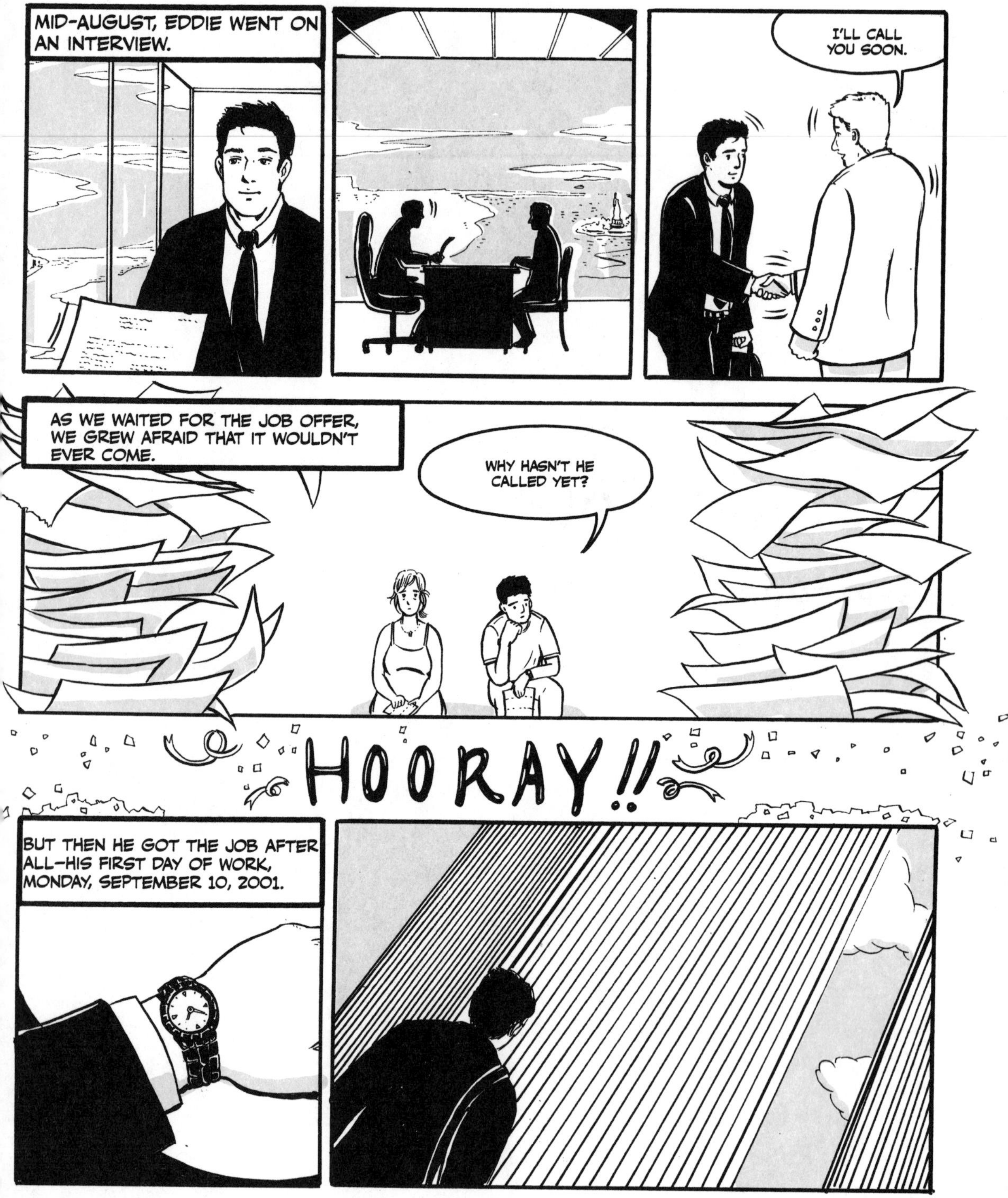
MID-AUGUST, EDDIE WENT ON AN INTERVIEW.
I'LL CALL YOU SOON.
AS WE WAITED FOR THE JOB OFFER, WE GREW AFRAID THAT IT WOULDN'T EVER COME.
WHY HASN'T HE CALLED YET?
HOORAY!!
BUT THEN HE GOT THE JOB AFTER ALL—HIS FIRST DAY OF WORK, MONDAY, SEPTEMBER 10, 2001.

Chapter Four

SEPTEMBER 11, 2001

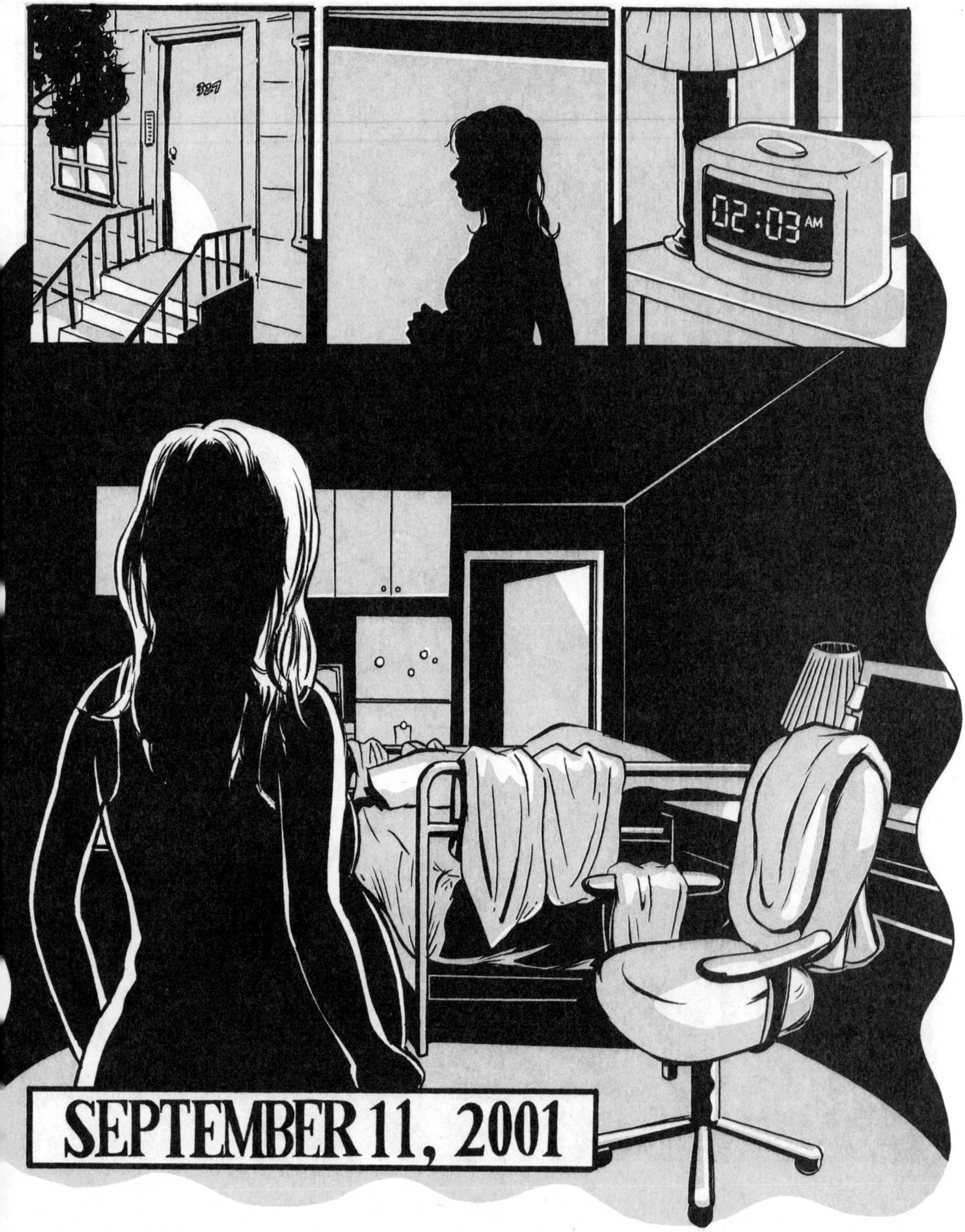
327
02:03 AM
SEPTEMBER 11, 2001

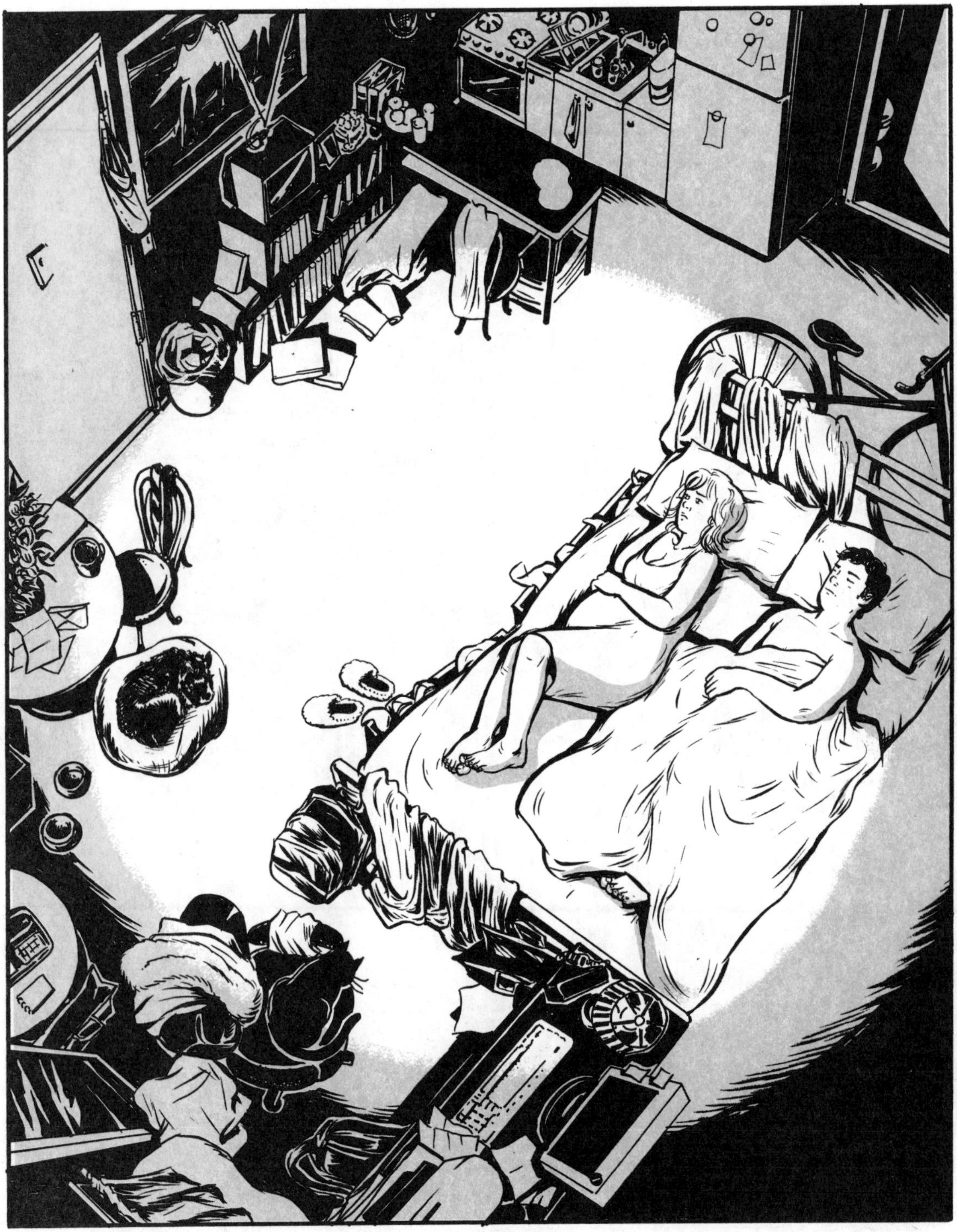

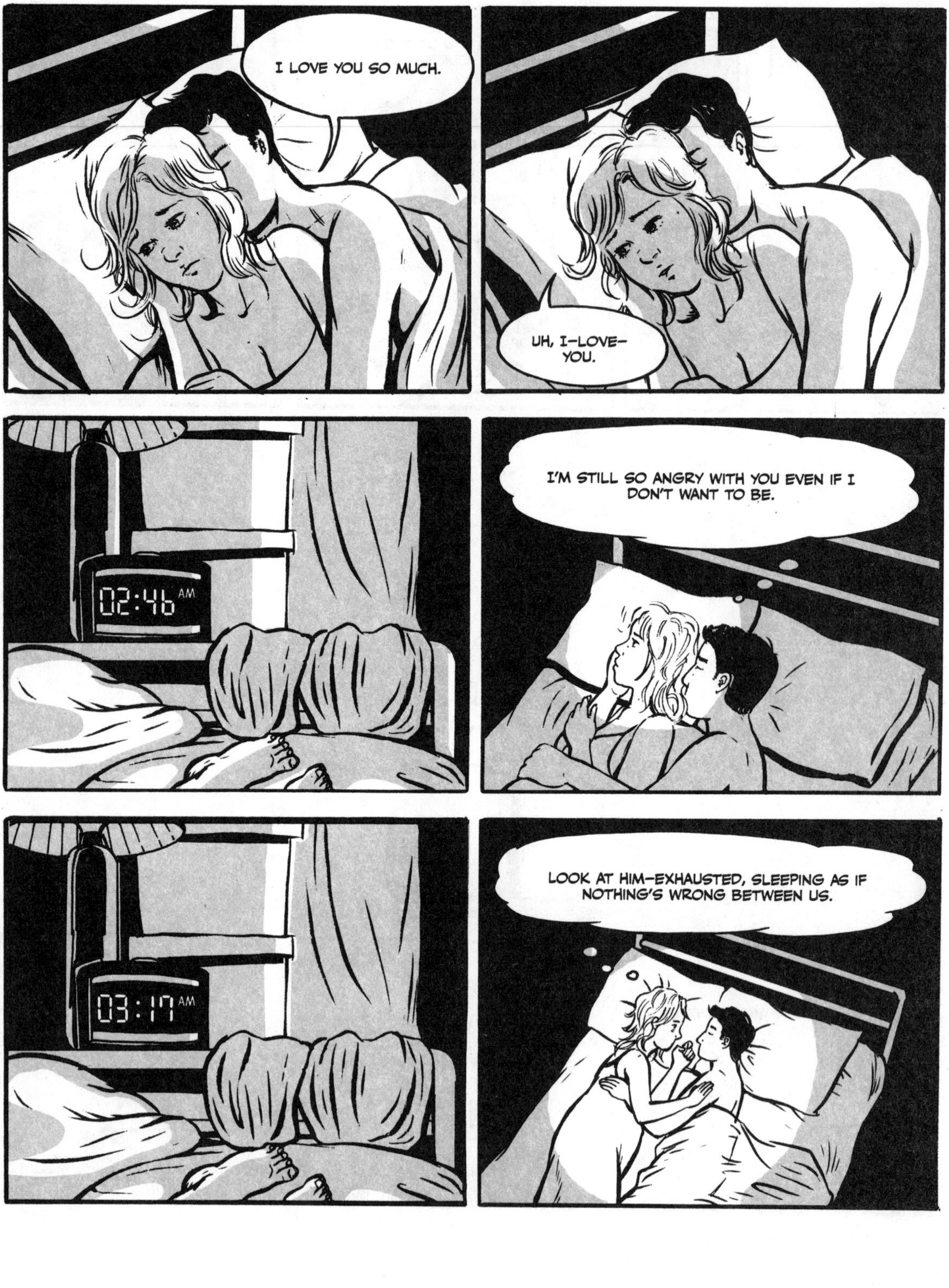
I LOVE YOU SO MUCH.
UH, I-LOVE-YOU.
02:46 AM
I'M STILL SO ANGRY WITH YOU EVEN IF I DON'T WANT TO BE.
03:17 AM
LOOK AT HIM-EXHAUSTED, SLEEPING AS IF NOTHING'S WRONG BETWEEN US.

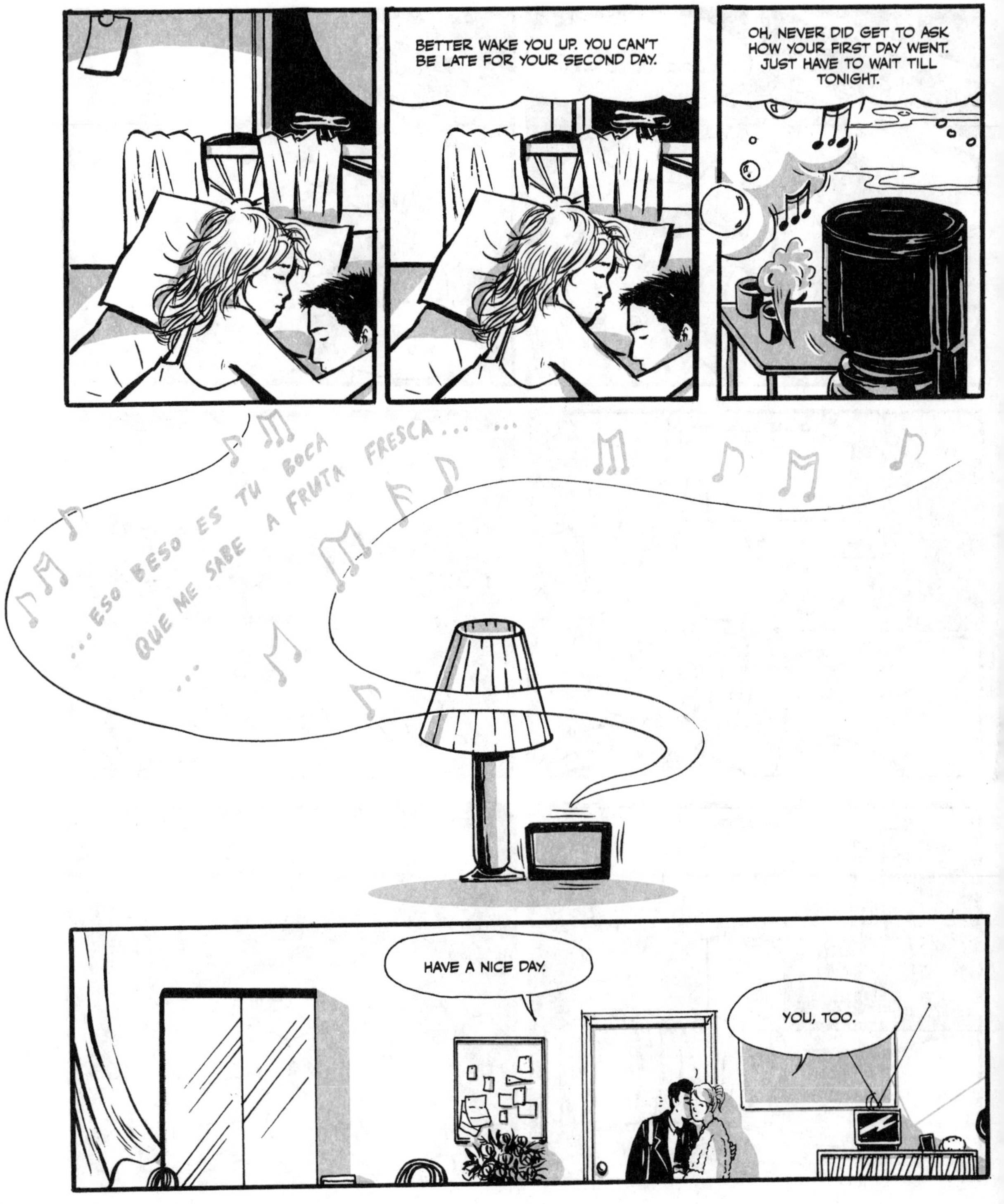
BETTER WAKE YOU UP. YOU CAN'T BE LATE FOR YOUR SECOND DAY.
OH, NEVER DID GET TO ASK HOW YOUR FIRST DAY WENT. JUST HAVE TO WAIT TILL TONIGHT.
...ESO BESO ES TU BOCA QUE ME SABE A FRUTA FRESCA... ...
HAVE A NICE DAY.
YOU, TOO.

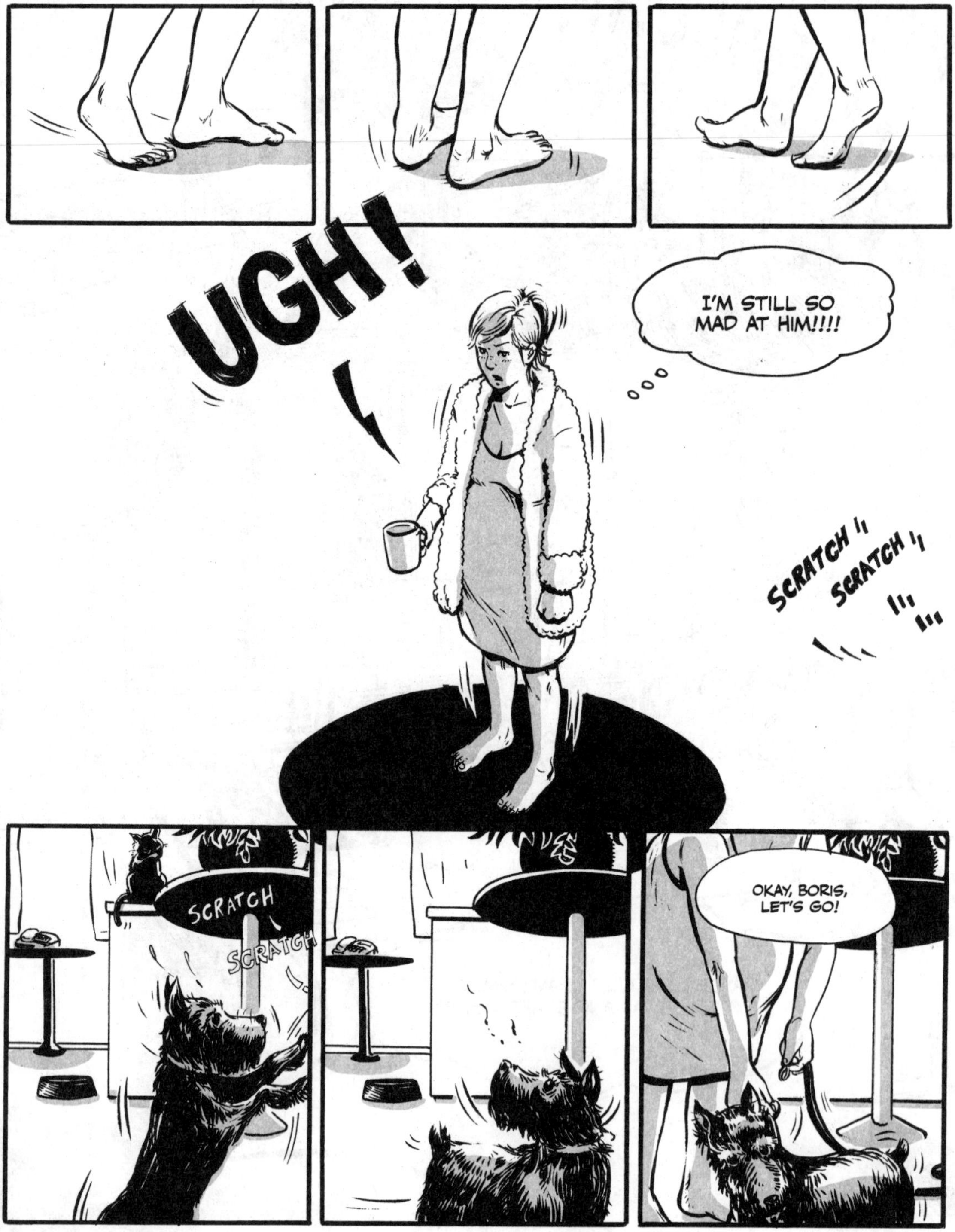
UGH!
I'M STILL SO MAD AT HIM!!!!
SCRATCH
SCRATCH
SCRATCH
SCRATCH
OKAY, BORIS, LET'S GO!

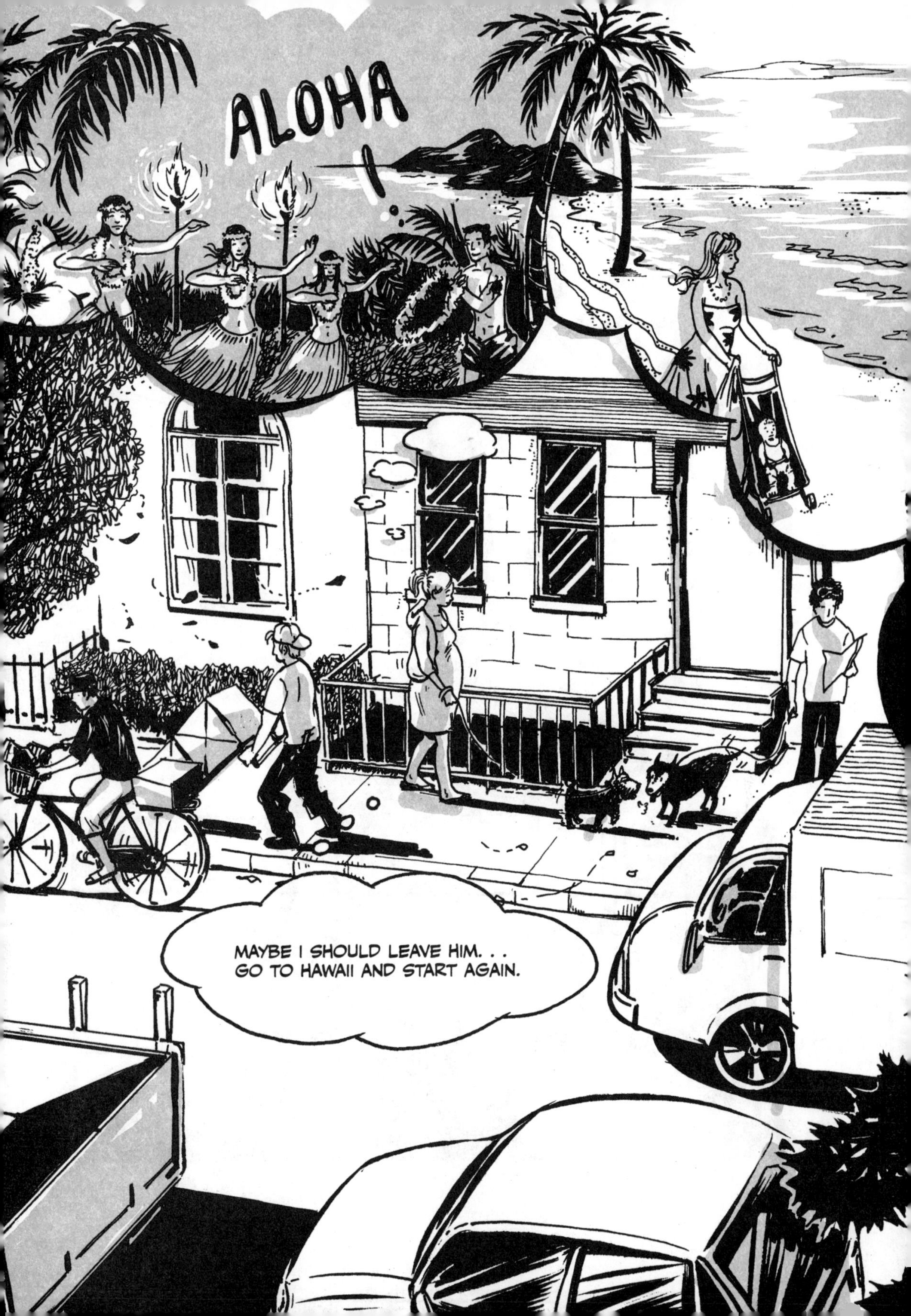
ALOHA!
MAYBE I SHOULD LEAVE HIM. . .
GO TO HAWAII AND START AGAIN.

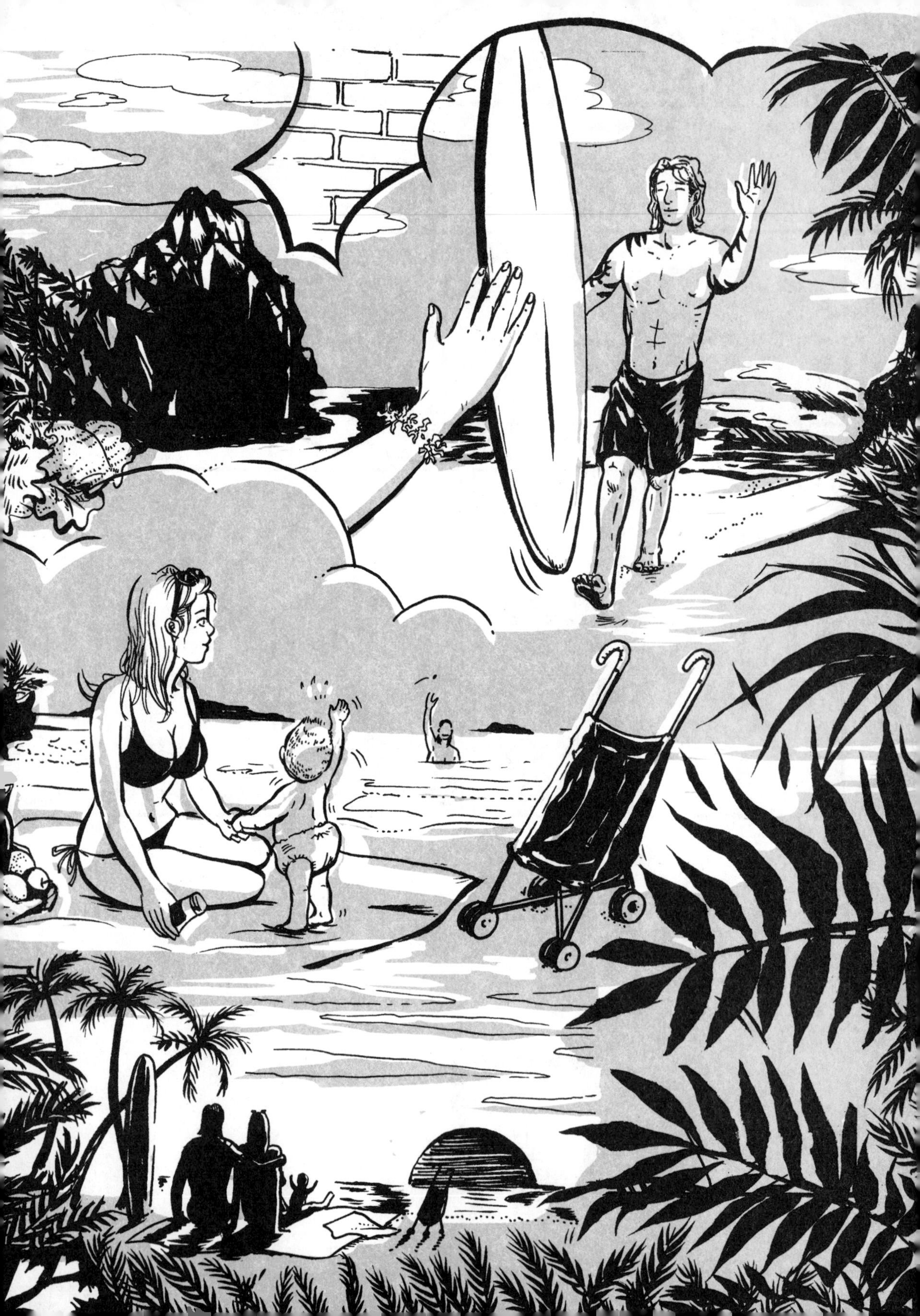

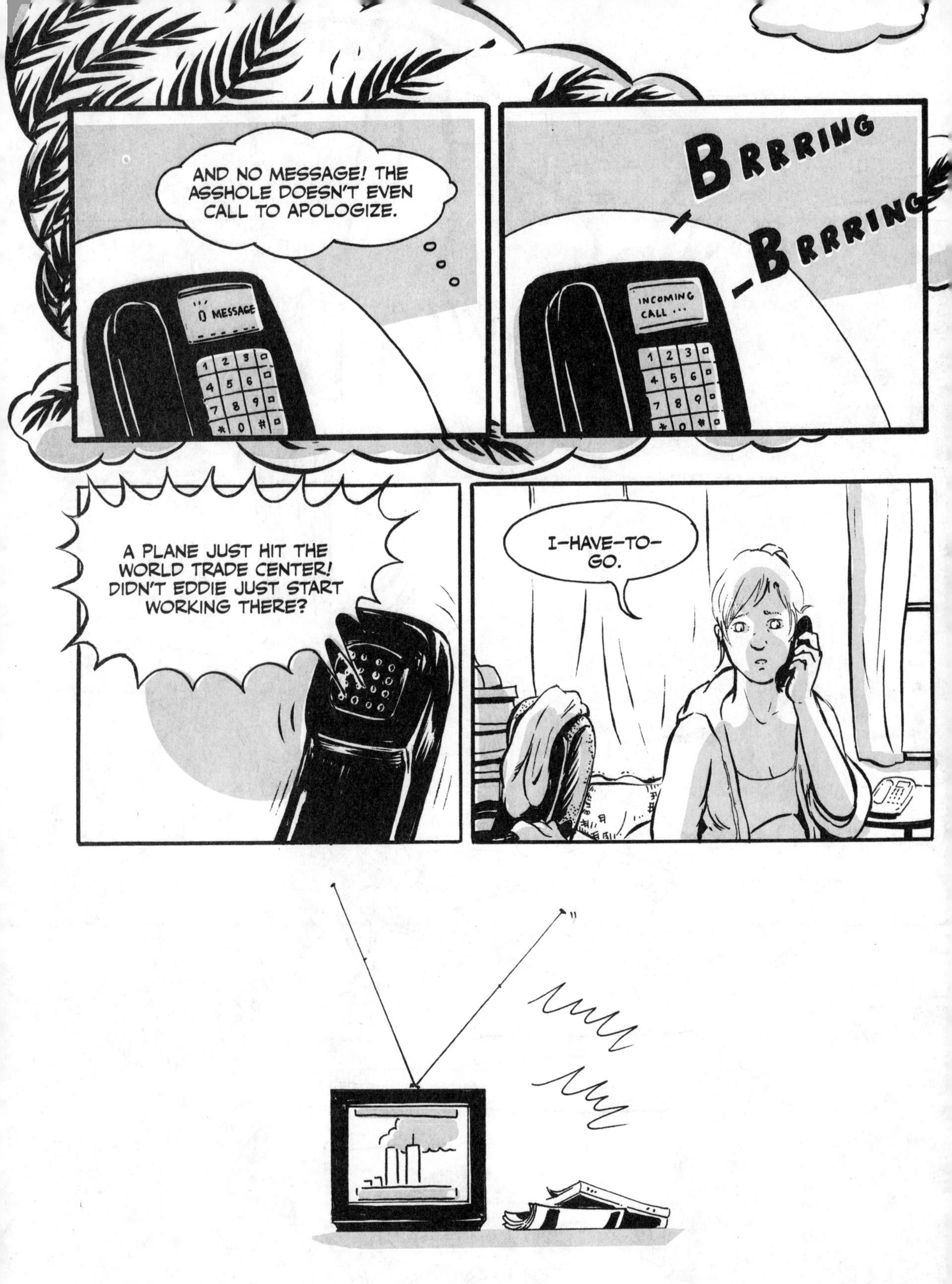
AND NO MESSAGE! THE ASSHOLE DOESN'T EVEN CALL TO APOLOGIZE.
0 MESSAGE
BRRRING-BRRRING
INCOMING CALL ...
A PLANE JUST HIT THE WORLD TRADE CENTER! DIDN'T EDDIE JUST START WORKING THERE?
I-HAVE-TO-GO.

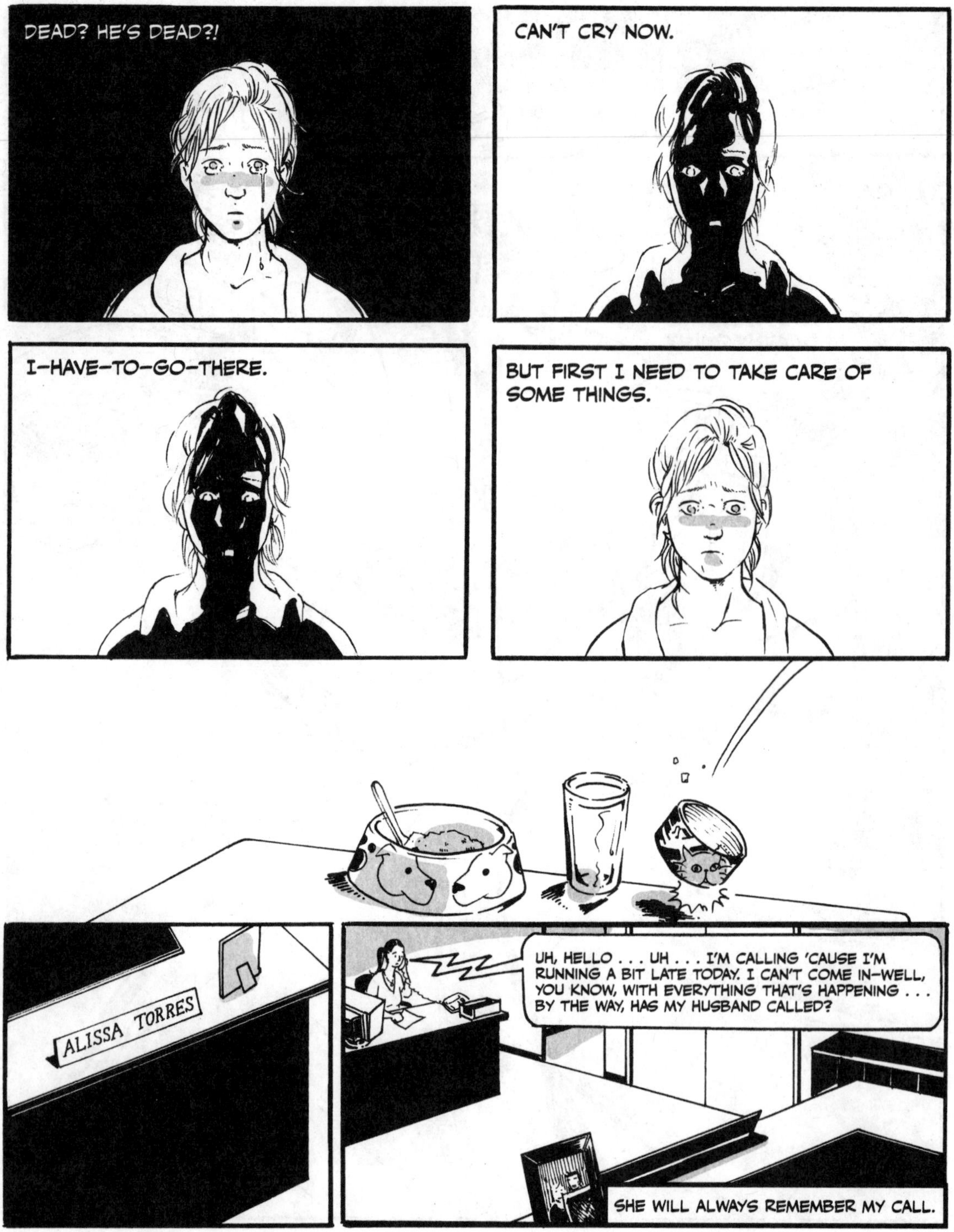
DEAD? HE'S DEAD?!
CAN'T CRY NOW.
I-HAVE-TO-GO-THERE.
BUT FIRST I NEED TO TAKE CARE OF SOME THINGS.
ALISSA TORRES
UH, HELLO . . . UH . . . I'M CALLING 'CAUSE I'M RUNNING A BIT LATE TODAY. I CAN'T COME IN—WELL, YOU KNOW, WITH EVERYTHING THAT'S HAPPENING . . . BY THE WAY, HAS MY HUSBAND CALLED?
SHE WILL ALWAYS REMEMBER MY CALL.

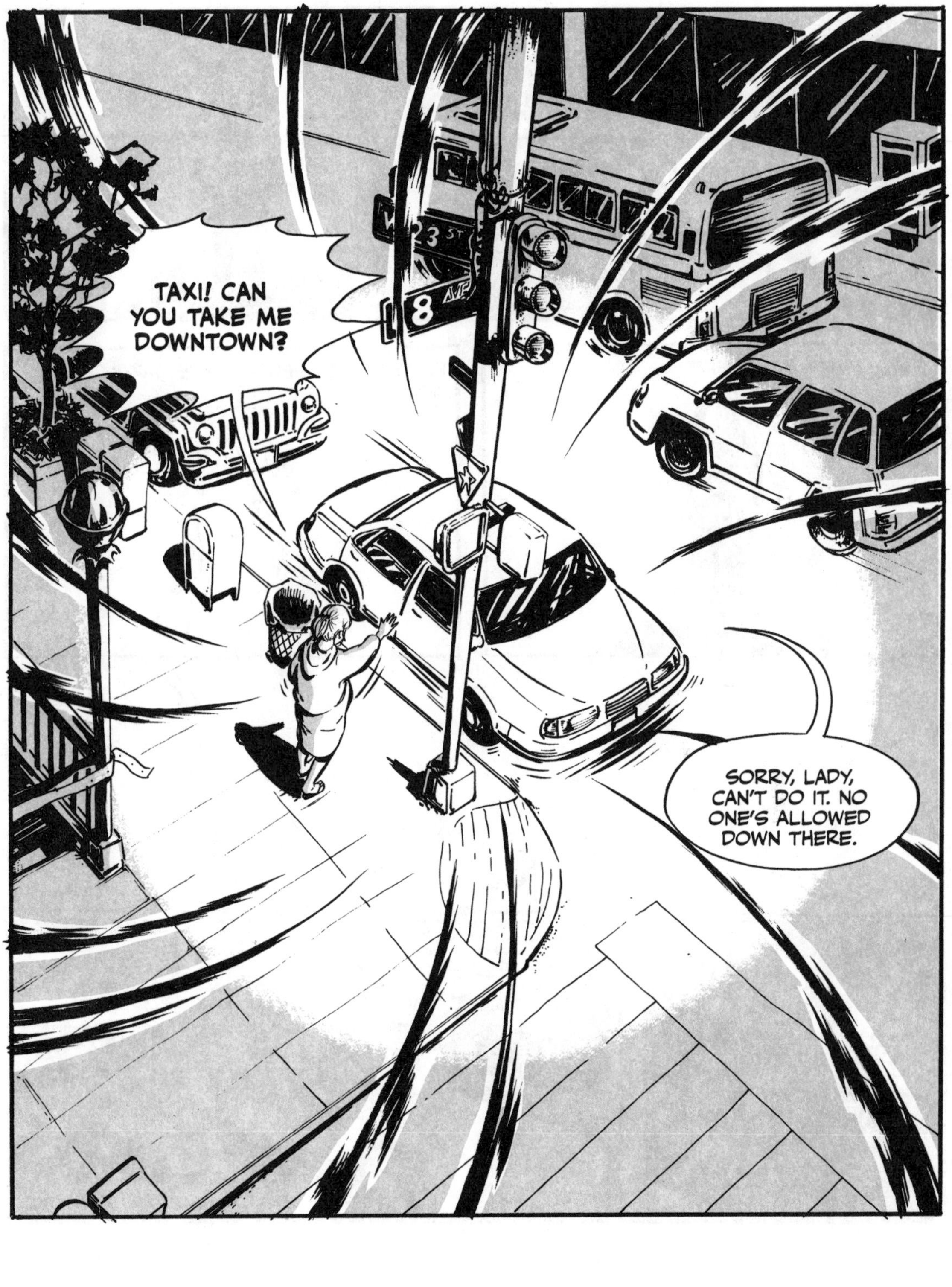
W 23 ST
8 AVE
TAXI! CAN YOU TAKE ME DOWNTOWN?
SORRY, LADY, CAN'T DO IT. NO ONE'S ALLOWED DOWN THERE.

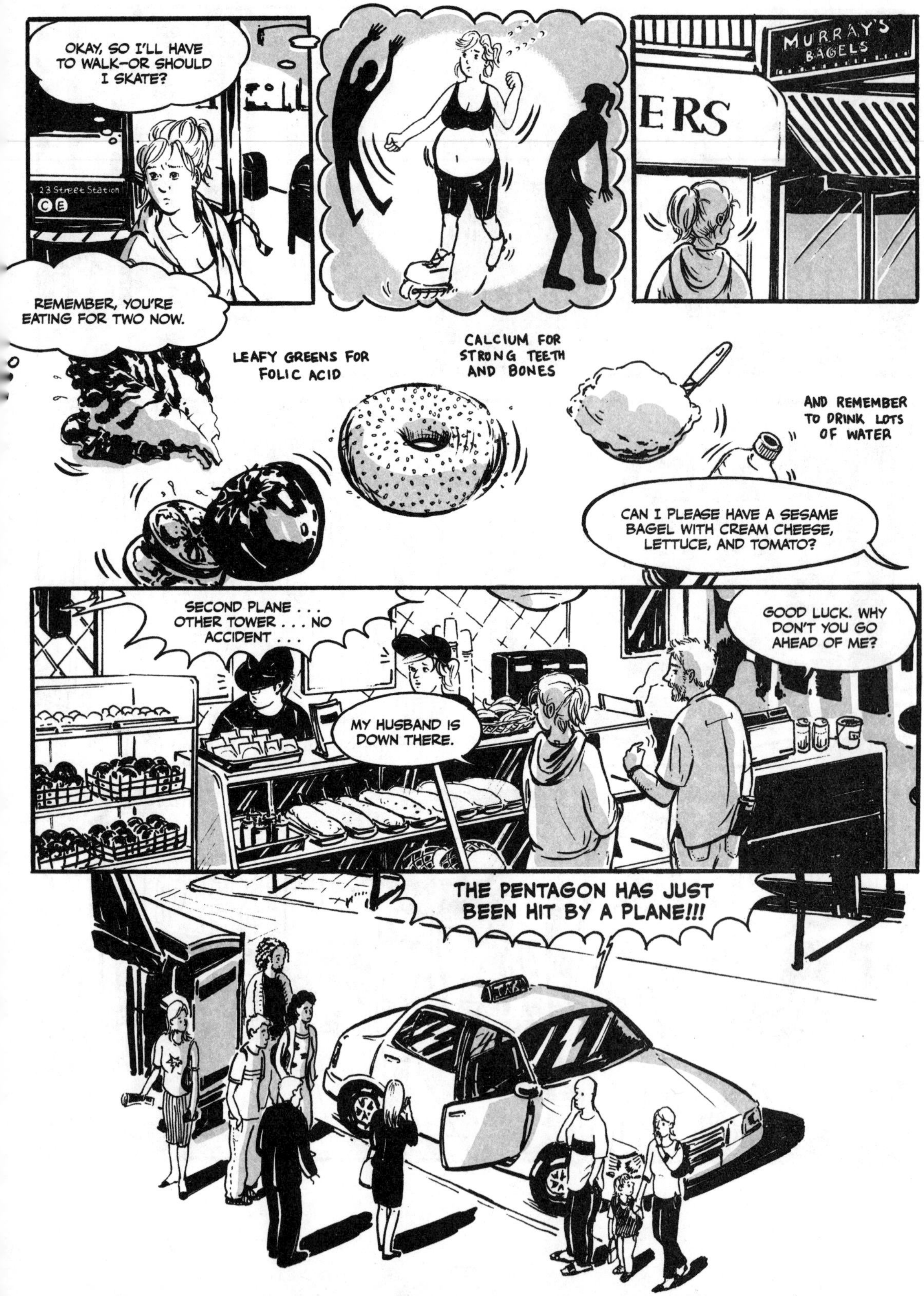
OKAY, SO I'LL HAVE TO WALK—OR SHOULD I SKATE?
23 Street Station
MURRAY'S BAGELS
ERS
REMEMBER, YOU'RE EATING FOR TWO NOW.
LEAFY GREENS FOR FOLIC ACID
CALCIUM FOR STRONG TEETH AND BONES
AND REMEMBER TO DRINK LOTS OF WATER
CAN I PLEASE HAVE A SESAME BAGEL WITH CREAM CHEESE, LETTUCE, AND TOMATO?
SECOND PLANE . . . OTHER TOWER . . . NO ACCIDENT . . .
GOOD LUCK. WHY DON'T YOU GO AHEAD OF ME?
MY HUSBAND IS DOWN THERE.
THE PENTAGON HAS JUST BEEN HIT BY A PLANE!!!

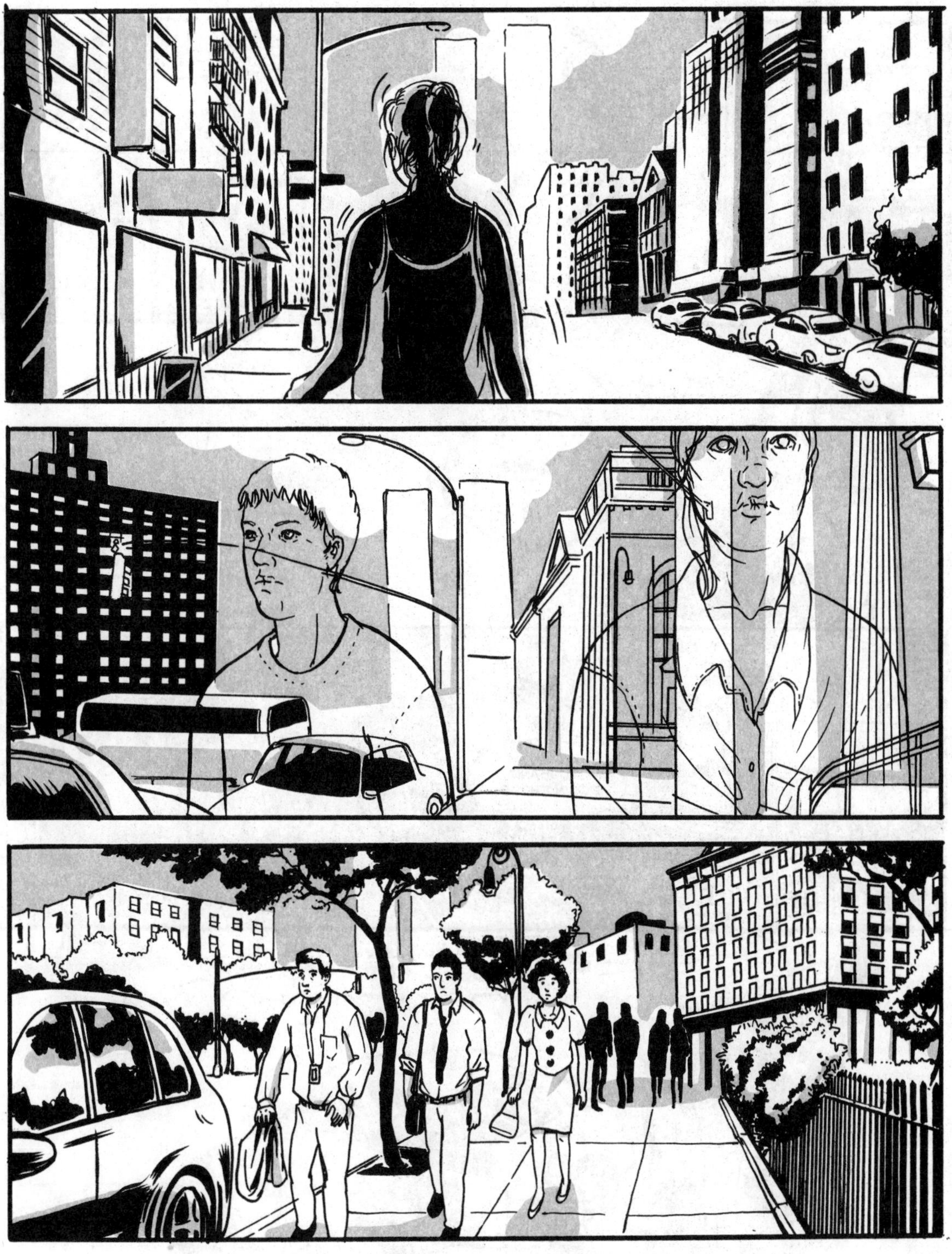

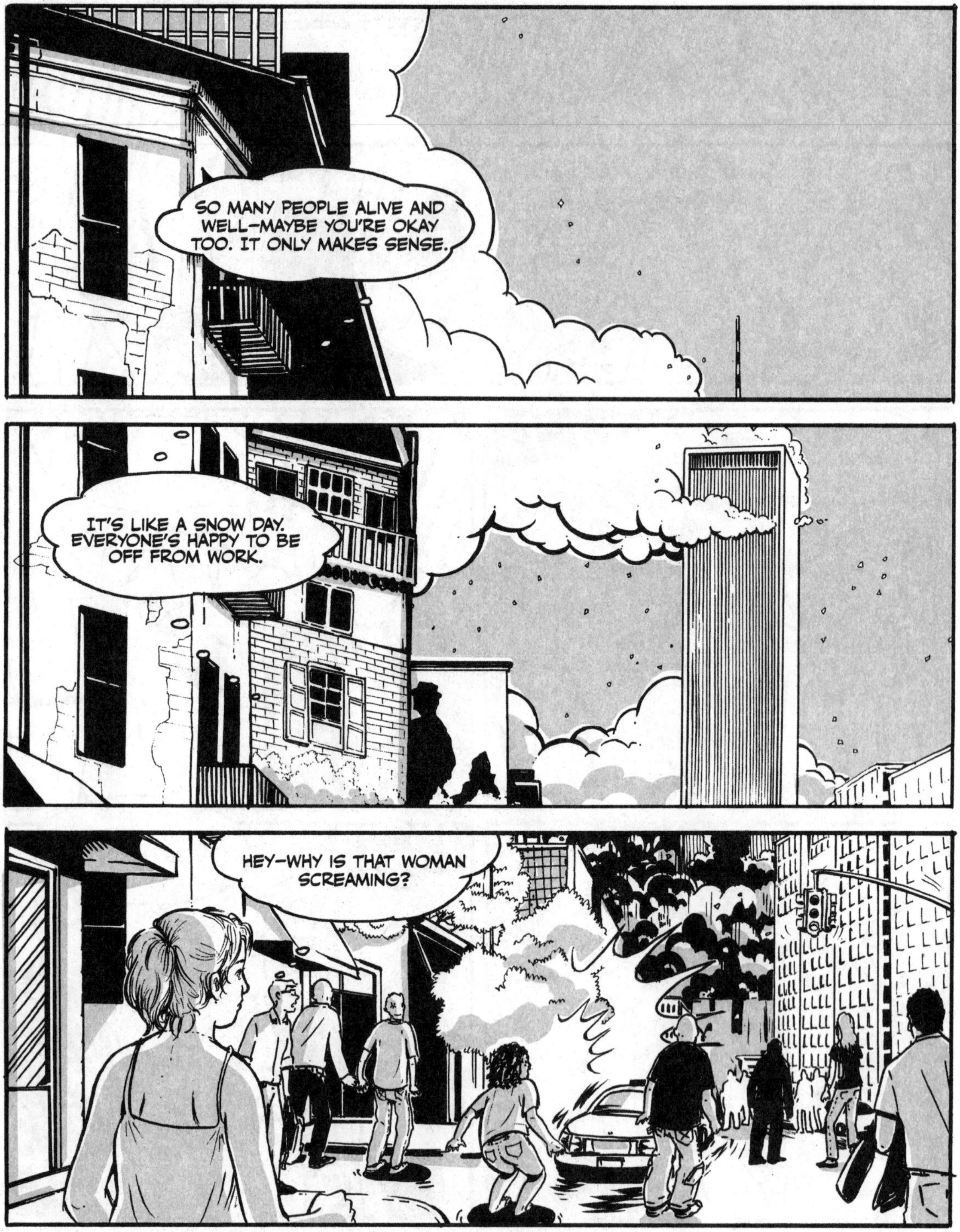
SO MANY PEOPLE ALIVE AND WELL—MAYBE YOU'RE OKAY TOO. IT ONLY MAKES SENSE.
IT'S LIKE A SNOW DAY. EVERYONE'S HAPPY TO BE OFF FROM WORK.
HEY—WHY IS THAT WOMAN SCREAMING?

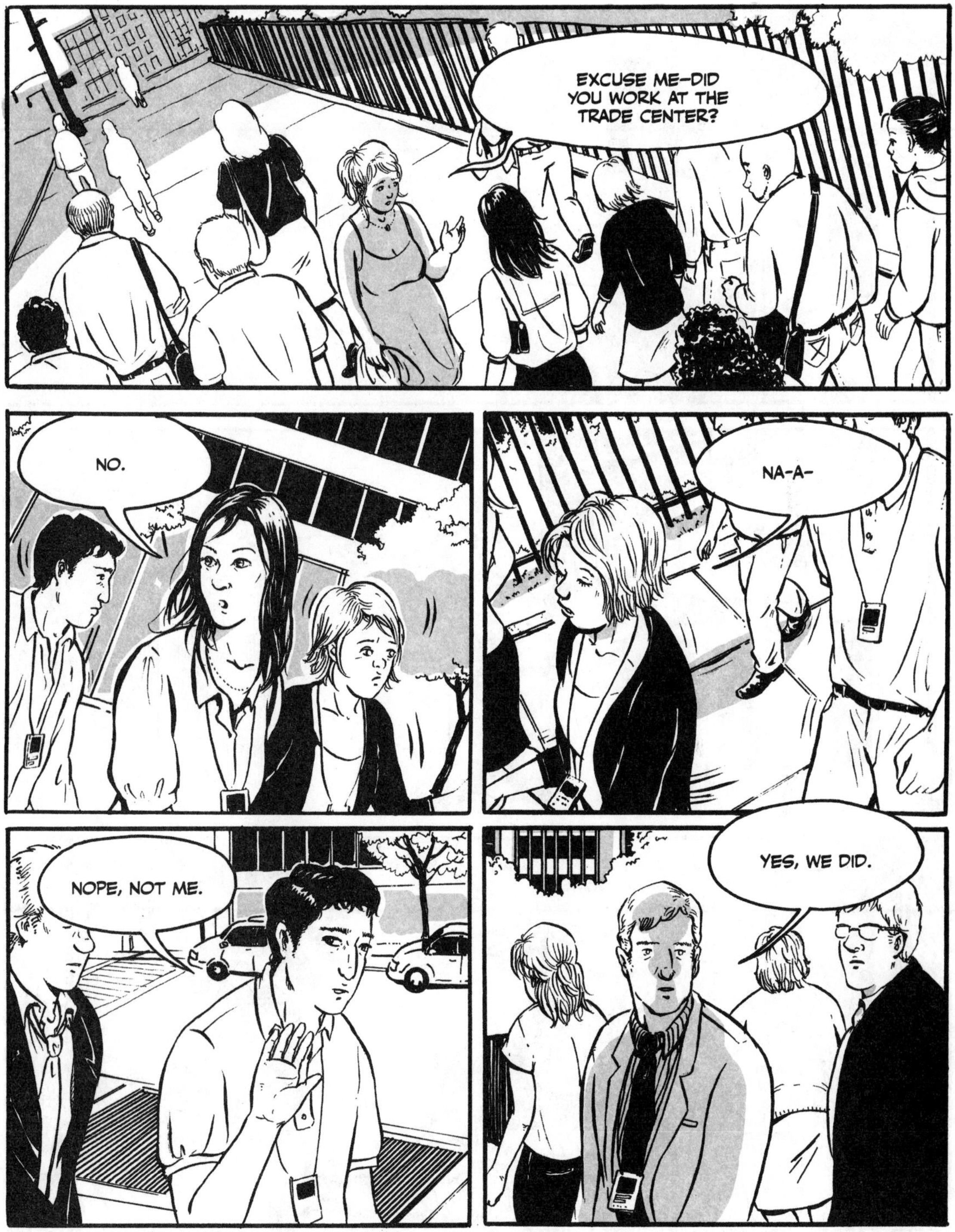
EXCUSE ME—DID YOU WORK AT THE TRADE CENTER?
NO.
NA-A-
NOPE, NOT ME.
YES, WE DID.

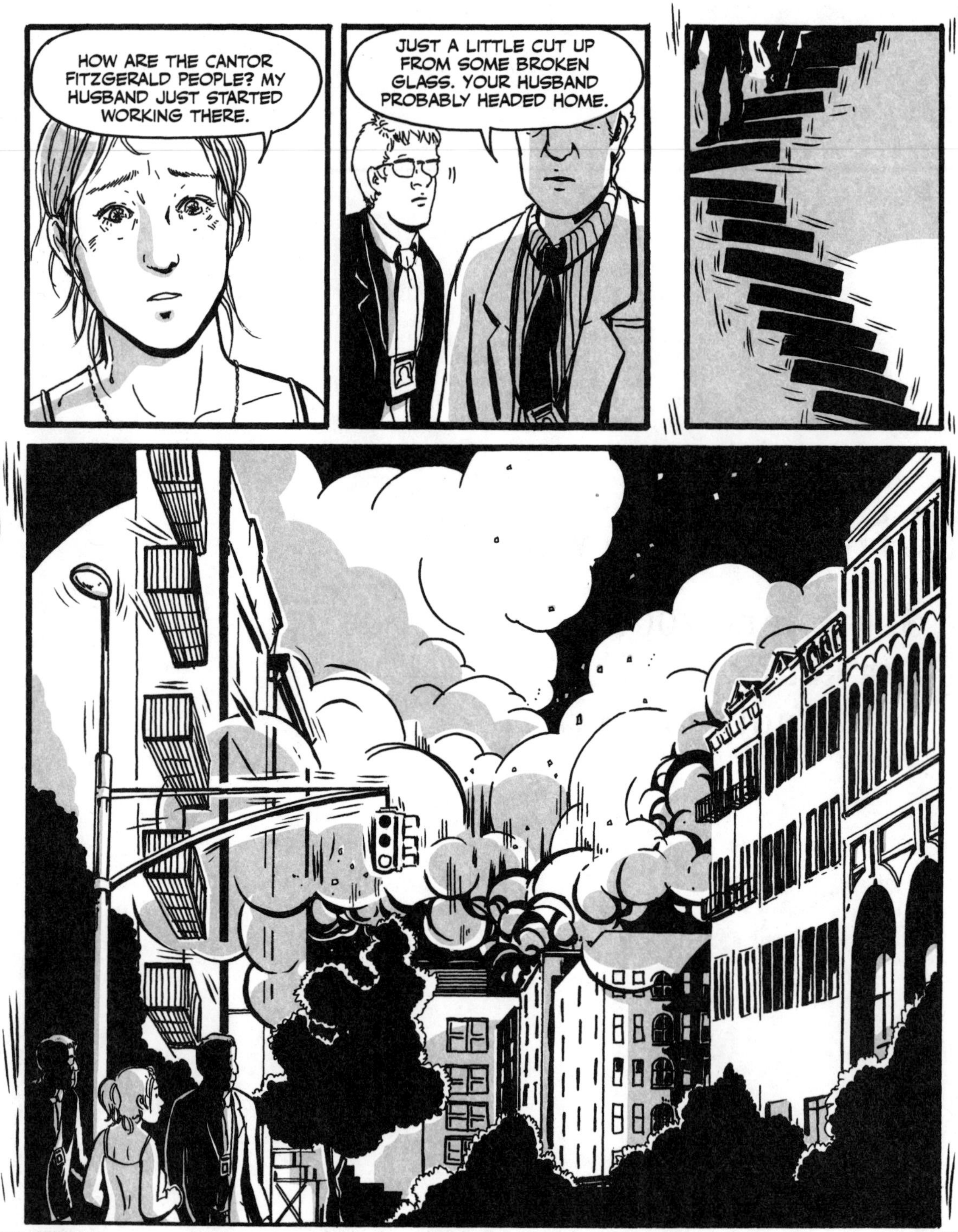
HOW ARE THE CANTOR FITZGERALD PEOPLE? MY HUSBAND JUST STARTED WORKING THERE.
JUST A LITTLE CUT UP FROM SOME BROKEN GLASS. YOUR HUSBAND PROBABLY HEADED HOME.

Chapter Five

Septemmber 2001
The Rest of
the Longest Month

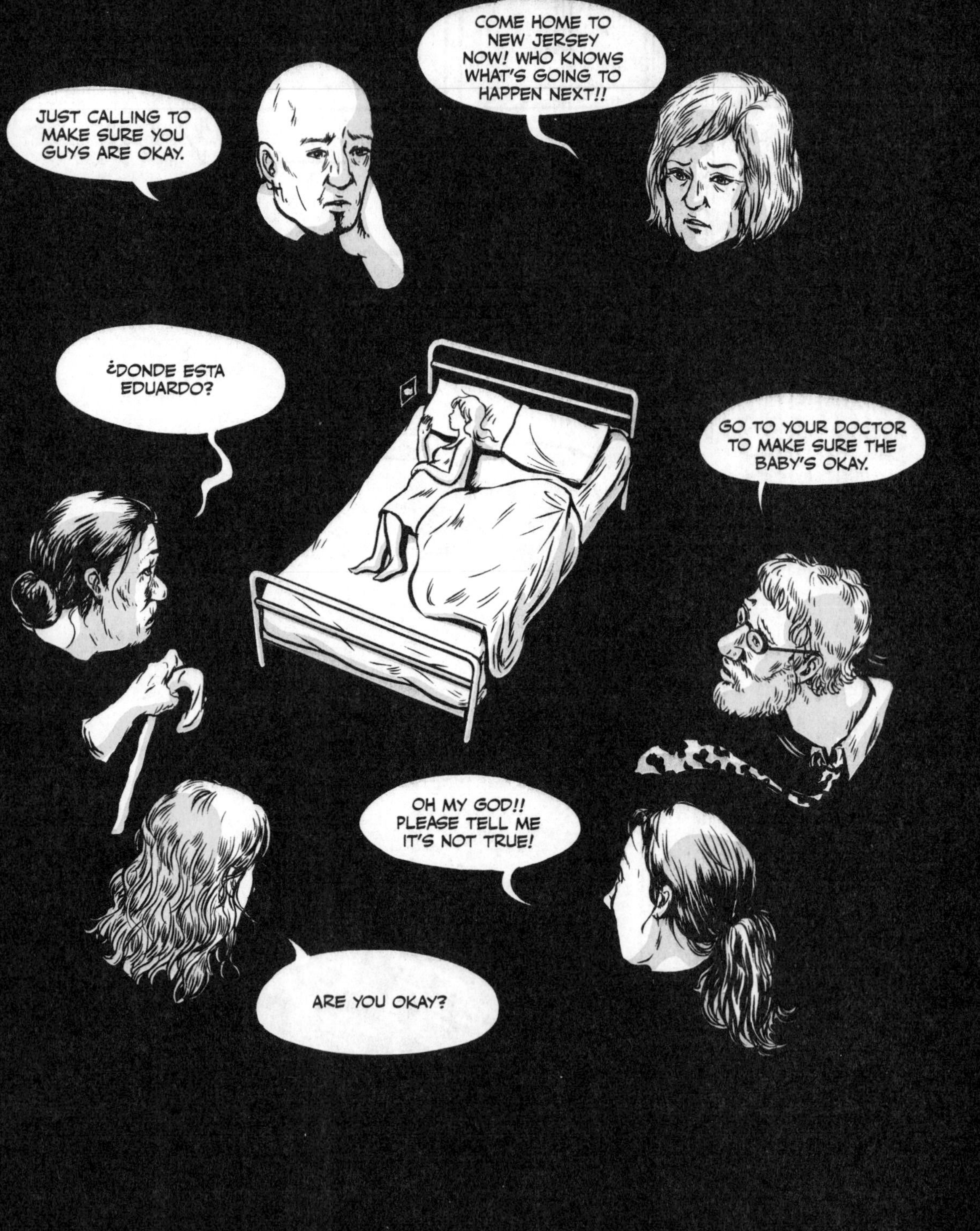
JUST CALLING TO MAKE SURE YOU GUYS ARE OKAY.
COME HOME TO NEW JERSEY NOW! WHO KNOWS WHAT'S GOING TO HAPPEN NEXT!!
¿DONDE ESTA EDUARDO?
GO TO YOUR DOCTOR TO MAKE SURE THE BABY'S OKAY.
OH MY GOD!! PLEASE TELL ME IT'S NOT TRUE!
ARE YOU OKAY?

IN THE BEGINNING THERE WAS A CLEAR BLUE SKY ON A BEAUTIFUL DAY.

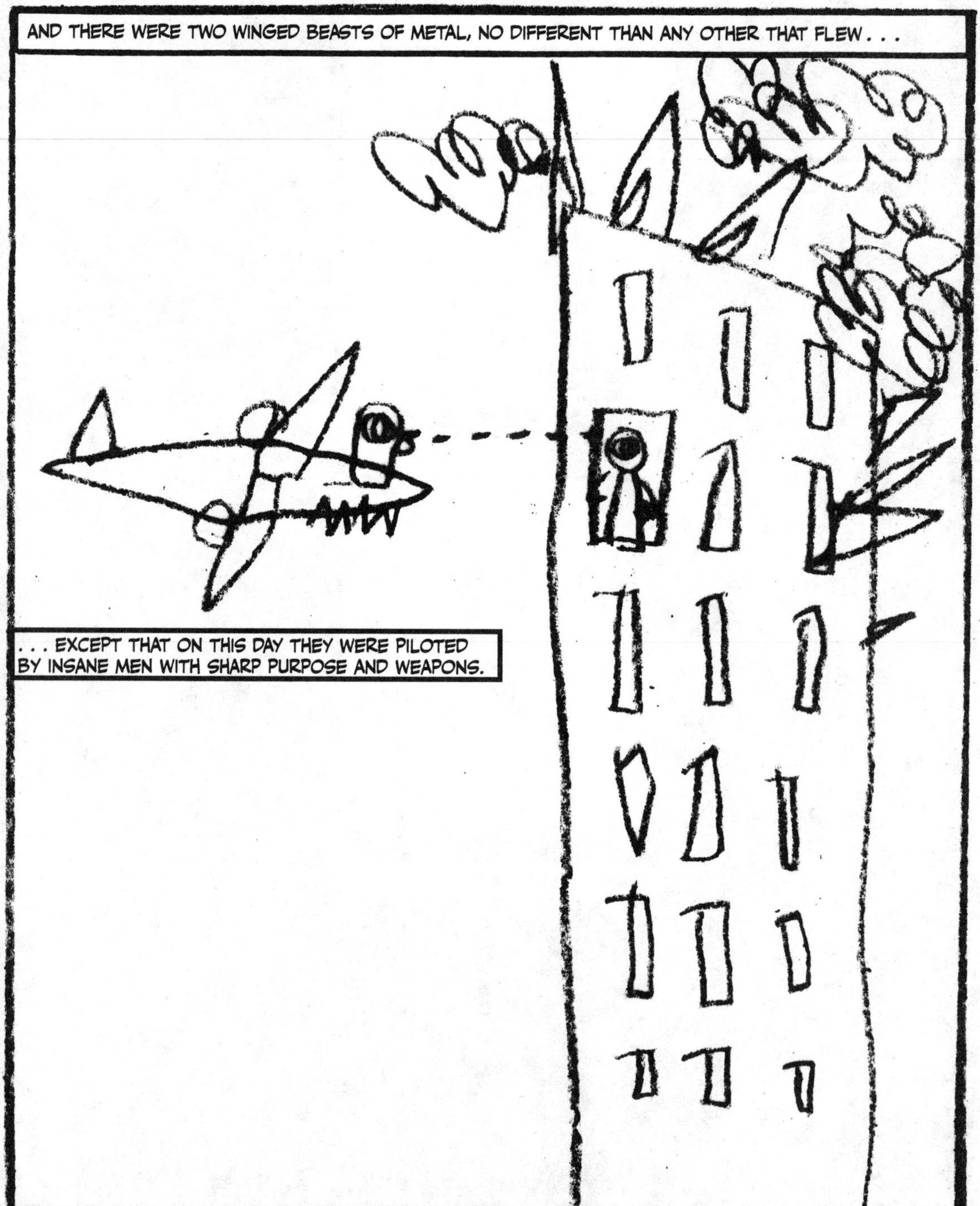
AND THERE WERE TWO WINGED BEASTS OF METAL, NO DIFFERENT THAN ANY OTHER THAT FLEW . . .
. . . EXCEPT THAT ON THIS DAY THEY WERE PILOTED BY INSANE MEN WITH SHARP PURPOSE AND WEAPONS.
AND THEN THE METAL BEASTS UNLEASHED MONSTERS OF FIRE THAT CONSUMED ALL THEY COULD.

YOU JUMPED.

YOU SAID, "FUCK IT, I'M OUT OF HERE."

AND THAT WAS THAT.

THAT WAS DAY 1.

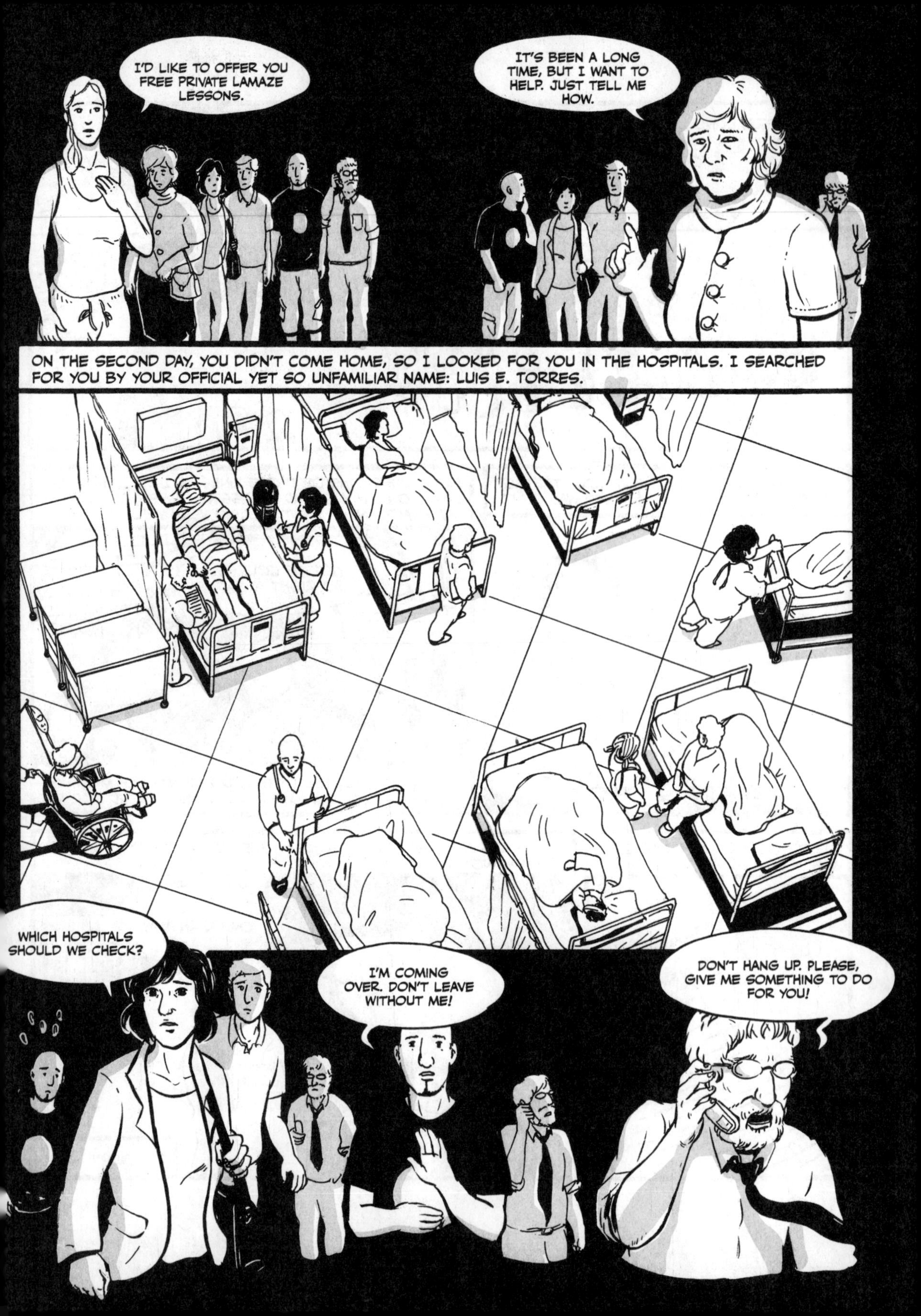
I'D LIKE TO OFFER YOU FREE PRIVATE LAMAZE LESSONS.
IT'S BEEN A LONG TIME, BUT I WANT TO HELP. JUST TELL ME HOW.
ON THE SECOND DAY, YOU DIDN'T COME HOME, SO I LOOKED FOR YOU IN THE HOSPITALS. I SEARCHED FOR YOU BY YOUR OFFICIAL YET SO UNFAMILIAR NAME: LUIS E. TORRES.
WHICH HOSPITALS SHOULD WE CHECK?
I'M COMING OVER. DON'T LEAVE WITHOUT ME!
DON'T HANG UP. PLEASE, GIVE ME SOMETHING TO DO FOR YOU!

EVERYWHERE, LONG LINES LED TO A TABLE WITH A PERSON HOLDING A LIST.

THE PERSON DID NOTHING BUT HOLD THE LIST AND REVEAL WHETHER YOUR NAME WAS ON IT.

NOPE!

I CUT EVERY ONE OF THOSE LINES AS I EXPLAINED MY SITUATION: MY HUSBAND IS MISSING, I'M SEVEN MONTHS PREGNANT, AND I'M NOT FEELING VERY WELL.

YES, OF COURSE. GO RIGHT AHEAD.

JUST A FEW MONTHS LATER, I'D FIND MYSELF MISSING THOSE MAGICAL DAYS WHEN ALL LINES PARTED FOR ME.

THERE WAS A LOUIS TORRES. HE WAS IN BELLEVUE.

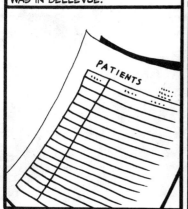

PATIENTS

THERE WAS A DORIS TORRES. I KNEW SHE WAS A WOMAN; I KNEW SHE WAS NOT YOU.

CHECK ANYWAY.

IT WASN'T YOU.

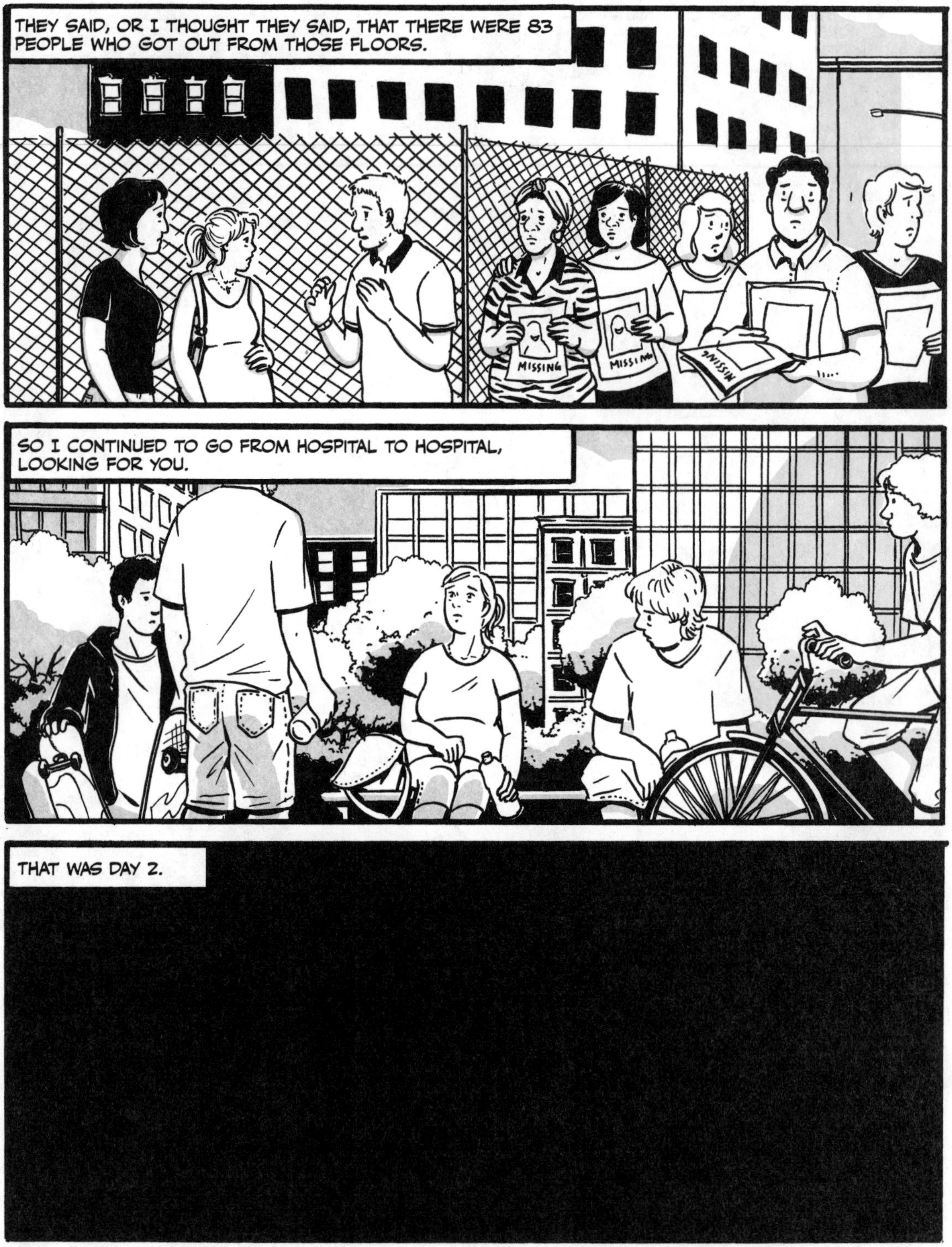
THEY SAID, OR I THOUGHT THEY SAID, THAT THERE WERE 83 PEOPLE WHO GOT OUT FROM THOSE FLOORS.
MISSING
MISSING
SO I CONTINUED TO GO FROM HOSPITAL TO HOSPITAL, LOOKING FOR YOU.
THAT WAS DAY 2.

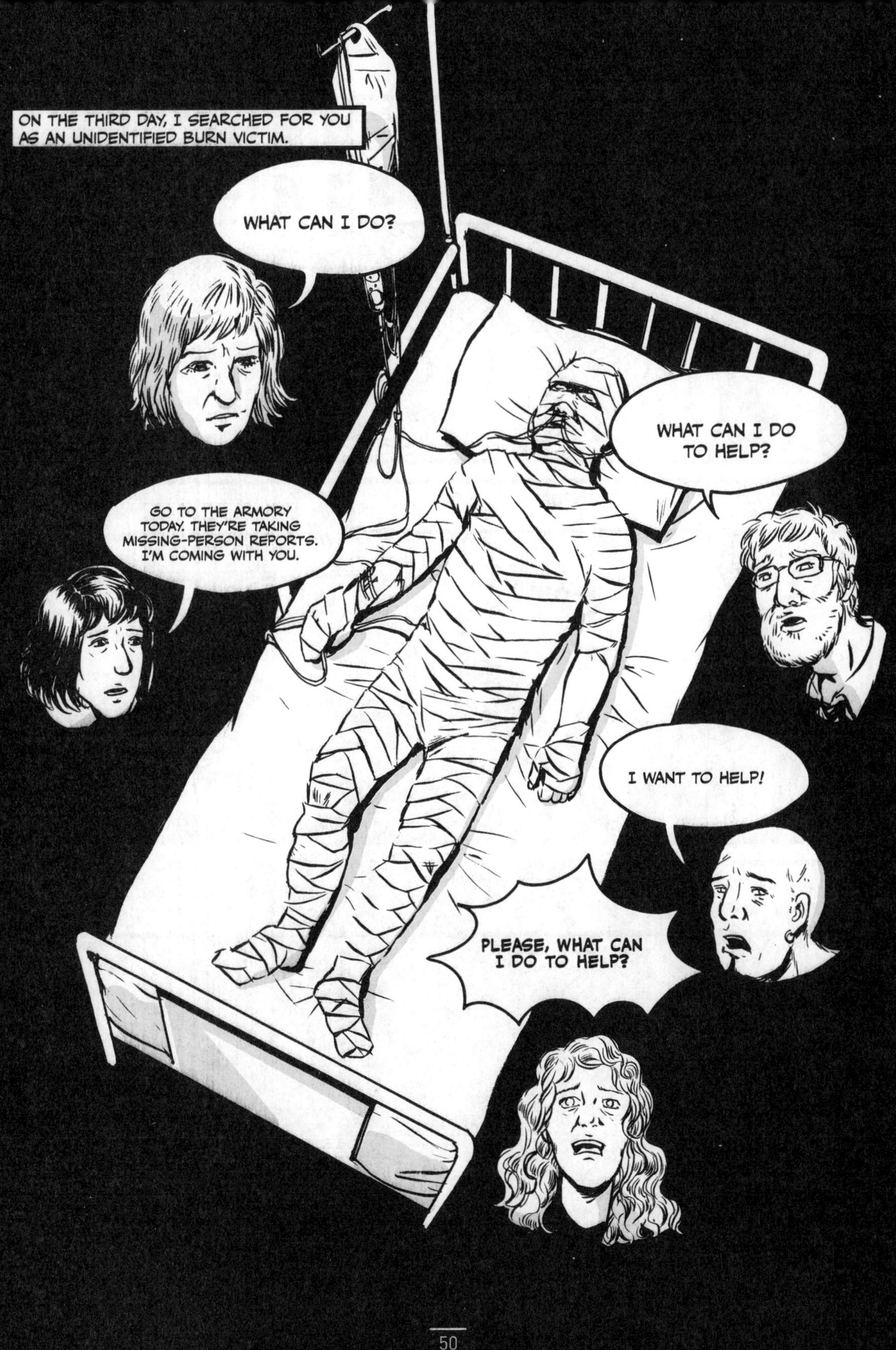
ON THE THIRD DAY, I SEARCHED FOR YOU AS AN UNIDENTIFIED BURN VICTIM.
WHAT CAN I DO?
WHAT CAN I DO TO HELP?
GO TO THE ARMORY TODAY. THEY'RE TAKING MISSING-PERSON REPORTS. I'M COMING WITH YOU.
I WANT TO HELP!
PLEASE, WHAT CAN I DO TO HELP?

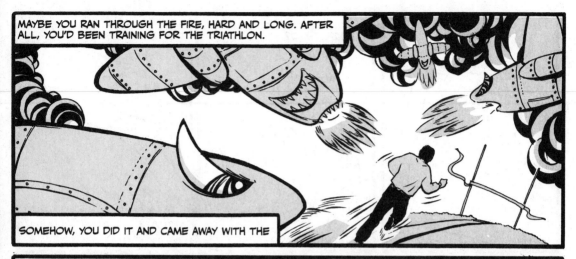

MAYBE YOU RAN THROUGH THE FIRE, HARD AND LONG. AFTER ALL, YOU'D BEEN TRAINING FOR THE TRIATHLON.

SOMEHOW, YOU DID IT AND CAME AWAY WITH THE

I CLUNG TO A STORY YOU TOLD ME OF A FIRE IN A QUEENS APARTMENT BUILDING. THE PARENTS DIED BUT SAVED THEIR SON BY PUTTING HIM INTO THE BATHTUB. YOU WERE ANGRY AT THEM FOR THEIR FOOLISHNESS.

YOU SAID:

WHY DIDN'T THEY RUN THROUGH THE FIRE, BECAUSE THEY WERE GOING TO DIE ANYWAY?

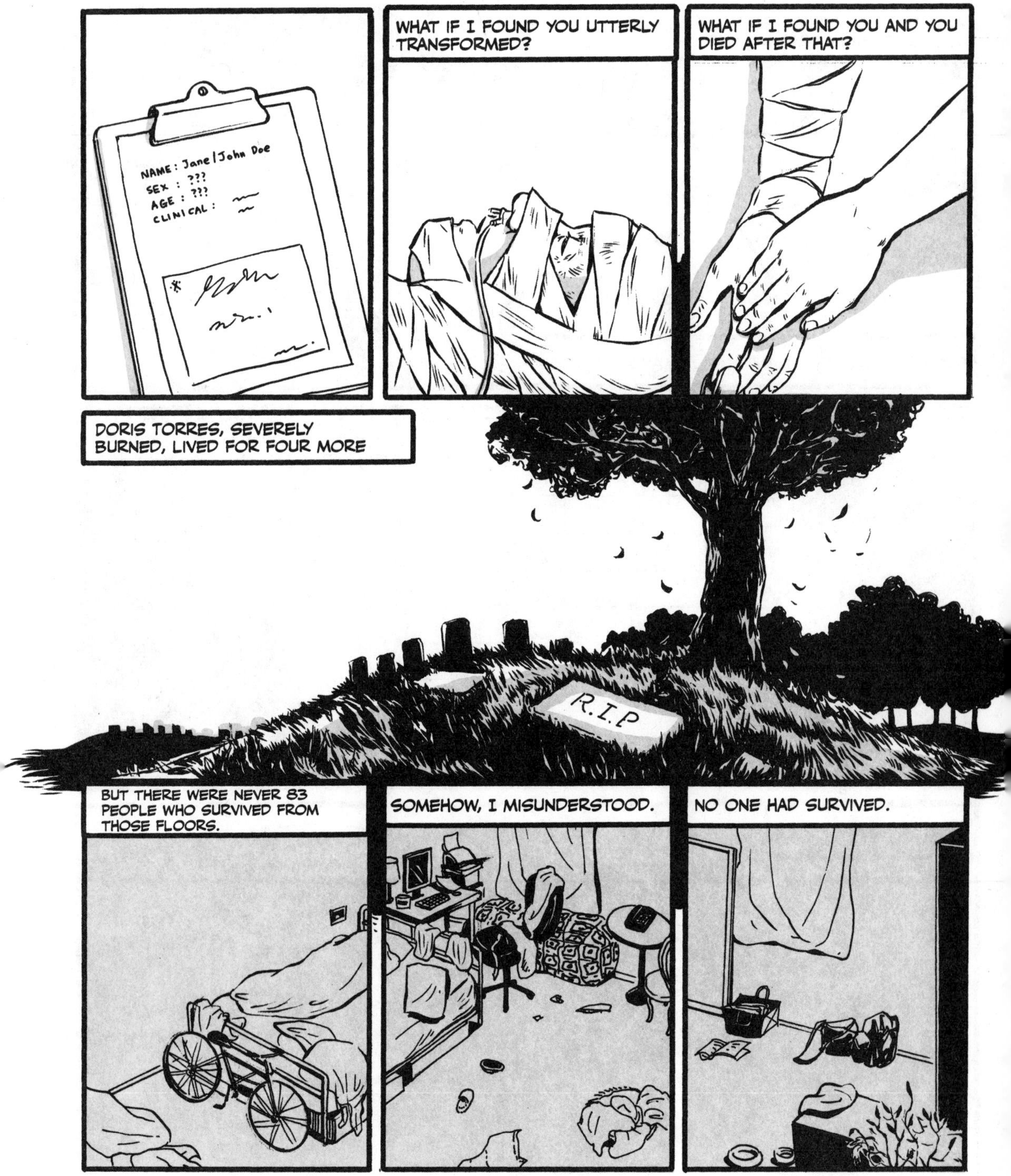
NAME: Jane/John Doe
SEX: ???
AGE: ???
CLINICAL:
WHAT IF I FOUND YOU UTTERLY TRANSFORMED?
WHAT IF I FOUND YOU AND YOU DIED AFTER THAT?
DORIS TORRES, SEVERELY BURNED, LIVED FOR FOUR MORE
R.I.P.
BUT THERE WERE NEVER 83 PEOPLE WHO SURVIVED FROM THOSE FLOORS.
SOMEHOW, I MISUNDERSTOOD.
NO ONE HAD SURVIVED.

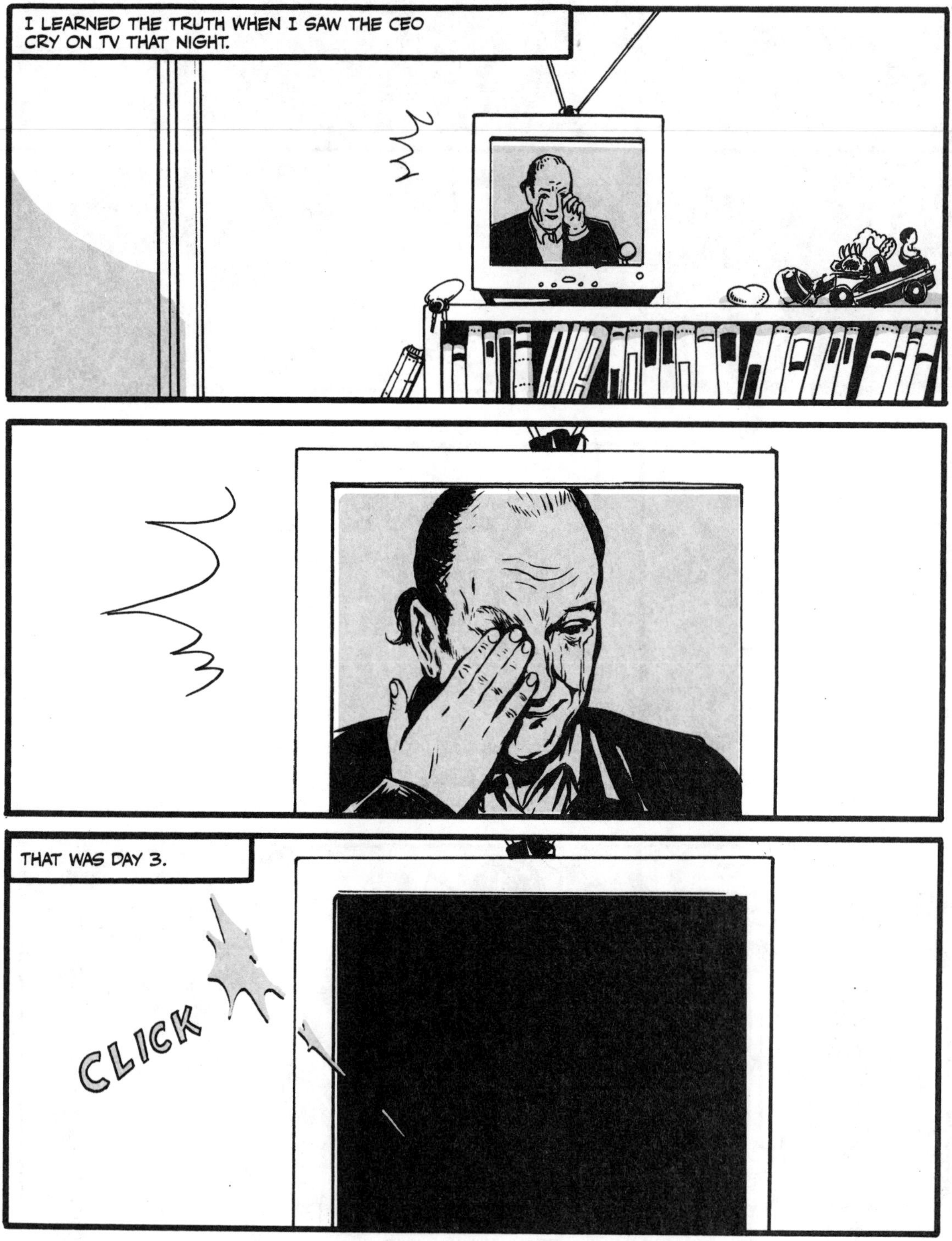
I LEARNED THE TRUTH WHEN I SAW THE CEO CRY ON TV THAT NIGHT.
THAT WAS DAY 3.
CLICK

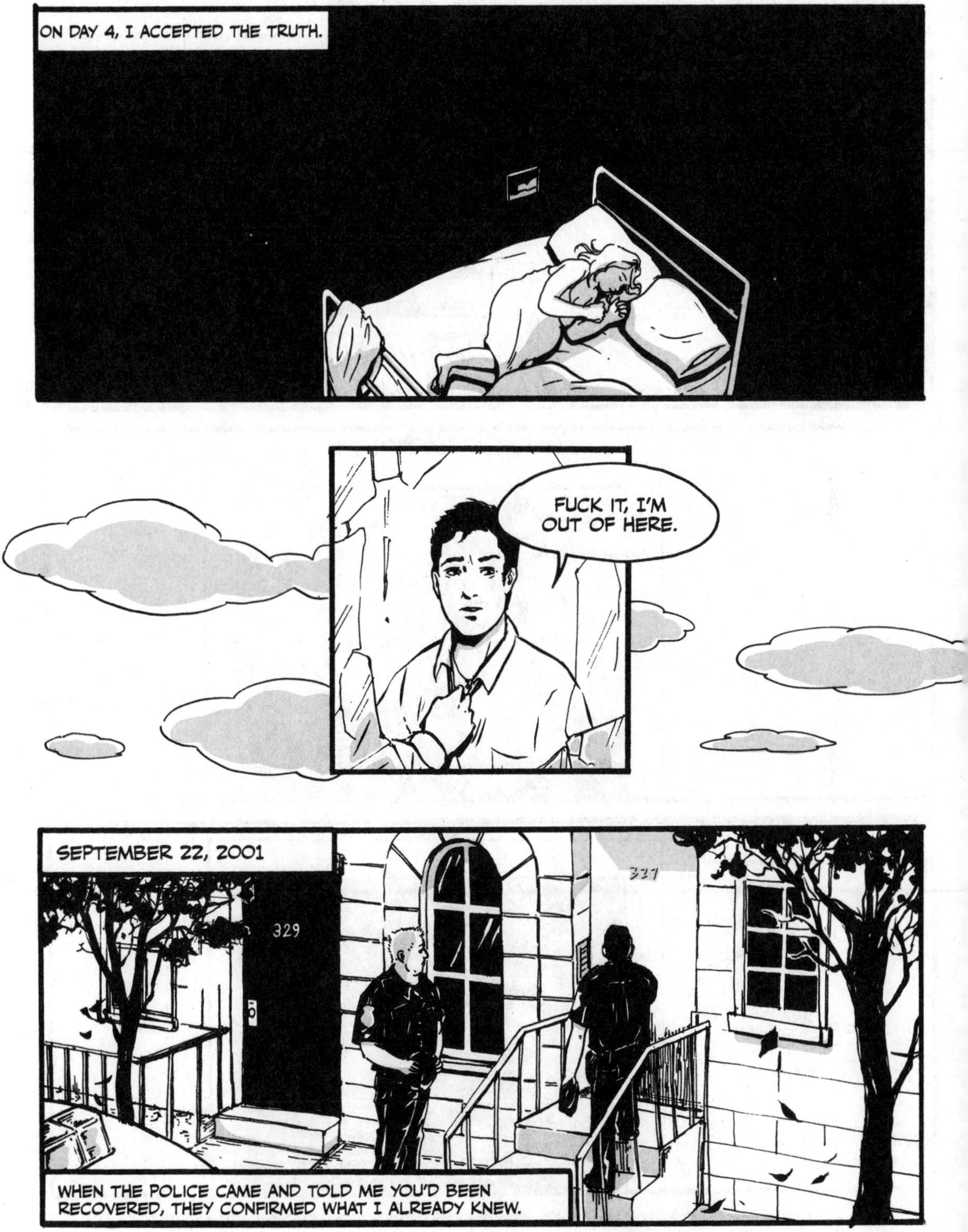
ON DAY 4, I ACCEPTED THE TRUTH.
FUCK IT, I'M OUT OF HERE.
SEPTEMBER 22, 2001
329
327
WHEN THE POLICE CAME AND TOLD ME YOU'D BEEN RECOVERED, THEY CONFIRMED WHAT I ALREADY KNEW.

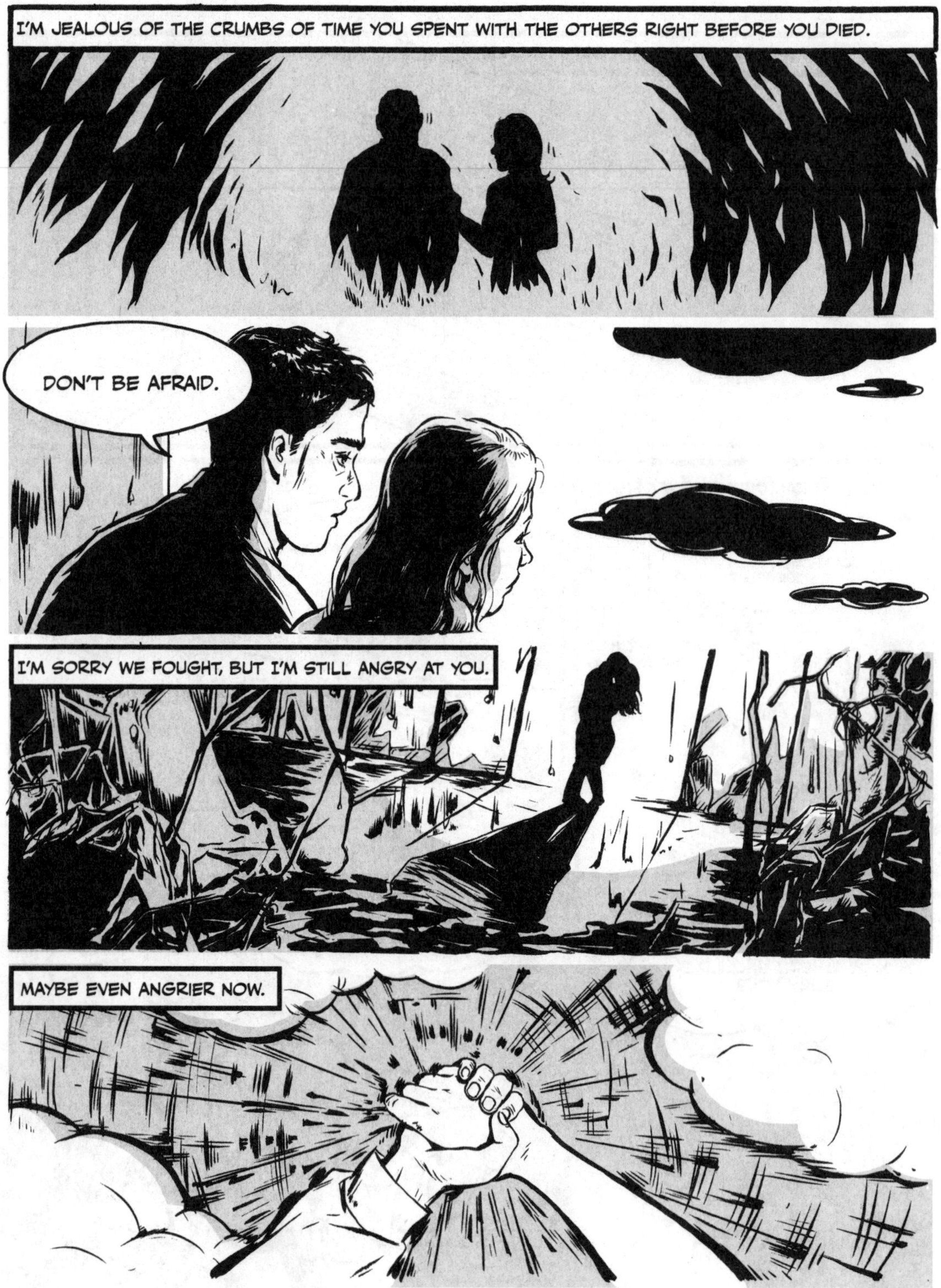
I'M JEALOUS OF THE CRUMBS OF TIME YOU SPENT WITH THE OTHERS RIGHT BEFORE YOU DIED.
DON'T BE AFRAID.
I'M SORRY WE FOUGHT, BUT I'M STILL ANGRY AT YOU.
MAYBE EVEN ANGRIER NOW.

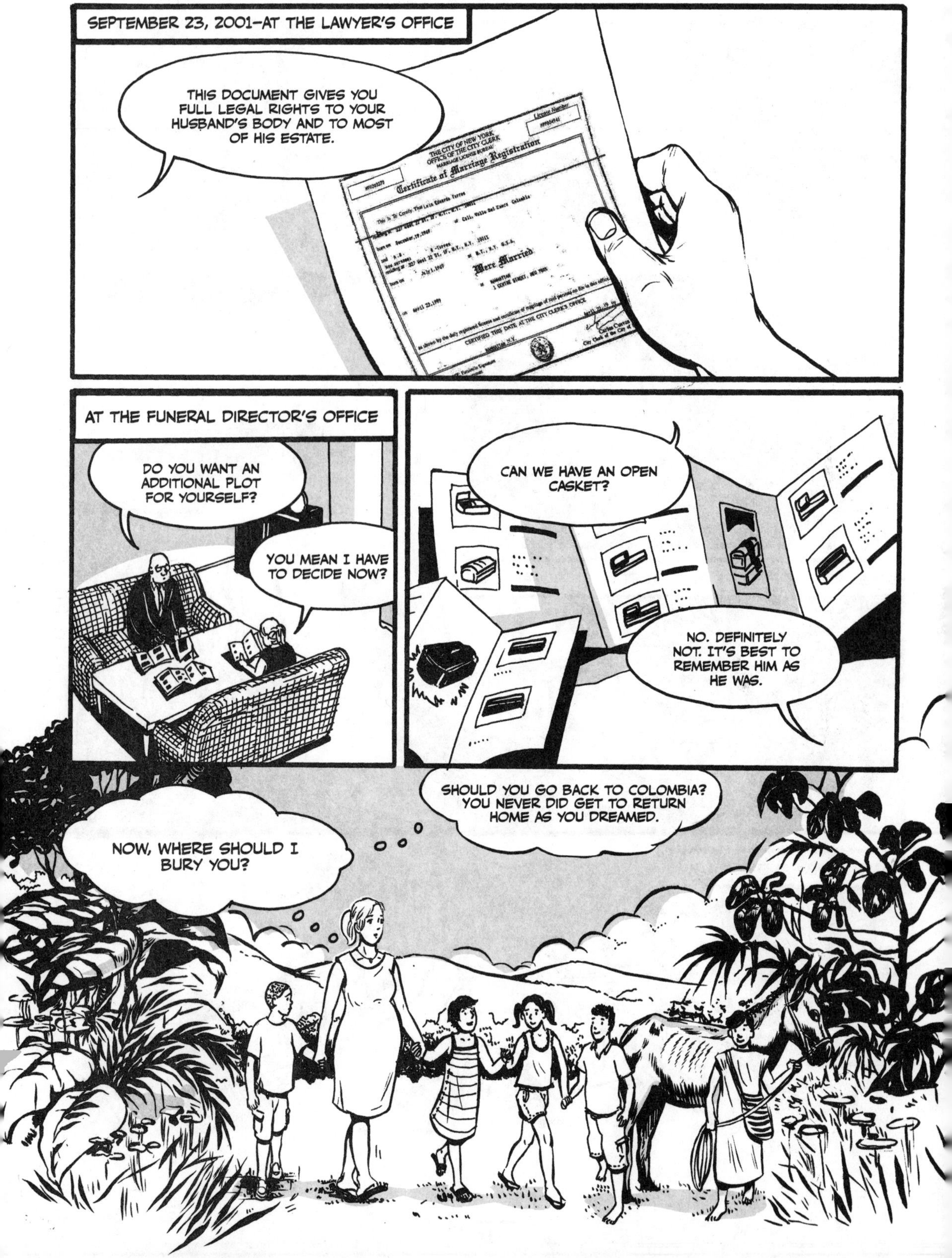
SEPTEMBER 23, 2001—AT THE LAWYER'S OFFICE
THIS DOCUMENT GIVES YOU FULL LEGAL RIGHTS TO YOUR HUSBAND'S BODY AND TO MOST OF HIS ESTATE.
Certificate of Marriage Registration
Were Married
AT THE FUNERAL DIRECTOR'S OFFICE
DO YOU WANT AN ADDITIONAL PLOT FOR YOURSELF?
YOU MEAN I HAVE TO DECIDE NOW?
CAN WE HAVE AN OPEN CASKET?
NO. DEFINITELY NOT. IT'S BEST TO REMEMBER HIM AS HE WAS.
NOW, WHERE SHOULD I BURY YOU?
SHOULD YOU GO BACK TO COLOMBIA? YOU NEVER DID GET TO RETURN HOME AS YOU DREAMED.

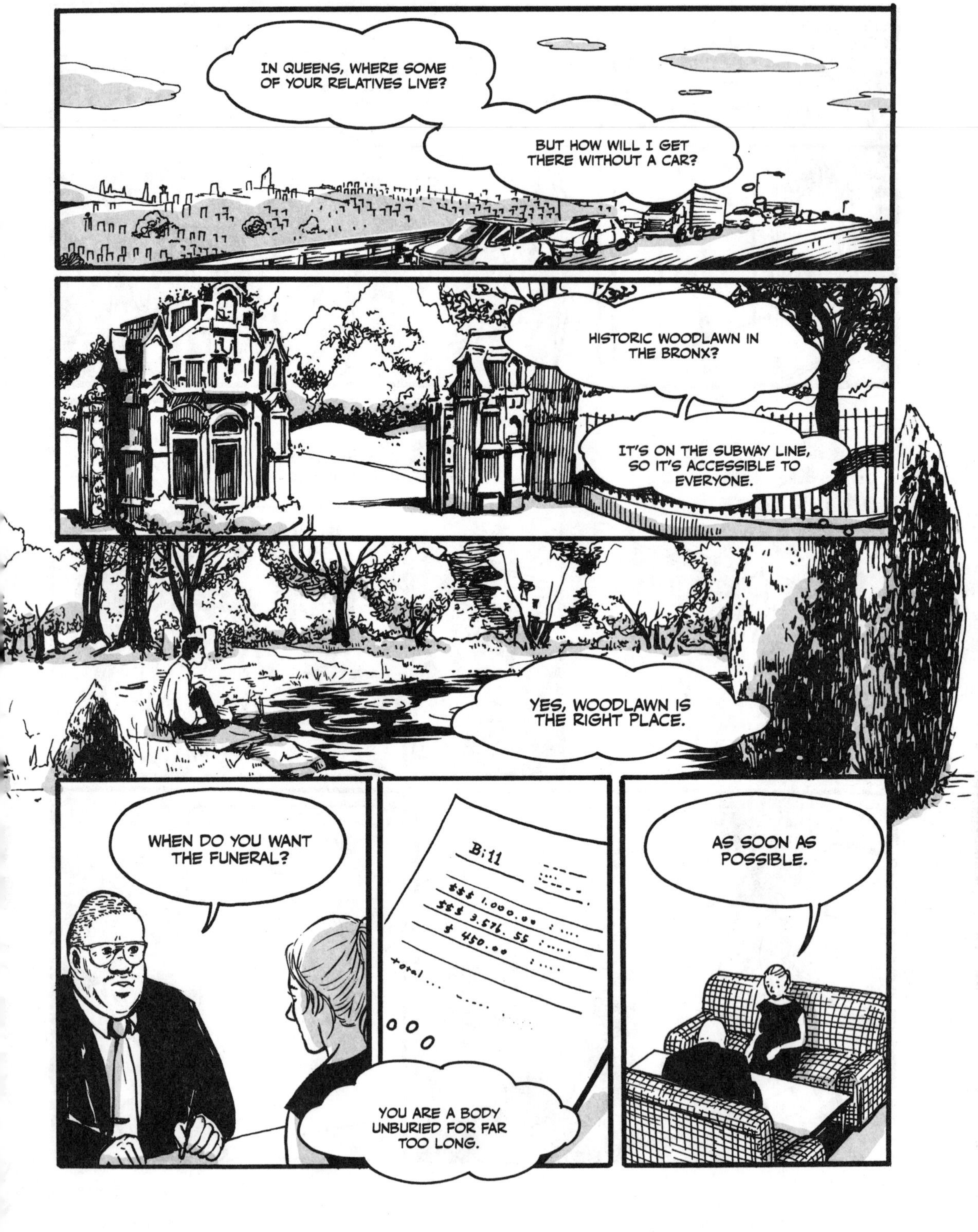
IN QUEENS, WHERE SOME OF YOUR RELATIVES LIVE?
BUT HOW WILL I GET THERE WITHOUT A CAR?
HISTORIC WOODLAWN IN THE BRONX?
IT'S ON THE SUBWAY LINE, SO IT'S ACCESSIBLE TO EVERYONE.
YES, WOODLAWN IS THE RIGHT PLACE.
WHEN DO YOU WANT THE FUNERAL?
Bill
$$$ 1.000.00
$$$ 3.576.55
$ 450.00
total
YOU ARE A BODY UNBURIED FOR FAR TOO LONG.
AS SOON AS POSSIBLE.

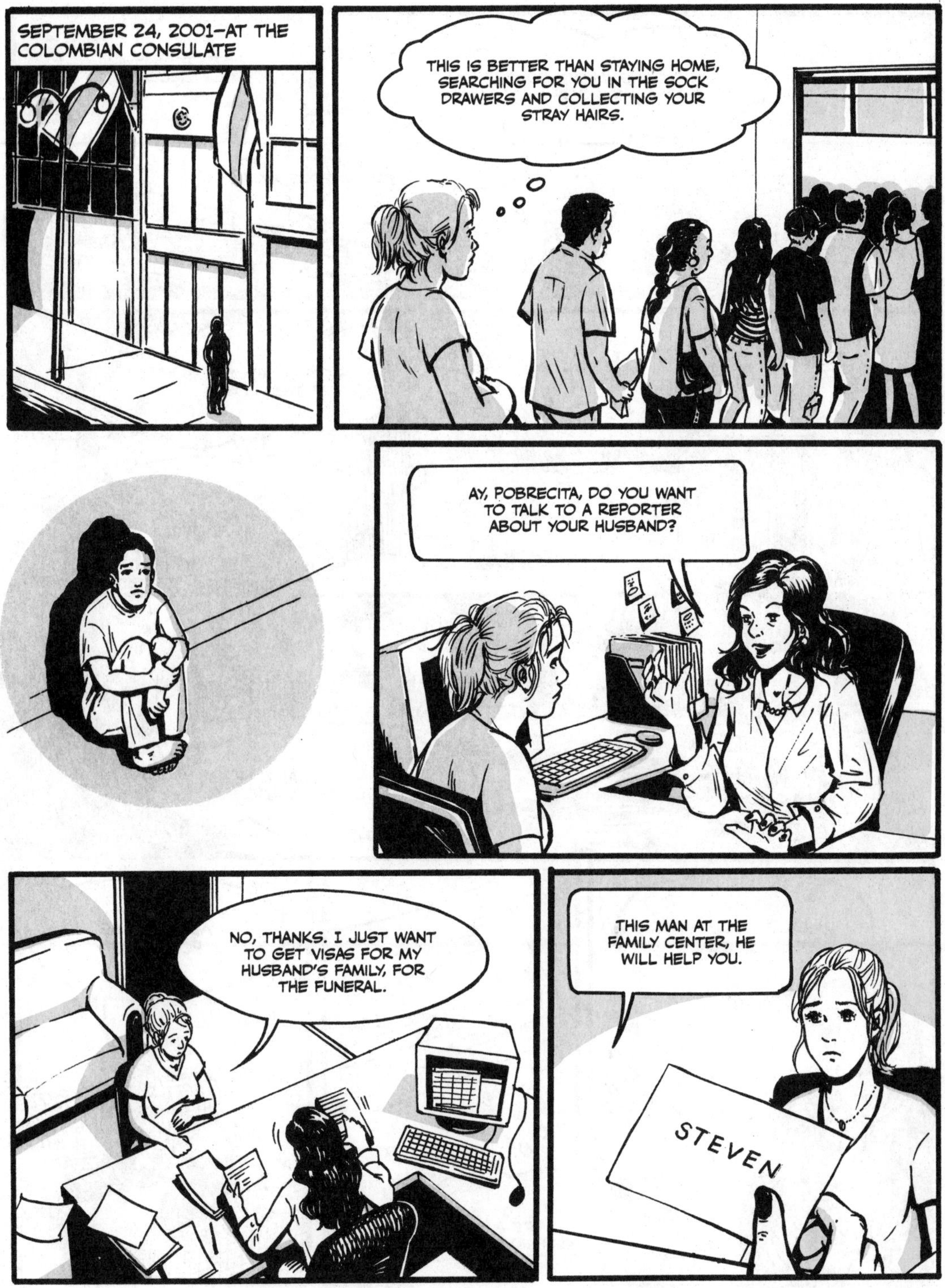
SEPTEMBER 24, 2001—AT THE COLOMBIAN CONSULATE
THIS IS BETTER THAN STAYING HOME, SEARCHING FOR YOU IN THE SOCK DRAWERS AND COLLECTING YOUR STRAY HAIRS.
AY, POBRECITA, DO YOU WANT TO TALK TO A REPORTER ABOUT YOUR HUSBAND?
NO, THANKS. I JUST WANT TO GET VISAS FOR MY HUSBAND'S FAMILY, FOR THE FUNERAL.
THIS MAN AT THE FAMILY CENTER, HE WILL HELP YOU.
STEVEN

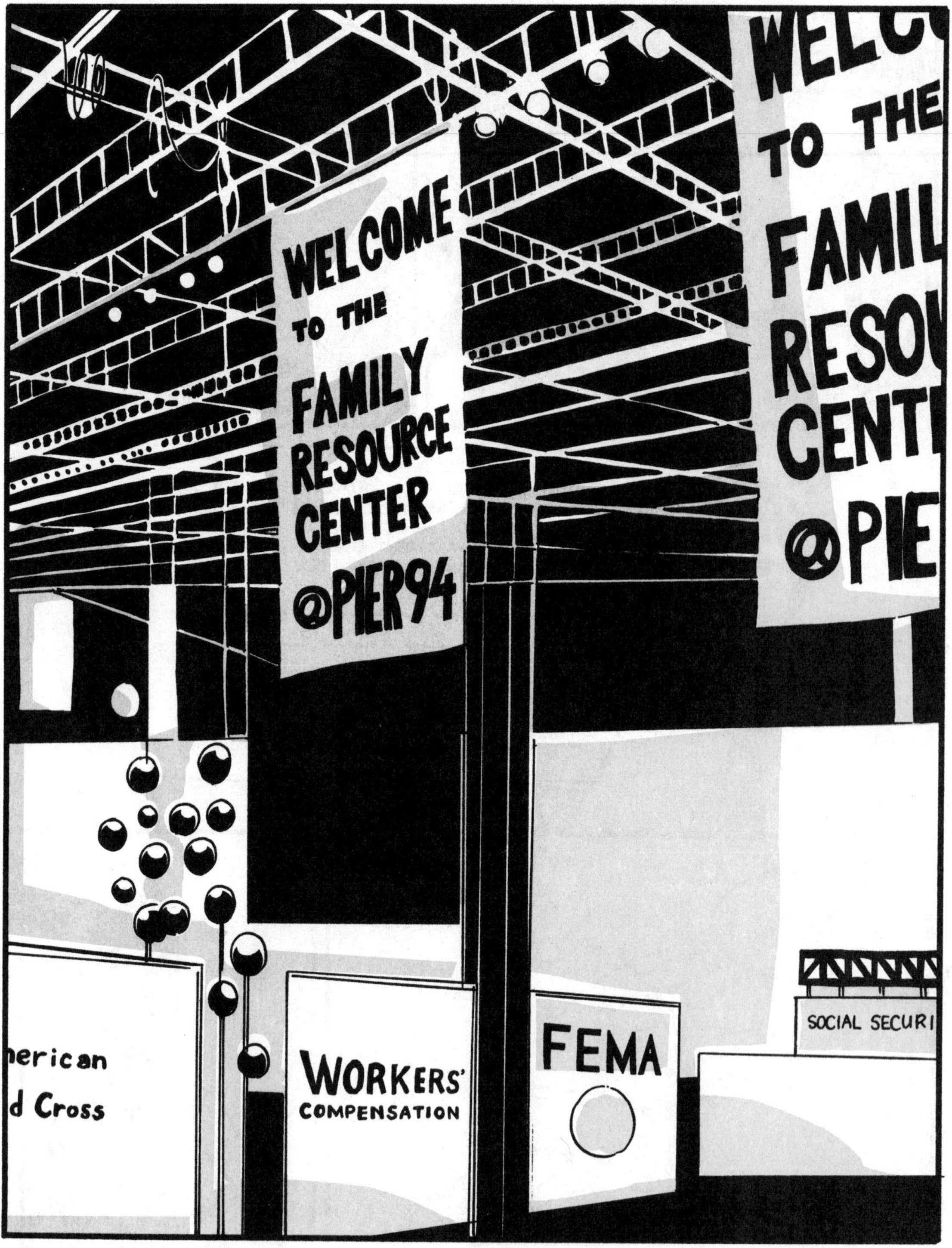
WELCOME
TO THE
FAMILY
RESOURCE
CENTER
@PIER94
WELC
TO THE
FAMIL
RESOU
CENT
@PIE
merican
d Cross
WORKERS'
COMPENSATION
FEMA
SOCIAL SECURI

MAYOR'S OFFICE

SO THIS IS STEVEN.

HELGA SHOULDN'T HAVE SENT YOU; SHE KNOWS BETTER.

THE CONSULATE IS SUPPOSED TO CONTACT THE EMBASSY IN D.C., THE EMBASSY CONTACTS THE STATE DEPARTMENT, THE STATE DEPARTMENT CONTACTS THE COLOMBIAN EMBASSY IN BOGOTÁ.

FOR A WHILE I WAS DIRECTING PEOPLE TO THE STATE DEPARTMENT BUT GOT IN TROUBLE.

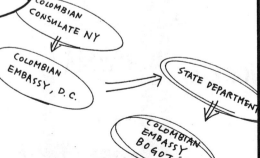

LET ME SHOW YOU HOW THIS WORKS.

COLOMBIAN CONSULATE NY

COLOMBIAN EMBASSY, D.C.

STATE DEPARTMENT

COLOMBIAN EMBASSY BOGOTÁ

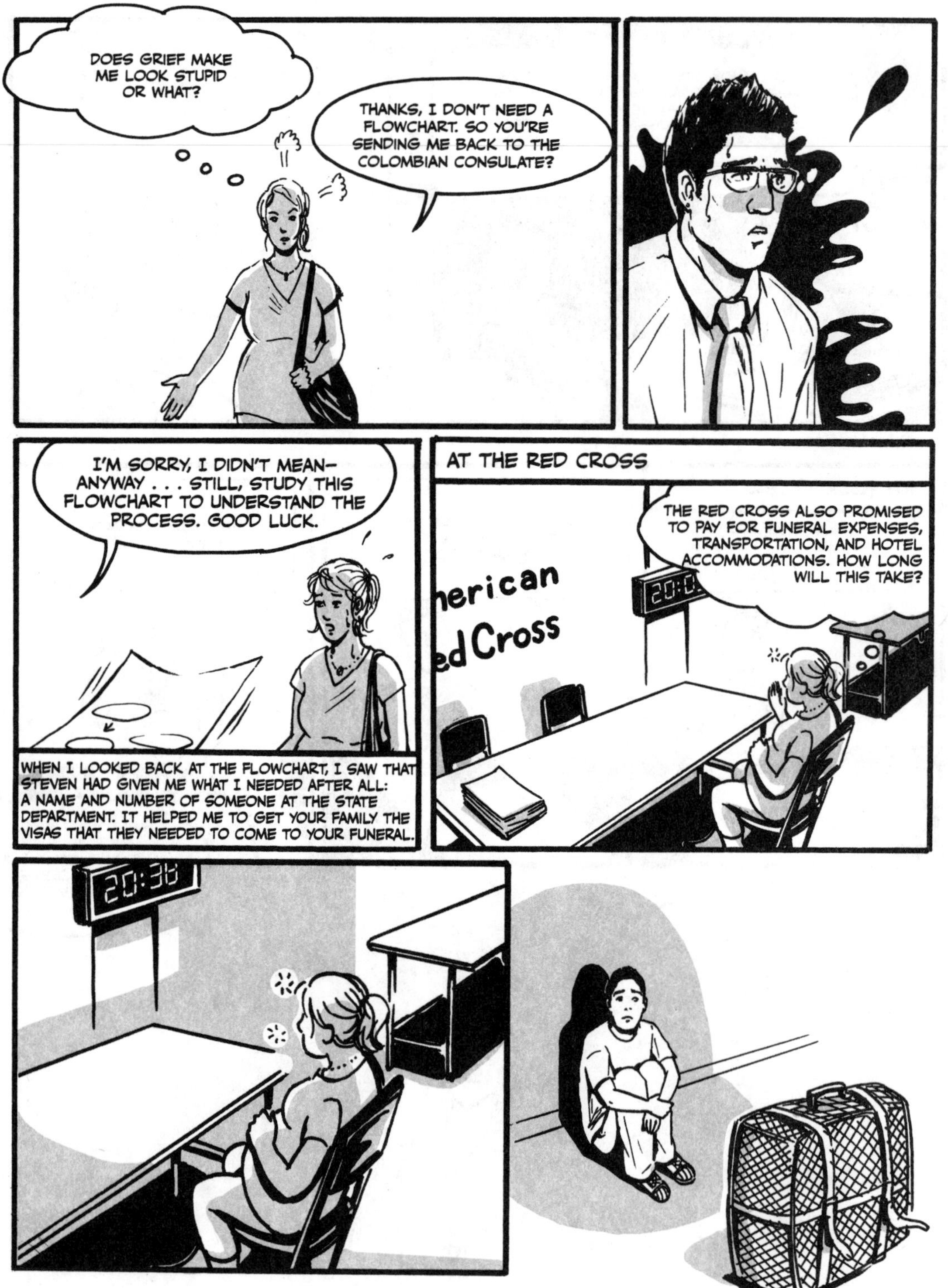
DOES GRIEF MAKE ME LOOK STUPID OR WHAT?
THANKS, I DON'T NEED A FLOWCHART. SO YOU'RE SENDING ME BACK TO THE COLOMBIAN CONSULATE?
I'M SORRY, I DIDN'T MEAN— ANYWAY . . . STILL, STUDY THIS FLOWCHART TO UNDERSTAND THE PROCESS. GOOD LUCK.
WHEN I LOOKED BACK AT THE FLOWCHART, I SAW THAT STEVEN HAD GIVEN ME WHAT I NEEDED AFTER ALL: A NAME AND NUMBER OF SOMEONE AT THE STATE DEPARTMENT. IT HELPED ME TO GET YOUR FAMILY THE VISAS THAT THEY NEEDED TO COME TO YOUR FUNERAL.
AT THE RED CROSS
THE RED CROSS ALSO PROMISED TO PAY FOR FUNERAL EXPENSES, TRANSPORTATION, AND HOTEL ACCOMMODATIONS. HOW LONG WILL THIS TAKE?
merican
ed Cross
20:38

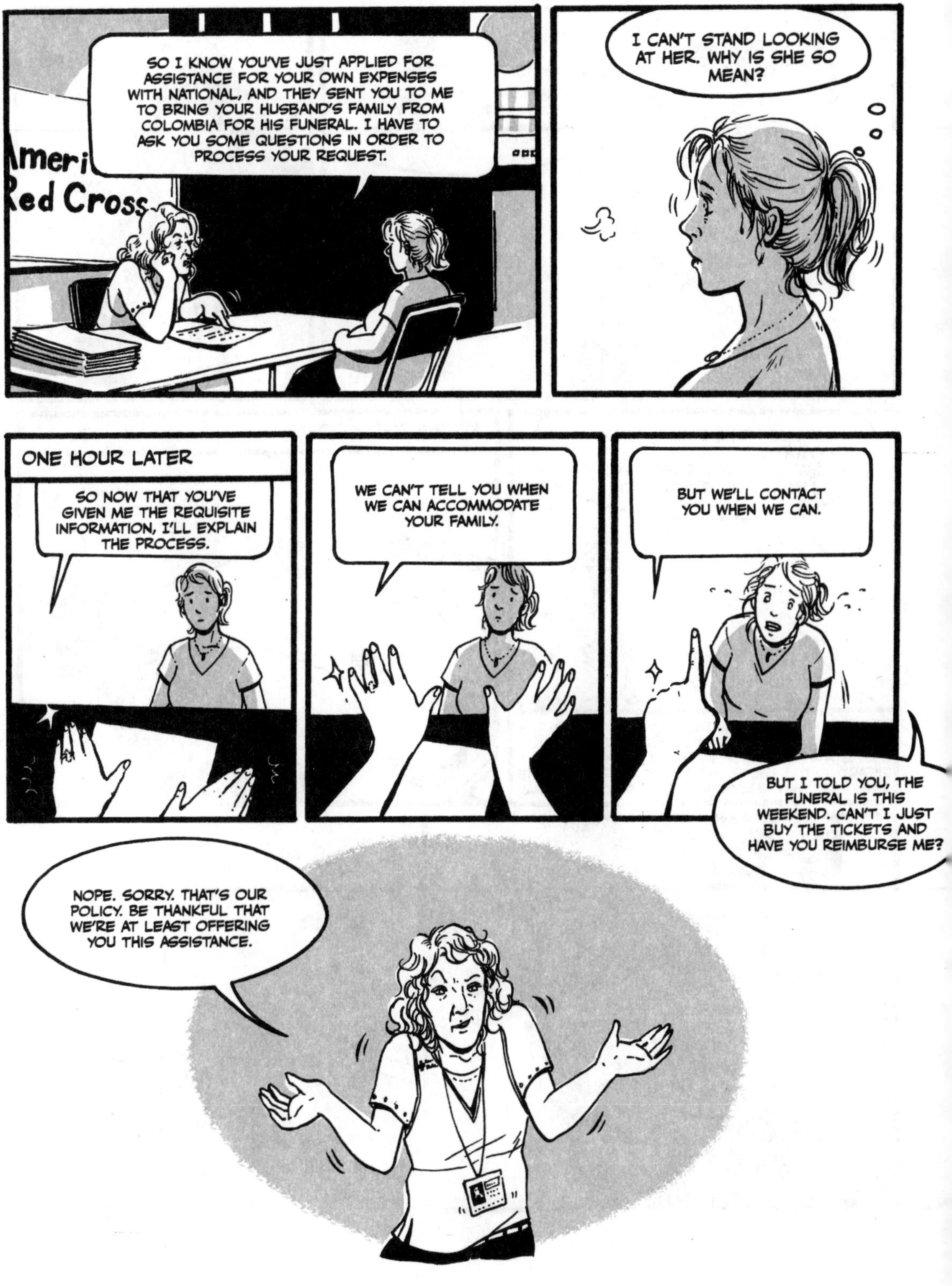

Ameri
Red Cross
SO I KNOW YOU'VE JUST APPLIED FOR ASSISTANCE FOR YOUR OWN EXPENSES WITH NATIONAL, AND THEY SENT YOU TO ME TO BRING YOUR HUSBAND'S FAMILY FROM COLOMBIA FOR HIS FUNERAL. I HAVE TO ASK YOU SOME QUESTIONS IN ORDER TO PROCESS YOUR REQUEST.
I CAN'T STAND LOOKING AT HER. WHY IS SHE SO MEAN?
ONE HOUR LATER
SO NOW THAT YOU'VE GIVEN ME THE REQUISITE INFORMATION, I'LL EXPLAIN THE PROCESS.
WE CAN'T TELL YOU WHEN WE CAN ACCOMMODATE YOUR FAMILY.
BUT WE'LL CONTACT YOU WHEN WE CAN.
BUT I TOLD YOU, THE FUNERAL IS THIS WEEKEND. CAN'T I JUST BUY THE TICKETS AND HAVE YOU REIMBURSE ME?
NOPE. SORRY. THAT'S OUR POLICY. BE THANKFUL THAT WE'RE AT LEAST OFFERING YOU THIS ASSISTANCE.

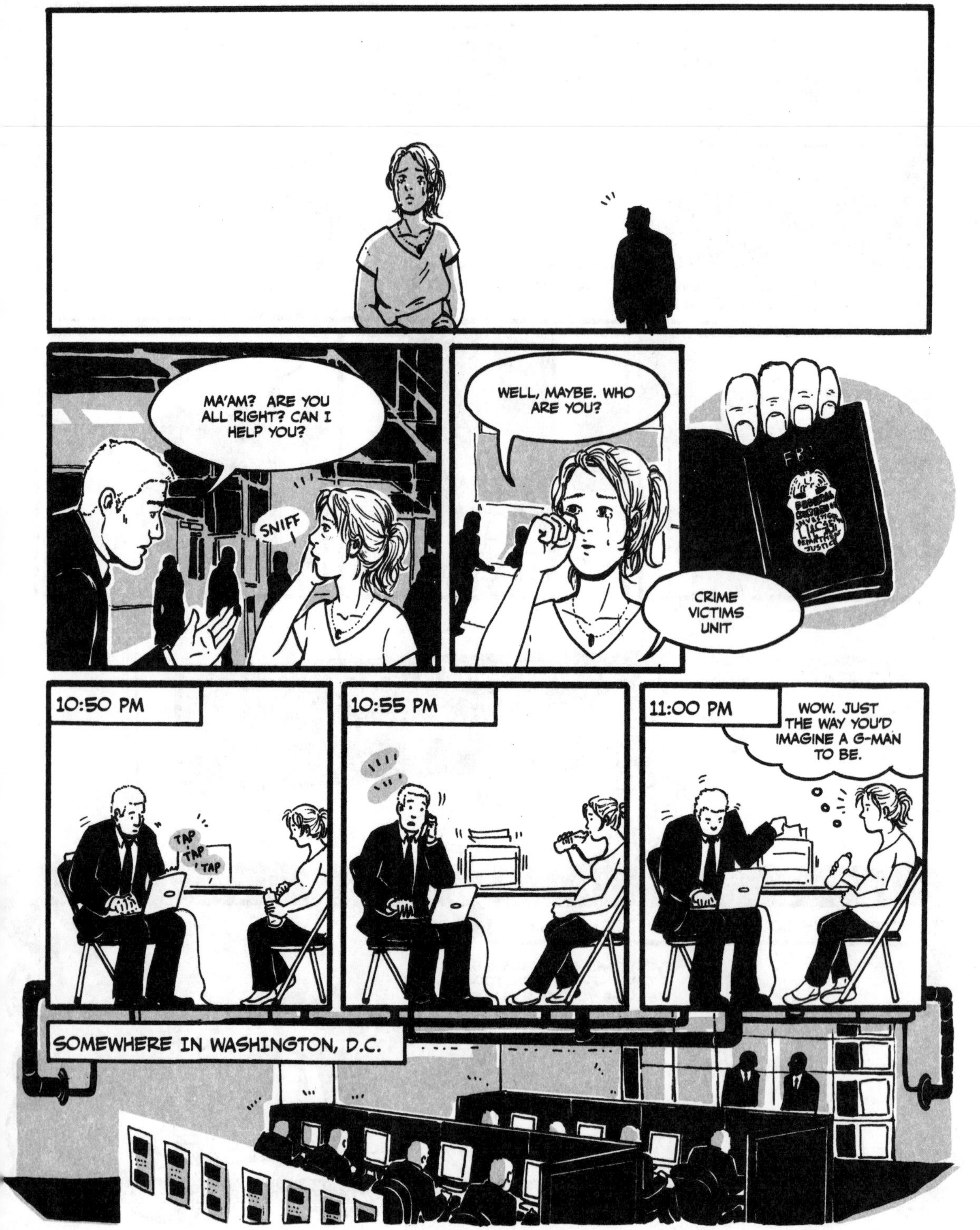
MA'AM? ARE YOU ALL RIGHT? CAN I HELP YOU?
SNIFF
WELL, MAYBE. WHO ARE YOU?
FBI
CRIME VICTIMS UNIT
10:50 PM
TAP TAP TAP
10:55 PM
11:00 PM
WOW. JUST THE WAY YOU'D IMAGINE A G-MAN TO BE.
SOMEWHERE IN WASHINGTON, D.C.

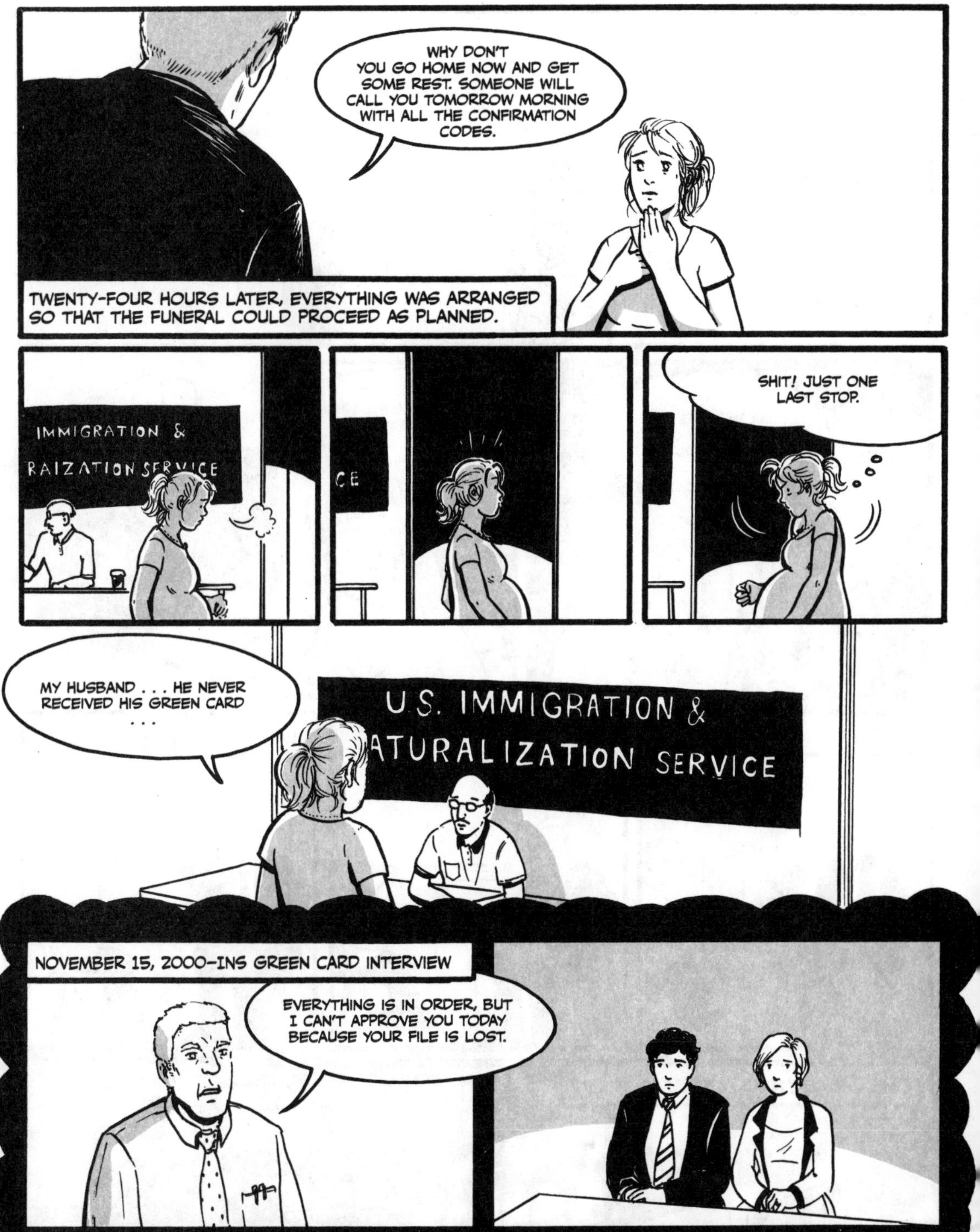
WHY DON'T YOU GO HOME NOW AND GET SOME REST. SOMEONE WILL CALL YOU TOMORROW MORNING WITH ALL THE CONFIRMATION CODES.
TWENTY-FOUR HOURS LATER, EVERYTHING WAS ARRANGED SO THAT THE FUNERAL COULD PROCEED AS PLANNED.
IMMIGRATION &
RAIZATION SERVICE
CE
SHIT! JUST ONE LAST STOP.
MY HUSBAND . . . HE NEVER RECEIVED HIS GREEN CARD . . .
U.S. IMMIGRATION &
ATURALIZATION SERVICE
NOVEMBER 15, 2000—INS GREEN CARD INTERVIEW
EVERYTHING IS IN ORDER, BUT I CAN'T APPROVE YOU TODAY BECAUSE YOUR FILE IS LOST.

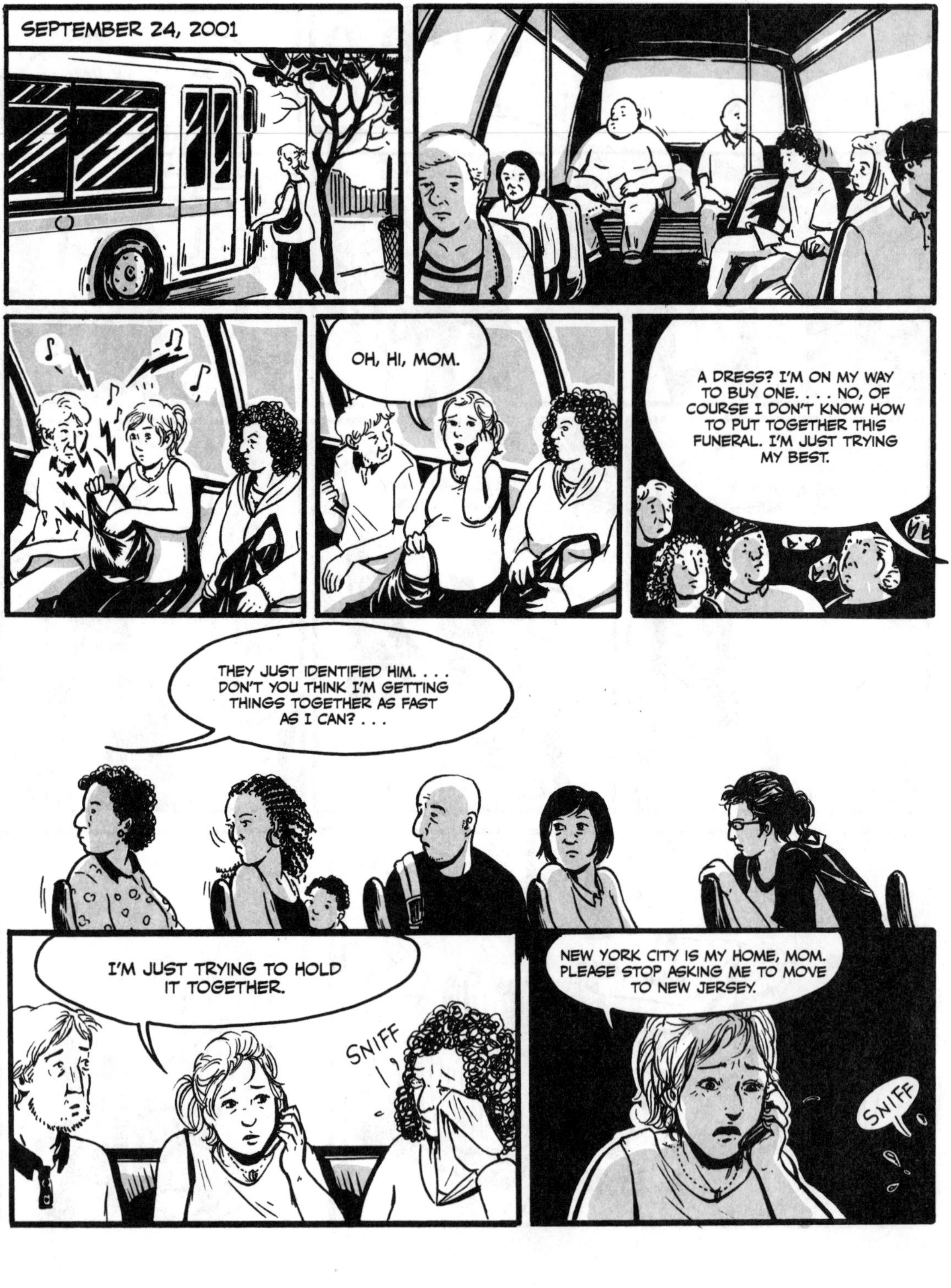
SEPTEMBER 24, 2001
OH, HI, MOM.
A DRESS? I'M ON MY WAY TO BUY ONE. . . . NO, OF COURSE I DON'T KNOW HOW TO PUT TOGETHER THIS FUNERAL. I'M JUST TRYING MY BEST.
THEY JUST IDENTIFIED HIM. . . . DON'T YOU THINK I'M GETTING THINGS TOGETHER AS FAST AS I CAN? . . .
I'M JUST TRYING TO HOLD IT TOGETHER.
SNIFF
NEW YORK CITY IS MY HOME, MOM. PLEASE STOP ASKING ME TO MOVE TO NEW JERSEY.
SNIFF

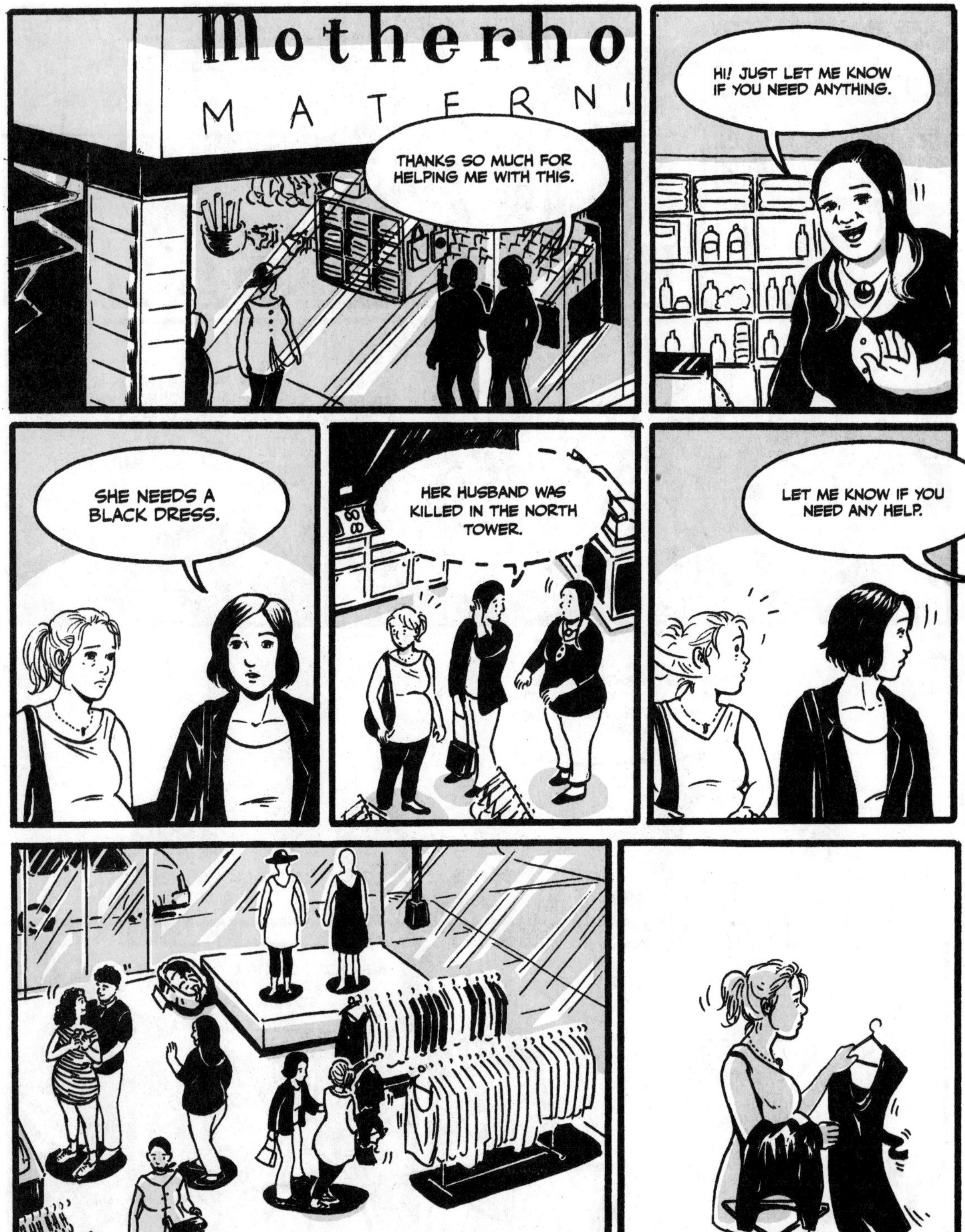
Motherho
MATERNI
THANKS SO MUCH FOR HELPING ME WITH THIS.
HI! JUST LET ME KNOW IF YOU NEED ANYTHING.
SHE NEEDS A BLACK DRESS.
HER HUSBAND WAS KILLED IN THE NORTH TOWER.
LET ME KNOW IF YOU NEED ANY HELP.

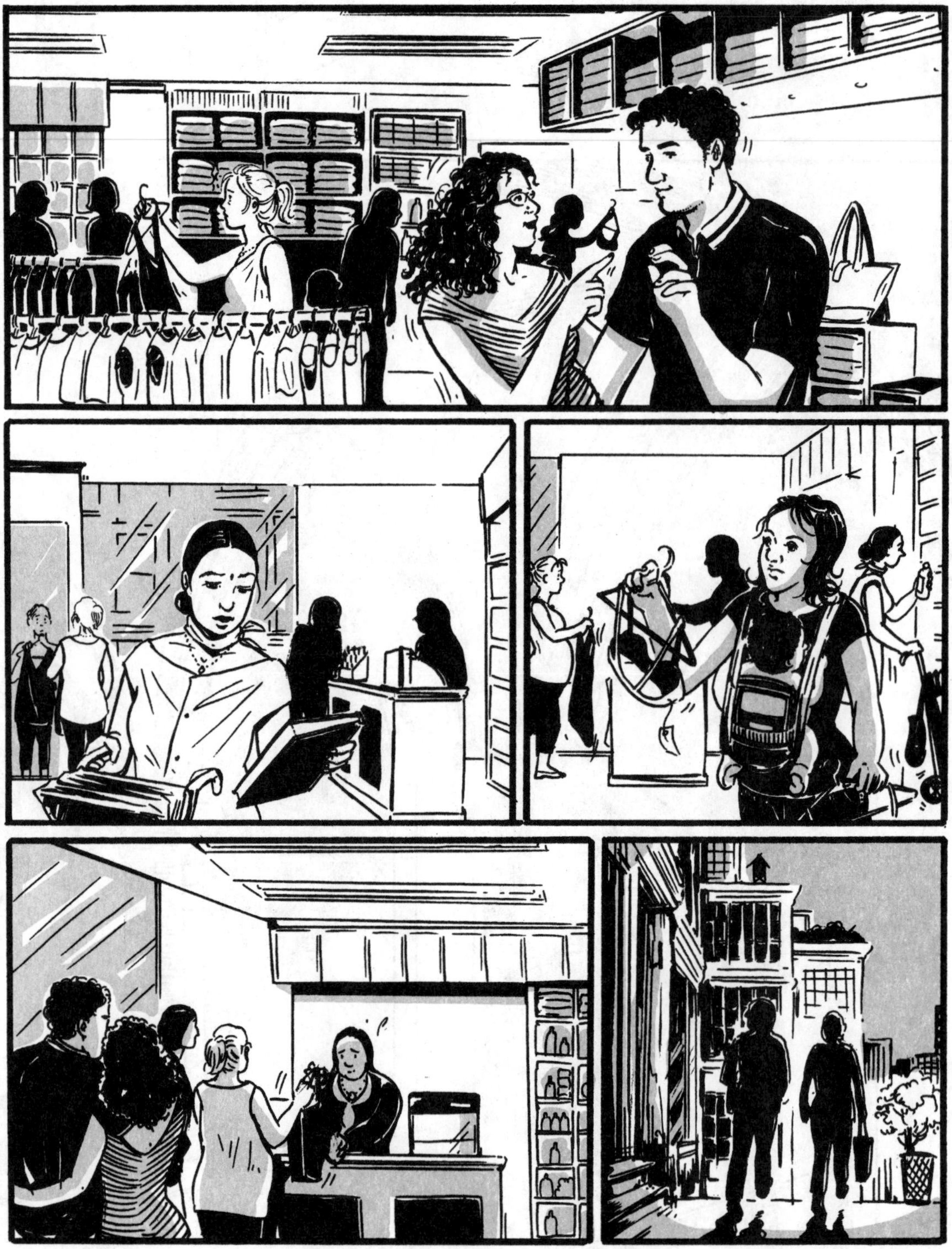

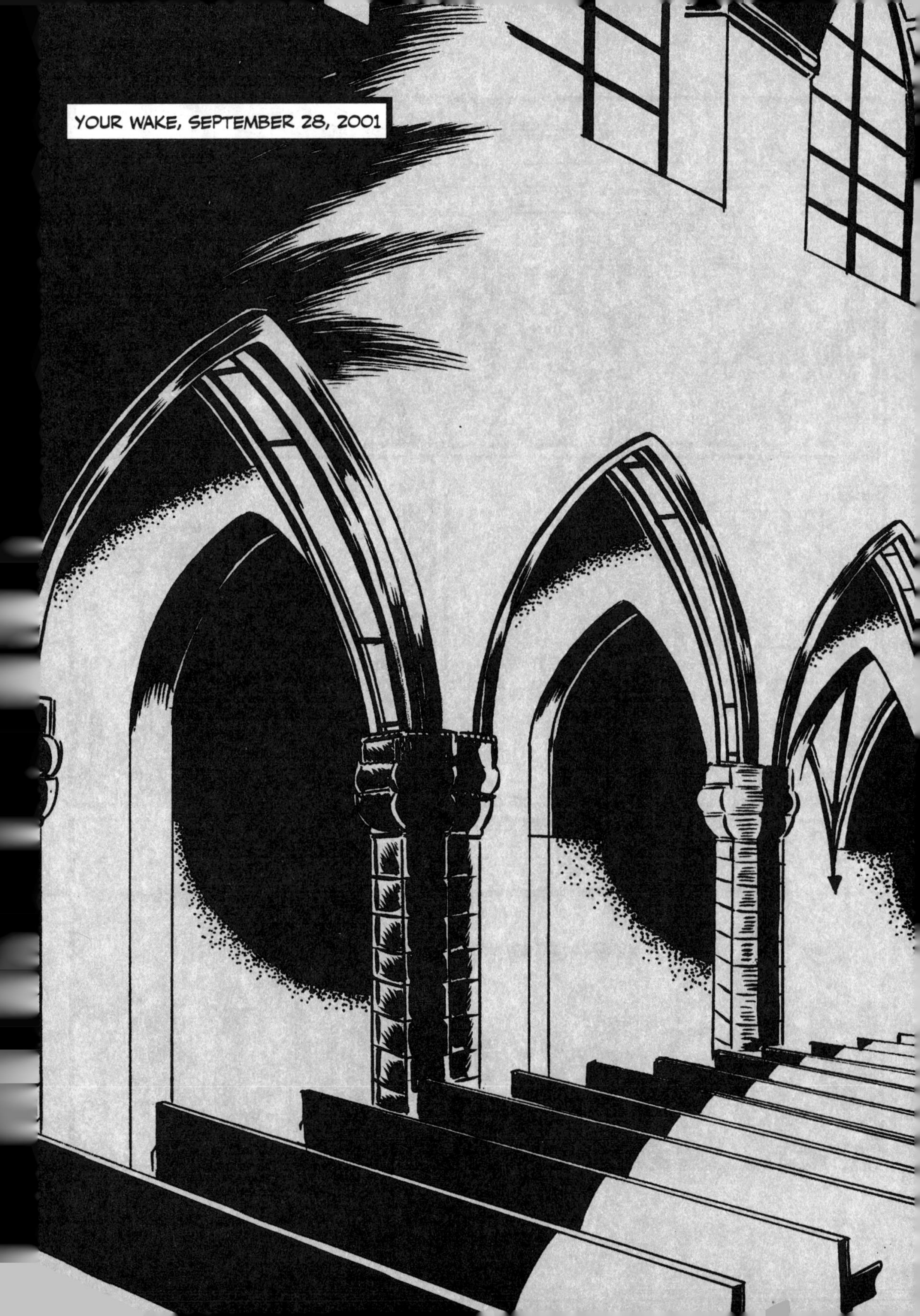
YOUR WAKE, SEPTEMBER 28, 2001

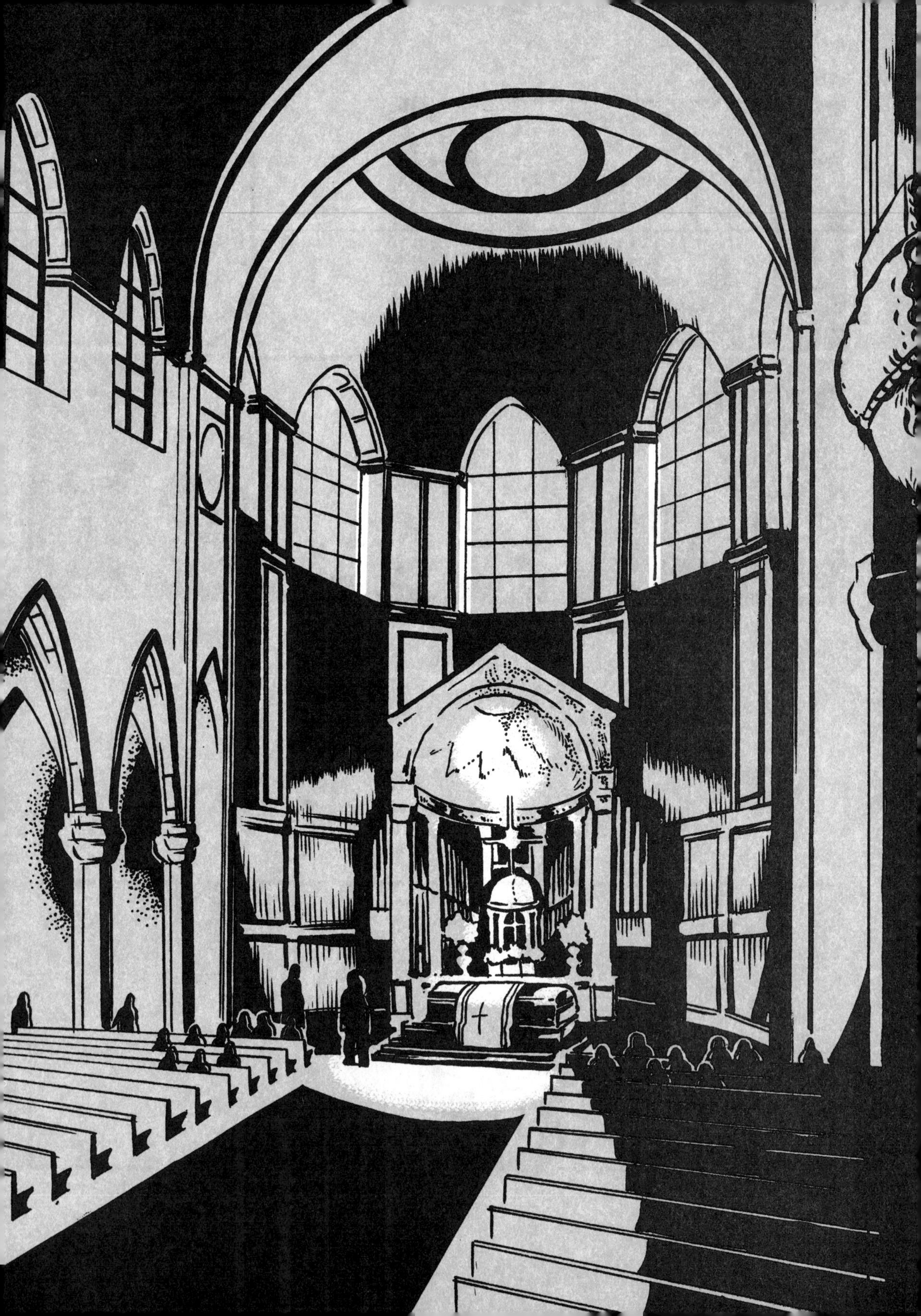

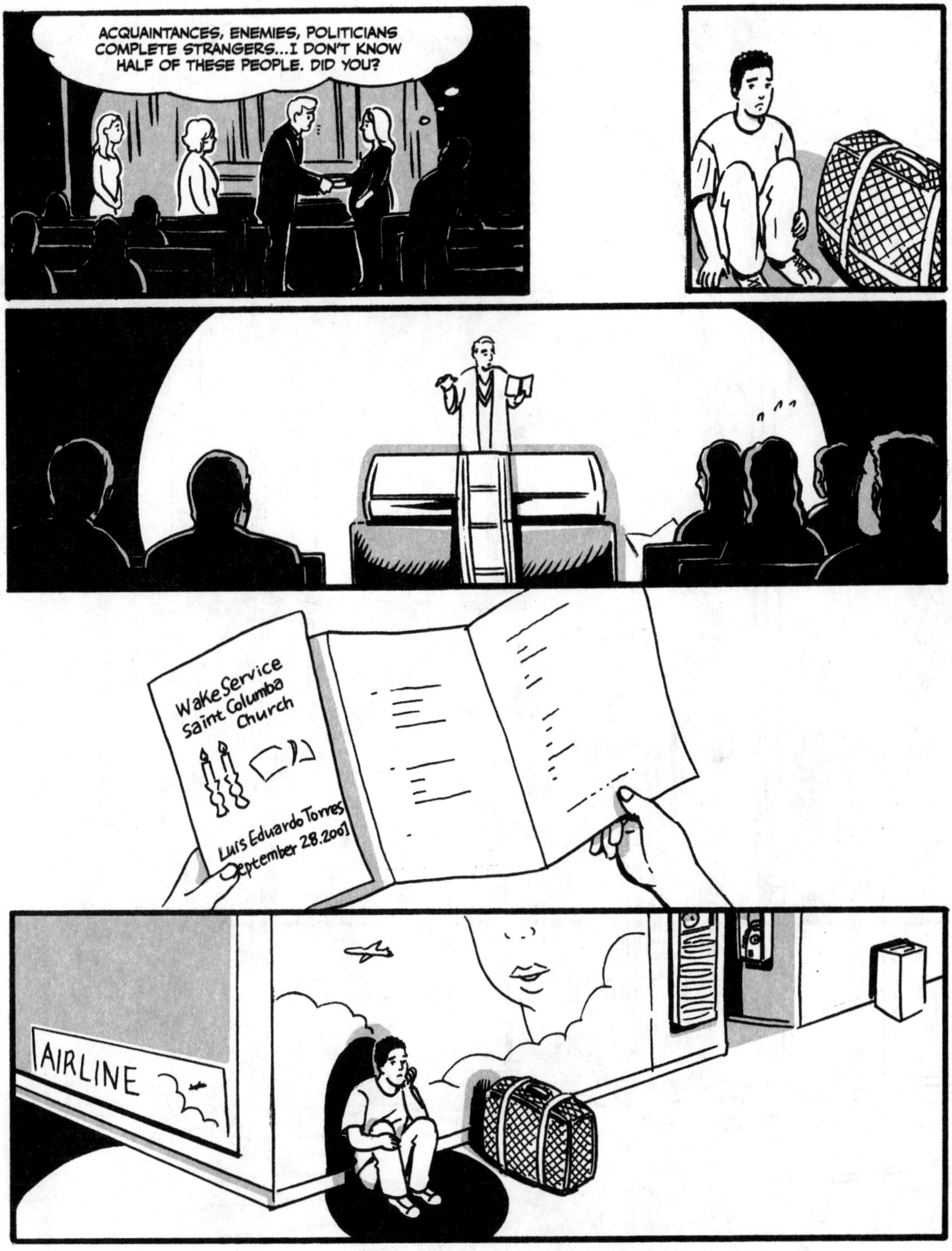
ACQUAINTANCES, ENEMIES, POLITICIANS COMPLETE STRANGERS...I DON'T KNOW HALF OF THESE PEOPLE. DID YOU?
WaKe Service
Saint Columba Church
Luis Eduardo Torres
September 28.2001
AIRLINE

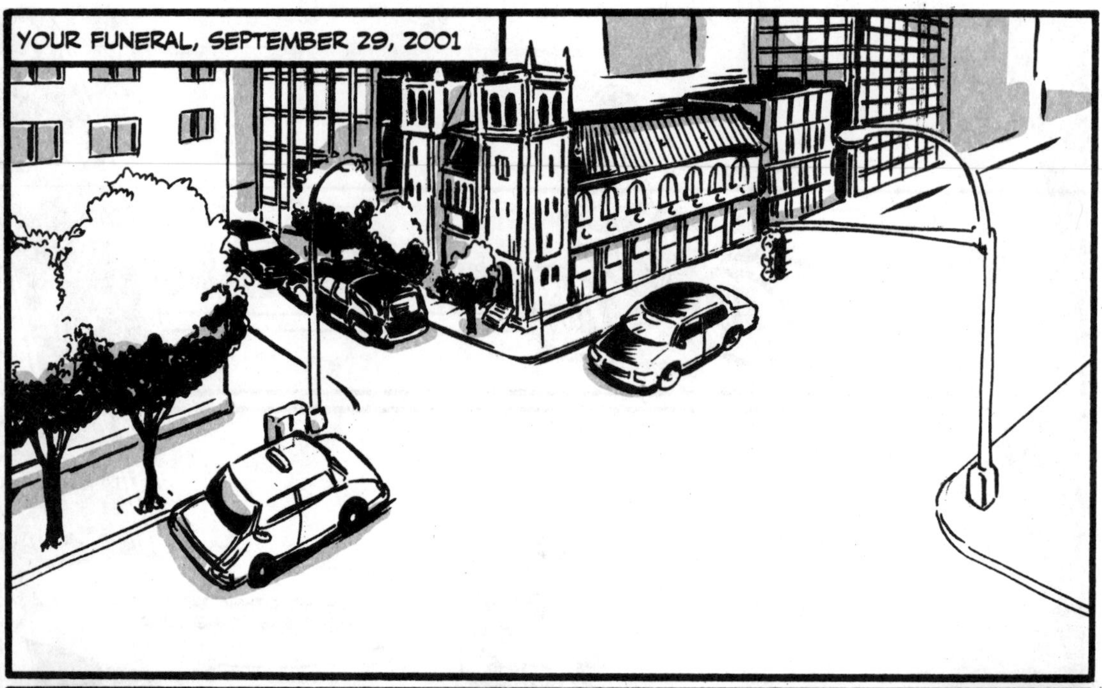
YOUR FUNERAL, SEPTEMBER 29, 2001

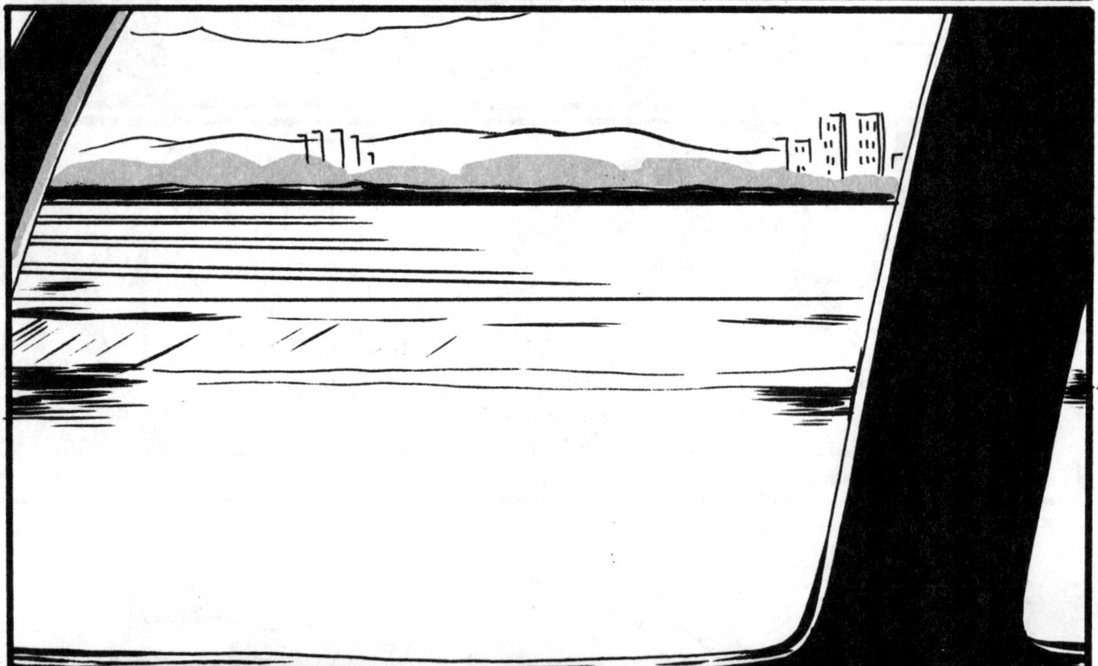

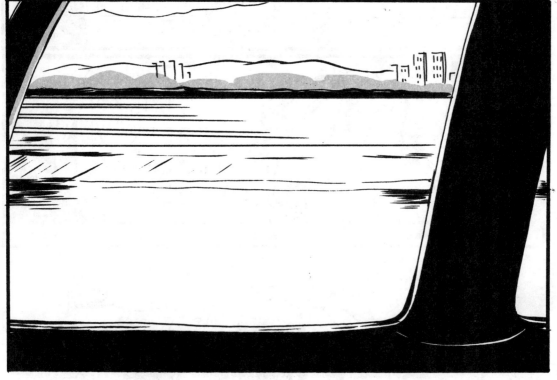

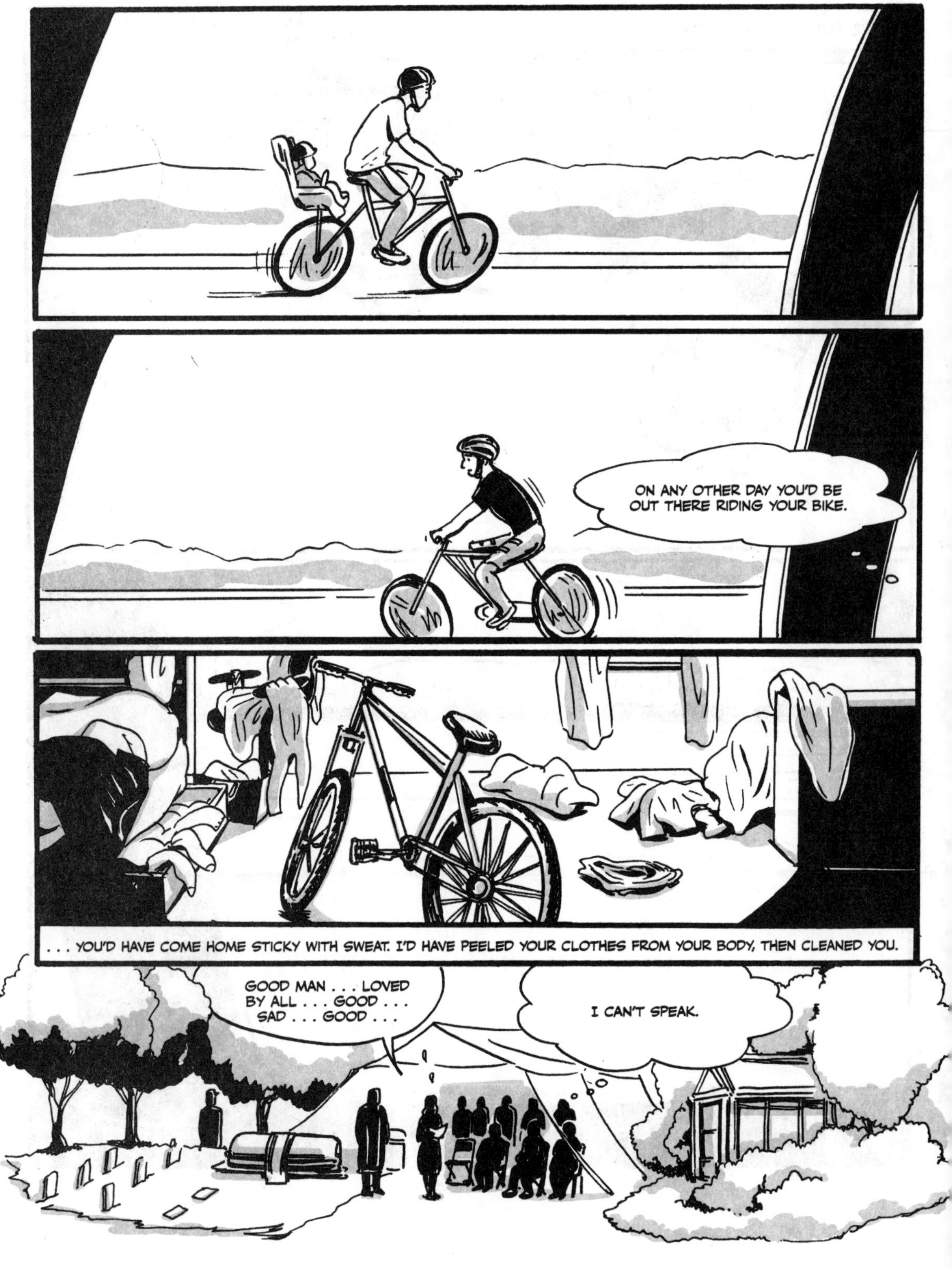
ON ANY OTHER DAY YOU'D BE OUT THERE RIDING YOUR BIKE.
. . . YOU'D HAVE COME HOME STICKY WITH SWEAT. I'D HAVE PEELED YOUR CLOTHES FROM YOUR BODY, THEN CLEANED YOU.
GOOD MAN . . . LOVED BY ALL . . . GOOD . . . SAD . . . GOOD . . .
I CAN'T SPEAK.

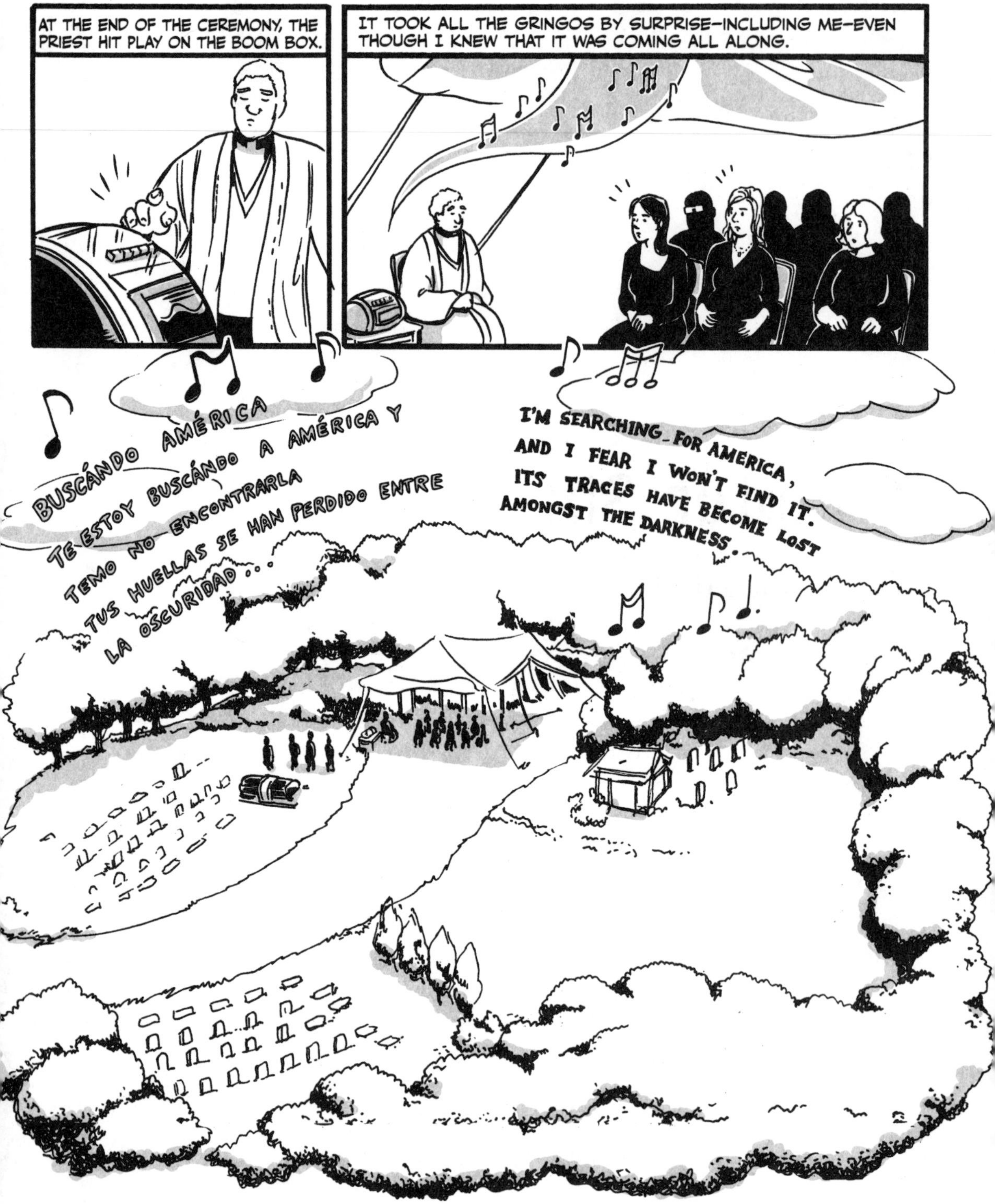
AT THE END OF THE CEREMONY, THE PRIEST HIT PLAY ON THE BOOM BOX.
IT TOOK ALL THE GRINGOS BY SURPRISE—INCLUDING ME—EVEN THOUGH I KNEW THAT IT WAS COMING ALL ALONG.
BUSCÁNDO AMÉRICA
TE ESTOY BUSCÁNDO A AMÉRICA Y
TEMO NO ENCONTRARLA
TUS HUELLAS SE HAN PERDIDO ENTRE
LA OSCURIDAD...
I'M SEARCHING FOR AMERICA,
AND I FEAR I WON'T FIND IT.
ITS TRACES HAVE BECOME LOST
AMONGST THE DARKNESS.

Chapter Six

OCTOBER 2001

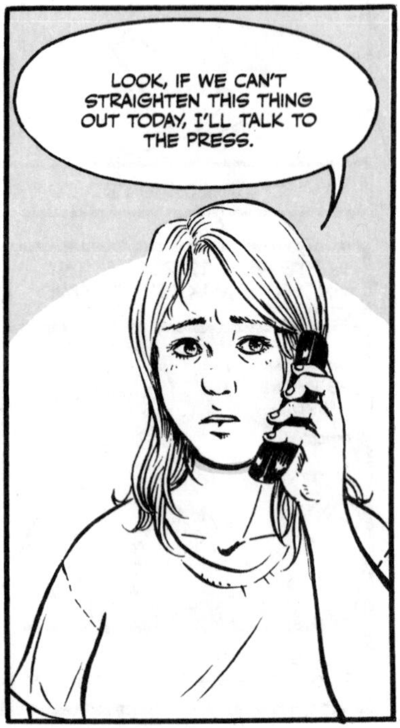
LOOK, IF WE CAN'T STRAIGHTEN THIS THING OUT TODAY, I'LL TALK TO THE PRESS.

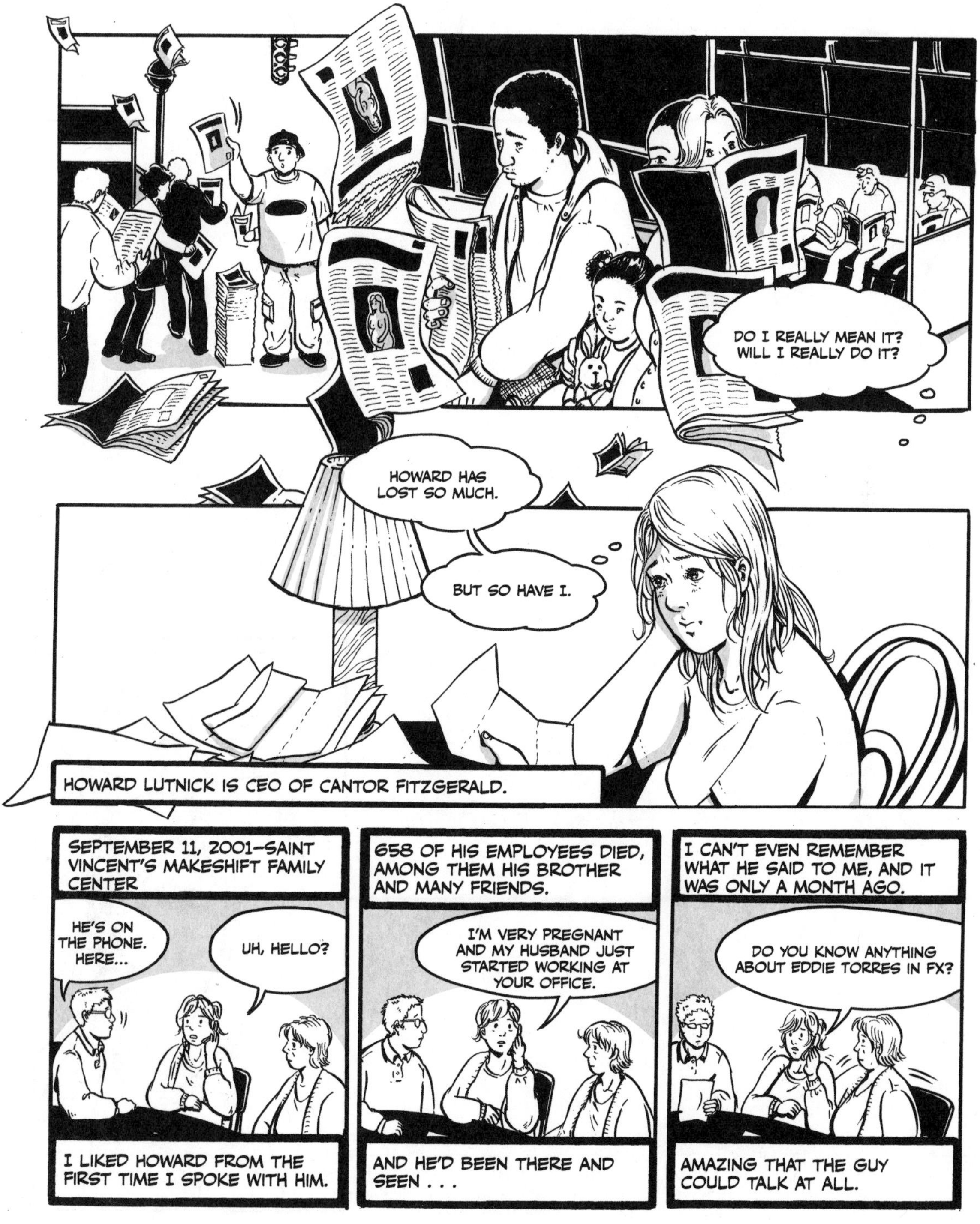
DO I REALLY MEAN IT? WILL I REALLY DO IT?
HOWARD HAS LOST SO MUCH.
BUT SO HAVE I.
HOWARD LUTNICK IS CEO OF CANTOR FITZGERALD.
SEPTEMBER 11, 2001—SAINT VINCENT'S MAKESHIFT FAMILY CENTER
HE'S ON THE PHONE. HERE...
UH, HELLO?
I LIKED HOWARD FROM THE FIRST TIME I SPOKE WITH HIM.
658 OF HIS EMPLOYEES DIED, AMONG THEM HIS BROTHER AND MANY FRIENDS.
I'M VERY PREGNANT AND MY HUSBAND JUST STARTED WORKING AT YOUR OFFICE.
AND HE'D BEEN THERE AND SEEN . . .
I CAN'T EVEN REMEMBER WHAT HE SAID TO ME, AND IT WAS ONLY A MONTH AGO.
DO YOU KNOW ANYTHING ABOUT EDDIE TORRES IN FX?
AMAZING THAT THE GUY COULD TALK AT ALL.

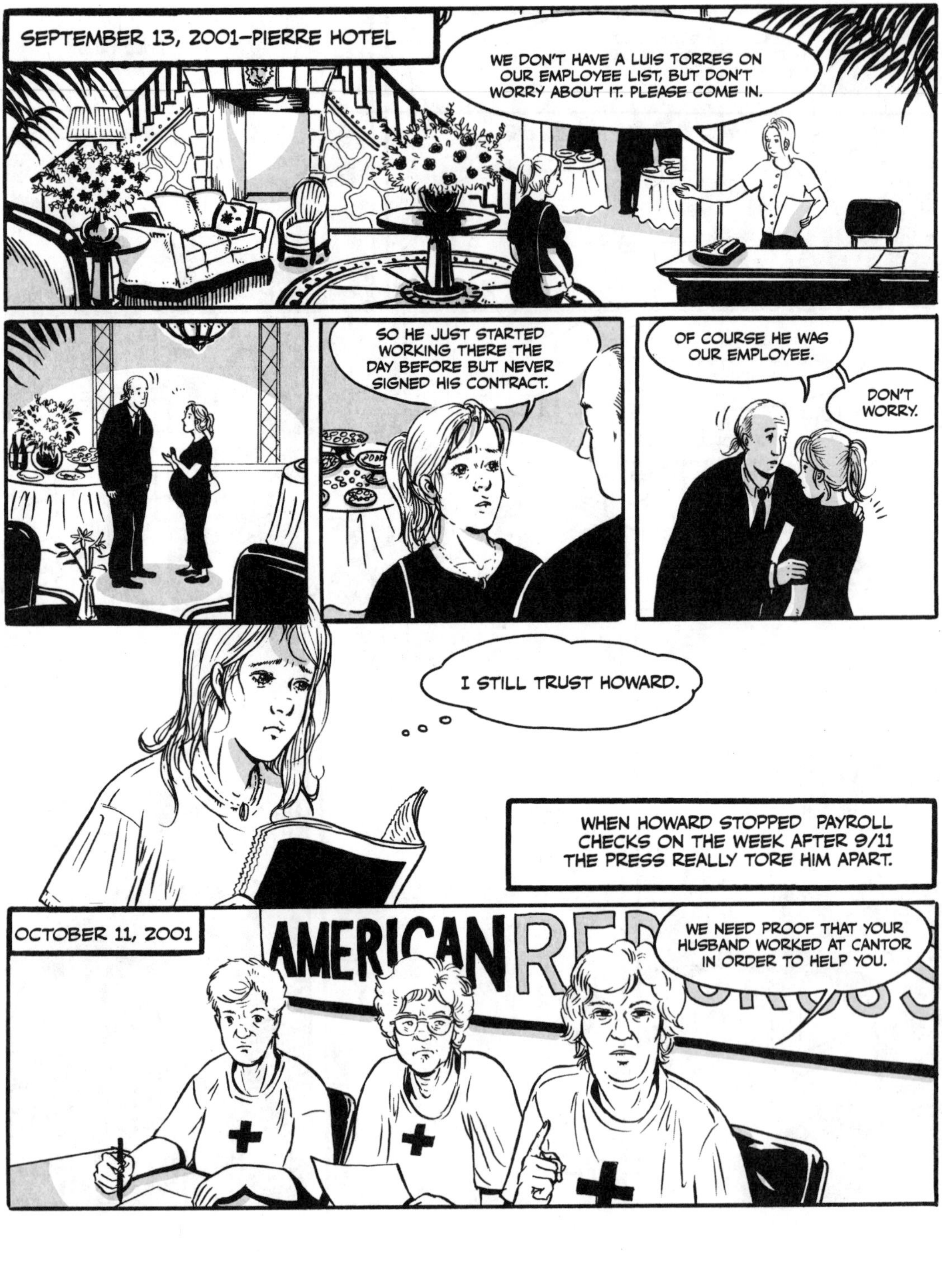
SEPTEMBER 13, 2001–PIERRE HOTEL
WE DON'T HAVE A LUIS TORRES ON OUR EMPLOYEE LIST, BUT DON'T WORRY ABOUT IT. PLEASE COME IN.
SO HE JUST STARTED WORKING THERE THE DAY BEFORE BUT NEVER SIGNED HIS CONTRACT.
OF COURSE HE WAS OUR EMPLOYEE.
DON'T WORRY.
I STILL TRUST HOWARD.
WHEN HOWARD STOPPED PAYROLL CHECKS ON THE WEEK AFTER 9/11 THE PRESS REALLY TORE HIM APART.
OCTOBER 11, 2001
AMERICAN
WE NEED PROOF THAT YOUR HUSBAND WORKED AT CANTOR IN ORDER TO HELP YOU.

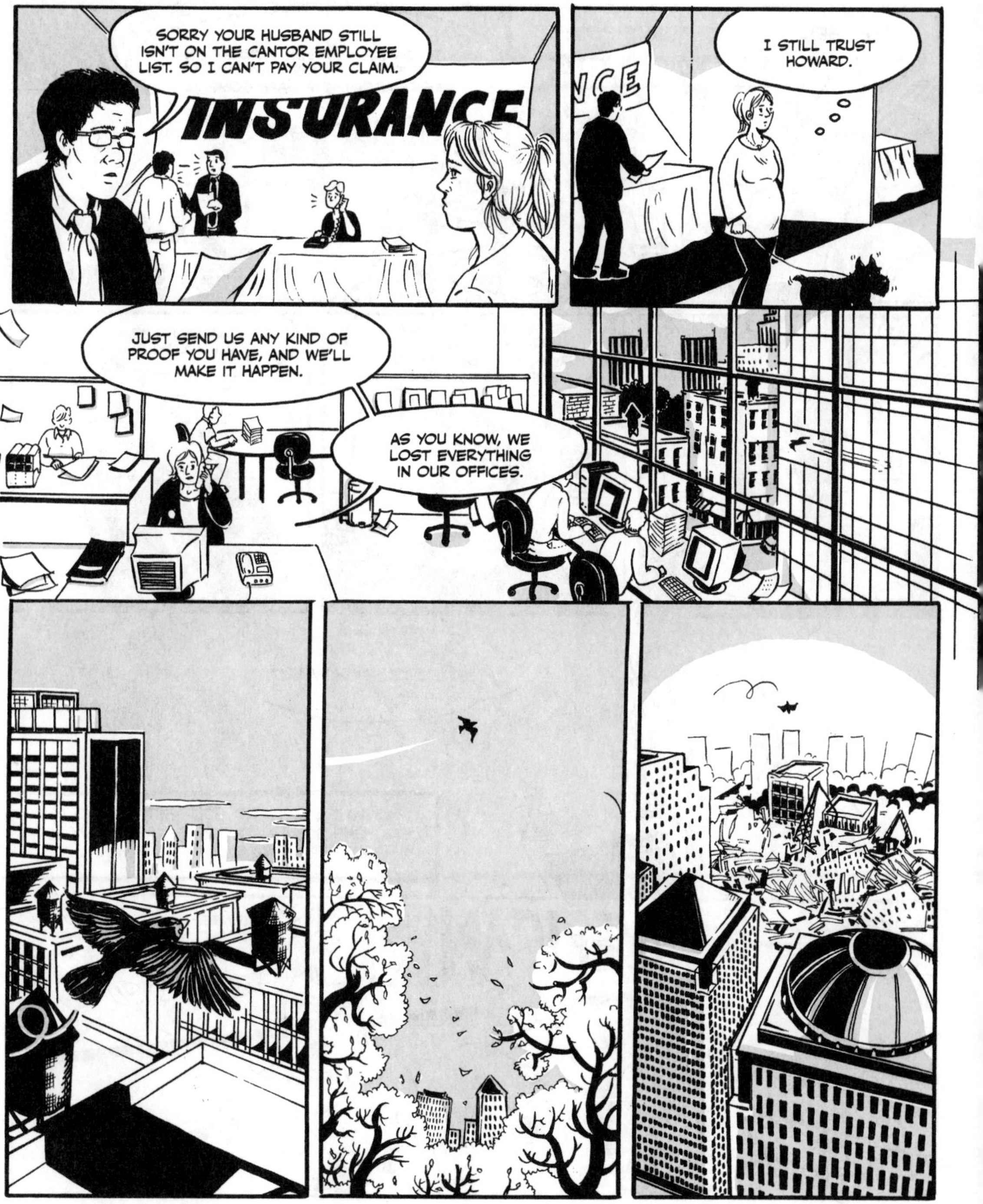
SORRY YOUR HUSBAND STILL ISN'T ON THE CANTOR EMPLOYEE LIST. SO I CAN'T PAY YOUR CLAIM.
INSURANCE
I STILL TRUST HOWARD.
JUST SEND US ANY KIND OF PROOF YOU HAVE, AND WE'LL MAKE IT HAPPEN.
AS YOU KNOW, WE LOST EVERYTHING IN OUR OFFICES.

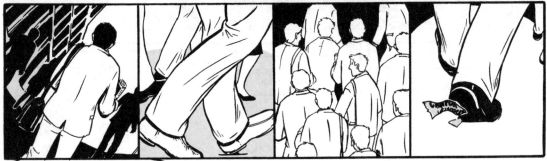

CAN YOU GIVE ME SOME MORE INFORMATION ABOUT THIS ACCOUNT THAT BELONGS TO MY DEAD HUSBAND?

I'M NOT SUPPOSED TO, BUT THIS ACCOUNT WAS SET UP ON SEPTEMBER 10, 2001, FOR PAYCHECK DIRECT DEPOSITS FROM CANTOR FITZGERALD.

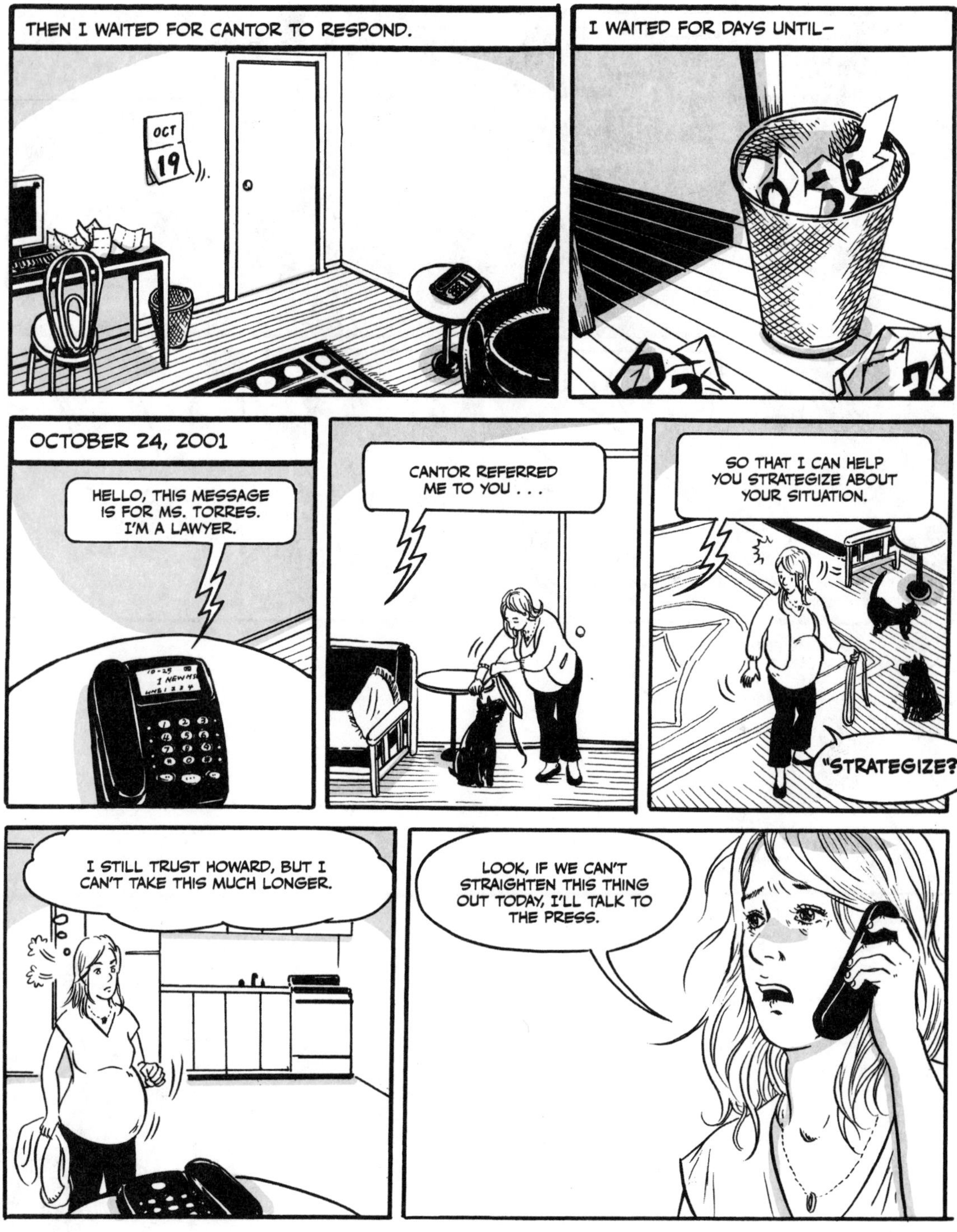
THEN I WAITED FOR CANTOR TO RESPOND.
OCT 19
I WAITED FOR DAYS UNTIL–
OCTOBER 24, 2001
HELLO, THIS MESSAGE IS FOR MS. TORRES. I'M A LAWYER.
CANTOR REFERRED ME TO YOU . . .
SO THAT I CAN HELP YOU STRATEGIZE ABOUT YOUR SITUATION.
"STRATEGIZE?"
I STILL TRUST HOWARD, BUT I CAN'T TAKE THIS MUCH LONGER.
LOOK, IF WE CAN'T STRAIGHTEN THIS THING OUT TODAY, I'LL TALK TO THE PRESS.

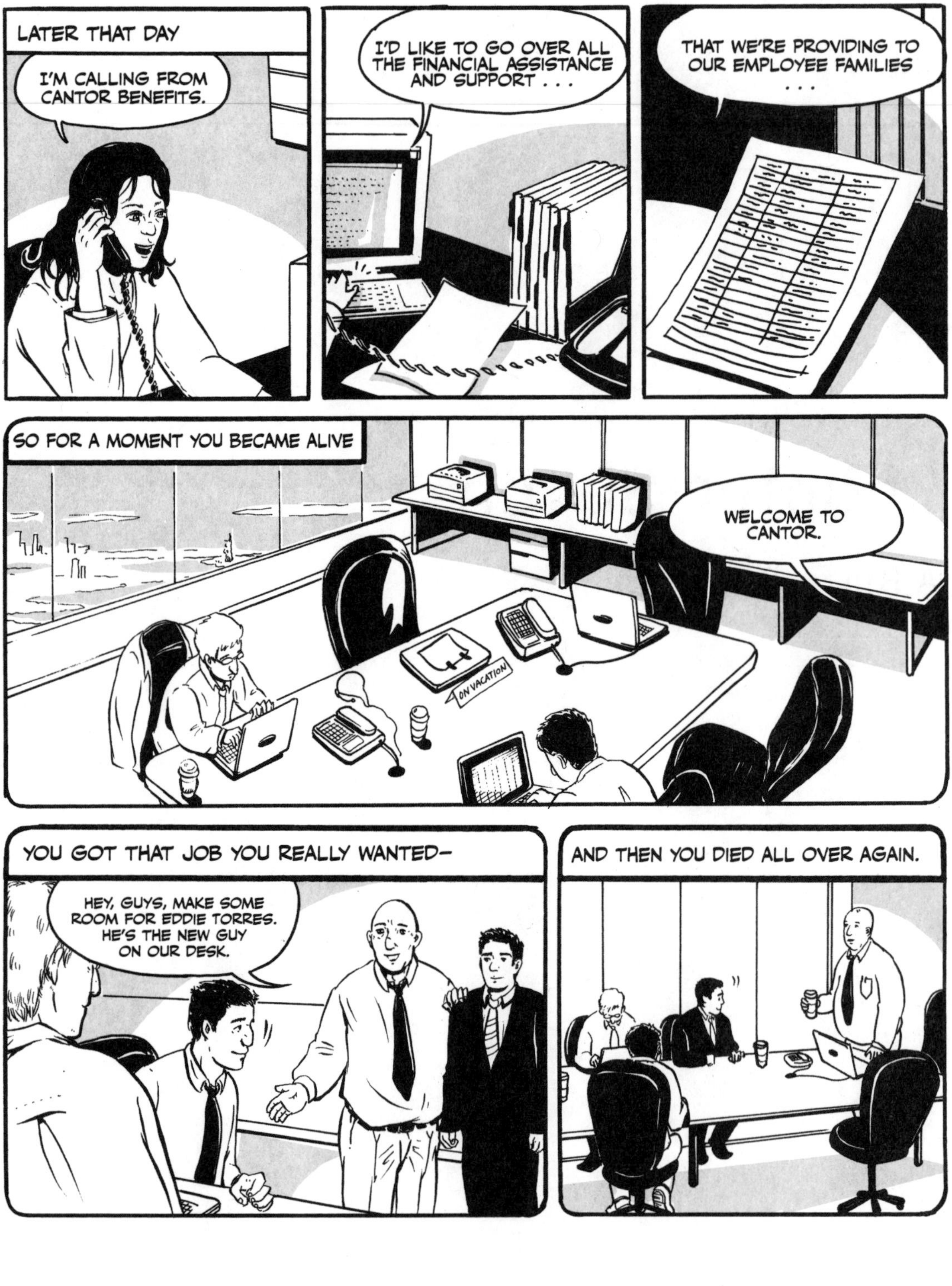
LATER THAT DAY
I'M CALLING FROM CANTOR BENEFITS.
I'D LIKE TO GO OVER ALL THE FINANCIAL ASSISTANCE AND SUPPORT . . .
THAT WE'RE PROVIDING TO OUR EMPLOYEE FAMILIES . . .
SO FOR A MOMENT YOU BECAME ALIVE
WELCOME TO CANTOR.
ON VACATION
YOU GOT THAT JOB YOU REALLY WANTED—
HEY, GUYS, MAKE SOME ROOM FOR EDDIE TORRES. HE'S THE NEW GUY ON OUR DESK.
AND THEN YOU DIED ALL OVER AGAIN.

Chapter Seven

A Birth Day

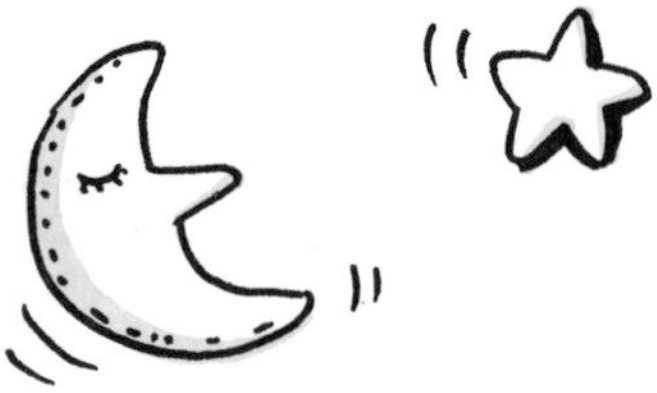

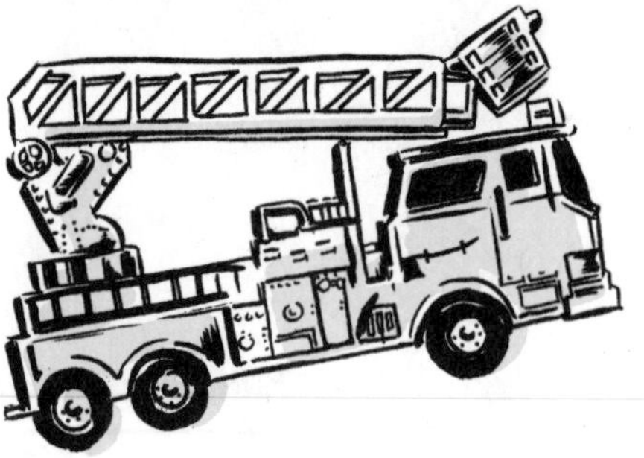

YOU ACCOMPANIED ME TO THE HOSPITAL TODAY IN AN ENVELOPE OF LARGE, VIBRANT PICTURES TAKEN AT THE BEACH ON SEPTEMBER 9, 2001, OUR LAST DAY TOGETHER. BECAUSE I WAS UNPREPARED FOR OUR SON TO COME 3 1/2 WEEKS EARLY, IT WAS ONE OF THE FEW THINGS I TOOK WITH ME. THAT AND THE STRANGE THOUGHT THAT I'D FIND A NEW LIFE AT THE HOSPITAL TO TAKE HOME. AT THAT TIME, I KNEW HOSPITALS ONLY AS THE PLACES TO GO TO FIND DEATH OR LESS, AND TO COME HOME EMPTY-HANDED.

I WELCOMED THE GRIEF IN THE SCREAMS OF MY HARD-EARNED LABOR. I INVITED YOU INTO EACH ONE, MOURNING YOU EACH TIME AS I HAD NOT DONE PREVIOUSLY. SO BADLY, I NOW WANTED THESE MOMENTS OF UNFETTERED NOISE THAT I DIDN'T HAVE TO EXPLAIN. AS I SCREAMED, IT FELT LIKE SEX. I INVOKED YOU IN MY MIND AS THE CONTRACTION ROSE TO MY LIPS. I REMEMBERED YOUR PHYSICALITY UPON ME AS I RODE EACH WAVE OF PAIN. MY FIRST INTENSE PHYSICAL SENSATION IN FIFTY DAYS. IT RECALLED THAT WORLD OF LUST AND BODY I USED TO INHABIT, NOW MADE MANIFEST ONLY IN GRIEF, WITH EACH THRUST OF LIFE.

AS MY BODY WAS TORN APART IN THE RHYTHMIC CONVULSIONS, SO TOO WAS MY HEART, IN THE SUDDEN FULL REALIZATION OF MY LOSS. THE SHOCK HAD PARTED DURING THESE MOMENTS OF CONTRACTION, AS A SUN OF REALITY PEERED IN, SHINING STRONG ON THE FACT THAT YOU WERE DEAD AND I WAS STILL ALIVE AND THIS BEING BEARING THE NAME OF TRAGEDY WOULD NEVER KNOW YOU EXCEPT AS I BUILT YOU IN HIS MEMORY.

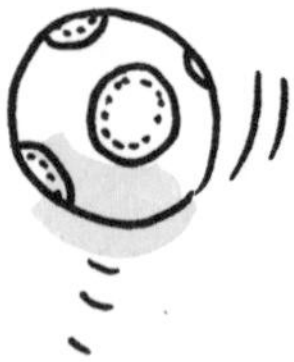

FIVE HOURS THAT FELT LIKE FIVE MINUTES.

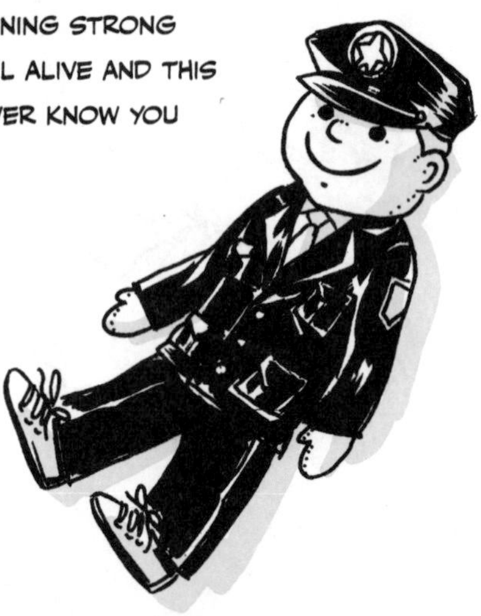

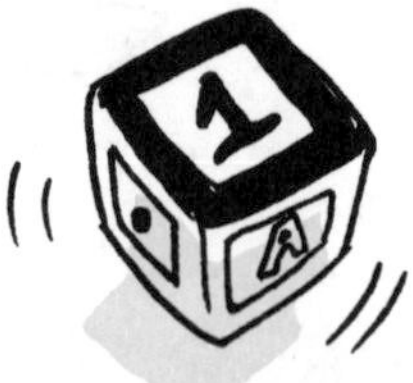
1
A

AND THEN THEY ANESTHETIZED ME.

THEY SAID: "YOUR BABY IS UPSIDE DOWN." I ANSWERED
UNDER THE UNWANTED HAZE: "OF COURSE HE IS; I'M
UPSIDE DOWN, TOO."

NO ONE, LEAST OF ALL ME, WANTED TO TAKE CHANCES WITH
A BREECH DELIVERY. INSTEAD, THEY HANDLED ME KINDLY, AS
A V.I.P., BECAUSE I HAD A POST-9/11 BABY TO DELIVER.
GENTLY, GENTLY, THEY CUT THE WIDOW OPEN AND TOOK OUT
THE PRIZE.

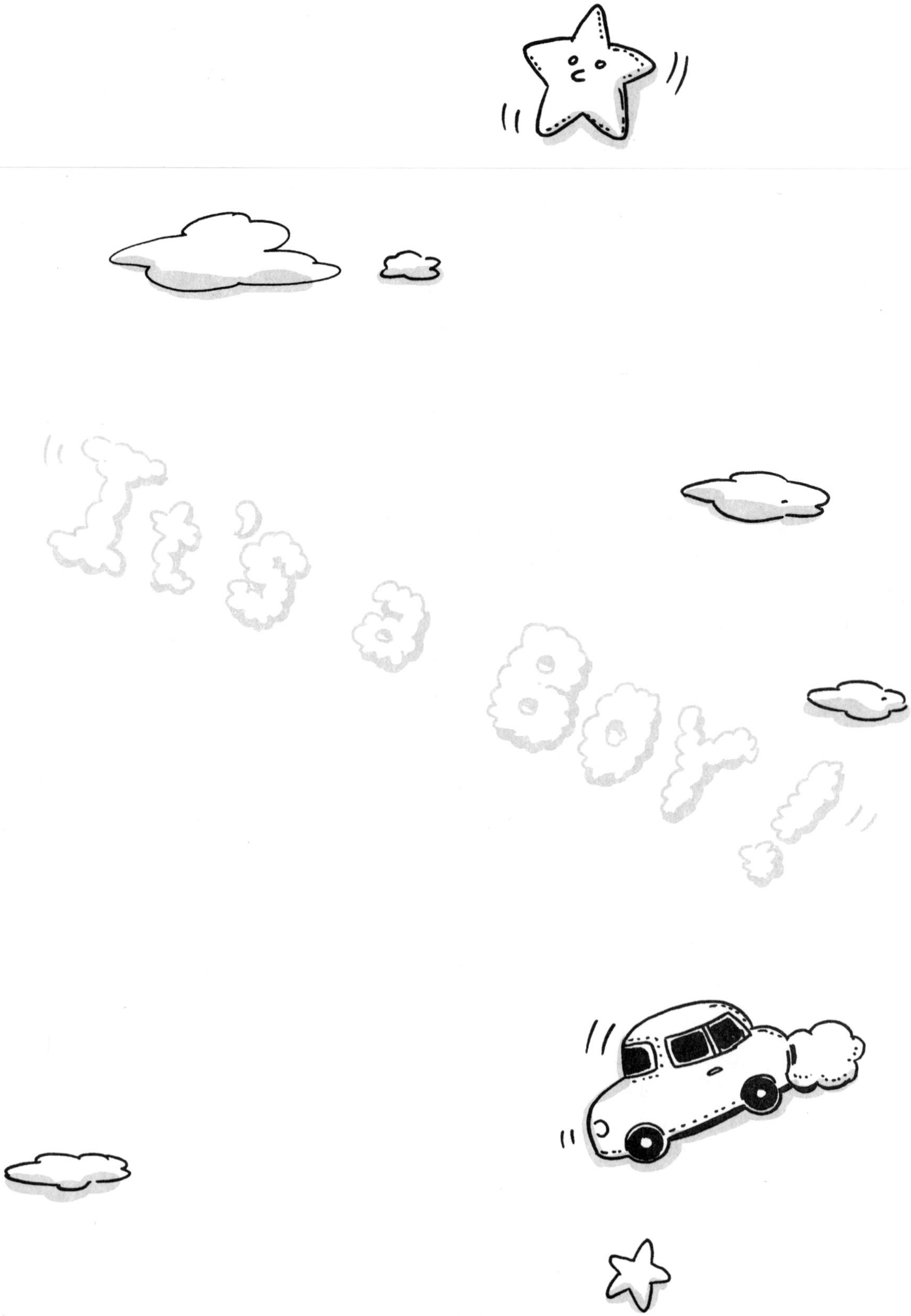
It's a Boy!

Chapter Eight

November 2001

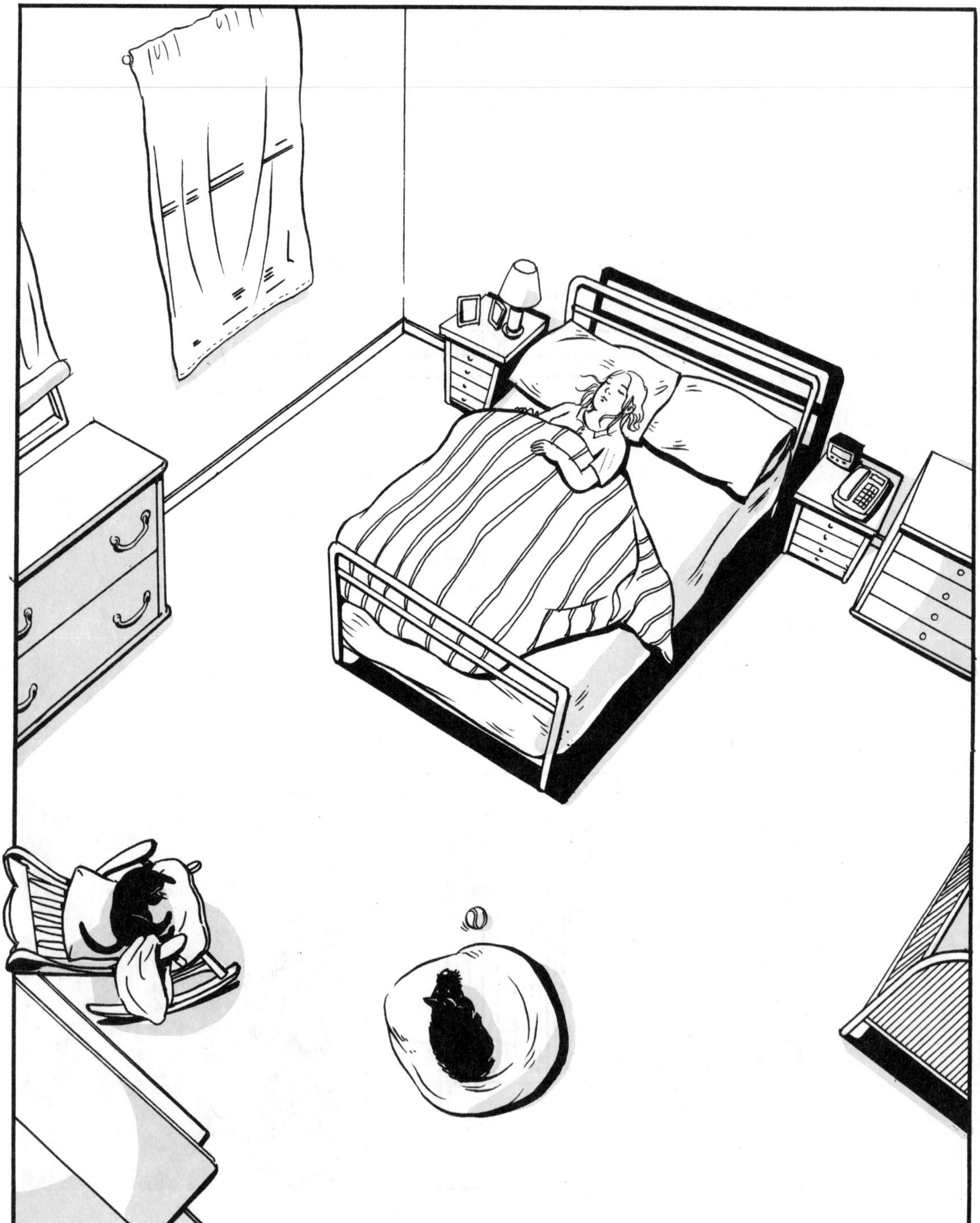

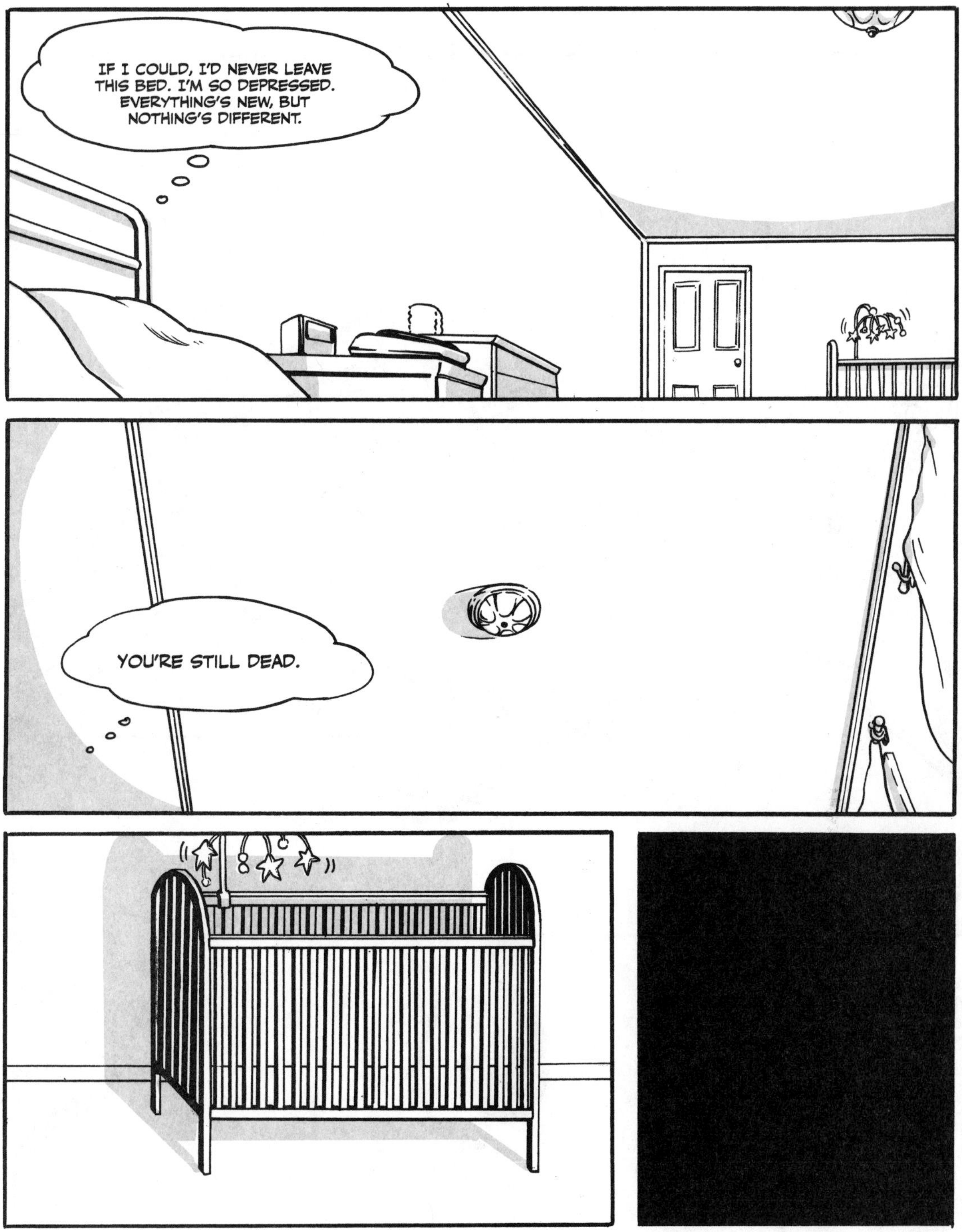
IF I COULD, I'D NEVER LEAVE THIS BED. I'M SO DEPRESSED. EVERYTHING'S NEW, BUT NOTHING'S DIFFERENT.
YOU'RE STILL DEAD.

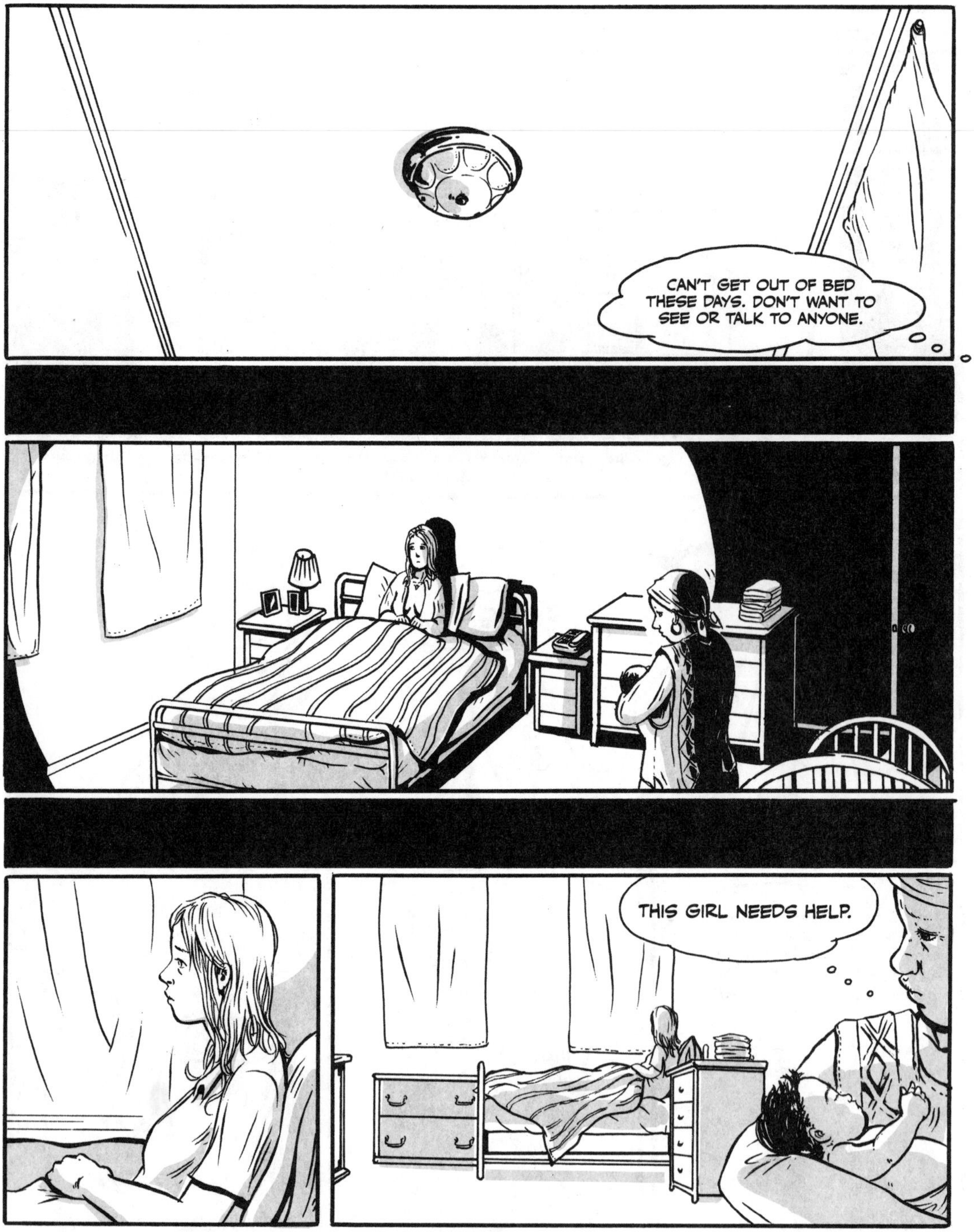
CAN'T GET OUT OF BED THESE DAYS. DON'T WANT TO SEE OR TALK TO ANYONE.
THIS GIRL NEEDS HELP.

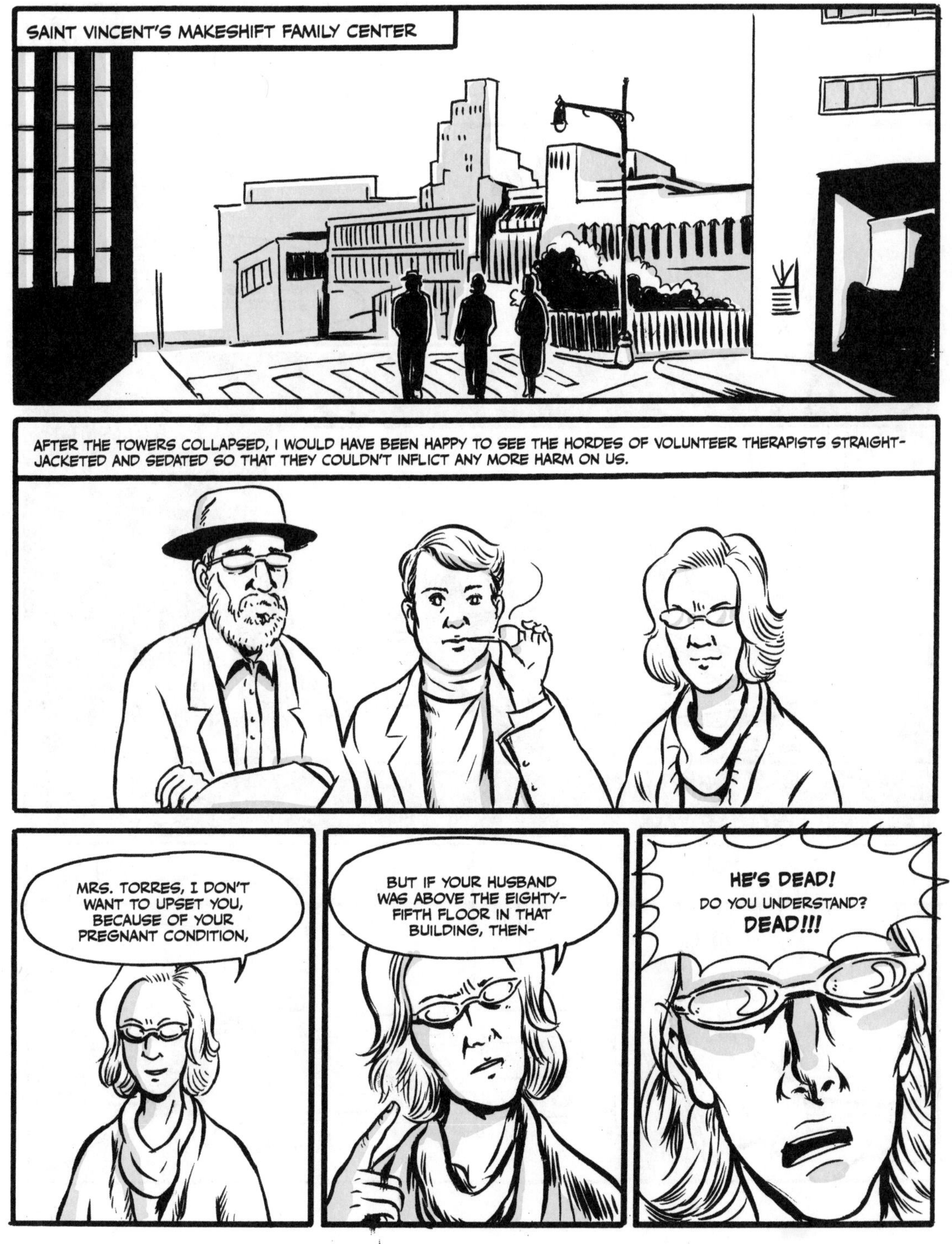
SAINT VINCENT'S MAKESHIFT FAMILY CENTER
AFTER THE TOWERS COLLAPSED, I WOULD HAVE BEEN HAPPY TO SEE THE HORDES OF VOLUNTEER THERAPISTS STRAIGHT-JACKETED AND SEDATED SO THAT THEY COULDN'T INFLICT ANY MORE HARM ON US.
MRS. TORRES, I DON'T WANT TO UPSET YOU, BECAUSE OF YOUR PREGNANT CONDITION,
BUT IF YOUR HUSBAND WAS ABOVE THE EIGHTY-FIFTH FLOOR IN THAT BUILDING, THEN-
HE'S DEAD! DO YOU UNDERSTAND? DEAD!!!

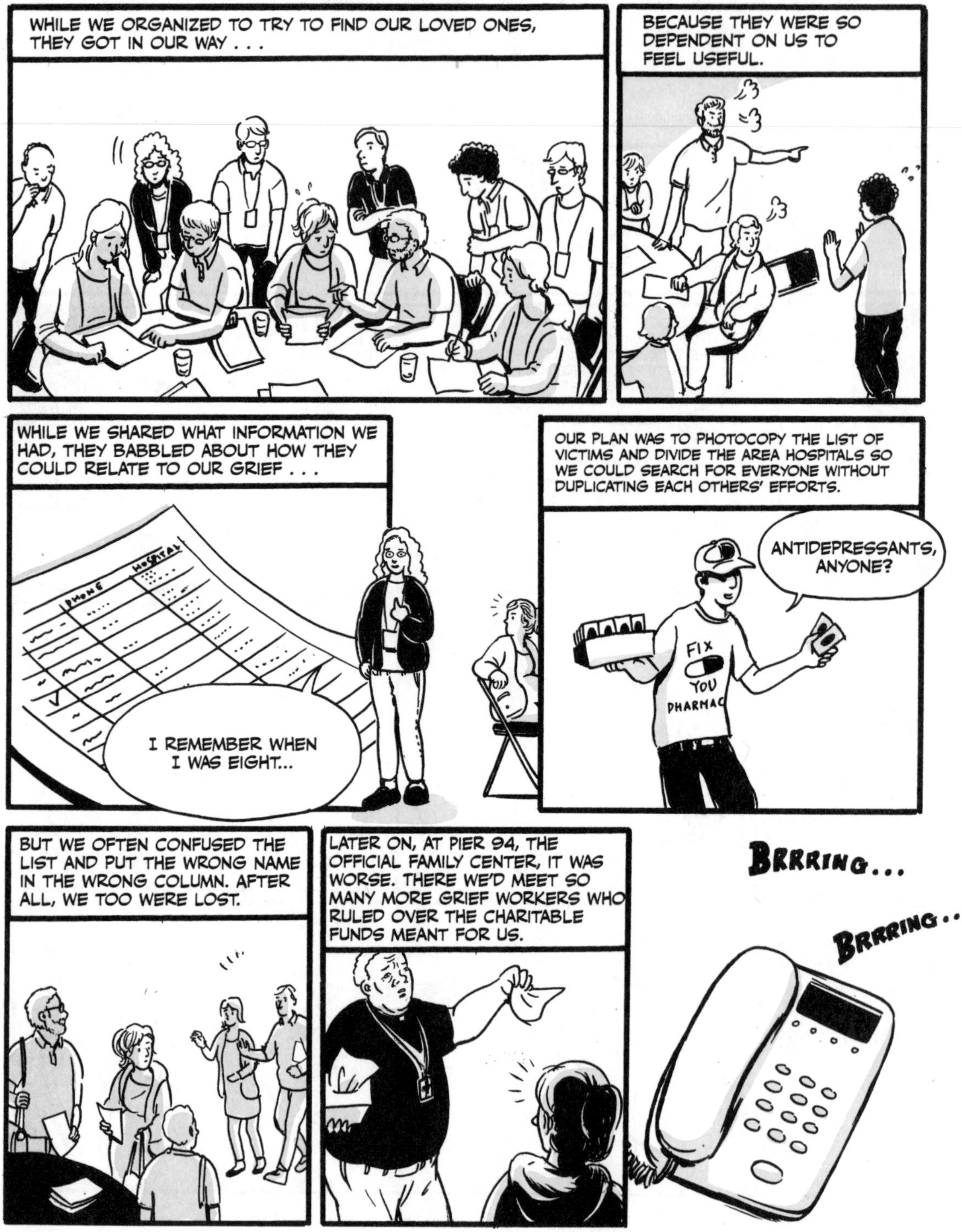
WHILE WE ORGANIZED TO TRY TO FIND OUR LOVED ONES, THEY GOT IN OUR WAY . . .
BECAUSE THEY WERE SO DEPENDENT ON US TO FEEL USEFUL.
WHILE WE SHARED WHAT INFORMATION WE HAD, THEY BABBLED ABOUT HOW THEY COULD RELATE TO OUR GRIEF . . .
PHONE
HOSPITAL
I REMEMBER WHEN I WAS EIGHT...
OUR PLAN WAS TO PHOTOCOPY THE LIST OF VICTIMS AND DIVIDE THE AREA HOSPITALS SO WE COULD SEARCH FOR EVERYONE WITHOUT DUPLICATING EACH OTHERS' EFFORTS.
ANTIDEPRESSANTS, ANYONE?
FIX YOU PHARMAC
BUT WE OFTEN CONFUSED THE LIST AND PUT THE WRONG NAME IN THE WRONG COLUMN. AFTER ALL, WE TOO WERE LOST.
LATER ON, AT PIER 94, THE OFFICIAL FAMILY CENTER, IT WAS WORSE. THERE WE'D MEET SO MANY MORE GRIEF WORKERS WHO RULED OVER THE CHARITABLE FUNDS MEANT FOR US.
BRRRING...
BRRRING...

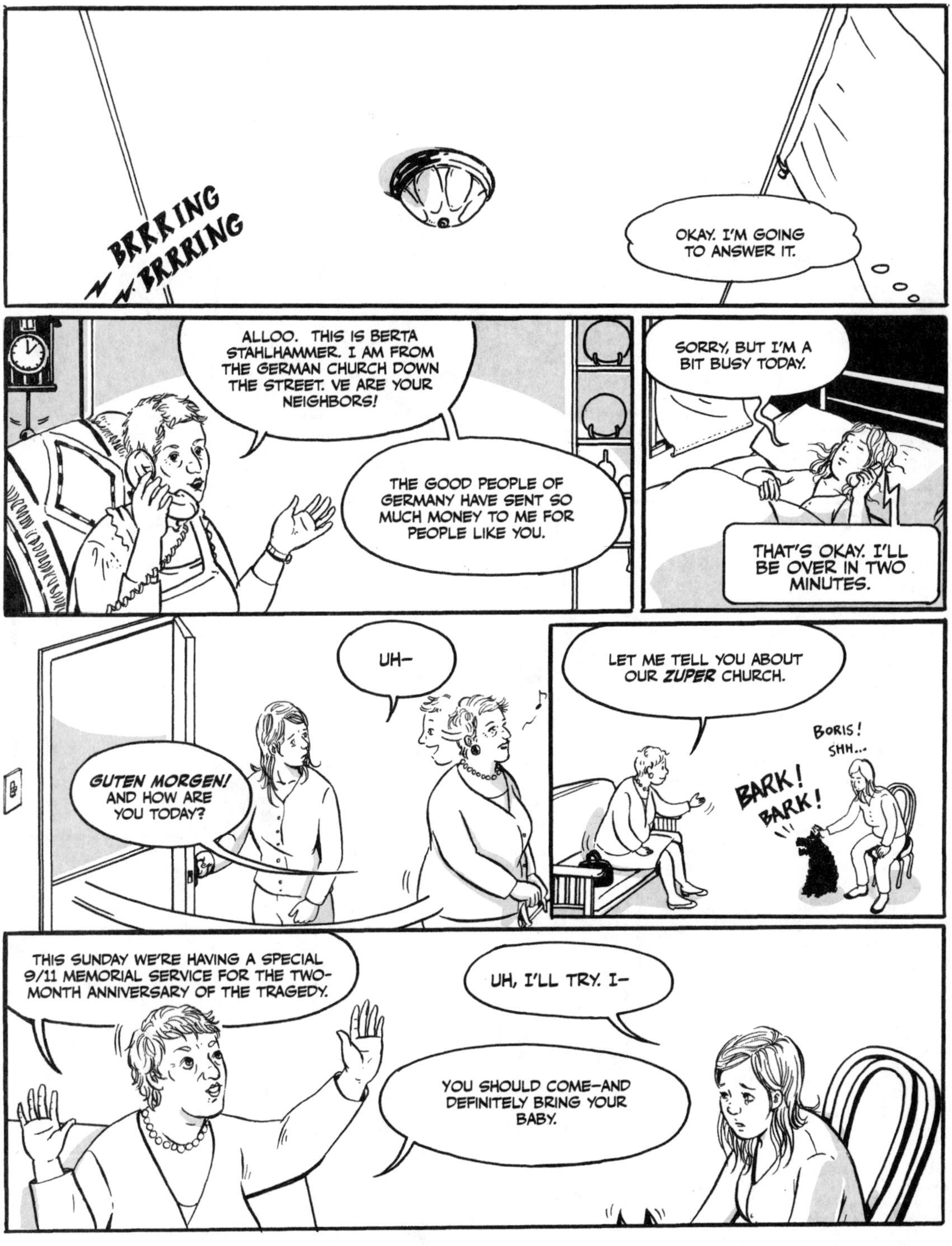
BRRRING
BRRRING
OKAY. I'M GOING TO ANSWER IT.
ALLOO. THIS IS BERTA STAHLHAMMER. I AM FROM THE GERMAN CHURCH DOWN THE STREET. VE ARE YOUR NEIGHBORS!
THE GOOD PEOPLE OF GERMANY HAVE SENT SO MUCH MONEY TO ME FOR PEOPLE LIKE YOU.
SORRY, BUT I'M A BIT BUSY TODAY.
THAT'S OKAY. I'LL BE OVER IN TWO MINUTES.
GUTEN MORGEN! AND HOW ARE YOU TODAY?
UH–
LET ME TELL YOU ABOUT OUR ZUPER CHURCH.
BARK! BARK!
BORIS! SHH...
THIS SUNDAY WE'RE HAVING A SPECIAL 9/11 MEMORIAL SERVICE FOR THE TWO-MONTH ANNIVERSARY OF THE TRAGEDY.
UH, I'LL TRY. I–
YOU SHOULD COME–AND DEFINITELY BRING YOUR BABY.

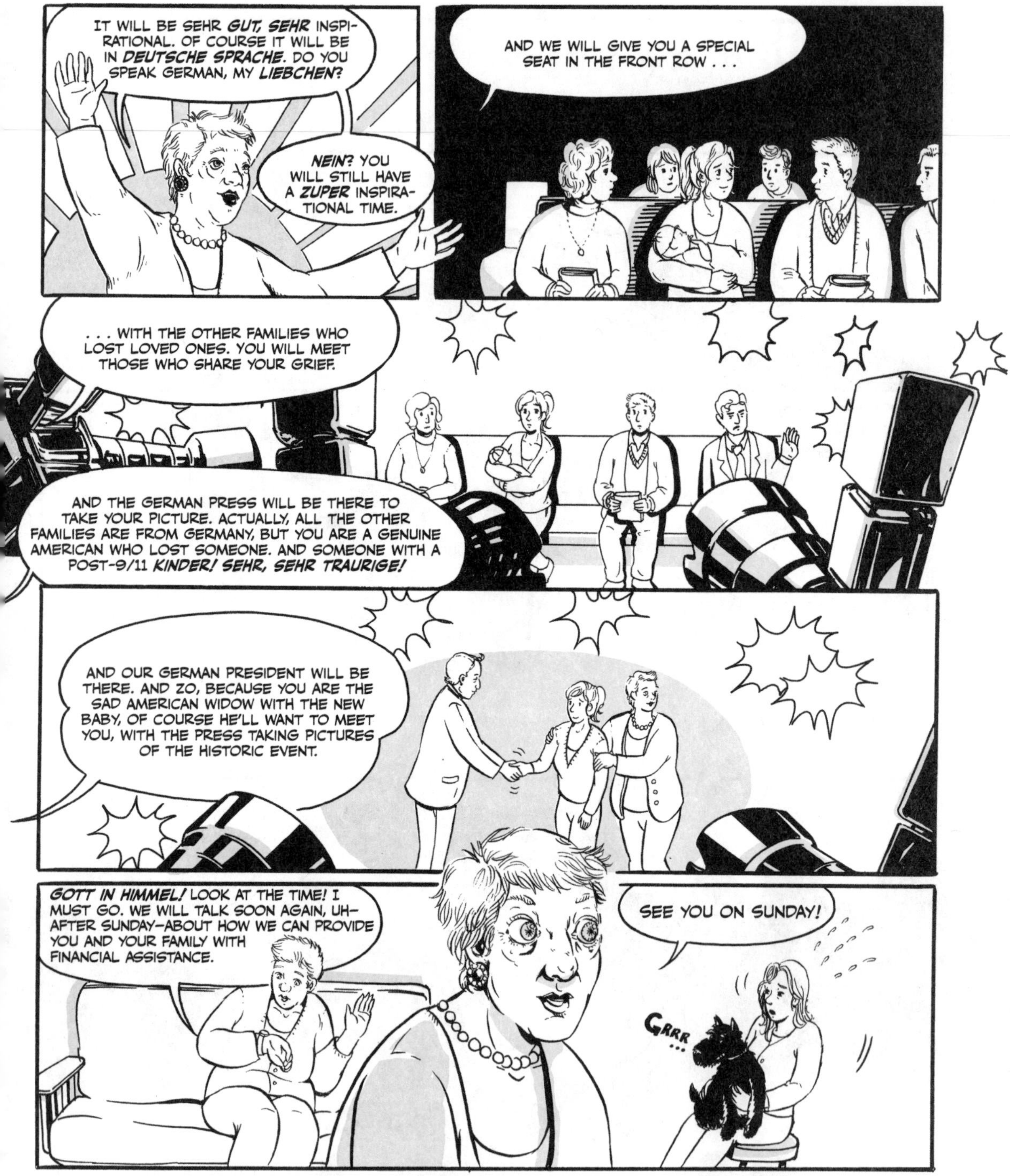
IT WILL BE SEHR GUT, SEHR INSPIRATIONAL. OF COURSE IT WILL BE IN DEUTSCHE SPRACHE. DO YOU SPEAK GERMAN, MY LIEBCHEN?
NEIN? YOU WILL STILL HAVE A ZUPER INSPIRATIONAL TIME.
AND WE WILL GIVE YOU A SPECIAL SEAT IN THE FRONT ROW . . .
. . . WITH THE OTHER FAMILIES WHO LOST LOVED ONES. YOU WILL MEET THOSE WHO SHARE YOUR GRIEF.
AND THE GERMAN PRESS WILL BE THERE TO TAKE YOUR PICTURE. ACTUALLY, ALL THE OTHER FAMILIES ARE FROM GERMANY, BUT YOU ARE A GENUINE AMERICAN WHO LOST SOMEONE. AND SOMEONE WITH A POST-9/11 KINDER! SEHR, SEHR TRAURIGE!
AND OUR GERMAN PRESIDENT WILL BE THERE. AND ZO, BECAUSE YOU ARE THE SAD AMERICAN WIDOW WITH THE NEW BABY, OF COURSE HE'LL WANT TO MEET YOU, WITH THE PRESS TAKING PICTURES OF THE HISTORIC EVENT.
GOTT IN HIMMEL! LOOK AT THE TIME! I MUST GO. WE WILL TALK SOON AGAIN, UH— AFTER SUNDAY—ABOUT HOW WE CAN PROVIDE YOU AND YOUR FAMILY WITH FINANCIAL ASSISTANCE.
SEE YOU ON SUNDAY!
GRRR . . .

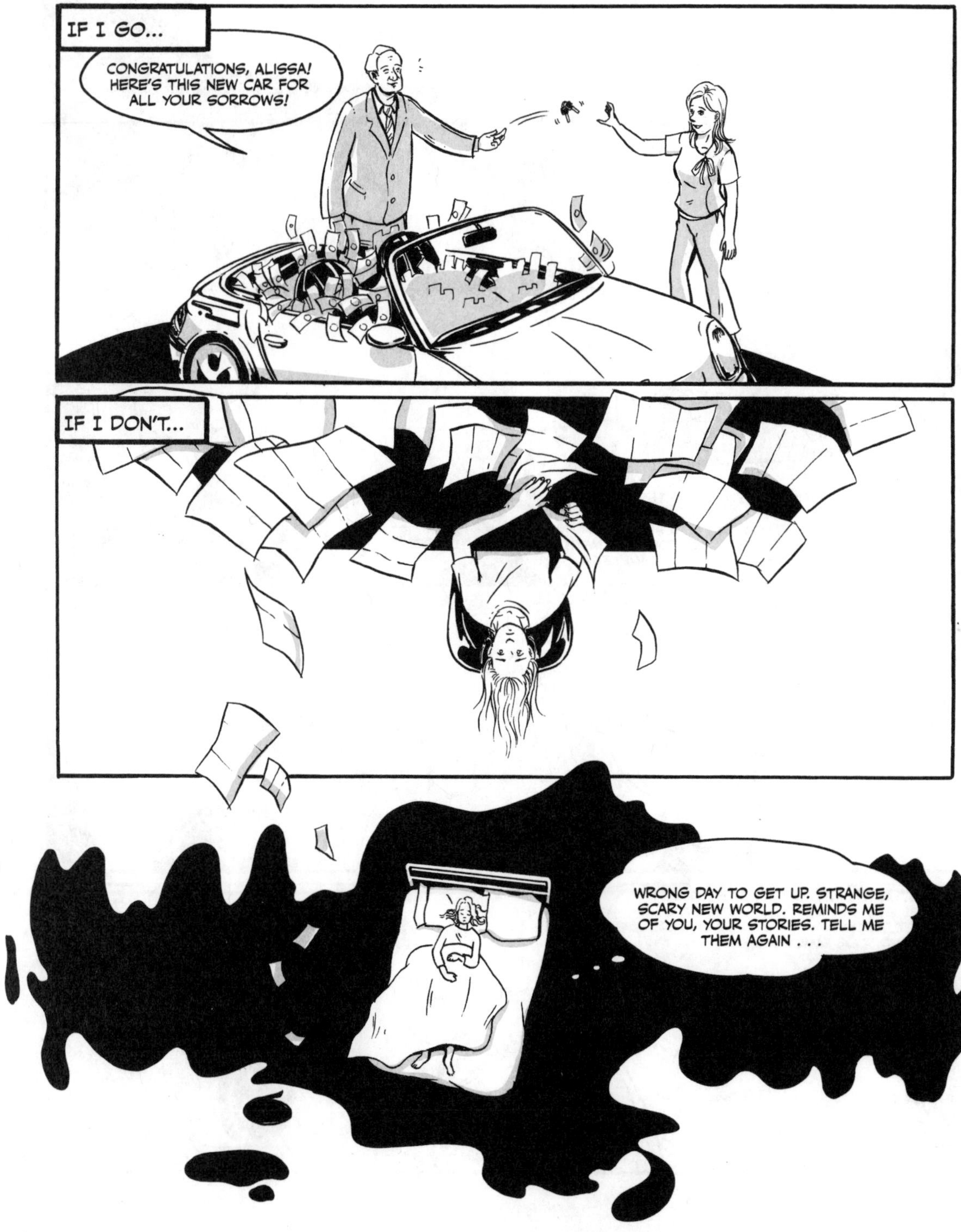
IF I GO...
CONGRATULATIONS, ALISSA! HERE'S THIS NEW CAR FOR ALL YOUR SORROWS!
IF I DON'T...
WRONG DAY TO GET UP. STRANGE, SCARY NEW WORLD. REMINDS ME OF YOU, YOUR STORIES. TELL ME THEM AGAIN . . .

I WAS SUCH A WET NOODLE.
I WORKED IN THE GARMENT DISTRICT . . .

1990

BOOM!!!

YOU'RE FIRED!!!

HEY, *GUAPO!* DOWN [...]
STREET THEY'RE AL[...]
HIRING. AND HERE, T[...]
MY NUMBER.

OH, SHIT, HOW I GET ANYTHING DONE WITH YOU PEOPLE!
SHAKE YOUR HEADS, ZI, ZI, ZI, BUT REALLY NO! ZO ONE
MORE TIME—I VANT THOSE BOXES IN ORDER:
AY, BEE, CEE . . . NOW, WHO CAN DO IT?

. . . MEESTER, I
CAN DO IT.

AND, IF NO, YOU OUT!
¿*COMPRENDE*?

*¡AY, NO!
POR FAVOR,*

. . . AND I HAD A WOMAN IN EVERY SWEATSHOP.

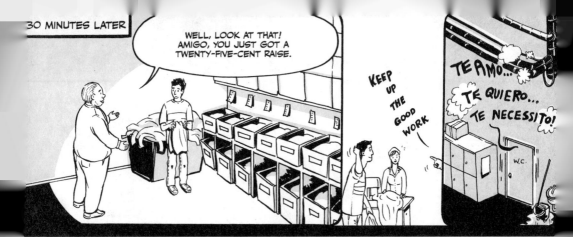

30 MINUTES LATER
WELL, LOOK AT THAT! AMIGO, YOU JUST GOT A TWENTY-FIVE-CENT RAISE.
KEEP UP THE GOOD WORK
TE AMO...
TE QUIERO...
TE NECESSITO!
W.C.
FOR THE NEXT SEVERAL YEARS, I WORKED MY ASS OFF AT ANY JOB I COULD GET, SO I COULD PAY MY BILLS AND TO SEND MONEY TO MY FAMILY.
7 AM–6 PM, MONDAY–FRIDAY
KID, YOU'RE LIKE MY RIGHT HAND. I'M GIVING YOU ANOTHER TWENTY-FIVE-CENT RAISE WITH THIS PROMOTION.
ER, THANK YOU, MR. MOJAK.
8 PM–1 AM
4H39
WEEKENDS
BEEF OR CHICKEN FOR YOUR ENTRÉE?
BRING IT HERE!
?
SORRY, I CAN'T ORDER IF MY WIFE ISN'T HERE!
HEY, KID, YOU REALLY DON'T NEED TO BUST YOUR BUTT LIKE THIS. I CAN HOOK YOU UP, IF YOU WANT TO MAKE LOCO DINERO, WITH A DEALERSHIP OF COLOMBIA'S FINEST IMPORT.
UH, I'LL THINK ABOUT IT.

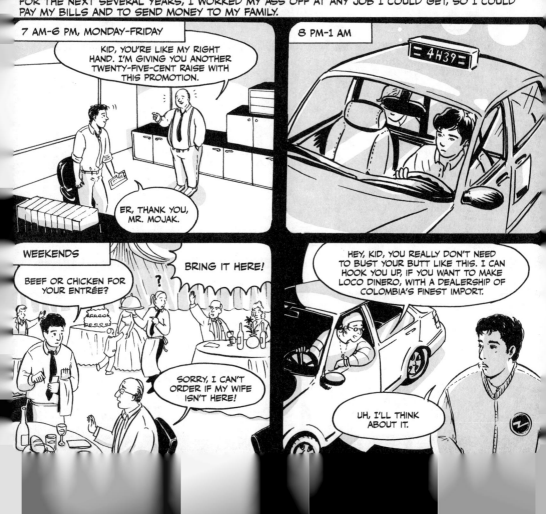

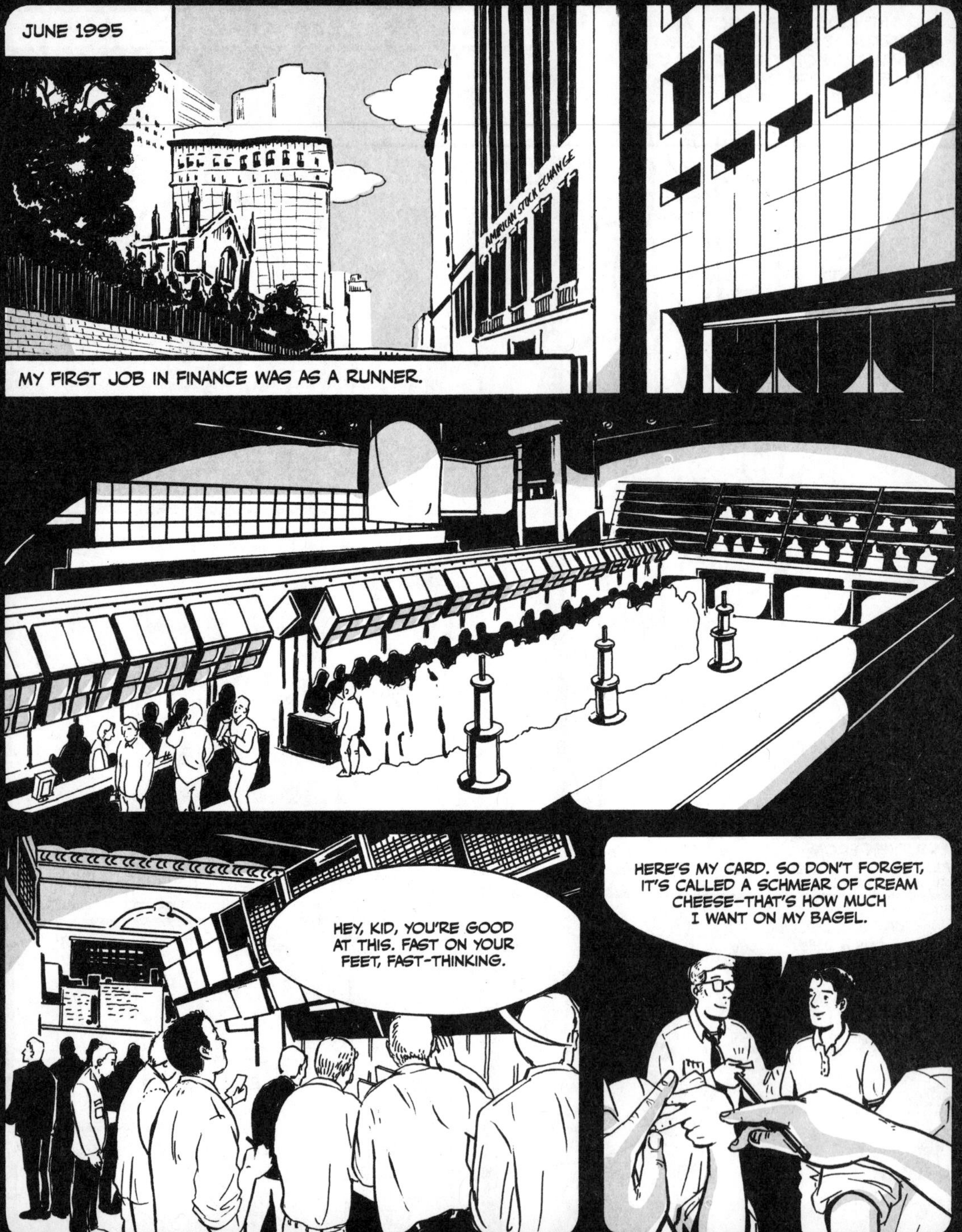
JUNE 1995
AMERICAN STOCK EXCHANGE
MY FIRST JOB IN FINANCE WAS AS A RUNNER.
HEY, KID, YOU'RE GOOD AT THIS. FAST ON YOUR FEET, FAST-THINKING.
HERE'S MY CARD. SO DON'T FORGET, IT'S CALLED A SCHMEAR OF CREAM CHEESE–THAT'S HOW MUCH I WANT ON MY BAGEL.

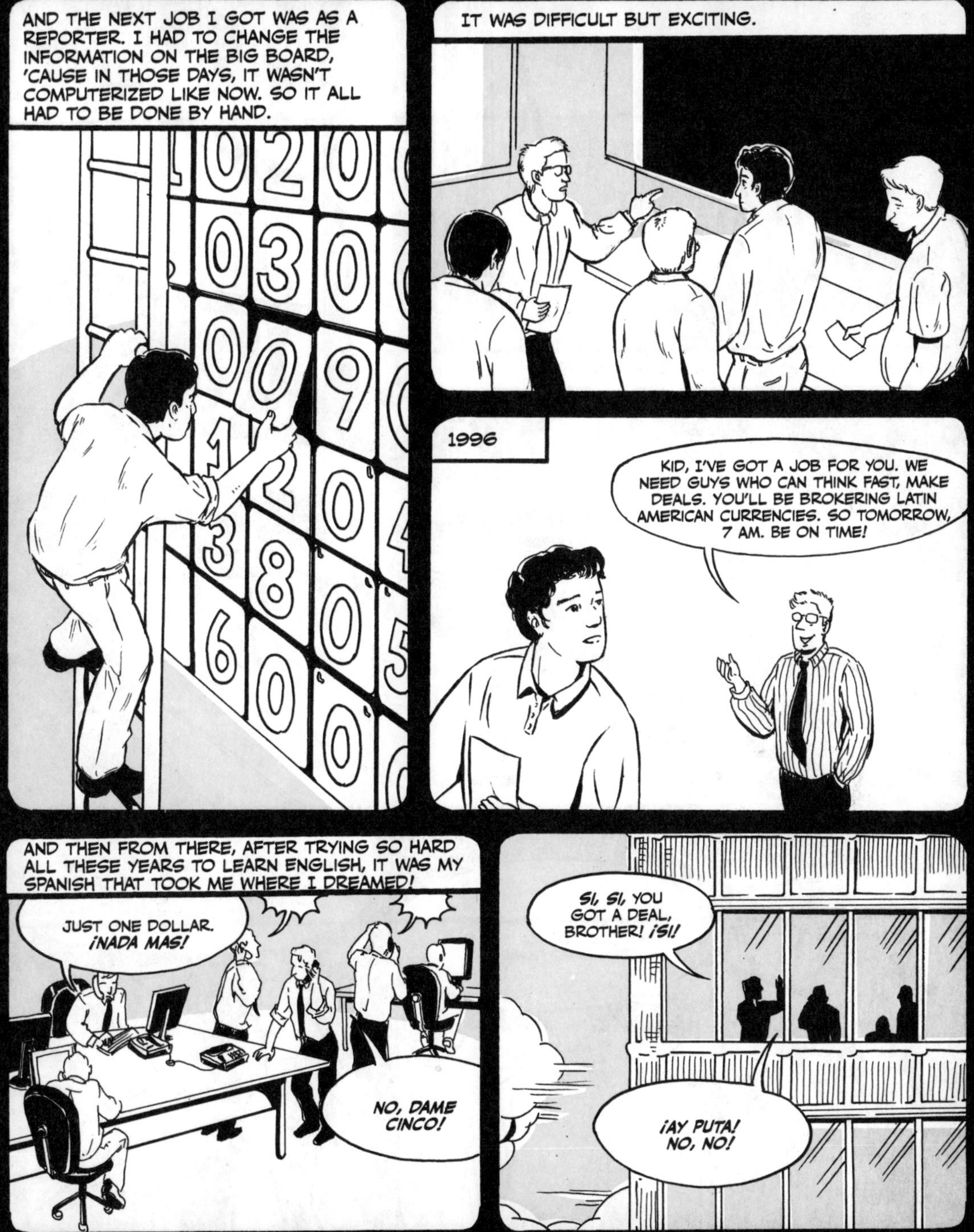
AND THE NEXT JOB I GOT WAS AS A REPORTER. I HAD TO CHANGE THE INFORMATION ON THE BIG BOARD, 'CAUSE IN THOSE DAYS, IT WASN'T COMPUTERIZED LIKE NOW. SO IT ALL HAD TO BE DONE BY HAND.
IT WAS DIFFICULT BUT EXCITING.
1996
KID, I'VE GOT A JOB FOR YOU. WE NEED GUYS WHO CAN THINK FAST, MAKE DEALS. YOU'LL BE BROKERING LATIN AMERICAN CURRENCIES. SO TOMORROW, 7 AM. BE ON TIME!
AND THEN FROM THERE, AFTER TRYING SO HARD ALL THESE YEARS TO LEARN ENGLISH, IT WAS MY SPANISH THAT TOOK ME WHERE I DREAMED!
JUST ONE DOLLAR. ¡NADA MAS!
NO, DAME CINCO!
SI, SI, YOU GOT A DEAL, BROTHER! ¡SI!
¡AY PUTA! NO, NO!

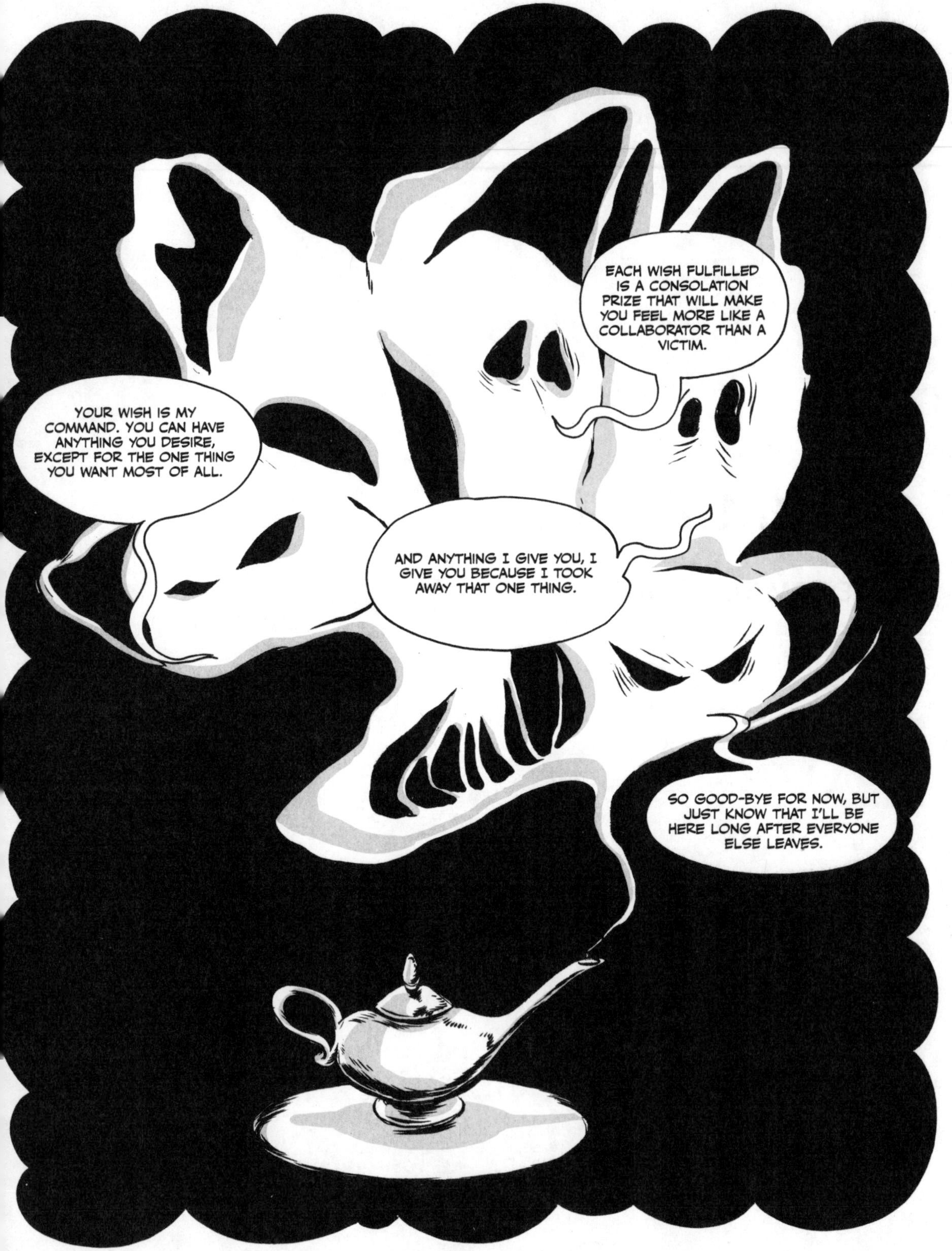
EACH WISH FULFILLED IS A CONSOLATION PRIZE THAT WILL MAKE YOU FEEL MORE LIKE A COLLABORATOR THAN A VICTIM.
YOUR WISH IS MY COMMAND. YOU CAN HAVE ANYTHING YOU DESIRE, EXCEPT FOR THE ONE THING YOU WANT MOST OF ALL.
AND ANYTHING I GIVE YOU, I GIVE YOU BECAUSE I TOOK AWAY THAT ONE THING.
SO GOOD-BYE FOR NOW, BUT JUST KNOW THAT I'LL BE HERE LONG AFTER EVERYONE ELSE LEAVES.

Chapter Nine

DECEMBER 2001

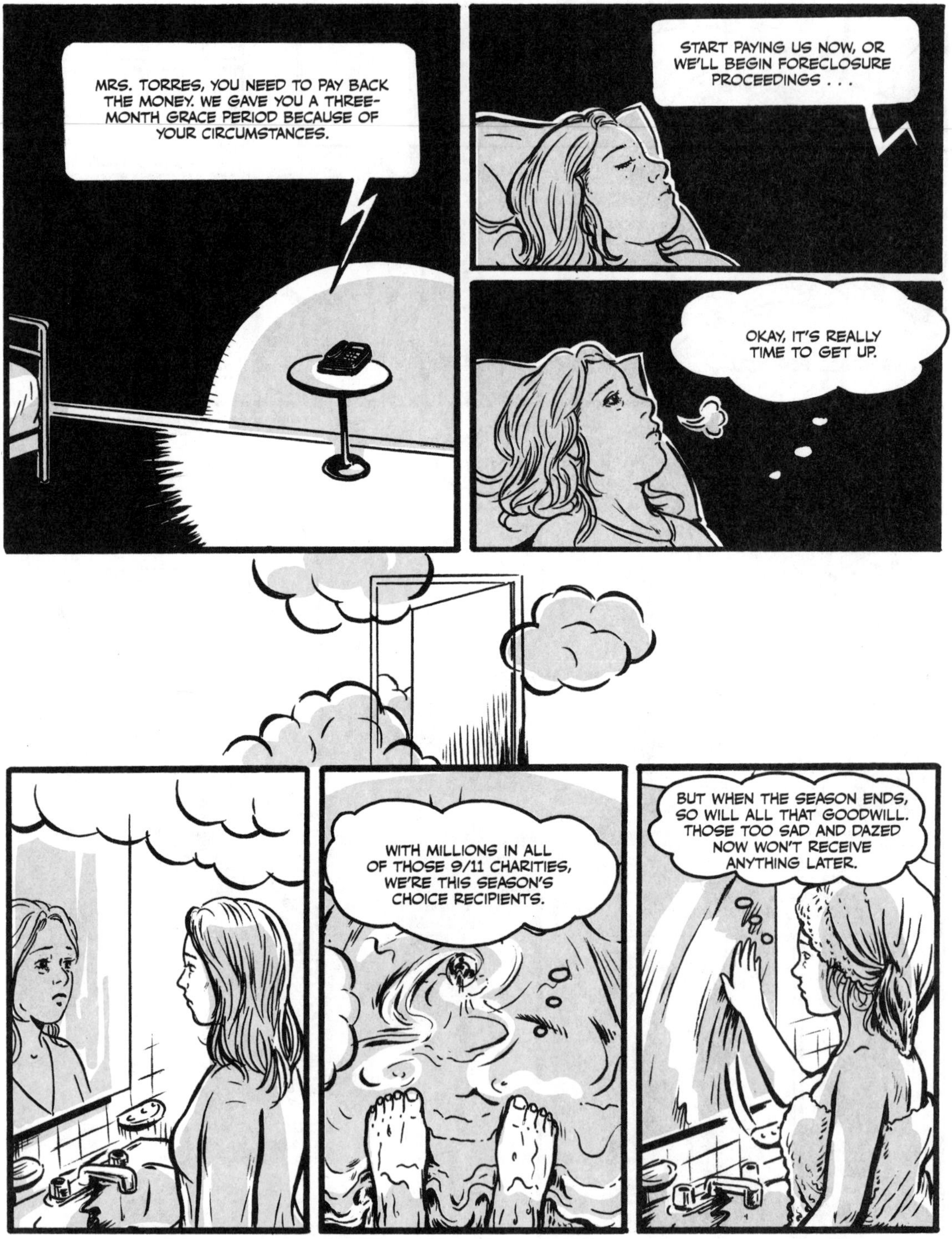
MRS. TORRES, YOU NEED TO PAY BACK THE MONEY. WE GAVE YOU A THREE-MONTH GRACE PERIOD BECAUSE OF YOUR CIRCUMSTANCES.
START PAYING US NOW, OR WE'LL BEGIN FORECLOSURE PROCEEDINGS . . .
OKAY, IT'S REALLY TIME TO GET UP.
WITH MILLIONS IN ALL OF THOSE 9/11 CHARITIES, WE'RE THIS SEASON'S CHOICE RECIPIENTS.
BUT WHEN THE SEASON ENDS, SO WILL ALL THAT GOODWILL. THOSE TOO SAD AND DAZED NOW WON'T RECEIVE ANYTHING LATER.

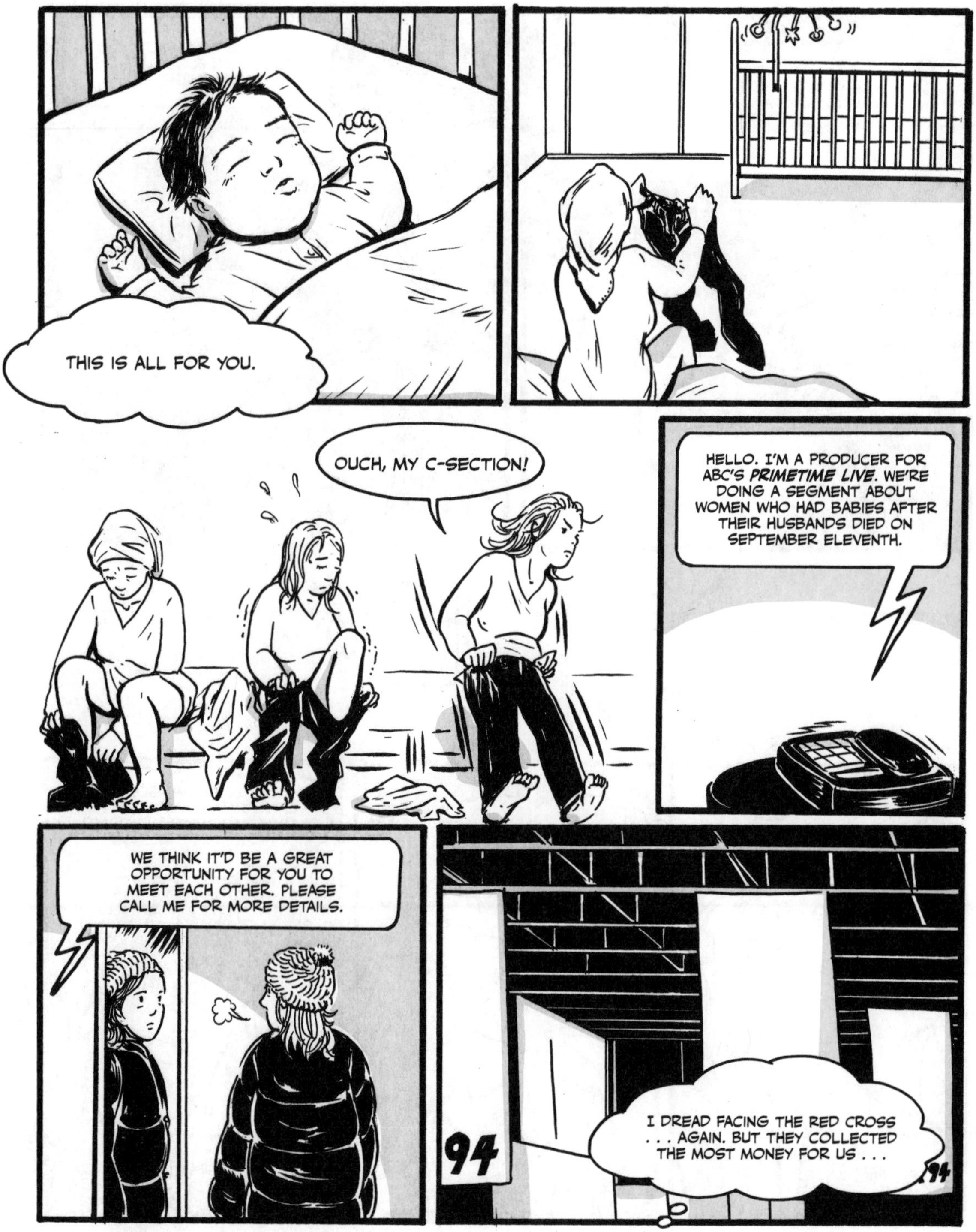
THIS IS ALL FOR YOU.
OUCH, MY C-SECTION!
HELLO. I'M A PRODUCER FOR ABC'S *PRIMETIME LIVE*. WE'RE DOING A SEGMENT ABOUT WOMEN WHO HAD BABIES AFTER THEIR HUSBANDS DIED ON SEPTEMBER ELEVENTH.
WE THINK IT'D BE A GREAT OPPORTUNITY FOR YOU TO MEET EACH OTHER. PLEASE CALL ME FOR MORE DETAILS.
94
I DREAD FACING THE RED CROSS . . . AGAIN. BUT THEY COLLECTED THE MOST MONEY FOR US . . .
94

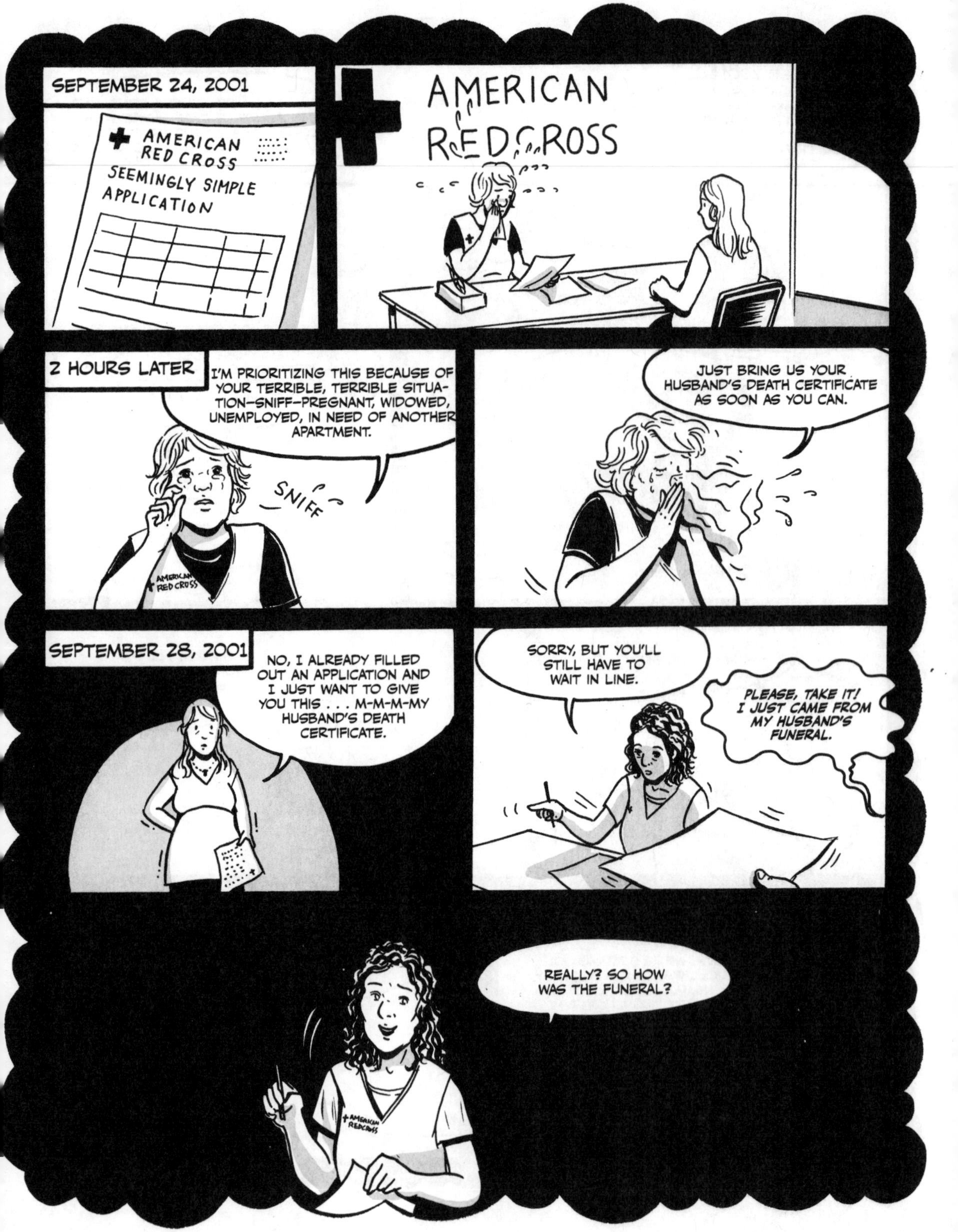
SEPTEMBER 24, 2001
AMERICAN RED CROSS
SEEMINGLY SIMPLE APPLICATION
AMERICAN RED CROSS
2 HOURS LATER
I'M PRIORITIZING THIS BECAUSE OF YOUR TERRIBLE, TERRIBLE SITUATION—SNIFF—PREGNANT, WIDOWED, UNEMPLOYED, IN NEED OF ANOTHER APARTMENT.
SNIFF
AMERICAN RED CROSS
JUST BRING US YOUR HUSBAND'S DEATH CERTIFICATE AS SOON AS YOU CAN.
SEPTEMBER 28, 2001
NO, I ALREADY FILLED OUT AN APPLICATION AND I JUST WANT TO GIVE YOU THIS . . . M-M-M-MY HUSBAND'S DEATH CERTIFICATE.
SORRY, BUT YOU'LL STILL HAVE TO WAIT IN LINE.
PLEASE, TAKE IT! I JUST CAME FROM MY HUSBAND'S FUNERAL.
REALLY? SO HOW WAS THE FUNERAL?
AMERICAN RED CROSS

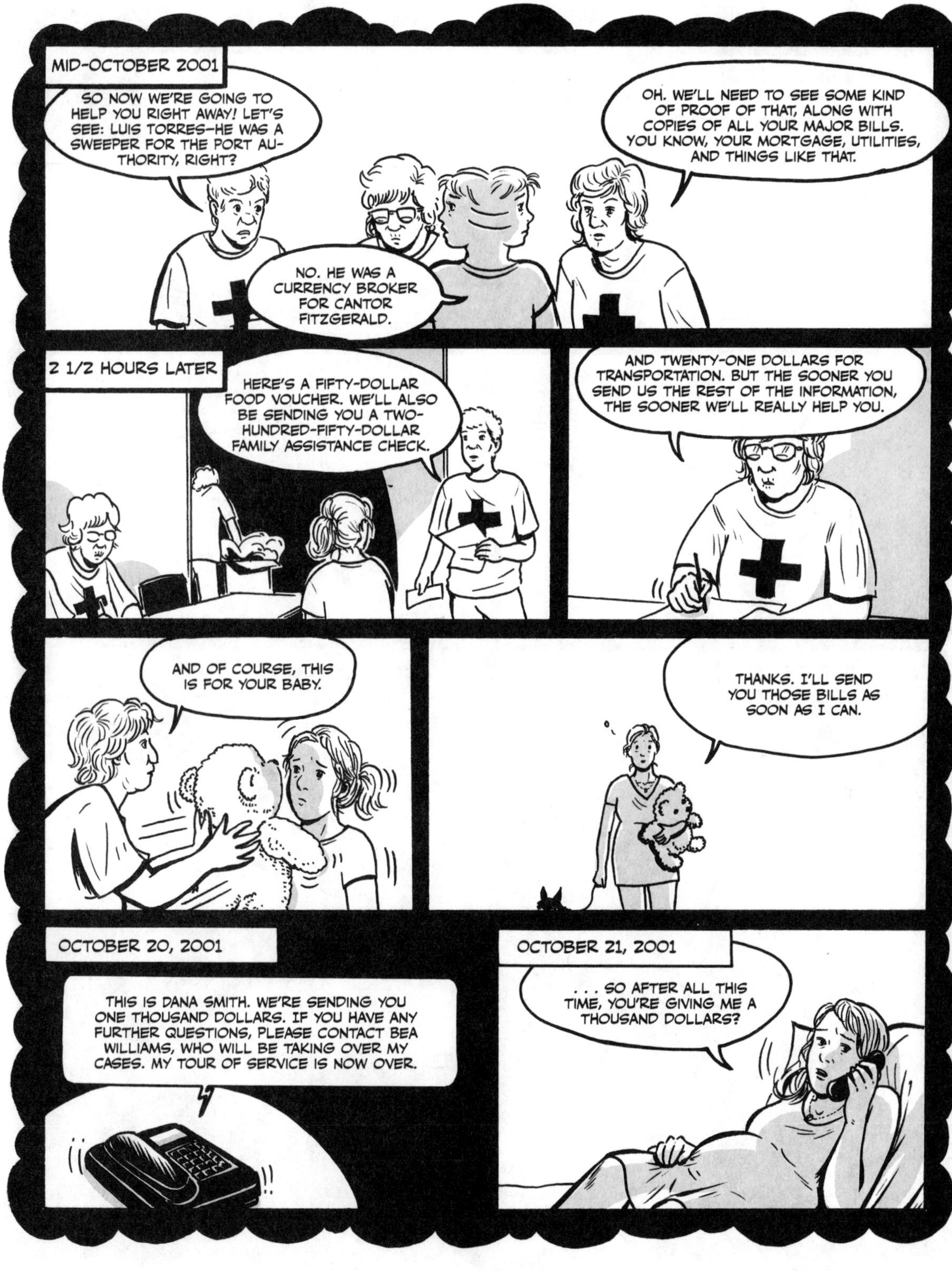
MID-OCTOBER 2001
SO NOW WE'RE GOING TO HELP YOU RIGHT AWAY! LET'S SEE: LUIS TORRES—HE WAS A SWEEPER FOR THE PORT AUTHORITY, RIGHT?
NO. HE WAS A CURRENCY BROKER FOR CANTOR FITZGERALD.
OH. WE'LL NEED TO SEE SOME KIND OF PROOF OF THAT, ALONG WITH COPIES OF ALL YOUR MAJOR BILLS. YOU KNOW, YOUR MORTGAGE, UTILITIES, AND THINGS LIKE THAT.
2 1/2 HOURS LATER
HERE'S A FIFTY-DOLLAR FOOD VOUCHER. WE'LL ALSO BE SENDING YOU A TWO-HUNDRED-FIFTY-DOLLAR FAMILY ASSISTANCE CHECK.
AND TWENTY-ONE DOLLARS FOR TRANSPORTATION. BUT THE SOONER YOU SEND US THE REST OF THE INFORMATION, THE SOONER WE'LL REALLY HELP YOU.
AND OF COURSE, THIS IS FOR YOUR BABY.
THANKS. I'LL SEND YOU THOSE BILLS AS SOON AS I CAN.
OCTOBER 20, 2001
THIS IS DANA SMITH. WE'RE SENDING YOU ONE THOUSAND DOLLARS. IF YOU HAVE ANY FURTHER QUESTIONS, PLEASE CONTACT BEA WILLIAMS, WHO WILL BE TAKING OVER MY CASES. MY TOUR OF SERVICE IS NOW OVER.
OCTOBER 21, 2001
. . . SO AFTER ALL THIS TIME, YOU'RE GIVING ME A THOUSAND DOLLARS?

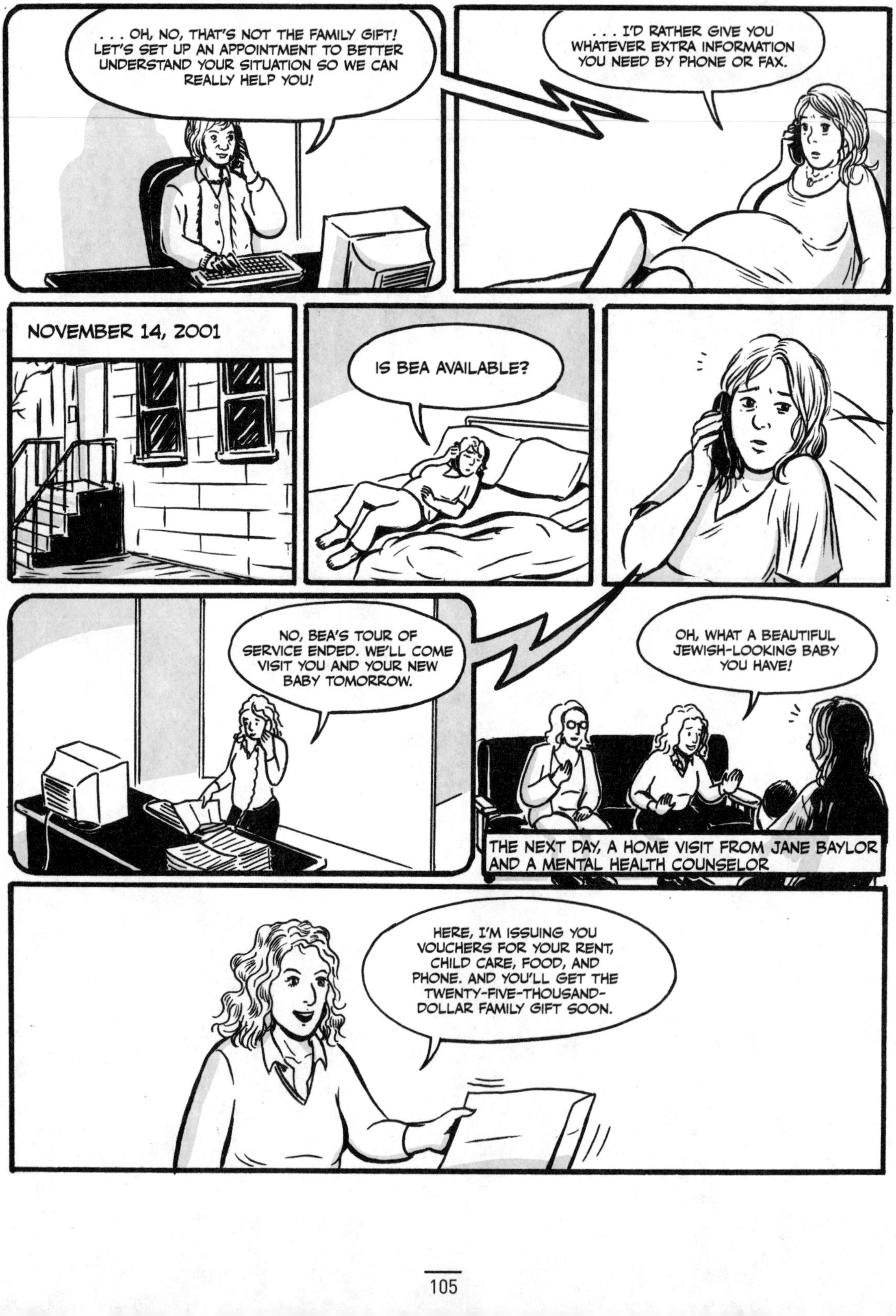
. . . OH, NO, THAT'S NOT THE FAMILY GIFT! LET'S SET UP AN APPOINTMENT TO BETTER UNDERSTAND YOUR SITUATION SO WE CAN REALLY HELP YOU!
. . . I'D RATHER GIVE YOU WHATEVER EXTRA INFORMATION YOU NEED BY PHONE OR FAX.
NOVEMBER 14, 2001
IS BEA AVAILABLE?
NO, BEA'S TOUR OF SERVICE ENDED. WE'LL COME VISIT YOU AND YOUR NEW BABY TOMORROW.
OH, WHAT A BEAUTIFUL JEWISH-LOOKING BABY YOU HAVE!
THE NEXT DAY, A HOME VISIT FROM JANE BAYLOR AND A MENTAL HEALTH COUNSELOR
HERE, I'M ISSUING YOU VOUCHERS FOR YOUR RENT, CHILD CARE, FOOD, AND PHONE. AND YOU'LL GET THE TWENTY-FIVE-THOUSAND-DOLLAR FAMILY GIFT SOON.

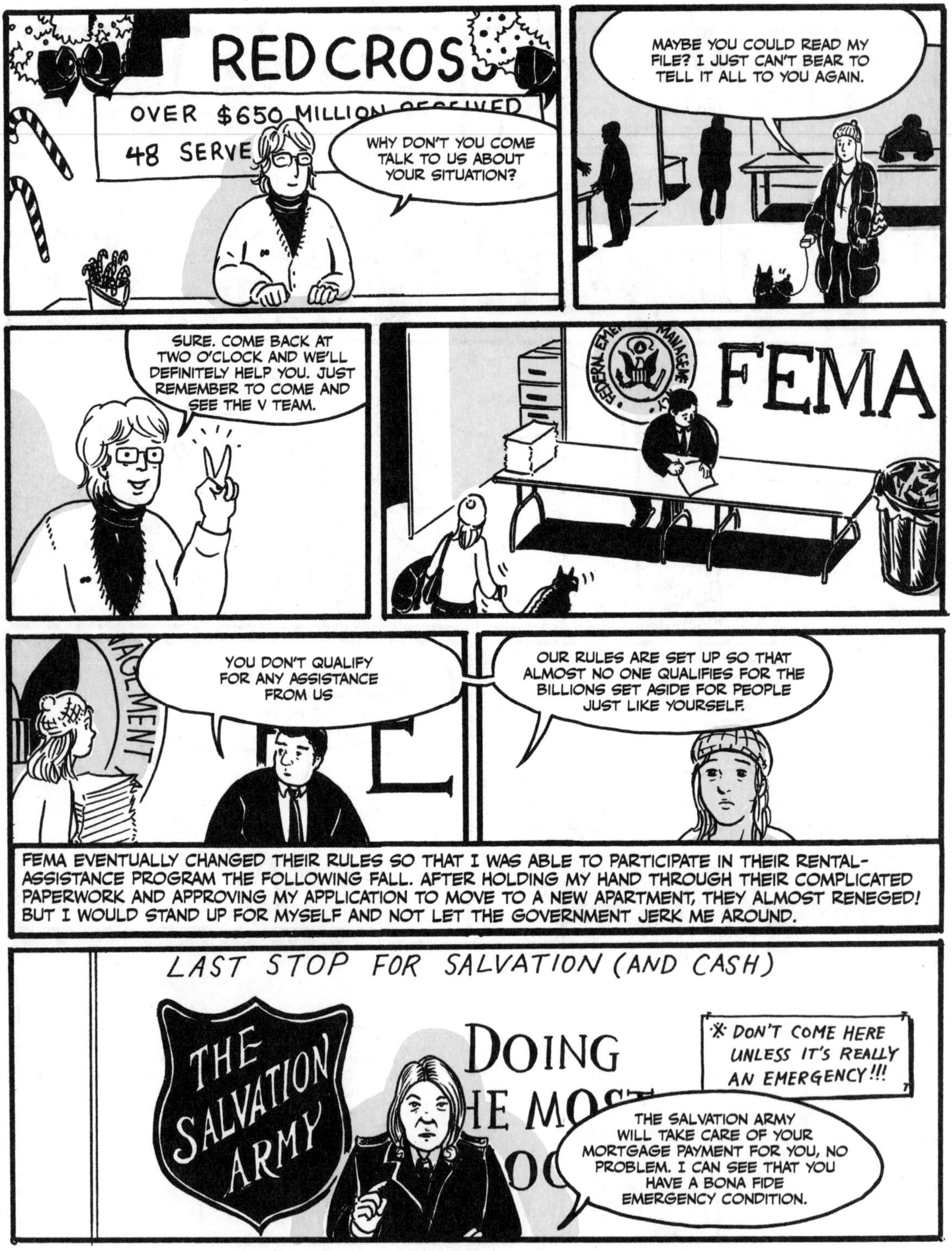
RED CROS
OVER $650 MILLION
48 SERVE
WHY DON'T YOU COME TALK TO US ABOUT YOUR SITUATION?
MAYBE YOU COULD READ MY FILE? I JUST CAN'T BEAR TO TELL IT ALL TO YOU AGAIN.
SURE. COME BACK AT TWO O'CLOCK AND WE'LL DEFINITELY HELP YOU. JUST REMEMBER TO COME AND SEE THE V TEAM.
FEMA
YOU DON'T QUALIFY FOR ANY ASSISTANCE FROM US
OUR RULES ARE SET UP SO THAT ALMOST NO ONE QUALIFIES FOR THE BILLIONS SET ASIDE FOR PEOPLE JUST LIKE YOURSELF.
FEMA EVENTUALLY CHANGED THEIR RULES SO THAT I WAS ABLE TO PARTICIPATE IN THEIR RENTAL-ASSISTANCE PROGRAM THE FOLLOWING FALL. AFTER HOLDING MY HAND THROUGH THEIR COMPLICATED PAPERWORK AND APPROVING MY APPLICATION TO MOVE TO A NEW APARTMENT, THEY ALMOST RENEGED! BUT I WOULD STAND UP FOR MYSELF AND NOT LET THE GOVERNMENT JERK ME AROUND.
LAST STOP FOR SALVATION (AND CASH)
THE SALVATION ARMY
DOING
※ DON'T COME HERE UNLESS IT'S REALLY AN EMERGENCY!!!
THE SALVATION ARMY WILL TAKE CARE OF YOUR MORTGAGE PAYMENT FOR YOU, NO PROBLEM. I CAN SEE THAT YOU HAVE A BONA FIDE EMERGENCY CONDITION.

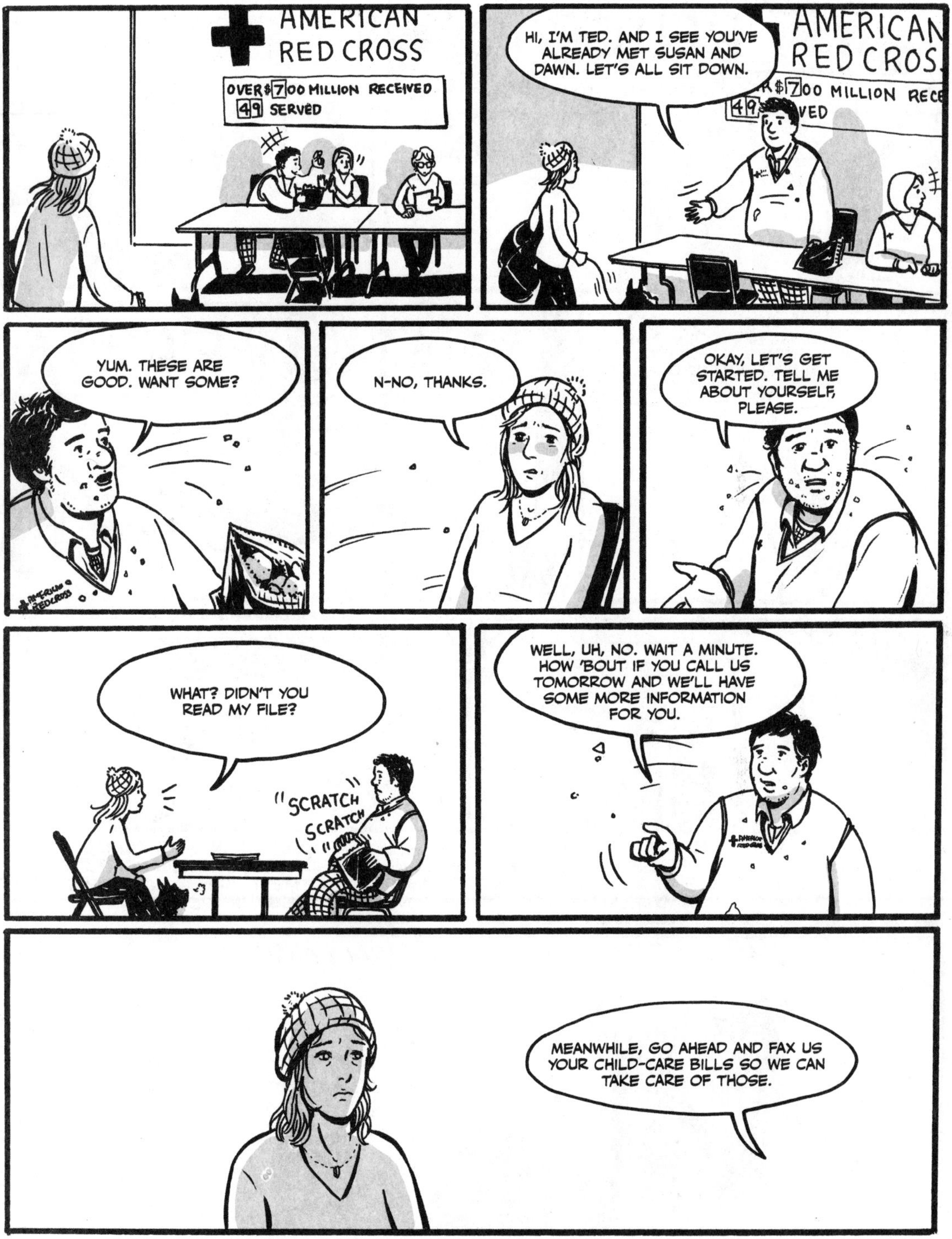
AMERICAN RED CROSS
OVER $700 MILLION RECEIVED
49 SERVED
HI, I'M TED. AND I SEE YOU'VE ALREADY MET SUSAN AND DAWN. LET'S ALL SIT DOWN.
YUM. THESE ARE GOOD. WANT SOME?
AMERICAN RED CROSS
N-NO, THANKS.
OKAY, LET'S GET STARTED. TELL ME ABOUT YOURSELF, PLEASE.
WHAT? DIDN'T YOU READ MY FILE?
SCRATCH SCRATCH
WELL, UH, NO. WAIT A MINUTE. HOW 'BOUT IF YOU CALL US TOMORROW AND WE'LL HAVE SOME MORE INFORMATION FOR YOU.
MEANWHILE, GO AHEAD AND FAX US YOUR CHILD-CARE BILLS SO WE CAN TAKE CARE OF THOSE.

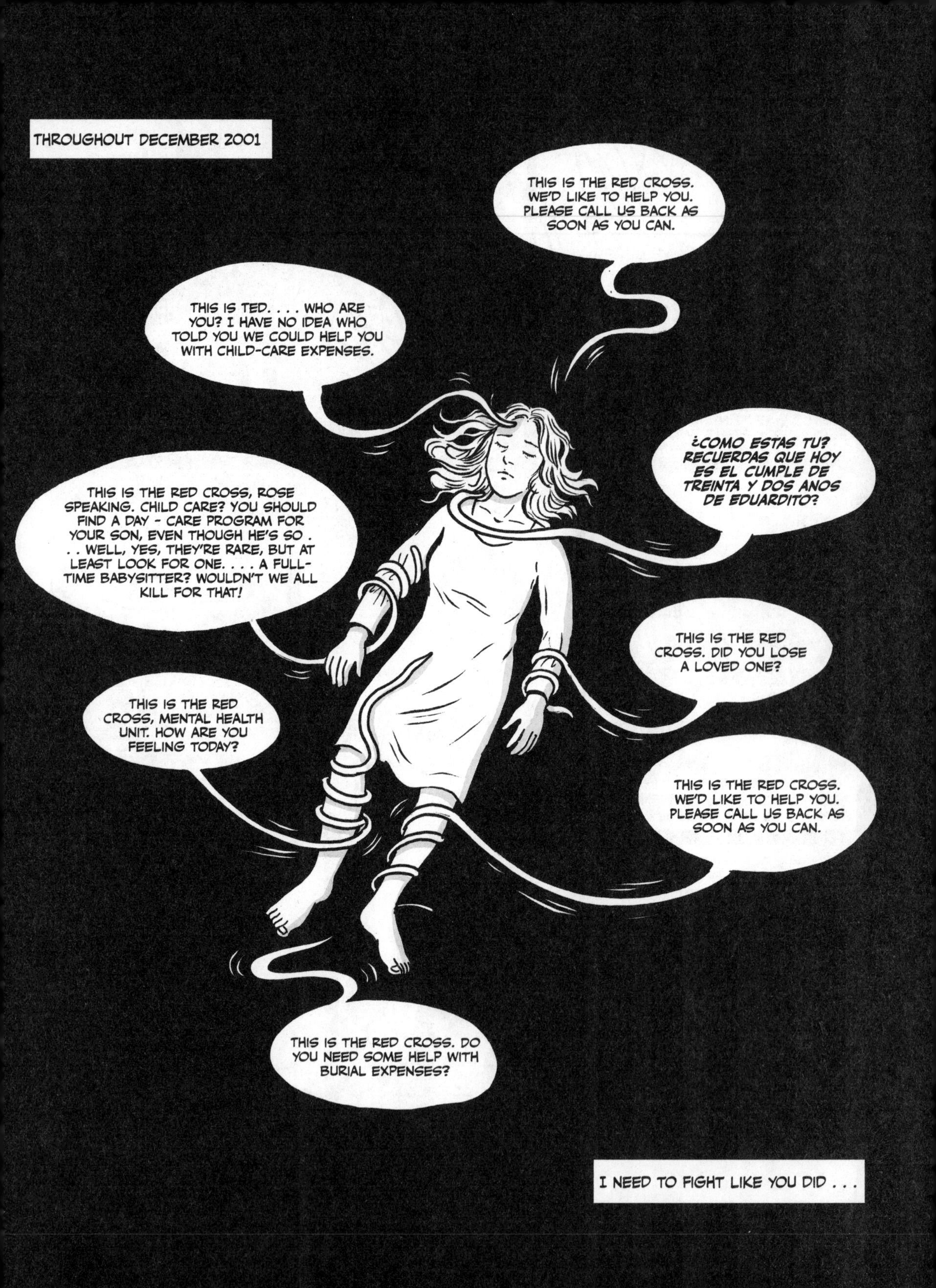
THROUGHOUT DECEMBER 2001
THIS IS THE RED CROSS. WE'D LIKE TO HELP YOU. PLEASE CALL US BACK AS SOON AS YOU CAN.
THIS IS TED. . . . WHO ARE YOU? I HAVE NO IDEA WHO TOLD YOU WE COULD HELP YOU WITH CHILD-CARE EXPENSES.
¿COMO ESTAS TU? RECUERDAS QUE HOY ES EL CUMPLE DE TREINTA Y DOS ANOS DE EDUARDITO?
THIS IS THE RED CROSS, ROSE SPEAKING. CHILD CARE? YOU SHOULD FIND A DAY - CARE PROGRAM FOR YOUR SON, EVEN THOUGH HE'S SO . . . WELL, YES, THEY'RE RARE, BUT AT LEAST LOOK FOR ONE. . . . A FULL-TIME BABYSITTER? WOULDN'T WE ALL KILL FOR THAT!
THIS IS THE RED CROSS. DID YOU LOSE A LOVED ONE?
THIS IS THE RED CROSS, MENTAL HEALTH UNIT. HOW ARE YOU FEELING TODAY?
THIS IS THE RED CROSS. WE'D LIKE TO HELP YOU. PLEASE CALL US BACK AS SOON AS YOU CAN.
THIS IS THE RED CROSS. DO YOU NEED SOME HELP WITH BURIAL EXPENSES?
I NEED TO FIGHT LIKE YOU DID . . .

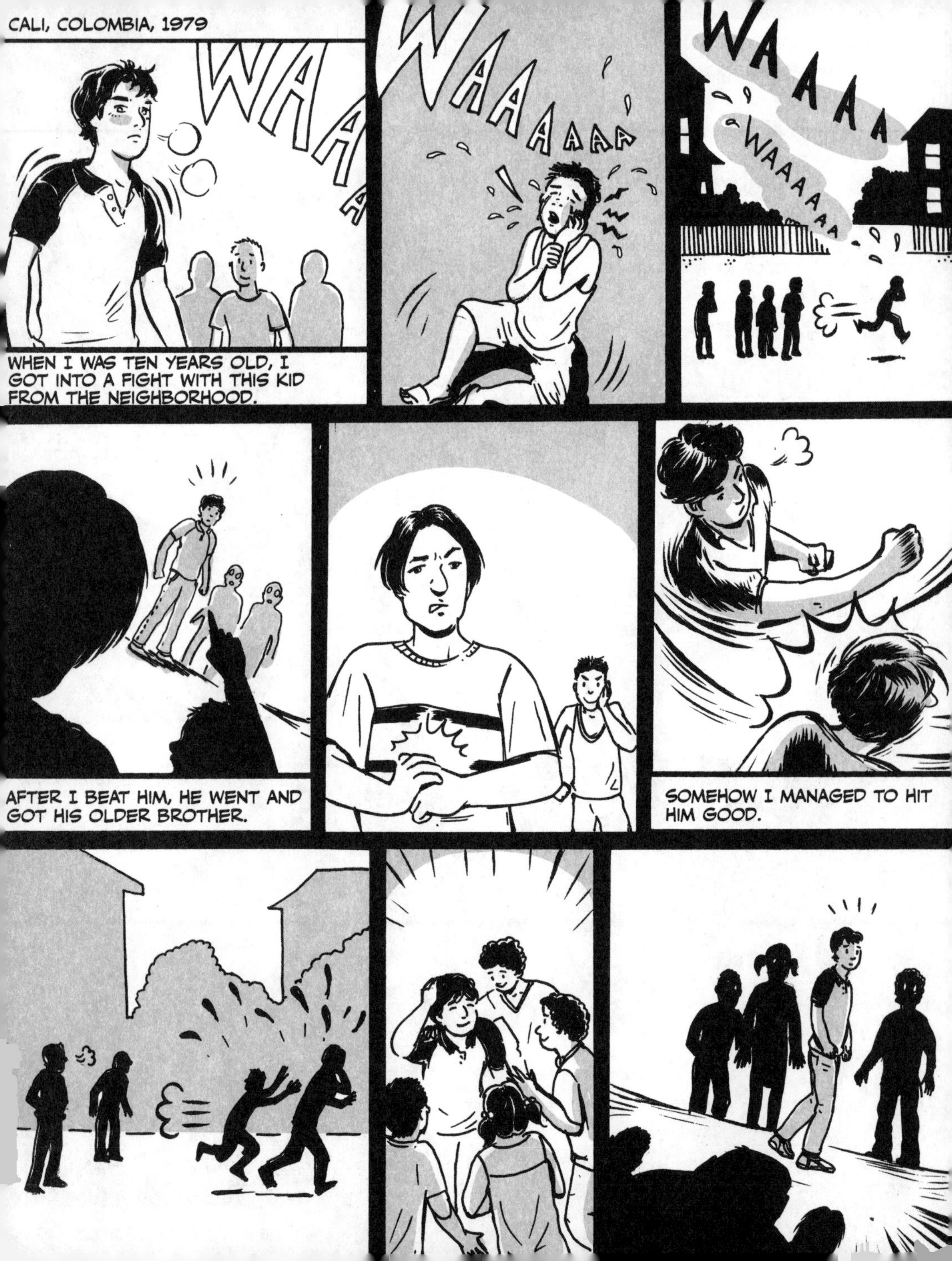
CALI, COLOMBIA, 1979
WAAA
WHEN I WAS TEN YEARS OLD, I GOT INTO A FIGHT WITH THIS KID FROM THE NEIGHBORHOOD.
WAAAAAAA
WAAAAA
WAAAAAAA
AFTER I BEAT HIM, HE WENT AND GOT HIS OLDER BROTHER.
SOMEHOW I MANAGED TO HIT HIM GOOD.

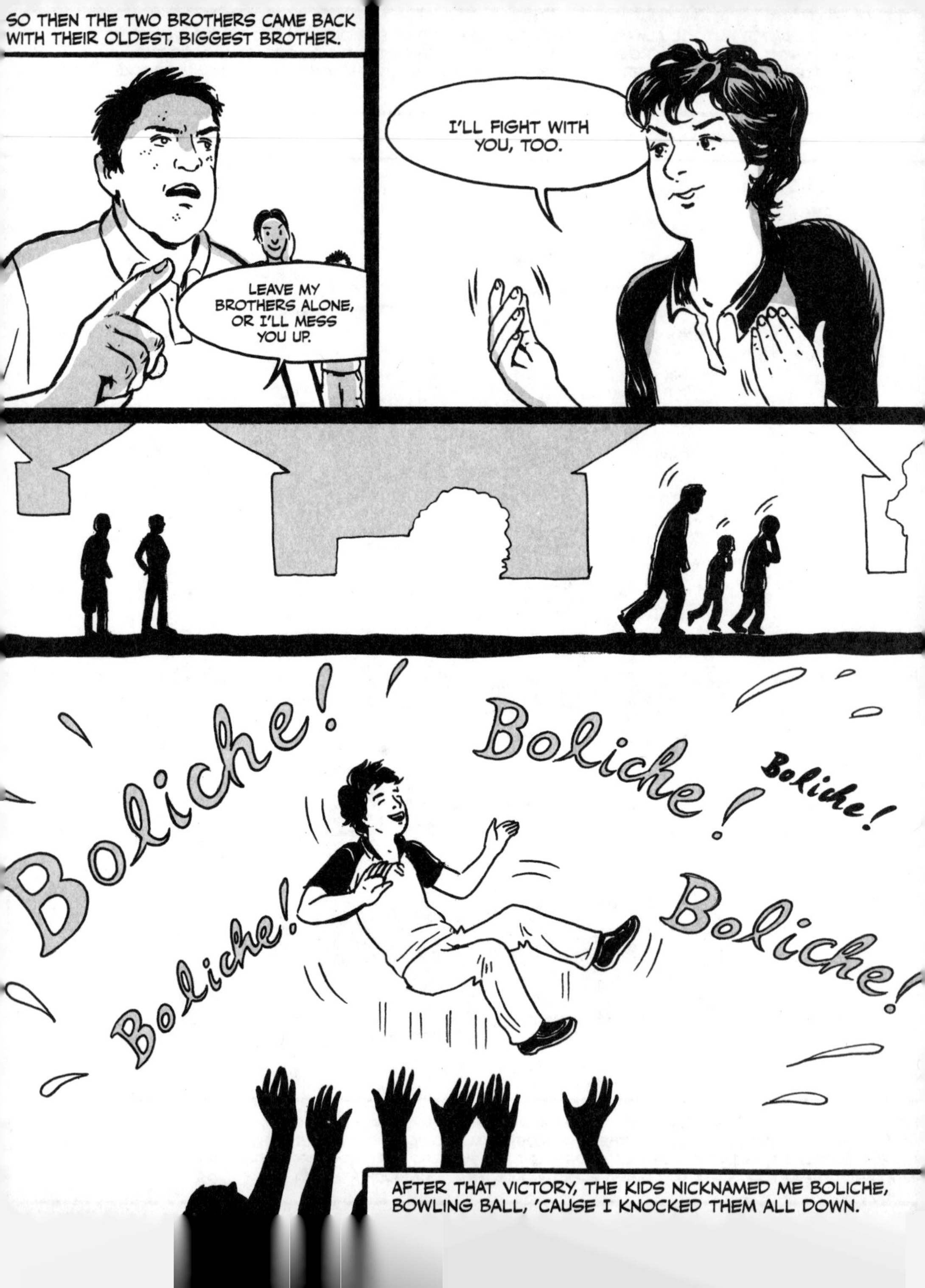
SO THEN THE TWO BROTHERS CAME BACK WITH THEIR OLDEST, BIGGEST BROTHER.
LEAVE MY BROTHERS ALONE, OR I'LL MESS YOU UP.
I'LL FIGHT WITH YOU, TOO.
Boliche!
Boliche!
Boliche!
Boliche!
Boliche!
AFTER THAT VICTORY, THE KIDS NICKNAMED ME BOLICHE, BOWLING BALL, 'CAUSE I KNOCKED THEM ALL DOWN.

I'M NOT YOU, *BOLICHE*, BUT I'LL ALWAYS TRY MY BEST TO STAND UP FOR OUR FAMILY. I WROTE A CERTIFIED LETTER AND SENT IT TO THE RED CROSS HEADQUARTERS IN WASHINGTON, D.C. I ADDRESSED IT TO THE CHAIRMAN AND SENT COPIES TO OTHER HIGH-RANKING OFFICERS IN THE CHARITY. IN MY LETTER, I DESCRIBED EVERY PAINFUL EXPERIENCE I HAD IN DEALING WITH THEM.

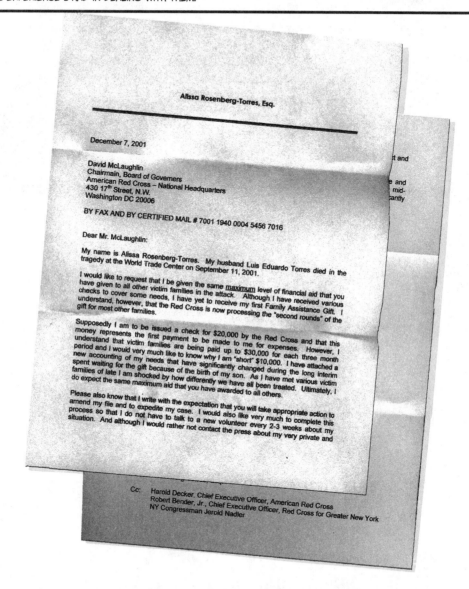

Alissa Rosenberg-Torres, Esq.

December 7, 2001

David McLaughlin
Chairmain, Board of Governers
American Red Cross – National Headquarters
430 17th Street, N.W.
Washington DC 20006

BY FAX AND BY CERTIFIED MAIL # 7001 1940 0004 5456 7016

Dear Mr. McLaughlin:

My name is Alissa Rosenberg-Torres. My husband Luis Eduardo Torres died in the tragedy at the World Trade Center on September 11, 2001.

I would like to request that I be given the same <u>maximum</u> level of financial aid that you have given to all other victim families in the attack. Although I have received various checks to cover some needs, I have yet to receive my first Family Assistance Gift. I understand, however, that the Red Cross is now processing the "second rounds" of the gift for most other families.

Supposedly I am to be issued a check for $20,000 by the Red Cross and that this money represents the first payment to be made to me for expenses. However, I understand that victim families are being paid up to $30,000 for each three month period and I would very much like to know why I am "short" $10,000. I have attached a new accounting of my needs that have significantly changed during the long interim spent waiting for the gift because of the birth of my son. As I have met various victim families of late I am shocked by how differently we have all been treated. Ultimately, I do expect the same maximum aid that you have awarded to all others.

Please also know that I write with the expectation that you will take appropriate action to amend my file and to expedite my case. I would also like very much to complete this process so that I do not have to talk to a new volunteer every 2-3 weeks about my situation. And although I would rather not contact the press about my very private and

Cc: Harold Decker, Chief Executive Officer, American Red Cross
Robert Bender, Jr., Chief Executive Officer, Red Cross for Greater New York
NY Congressman Jerold Nadler

IN RESPONSE TO MY LETTER, SOMEONE WITH AUTHORITY AND COMPETENCE HELPED ME, SO THAT AT LAST, THREE MONTHS AFTER MY INITIAL REQUEST, I RECEIVED THE RED CROSS FAMILY GIFT. UNFORTUNATELY, THIS WAS JUST THE FIRST OF MANY CERTIFIED LETTERS I'D SEND TO THE RED CROSS AS I MANEUVERED THROUGH THEIR INTRICATE SYSTEMS OF 9/11 ASSISTANCE. WHO'D HAVE THOUGHT THAT BEING HELPED WOULD FEEL LIKE SUCH A BEATING?

Chapter Ten

January 2002

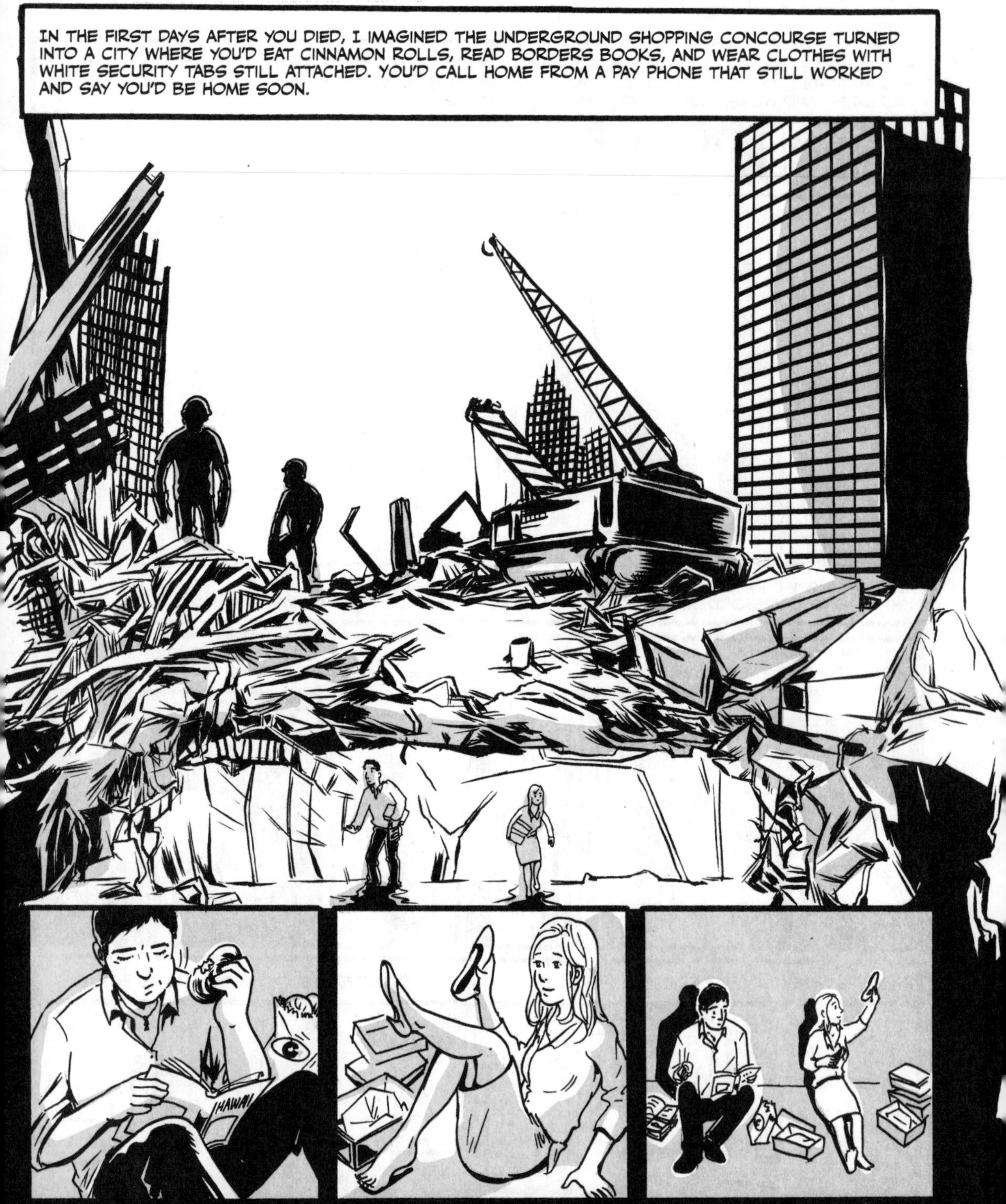
IN THE FIRST DAYS AFTER YOU DIED, I IMAGINED THE UNDERGROUND SHOPPING CONCOURSE TURNED INTO A CITY WHERE YOU'D EAT CINNAMON ROLLS, READ BORDERS BOOKS, AND WEAR CLOTHES WITH WHITE SECURITY TABS STILL ATTACHED. YOU'D CALL HOME FROM A PAY PHONE THAT STILL WORKED AND SAY YOU'D BE HOME SOON.
HAWAII

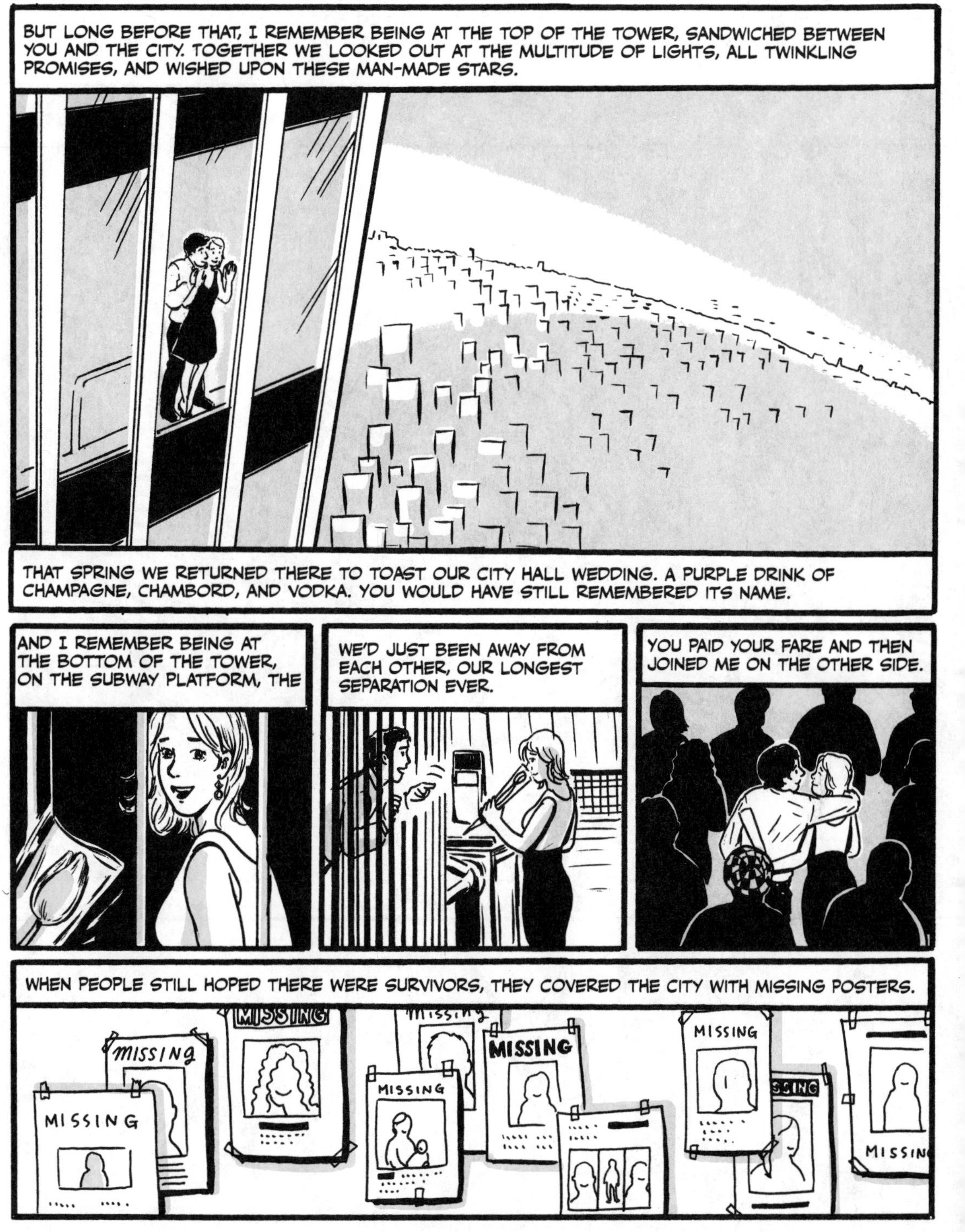
BUT LONG BEFORE THAT, I REMEMBER BEING AT THE TOP OF THE TOWER, SANDWICHED BETWEEN YOU AND THE CITY. TOGETHER WE LOOKED OUT AT THE MULTITUDE OF LIGHTS, ALL TWINKLING PROMISES, AND WISHED UPON THESE MAN-MADE STARS.
THAT SPRING WE RETURNED THERE TO TOAST OUR CITY HALL WEDDING. A PURPLE DRINK OF CHAMPAGNE, CHAMBORD, AND VODKA. YOU WOULD HAVE STILL REMEMBERED ITS NAME.
AND I REMEMBER BEING AT THE BOTTOM OF THE TOWER, ON THE SUBWAY PLATFORM, THE
WE'D JUST BEEN AWAY FROM EACH OTHER, OUR LONGEST SEPARATION EVER.
YOU PAID YOUR FARE AND THEN JOINED ME ON THE OTHER SIDE.
WHEN PEOPLE STILL HOPED THERE WERE SURVIVORS, THEY COVERED THE CITY WITH MISSING POSTERS.
MISSING
MISSING
MISSING
MISSING
MISSING
MISSING
MISSING

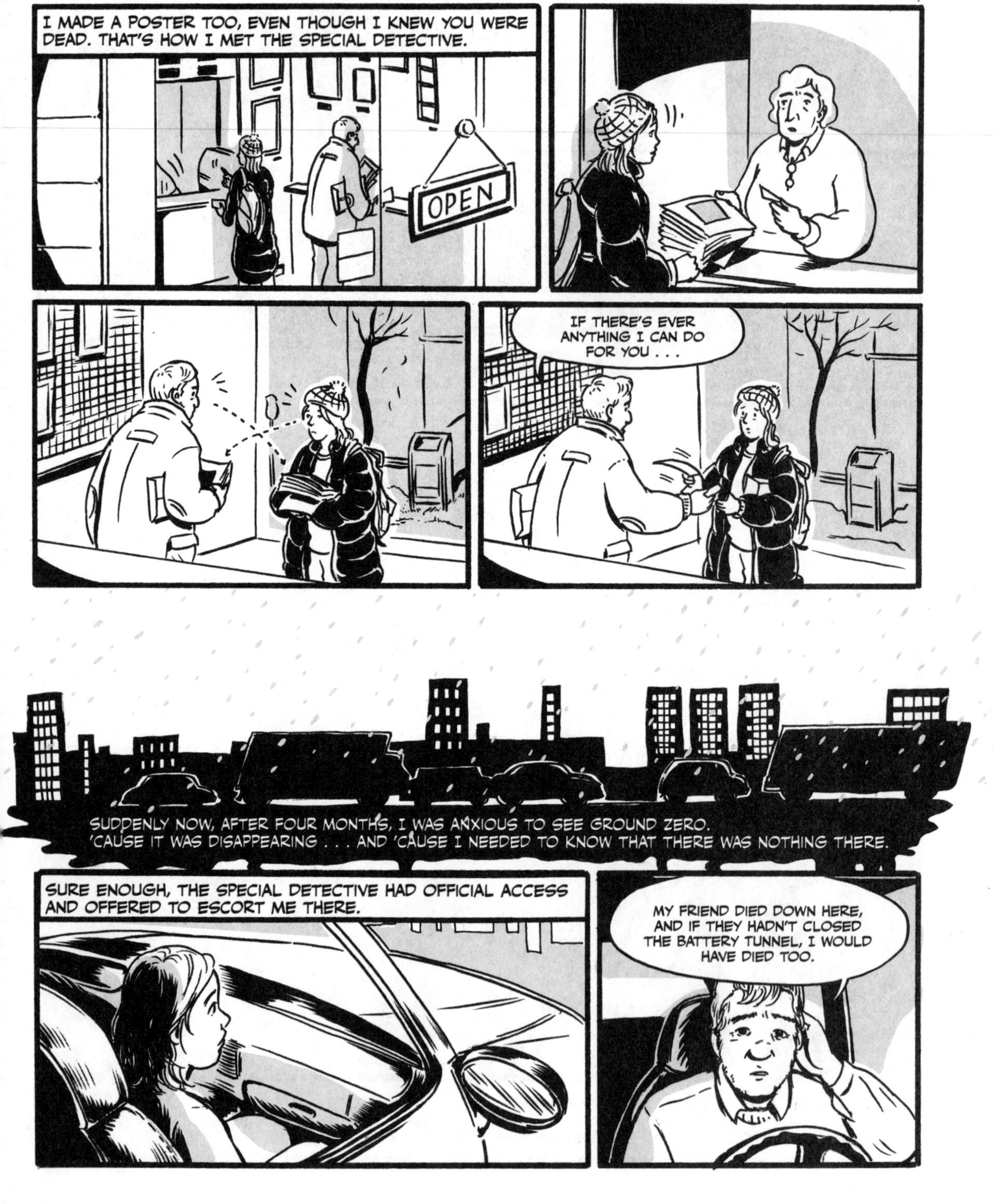
I MADE A POSTER TOO, EVEN THOUGH I KNEW YOU WERE DEAD. THAT'S HOW I MET THE SPECIAL DETECTIVE.
OPEN
IF THERE'S EVER ANYTHING I CAN DO FOR YOU . . .
SUDDENLY NOW, AFTER FOUR MONTHS, I WAS ANXIOUS TO SEE GROUND ZERO.
'CAUSE IT WAS DISAPPEARING . . . AND 'CAUSE I NEEDED TO KNOW THAT THERE WAS NOTHING THERE.
SURE ENOUGH, THE SPECIAL DETECTIVE HAD OFFICIAL ACCESS AND OFFERED TO ESCORT ME THERE.
MY FRIEND DIED DOWN HERE, AND IF THEY HADN'T CLOSED THE BATTERY TUNNEL, I WOULD HAVE DIED TOO.

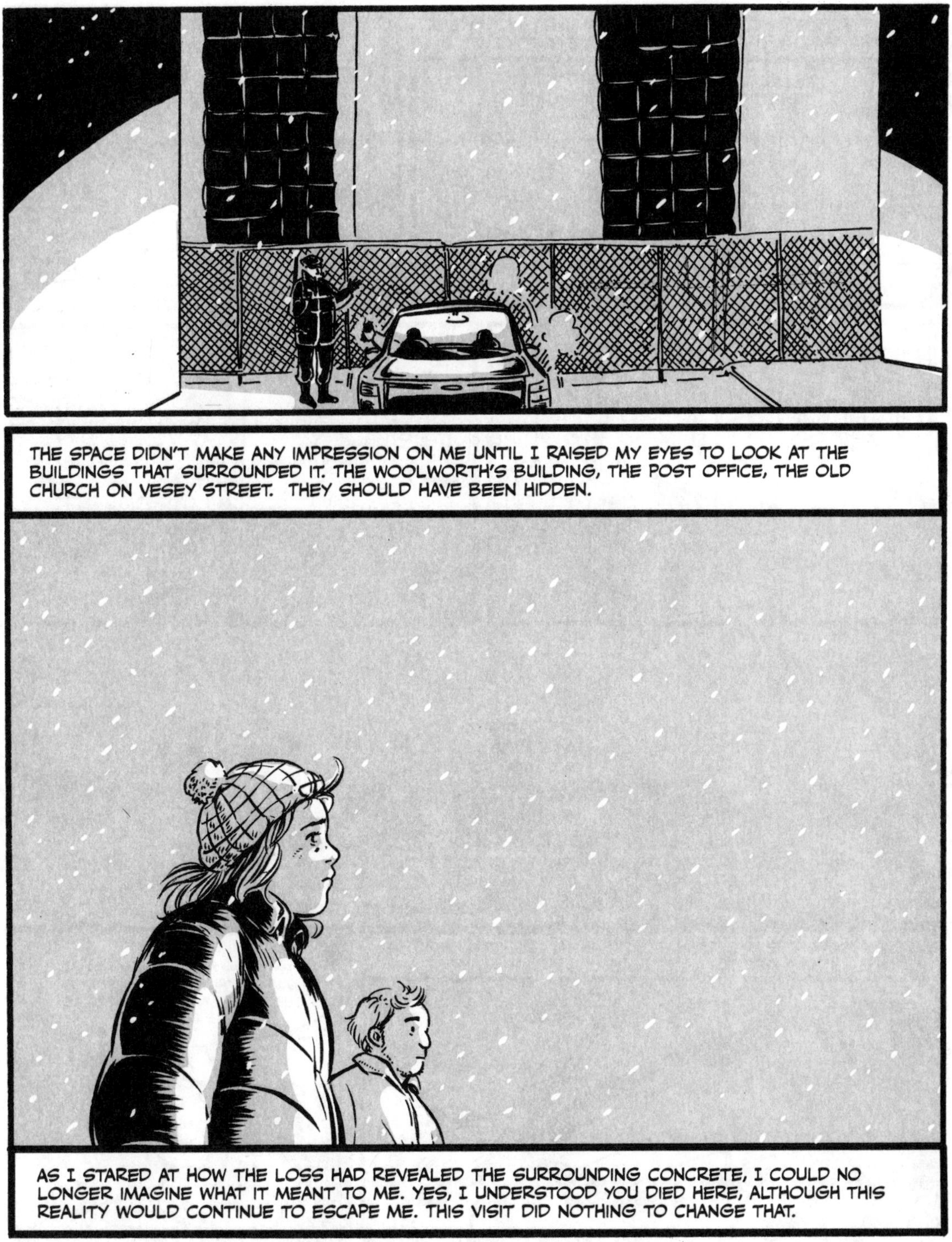
THE SPACE DIDN'T MAKE ANY IMPRESSION ON ME UNTIL I RAISED MY EYES TO LOOK AT THE BUILDINGS THAT SURROUNDED IT. THE WOOLWORTH'S BUILDING, THE POST OFFICE, THE OLD CHURCH ON VESEY STREET. THEY SHOULD HAVE BEEN HIDDEN.
AS I STARED AT HOW THE LOSS HAD REVEALED THE SURROUNDING CONCRETE, I COULD NO LONGER IMAGINE WHAT IT MEANT TO ME. YES, I UNDERSTOOD YOU DIED HERE, ALTHOUGH THIS REALITY WOULD CONTINUE TO ESCAPE ME. THIS VISIT DID NOTHING TO CHANGE THAT.

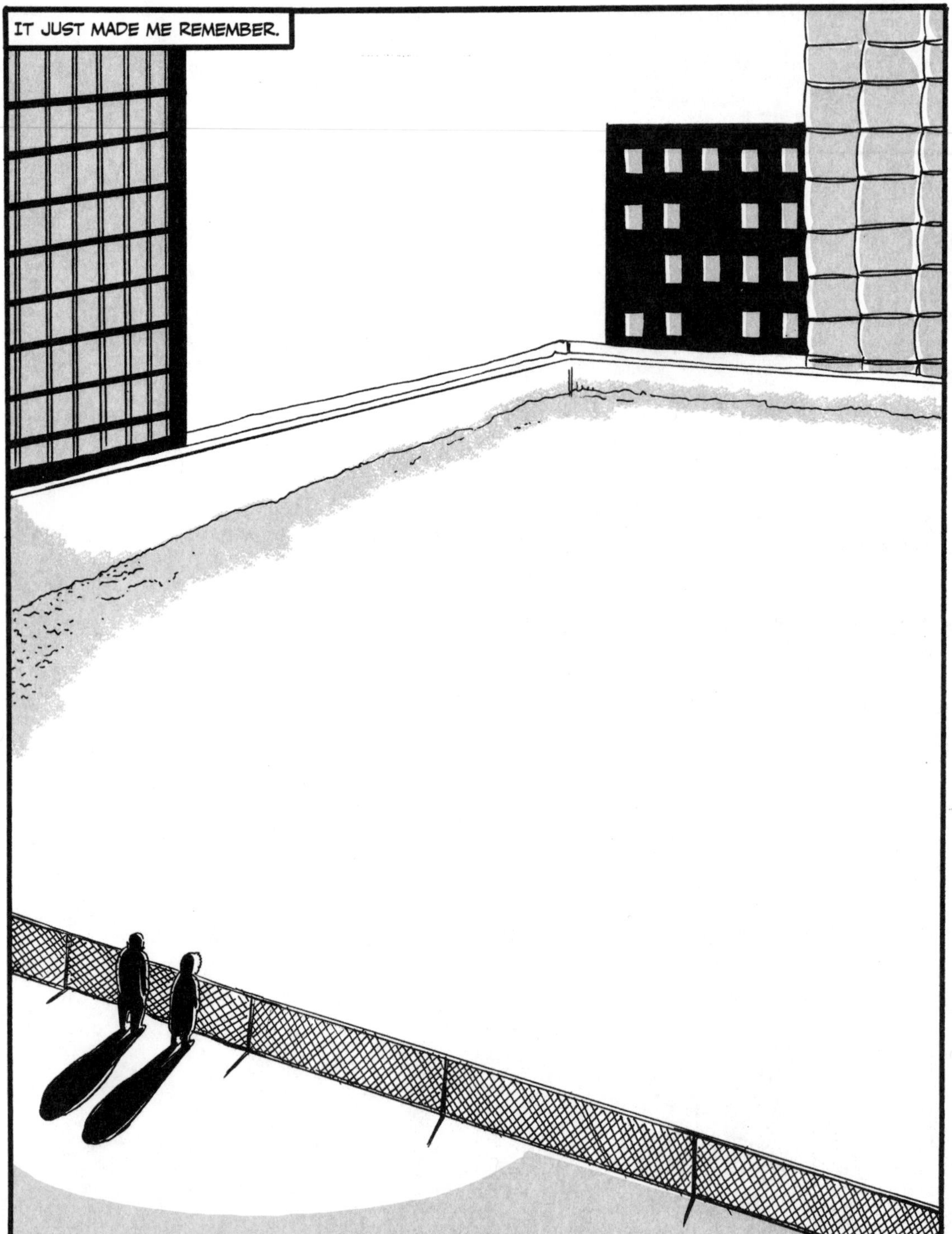
IT JUST MADE ME REMEMBER.

Chapter Eleven

February 2002

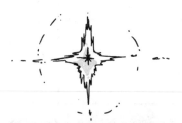

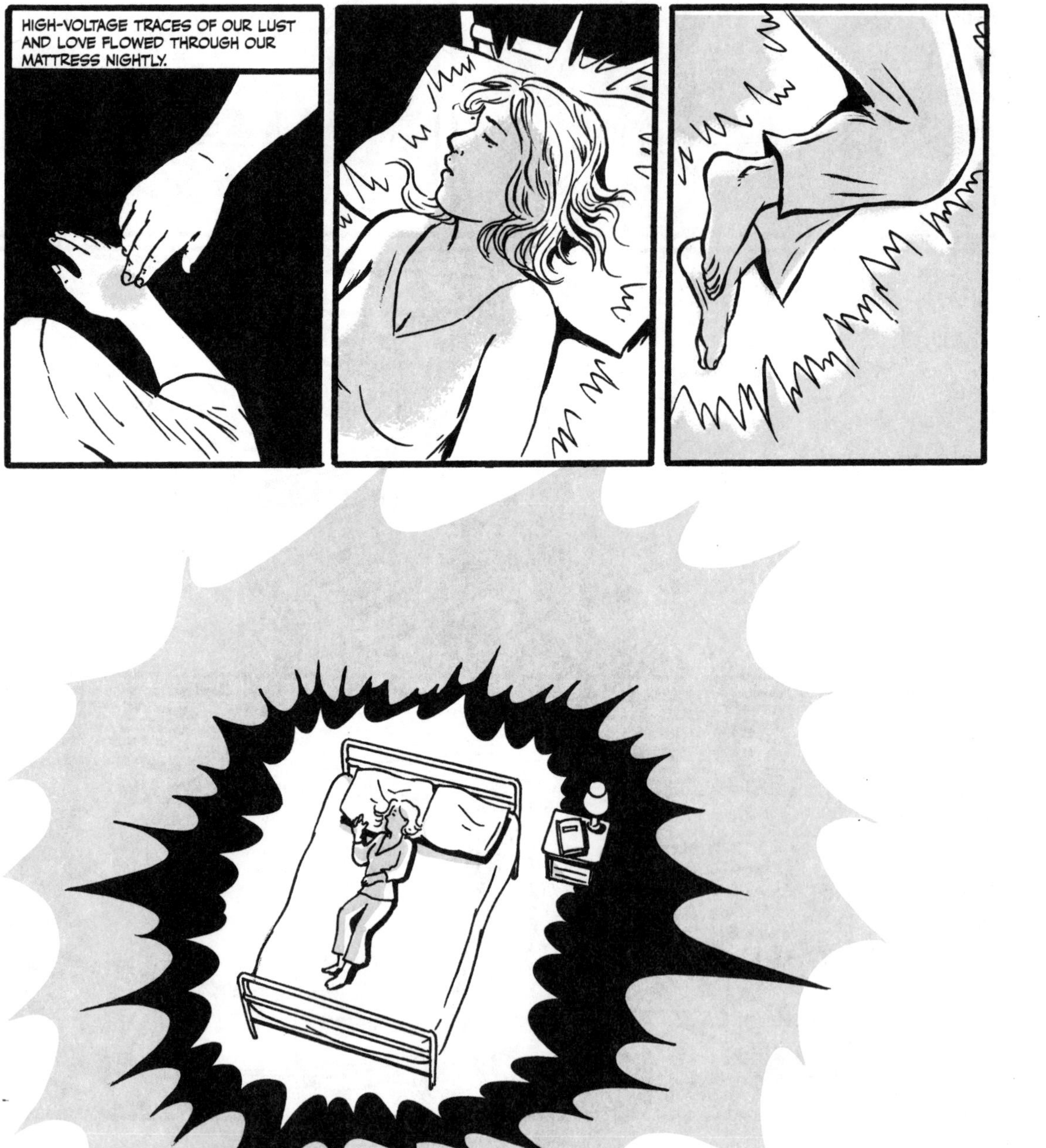
HIGH-VOLTAGE TRACES OF OUR LUST AND LOVE FLOWED THROUGH OUR MATTRESS NIGHTLY.

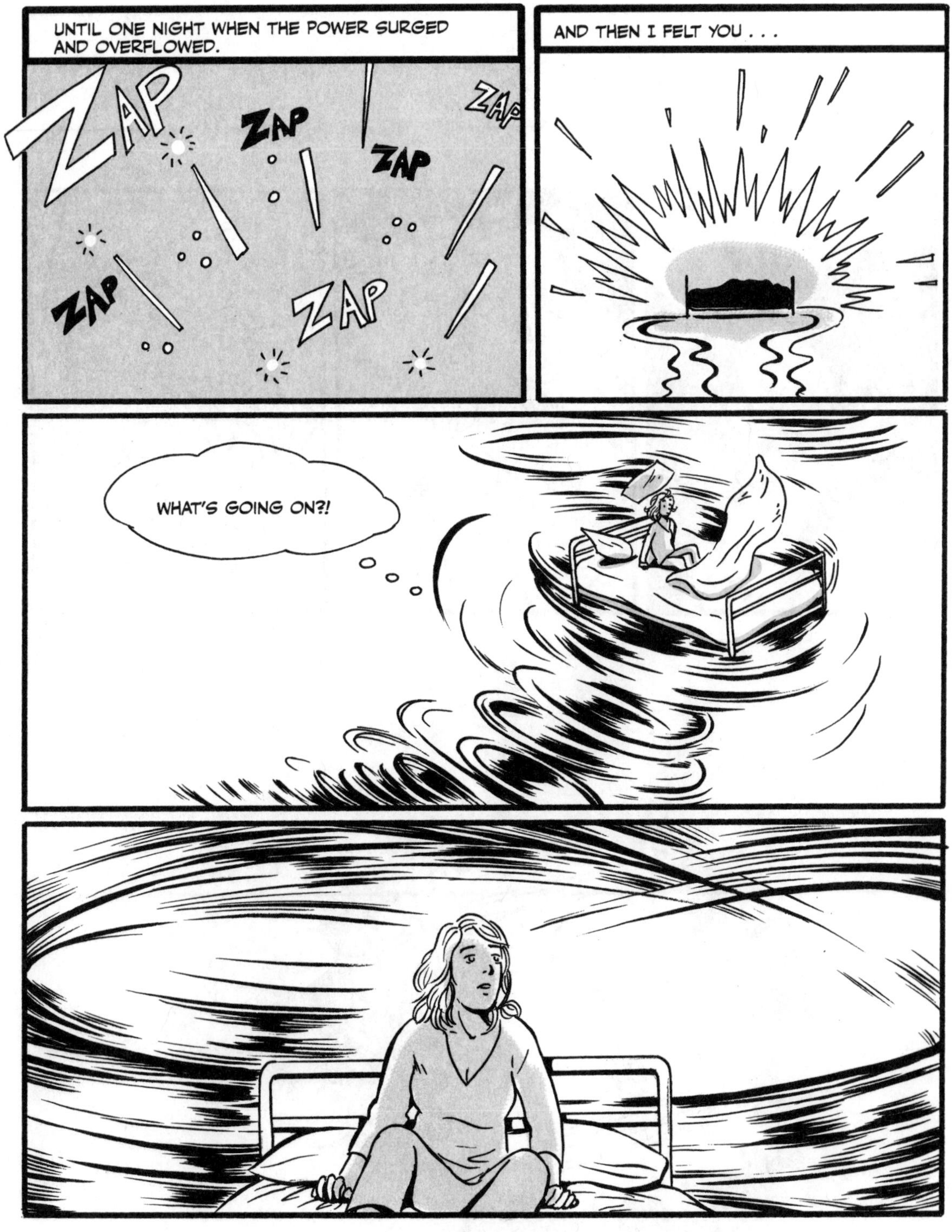
UNTIL ONE NIGHT WHEN THE POWER SURGED AND OVERFLOWED.
ZAP
ZAP
ZAP
ZAP
ZAP
ZAP
AND THEN I FELT YOU . . .
WHAT'S GOING ON?!

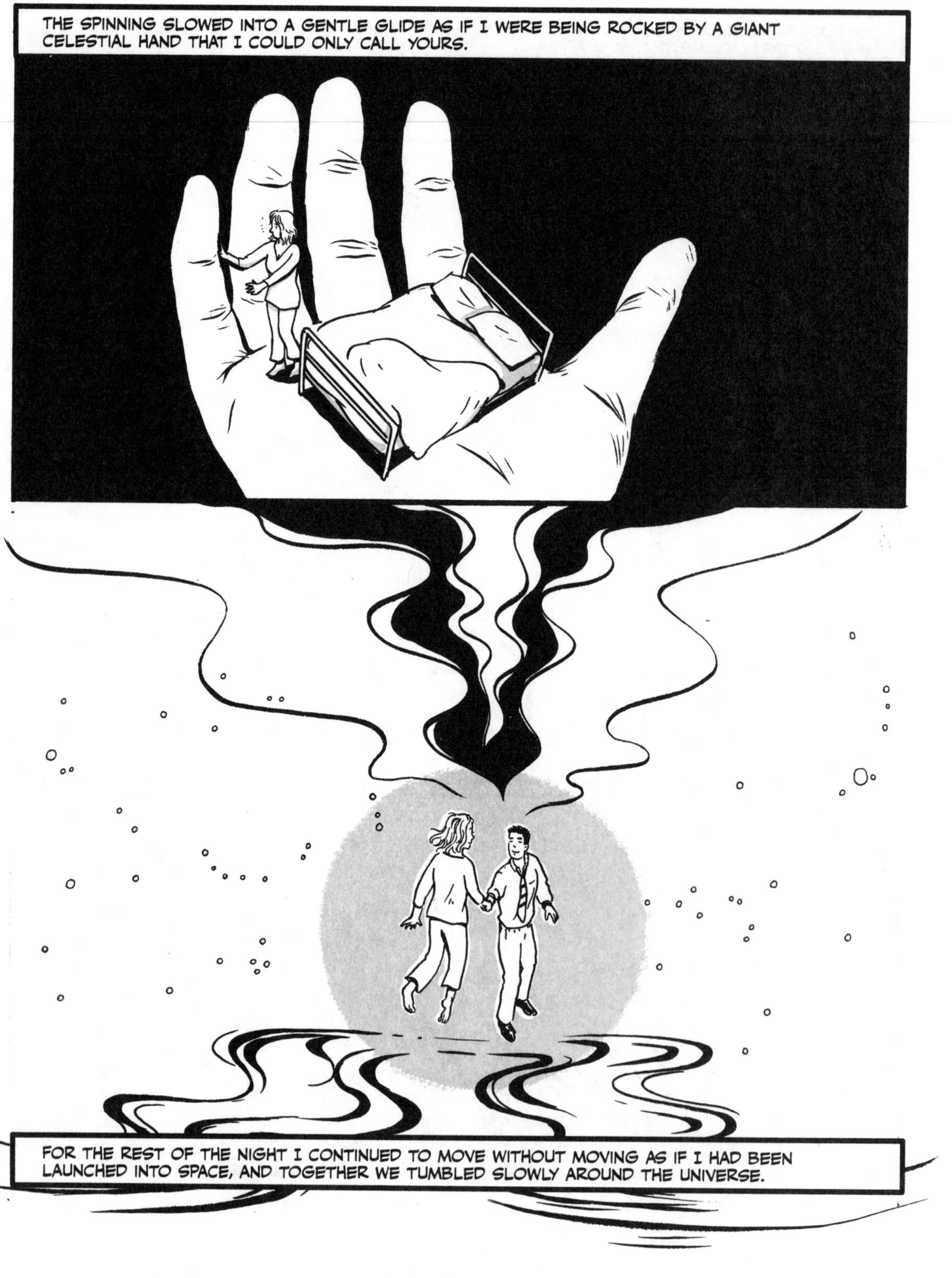

THE SPINNING SLOWED INTO A GENTLE GLIDE AS IF I WERE BEING ROCKED BY A GIANT CELESTIAL HAND THAT I COULD ONLY CALL YOURS.
FOR THE REST OF THE NIGHT I CONTINUED TO MOVE WITHOUT MOVING AS IF I HAD BEEN LAUNCHED INTO SPACE, AND TOGETHER WE TUMBLED SLOWLY AROUND THE UNIVERSE.

I'M LOOKING THROUGH ALL THE PARTICLES OF THE UNIVERSE FOR YOU, AND IT'S ONLY WHEN I STOP LOOKING THAT YOU APPEAR.

ALTHOUGH I NEVER AGAIN EXPERIENCE ANYTHING LIKE THE BED SPINS, SOMETIMES I STILL FEEL THE ELECTRICITY.

IT PERCHES ON MY LIPS LIKE A DETERMINED SPARROW OR CIRCLES MY HAND, LIKE A THOUSAND LIGHTNING BUGS, EACH EMITTING A TINY BUZZ.

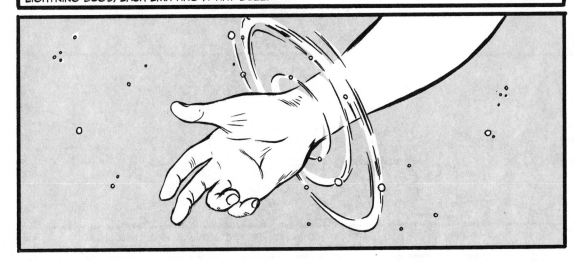

BUT AS I COMMUNICATE BACK, TO TELL YOU THAT I KNOW YOU'RE HERE . . .

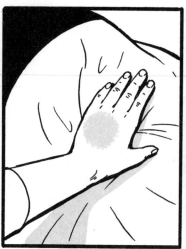

. . . I MAKE CONTACT ONLY WITH MY OWN SKIN.

Chapter Twelve

MARCH 2002

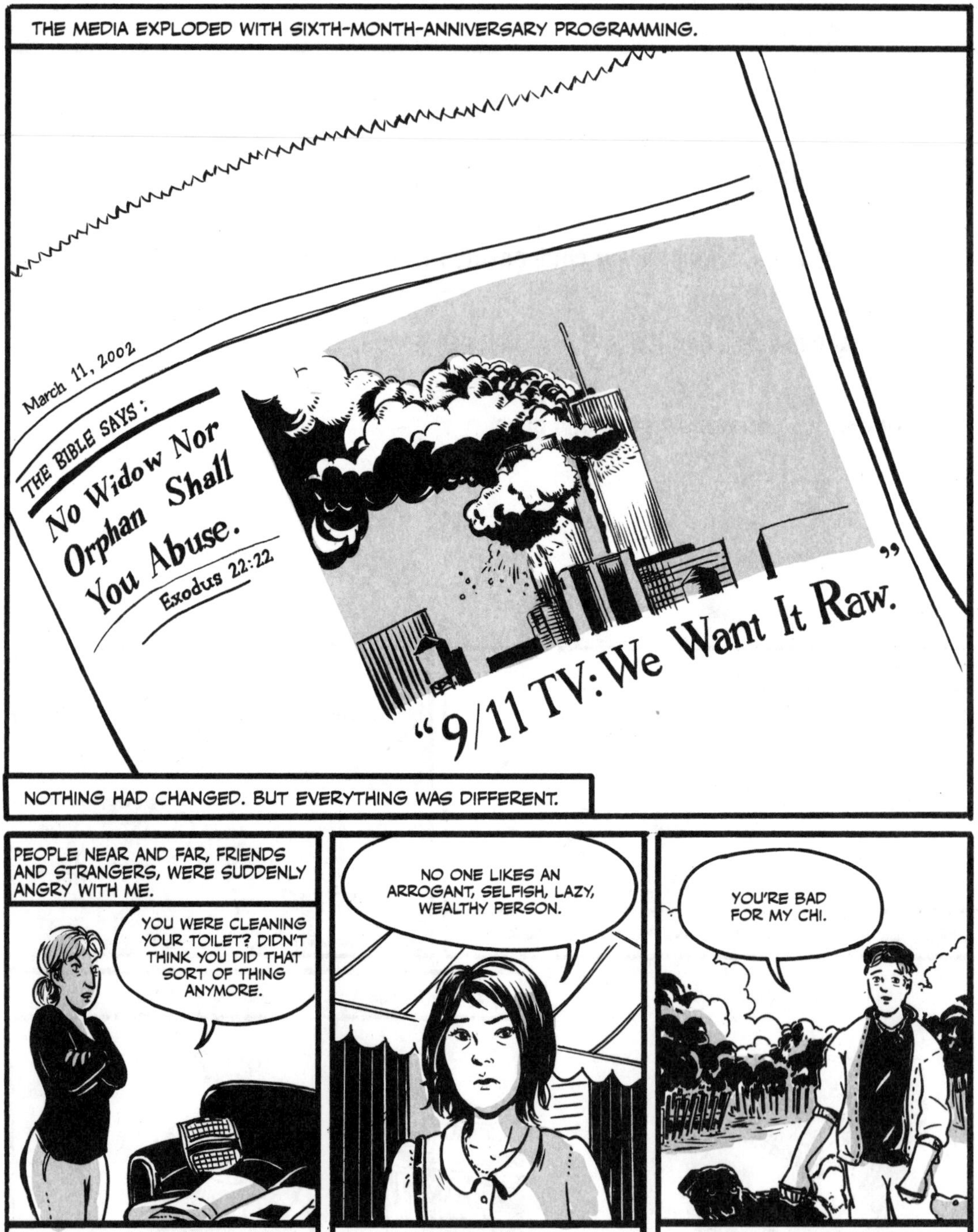
THE MEDIA EXPLODED WITH SIXTH-MONTH-ANNIVERSARY PROGRAMMING.
March 11, 2002
THE BIBLE SAYS:
No Widow Nor Orphan Shall You Abuse.
Exodus 22:22
"9/11 TV: We Want It Raw."
NOTHING HAD CHANGED. BUT EVERYTHING WAS DIFFERENT.
PEOPLE NEAR AND FAR, FRIENDS AND STRANGERS, WERE SUDDENLY ANGRY WITH ME.
YOU WERE CLEANING YOUR TOILET? DIDN'T THINK YOU DID THAT SORT OF THING ANYMORE.
CHILDHOOD PAL
NO ONE LIKES AN ARROGANT, SELFISH, LAZY, WEALTHY PERSON.
CLOSE FRIEND
YOU'RE BAD FOR MY CHI.
PETE THE DOGWALKER

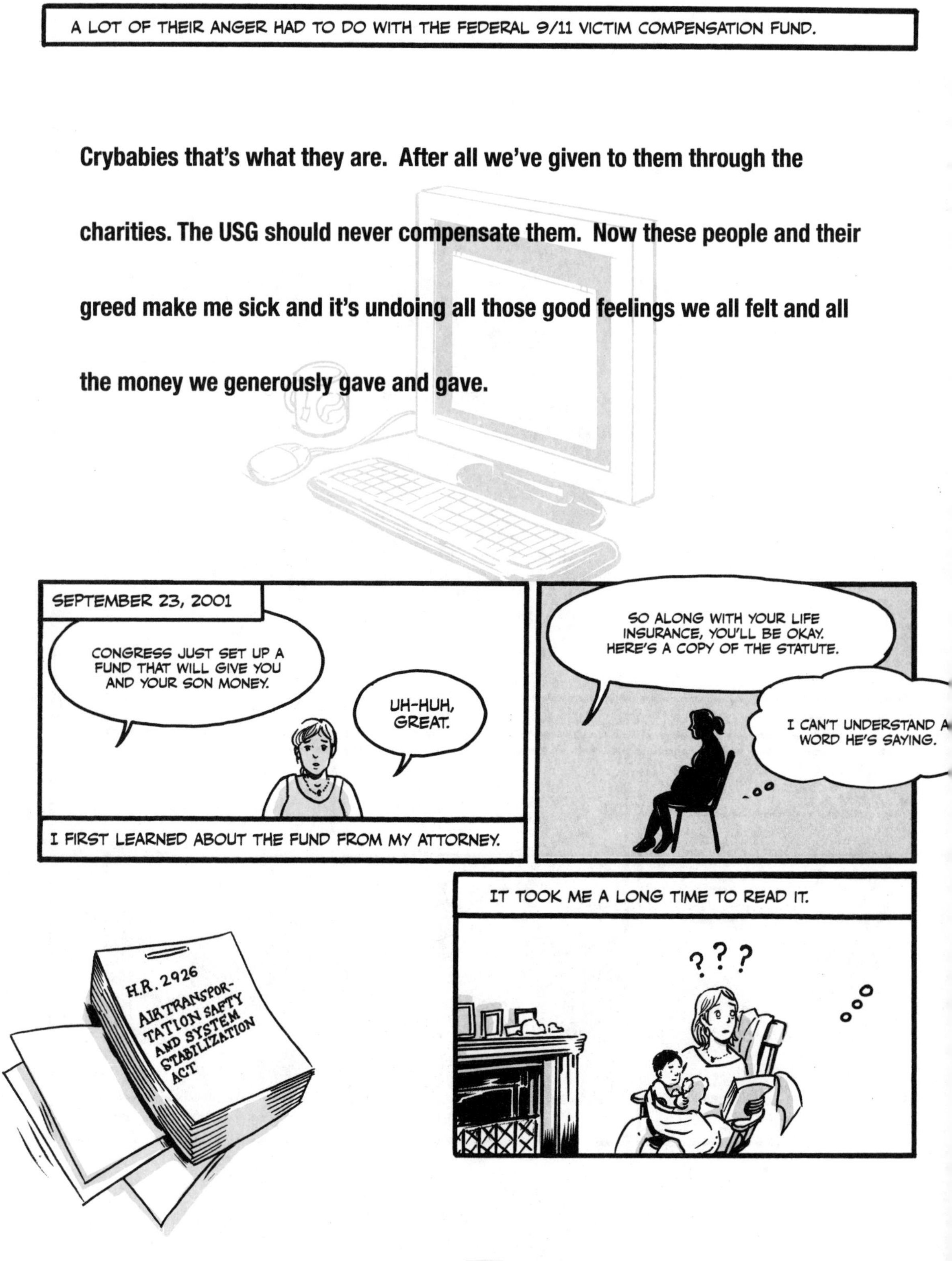
A LOT OF THEIR ANGER HAD TO DO WITH THE FEDERAL 9/11 VICTIM COMPENSATION FUND.
Crybabies that's what they are. After all we've given to them through the charities. The USG should never compensate them. Now these people and their greed make me sick and it's undoing all those good feelings we all felt and all the money we generously gave and gave.
SEPTEMBER 23, 2001
CONGRESS JUST SET UP A FUND THAT WILL GIVE YOU AND YOUR SON MONEY.
UH-HUH, GREAT.
I FIRST LEARNED ABOUT THE FUND FROM MY ATTORNEY.
SO ALONG WITH YOUR LIFE INSURANCE, YOU'LL BE OKAY. HERE'S A COPY OF THE STATUTE.
I CAN'T UNDERSTAND A WORD HE'S SAYING.
H.R. 2926
AIR TRANSPORTATION SAFTY AND SYSTEM STABILIZATION ACT
IT TOOK ME A LONG TIME TO READ IT.
? ? ?

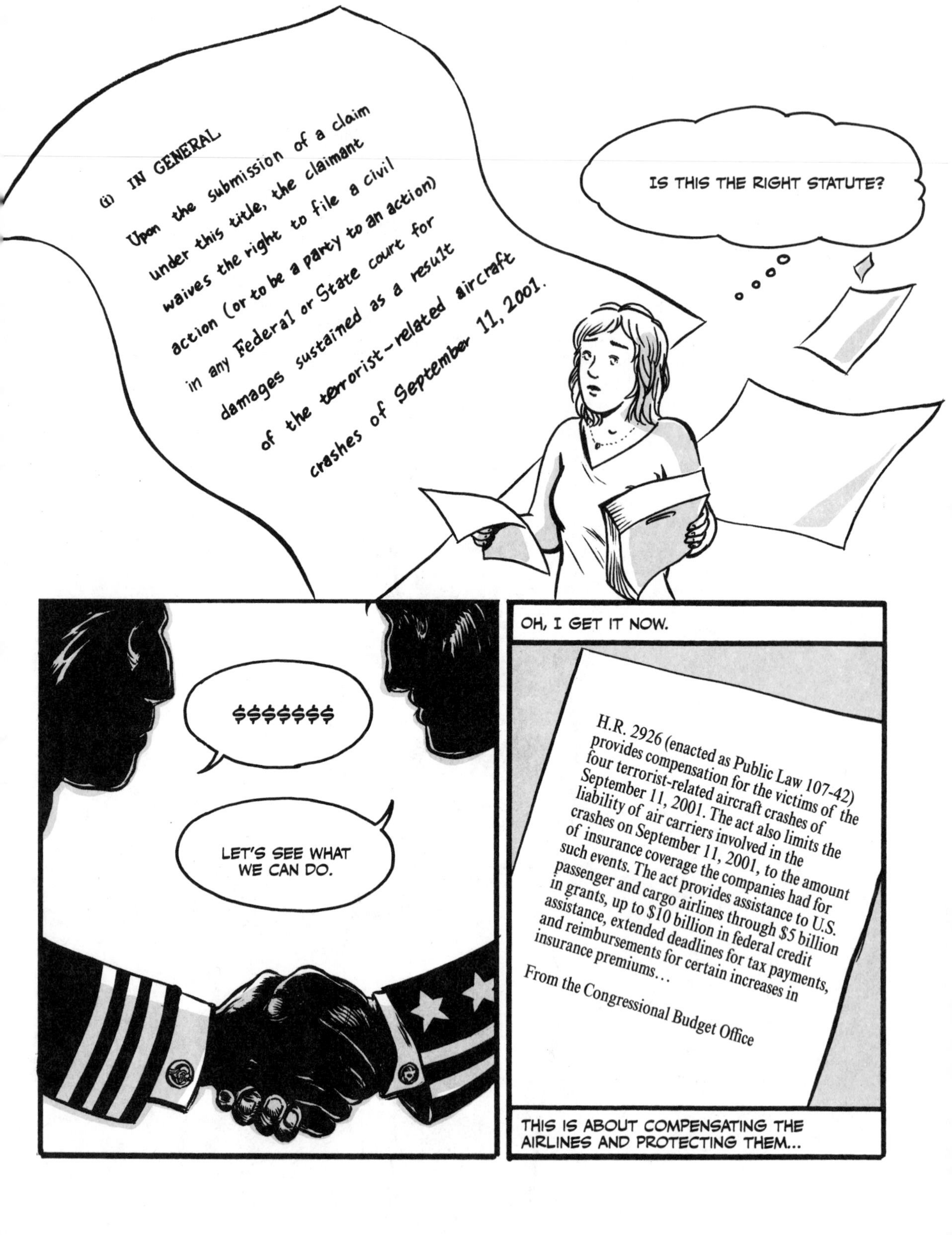

(i) IN GENERAL
Upon the submission of a claim under this title, the claimant waives the right to file a civil action (or to be a party to an action) in any Federal or State court for damages sustained as a result of the terrorist-related aircraft crashes of September 11, 2001.
IS THIS THE RIGHT STATUTE?
$$$$$$$
LET'S SEE WHAT WE CAN DO.
OH, I GET IT NOW.
H.R. 2926 (enacted as Public Law 107-42) provides compensation for the victims of the four terrorist-related aircraft crashes of September 11, 2001. The act also limits the liability of air carriers involved in the crashes on September 11, 2001, to the amount of insurance coverage the companies had for such events. The act provides assistance to U.S. passenger and cargo airlines through $5 billion in grants, up to $10 billion in federal credit assistance, extended deadlines for tax payments, and reimbursements for certain increases in insurance premiums…
From the Congressional Budget Office
THIS IS ABOUT COMPENSATING THE AIRLINES AND PROTECTING THEM...

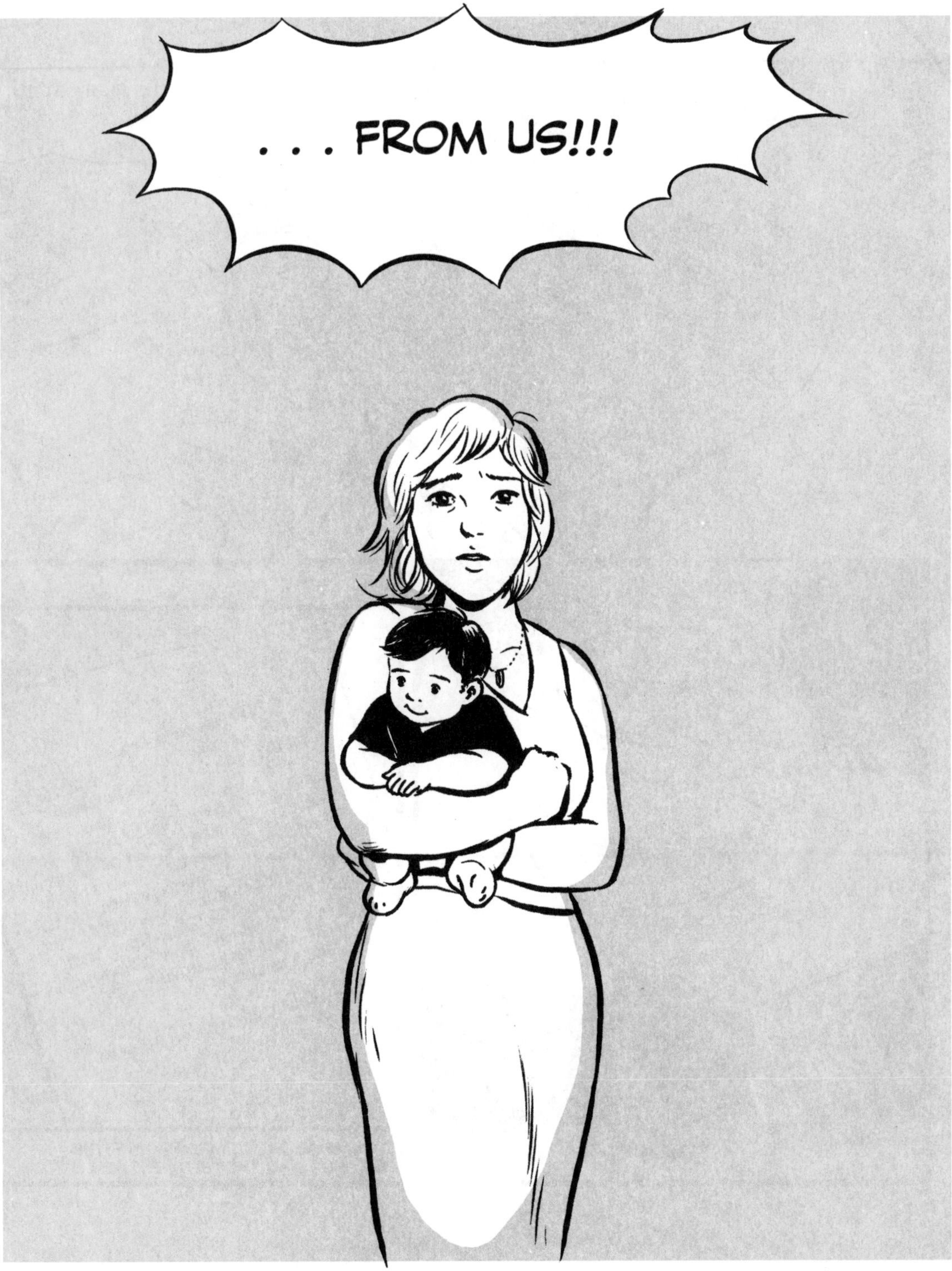
. . . FROM US!!!

THE FUND WAS TOUTED AS AN ACT OF COMPASSION AND KINDNESS, ALLOWING THE FAMILIES TO RECEIVE A SUBSTANTIAL FINANCIAL AWARD WITHOUT A LENGTHY LEGAL BATTLE. IT SOUNDED GREAT BUT YOU SHOULD ALWAYS LOOK AT THE FINE PRINT WHEN THE GOVERNMENT STARTS HANDING OUT MONEY.

GOOD EVENING...

KENNETH FEINBERG

SPECIAL MASTER

THIS POSITION WAS DESIGNATED BY CONGRESS

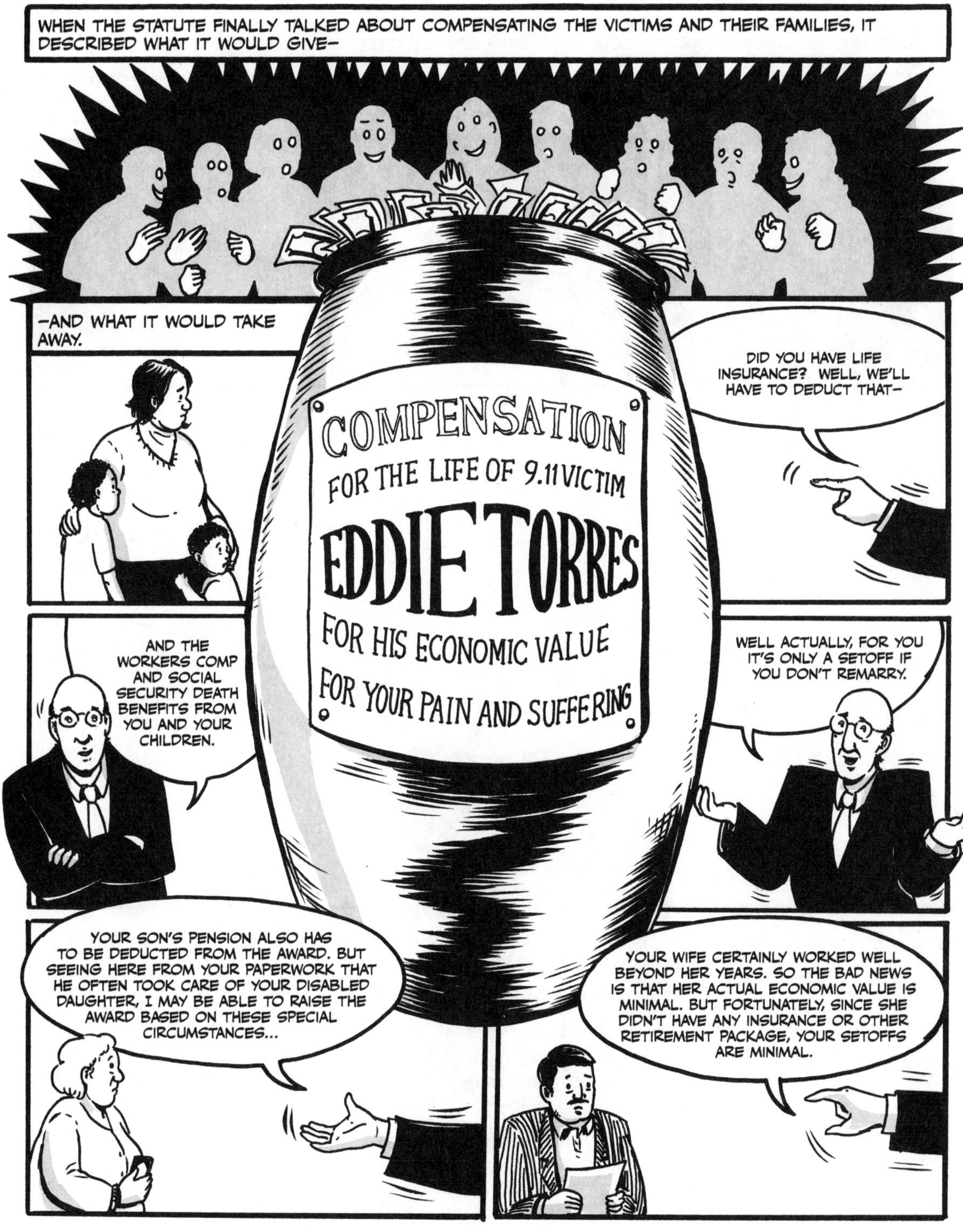

WHEN THE STATUTE FINALLY TALKED ABOUT COMPENSATING THE VICTIMS AND THEIR FAMILIES, IT DESCRIBED WHAT IT WOULD GIVE–
–AND WHAT IT WOULD TAKE AWAY.
COMPENSATION
FOR THE LIFE OF 9.11 VICTIM
EDDIE TORRES
FOR HIS ECONOMIC VALUE
FOR YOUR PAIN AND SUFFERING
DID YOU HAVE LIFE INSURANCE? WELL, WE'LL HAVE TO DEDUCT THAT–
AND THE WORKERS COMP AND SOCIAL SECURITY DEATH BENEFITS FROM YOU AND YOUR CHILDREN.
WELL ACTUALLY, FOR YOU IT'S ONLY A SETOFF IF YOU DON'T REMARRY.
YOUR SON'S PENSION ALSO HAS TO BE DEDUCTED FROM THE AWARD. BUT SEEING HERE FROM YOUR PAPERWORK THAT HE OFTEN TOOK CARE OF YOUR DISABLED DAUGHTER, I MAY BE ABLE TO RAISE THE AWARD BASED ON THESE SPECIAL CIRCUMSTANCES...
YOUR WIFE CERTAINLY WORKED WELL BEYOND HER YEARS. SO THE BAD NEWS IS THAT HER ACTUAL ECONOMIC VALUE IS MINIMAL. BUT FORTUNATELY, SINCE SHE DIDN'T HAVE ANY INSURANCE OR OTHER RETIREMENT PACKAGE, YOUR SETOFFS ARE MINIMAL.

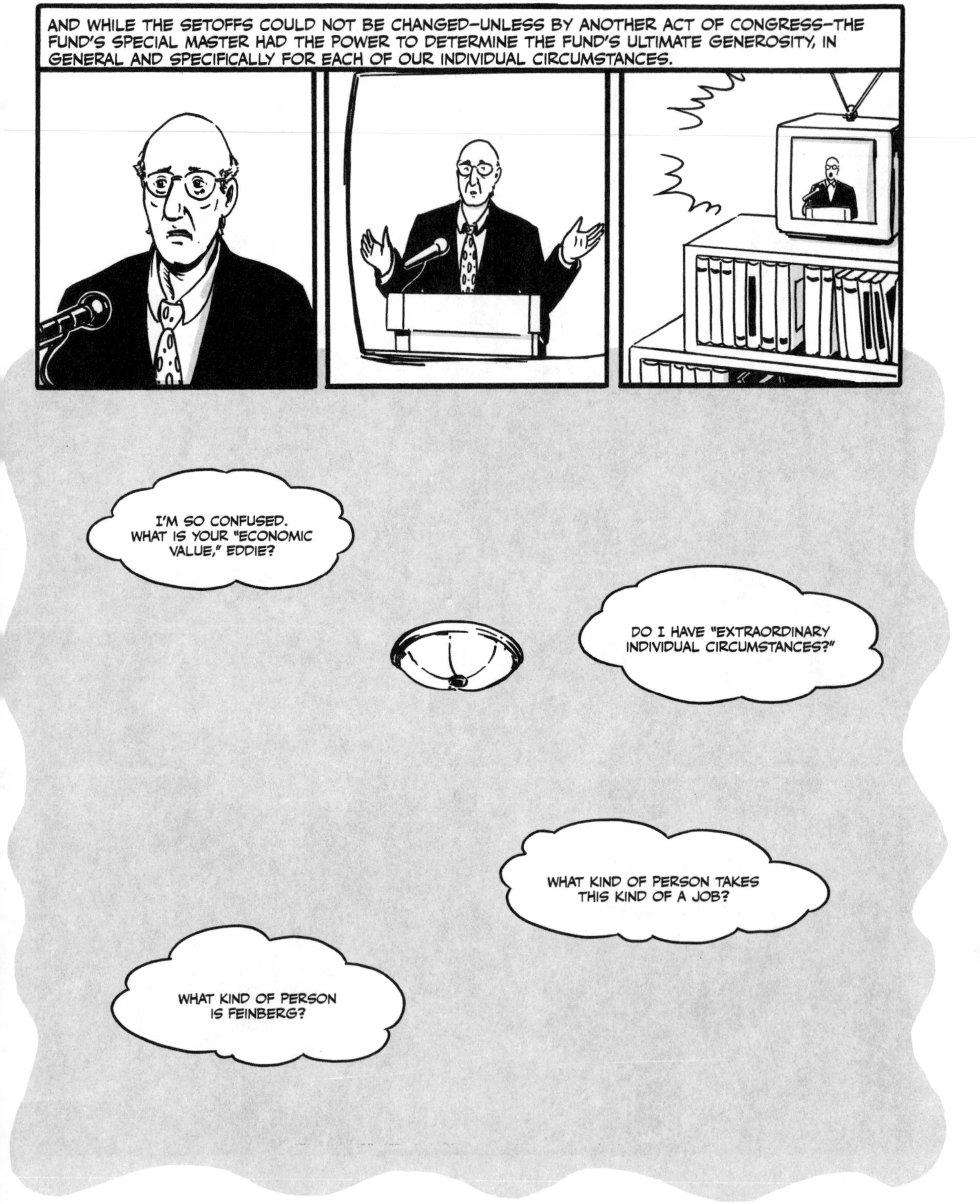
AND WHILE THE SETOFFS COULD NOT BE CHANGED—UNLESS BY ANOTHER ACT OF CONGRESS—THE FUND'S SPECIAL MASTER HAD THE POWER TO DETERMINE THE FUND'S ULTIMATE GENEROSITY, IN GENERAL AND SPECIFICALLY FOR EACH OF OUR INDIVIDUAL CIRCUMSTANCES.
I'M SO CONFUSED. WHAT IS YOUR "ECONOMIC VALUE," EDDIE?
DO I HAVE "EXTRAORDINARY INDIVIDUAL CIRCUMSTANCES?"
WHAT KIND OF PERSON TAKES THIS KIND OF A JOB?
WHAT KIND OF PERSON IS FEINBERG?

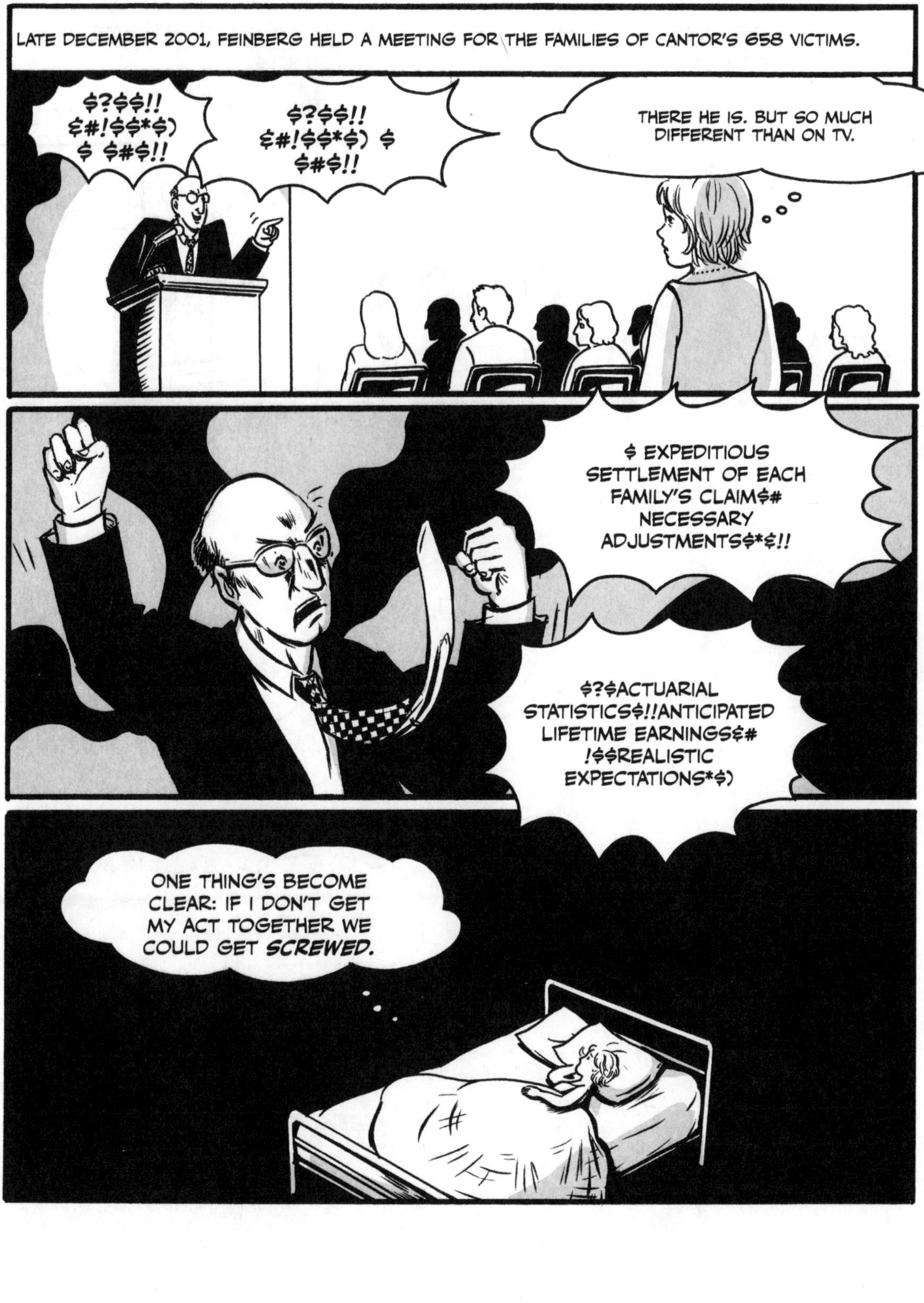
LATE DECEMBER 2001, FEINBERG HELD A MEETING FOR THE FAMILIES OF CANTOR'S 658 VICTIMS.
$?$$!! $#!$$*$) $ $#$!!
$?$$!! $#!$$*$) $ $#$!!
THERE HE IS. BUT SO MUCH DIFFERENT THAN ON TV.
$ EXPEDITIOUS SETTLEMENT OF EACH FAMILY'S CLAIM$# NECESSARY ADJUSTMENTS$*$!!
$?$ACTUARIAL STATISTICS$!!ANTICIPATED LIFETIME EARNINGS$# !$$REALISTIC EXPECTATIONS*$)
ONE THING'S BECOME CLEAR: IF I DON'T GET MY ACT TOGETHER WE COULD GET ***SCREWED.***

SOON AFTER THAT NIGHT, FEINBERG PUBLICLY RELEASED THE ECONOMIC CHART HE'D USE TO CALCULATE OUR LOVED ONES' VALUE. THE CHART PROJECTED OUR LOVED ONES AS FAILURES—PEOPLE WHO RARELY EARNED.

Presumed Economic and Non-Economic Loss
For a Married Decedent With 2 Dependent Children
(Ages Newborn and 9 at Date of Death of Victim)
Before Any Collateral Offset

Income

Age	$10,000	$15,000	$25,000	$30,000	$35,000	$40,000
25	741,554	1,025,749	1,174,577	1,314,621	1,462,012	1,610,618
30	694,588	938,778	1,066,058	1,186,481	1,312,022	1,438,321
35	613,714	789,016	879,190	965,827	1,053,744	1,141,629
40	582,244	730,739	806,473	876,963	953,239	1,026,177
45	547,827	667,771	728,683	788,109	846,791	905,063
50	513,199	604,721	651,110	696,510	741,078	785,269
55	500,000	541,474	573,385	604,733	635,293	665,541
60	500,000	500,000	517,548	538,800	559,518	580,025
65	500,000	500,000	500,000	500,000	513,452	528,037

Age	$45,000	$50,000	$60,000	$70,000	$80,000	$90,000
25	1,764,000	1,920,345	2,194,988	2,456,664	2,746,651	3,013,408
30	1,568,870	1,700,548	1,935,173	2,158,621	2,403,849	2,629,654
35	1,231,730	1,322,061	1,487,780	1,645,396	1,813,552	1,968,567
40	1,100,538	1,174,779	1,313,683	1,445,683	1,583,848	1,711,355
45	964,250	1,023,196	1,134,755	1,240,714	1,350,342	1,451,698
50	830,007	874,486	959,327	1,039,876	1,122,505	1,198,875
55	696,046	726,311	784,578	839,871	896,019	947,957
60	600,706	621,224	660,727	698,214	736,279	771,491
65	542,746	557,339	585,434	612,095	639,168	664,212

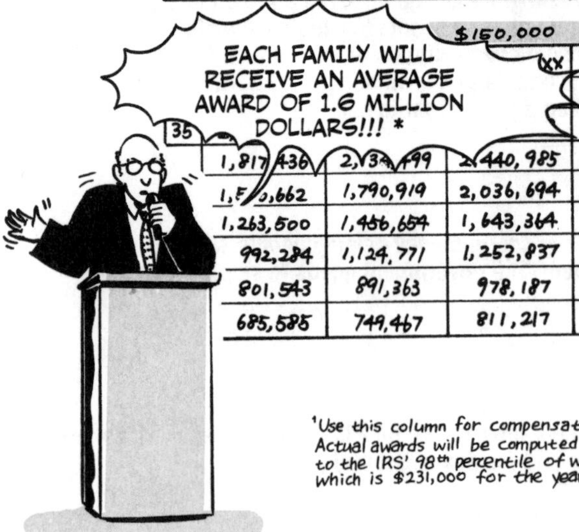

EACH FAMILY WILL RECEIVE AN AVERAGE AWARD OF 1.6 MILLION DOLLARS!!! *

Age			$150,000	$175,000	$200,000	$225,000
			XX	X,XXX,XXX	X,XXX,XXX	X,XXX,XXX
				4,351,060	X,XXX,XXX	X,XXX,XXX
35				3,179,705	3,500,964	3,805,087
	1,817,436	[illegible]	2,440,985	2,723,892	2,992,470	3,246,723
	[illegible]	1,790,919	2,036,694	2,263,561	2,478,938	2,682,827
	1,263,500	1,456,654	1,643,364	1,815,711	1,979,328	2,134,219
	992,284	1,124,771	1,252,837	1,371,052	1,483,279	1,589,520
	801,543	891,363	978,187	1,058,331	1,134,416	1,206,443
	685,585	749,467	811,217	868,217	922,330	973,557

[1]Use this column for compensation of $225,000 and higher. Actual awards will be computed on compensation levels up to the IRS' 98th percentile of wage earners, which is $231,000 for the year 2000.

*DOES NOT INCLUDE ANY SETOFFS (LIFE INSURANCE, SOCIAL SECURITY, WORKERS COMPENSATION, RETIREMENT FUNDS, PENSIONS, ETC.)

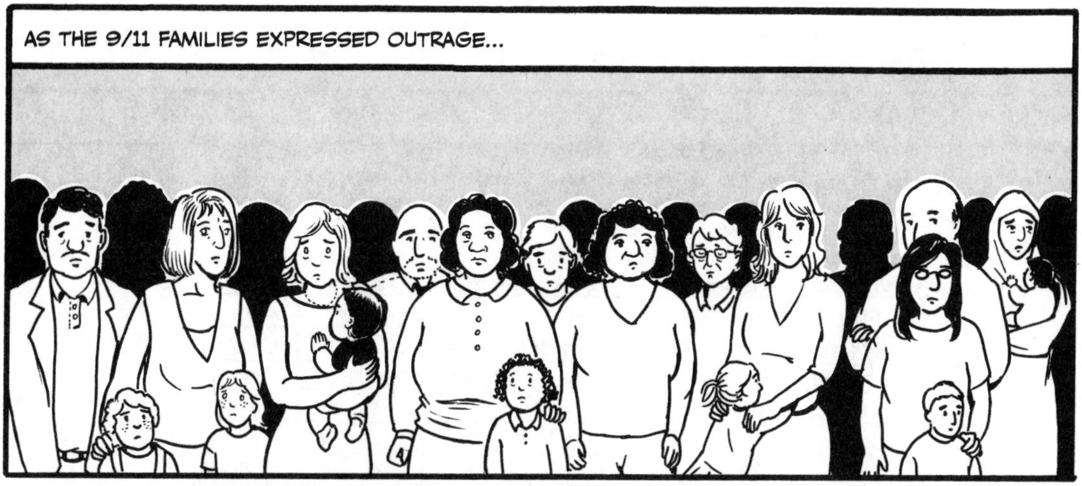
AS THE 9/11 FAMILIES EXPRESSED OUTRAGE...

. . . SOME OF THE PUBLIC-AT-LARGE EXPRESSED THEIR OUTRAGE TOO. THEY COMMENTED ABOUT IT ON THE FUND'S WEBSITE:

Life's a bitch and then you die. Why didn't those people have insurance? We didn't kill their loved ones so WE, THE PEOPLE, shouldn't have to pay anything. Not one penny. Sorry they died, but people lose loved ones every day in all kinds of tragic ways. If they chose not to buy insurance then, sorry, BUT their loss is THEIR LOSS. Then they have real nerve to want more and the govt has the nerve to give them MY hard earned money. We need our constitution in force again NOW!
Individual Comment
Wednesday, February 02, 2002 02:53 AM

GreedY!

My brother died and let me tell you, some people just sit on their butt all day at home and watch tv, soap operas and MTV videos in bikini. I say get up and get a job, go now. Get a life friends and inlaws cause if your spouse dies then it was their time. And unhappy people too, life's not all like roses. Some were getting divorced, others having affairs some even with contracts on their loved ones. So forget all this sad business and get off your butts friends and inlaws and get a job. Stop holding the government hostage and repuplicans and dems should go straight to hell.
Mr. Iknowalot
Individual Comment

We need to support our troops in Afghanistan and not spend money helping people. No matter how much we give, it will never be enough to satisfy them. The government needs to stop being such a girl.
A Patriot
Individual Comment

Don't give my money to illegals. Bad enough they take jobs. Now cause their loved ones died, we are giving them even more of my tax dollars. Terrorists and Mexicans get out!
A Legal Citizen
Individual Comment

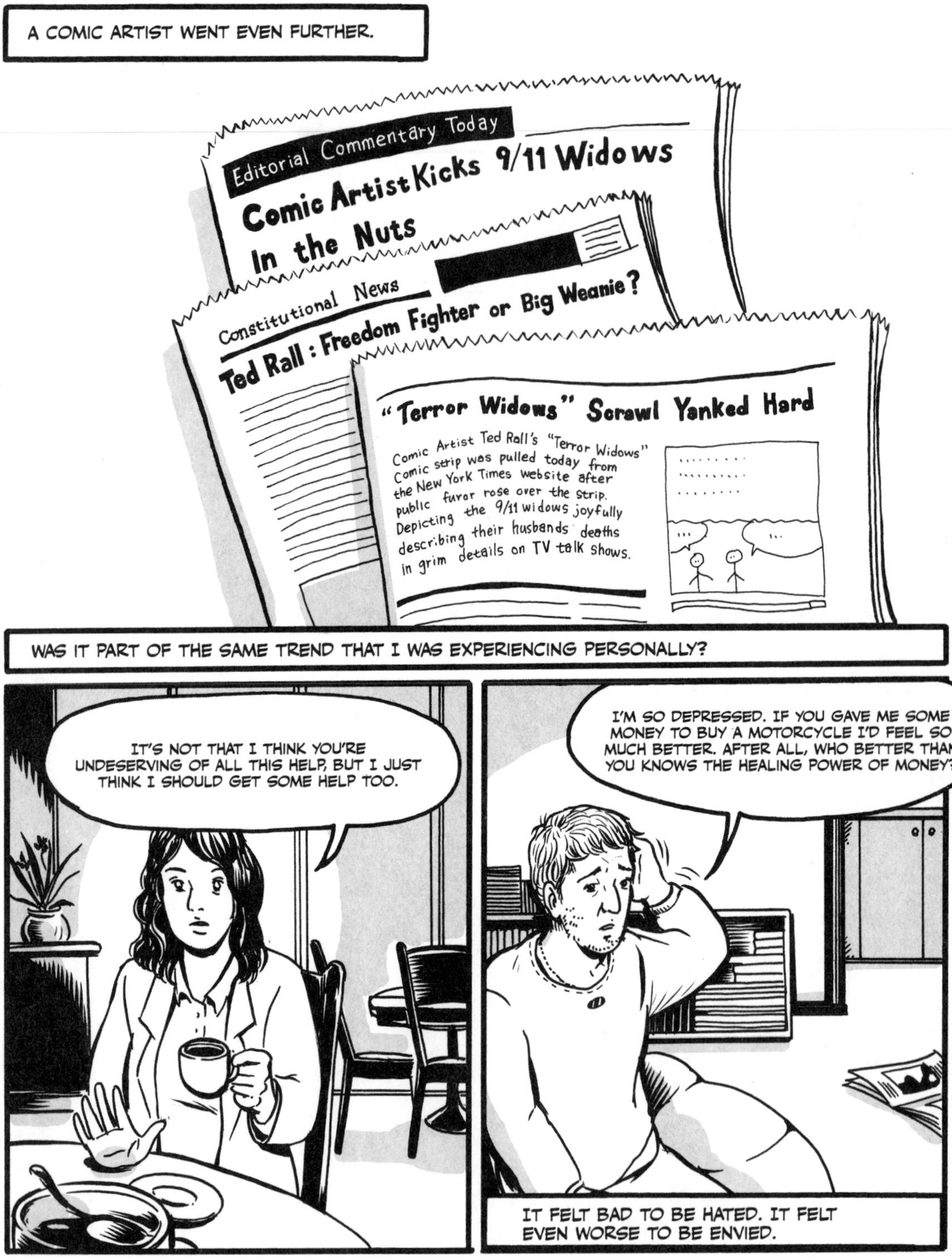
A COMIC ARTIST WENT EVEN FURTHER.
Editorial Commentary Today
Comic Artist Kicks 9/11 Widows In the Nuts
Constitutional News
Ted Rall : Freedom Fighter or Big Weanie?
"Terror Widows" Scrawl Yanked Hard
Comic Artist Ted Rall's "Terror Widows" Comic strip was pulled today from the New York Times website after public furor rose over the strip. Depicting the 9/11 widows joyfully describing their husbands' deaths in grim details on TV talk shows.
WAS IT PART OF THE SAME TREND THAT I WAS EXPERIENCING PERSONALLY?
IT'S NOT THAT I THINK YOU'RE UNDESERVING OF ALL THIS HELP, BUT I JUST THINK I SHOULD GET SOME HELP TOO.
I'M SO DEPRESSED. IF YOU GAVE ME SOME MONEY TO BUY A MOTORCYCLE I'D FEEL SO MUCH BETTER. AFTER ALL, WHO BETTER THAN YOU KNOWS THE HEALING POWER OF MONEY?
IT FELT BAD TO BE HATED. IT FELT EVEN WORSE TO BE ENVIED.

Chapter Thirteen

April 2002

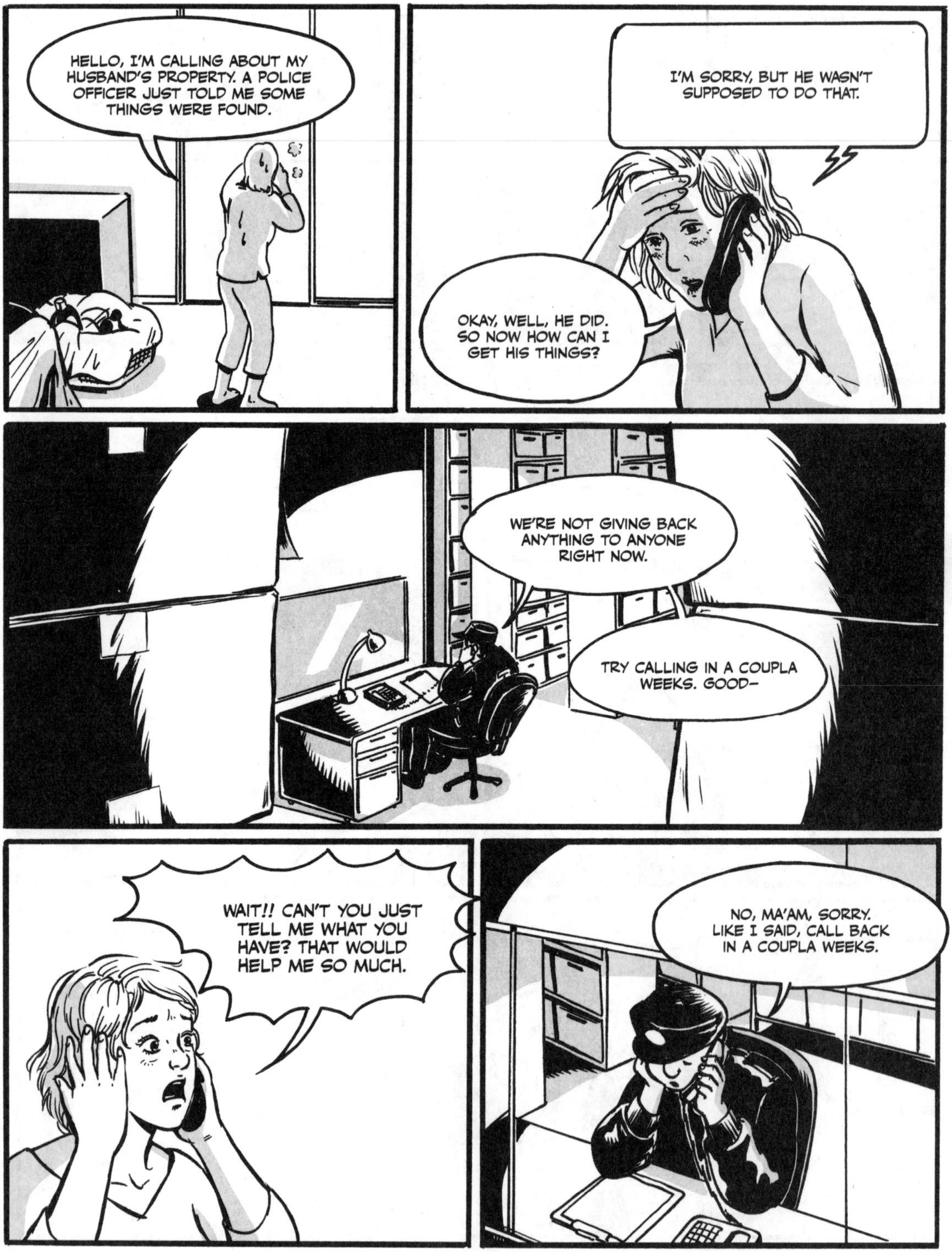
HELLO, I'M CALLING ABOUT MY HUSBAND'S PROPERTY. A POLICE OFFICER JUST TOLD ME SOME THINGS WERE FOUND.
I'M SORRY, BUT HE WASN'T SUPPOSED TO DO THAT.
OKAY, WELL, HE DID. SO NOW HOW CAN I GET HIS THINGS?
WE'RE NOT GIVING BACK ANYTHING TO ANYONE RIGHT NOW.
TRY CALLING IN A COUPLA WEEKS. GOOD–
WAIT!! CAN'T YOU JUST TELL ME WHAT YOU HAVE? THAT WOULD HELP ME SO MUCH.
NO, MA'AM, SORRY. LIKE I SAID, CALL BACK IN A COUPLA WEEKS.

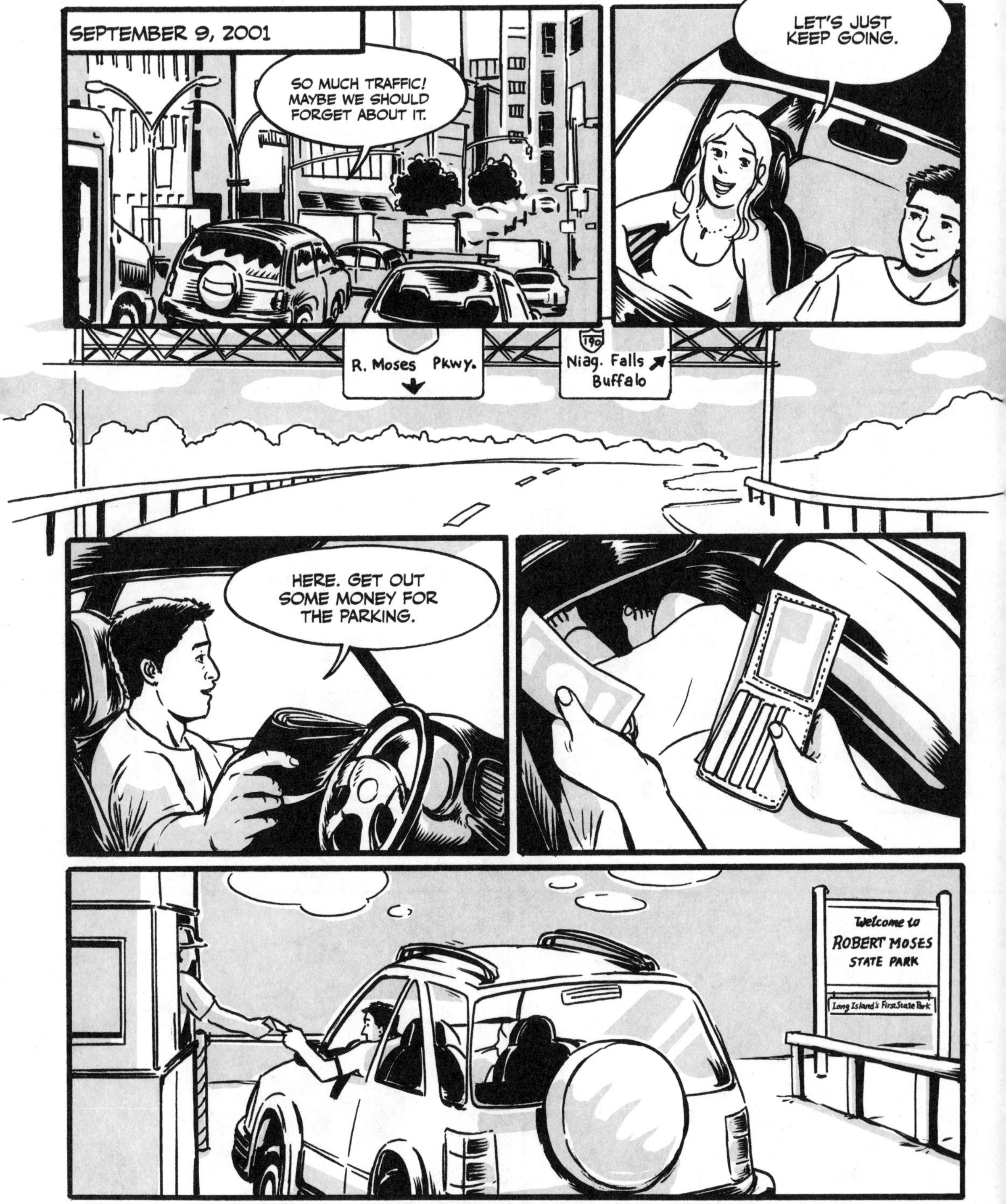
SEPTEMBER 9, 2001
SO MUCH TRAFFIC! MAYBE WE SHOULD FORGET ABOUT IT.
LET'S JUST KEEP GOING.
R. Moses Pkwy.
190
Niag. Falls Buffalo
HERE. GET OUT SOME MONEY FOR THE PARKING.
Welcome to ROBERT MOSES STATE PARK
Long Island's First State Park

WELL, I KNOW IT'S NOT YOUR WEDDING RING. YOU LOST IT IN THE OCEAN A MONTH BEFORE YOU DIED. WAS THAT THE FIRST SIGN I FAILED TO SEE?

I WANT IT TO BE YOUR SCUBA DIVER WATCH.

AND YOUR WALLET WITH LICENSE, CREDIT CARDS, FAMILY PICTURES— AND ALL THOSE LAMINATED SAINTS WHO FAILED TO PROTECT YOU.

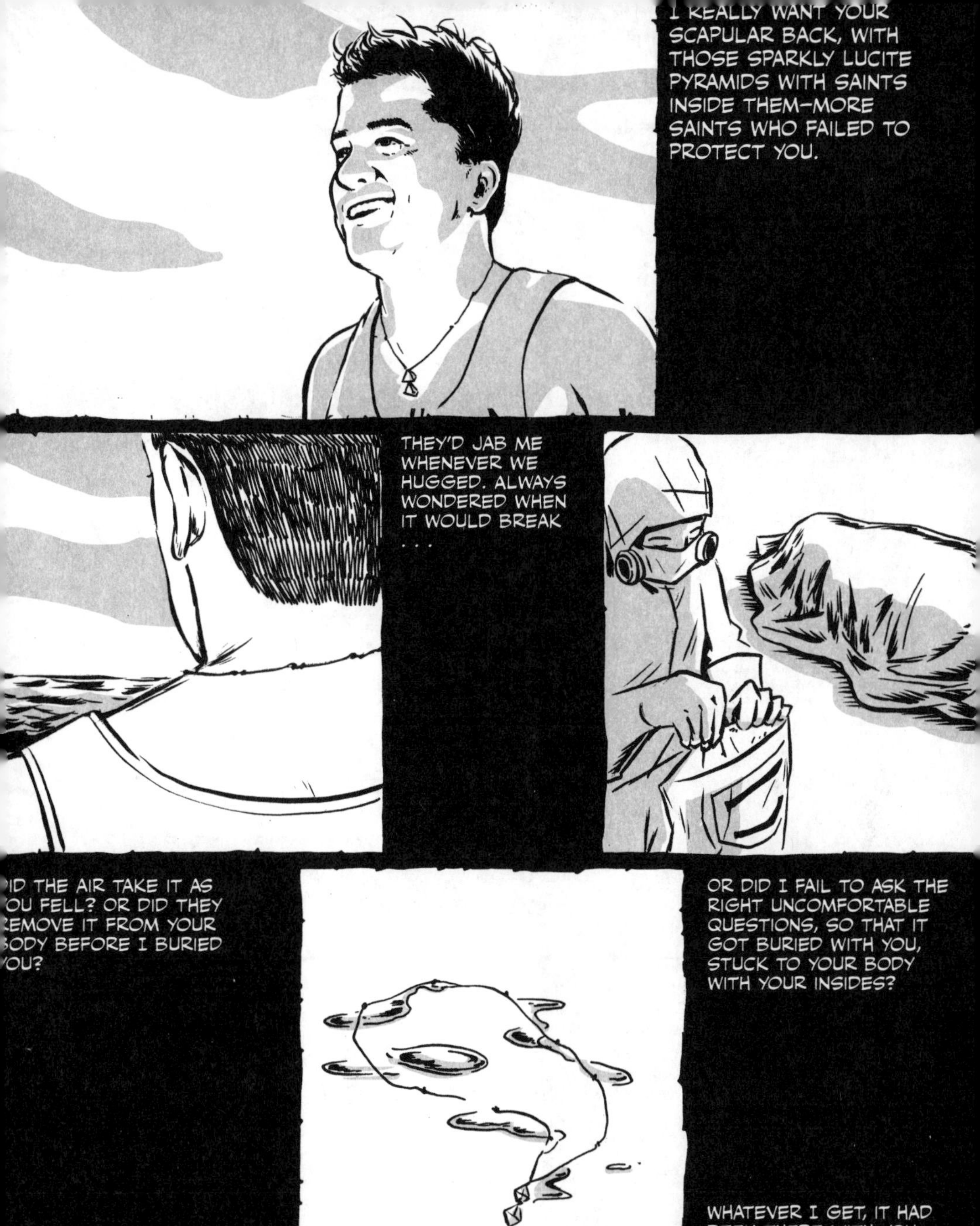

I REALLY WANT YOUR SCAPULAR BACK, WITH THOSE SPARKLY LUCITE PYRAMIDS WITH SAINTS INSIDE THEM—MORE SAINTS WHO FAILED TO PROTECT YOU.

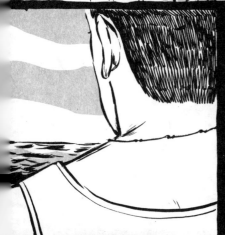

THEY'D JAB ME WHENEVER WE HUGGED. ALWAYS WONDERED WHEN IT WOULD BREAK . . .

DID THE AIR TAKE IT AS YOU FELL? OR DID THEY REMOVE IT FROM YOUR BODY BEFORE I BURIED YOU?

OR DID I FAIL TO ASK THE RIGHT UNCOMFORTABLE QUESTIONS, SO THAT IT GOT BURIED WITH YOU, STUCK TO YOUR BODY WITH YOUR INSIDES?

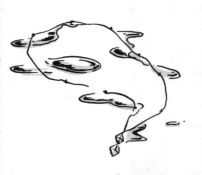

WHATEVER I GET, IT HAD BEEN THERE WITH YOU. I'LL TOUCH IT AND REALLY KNOW YOU DIED.

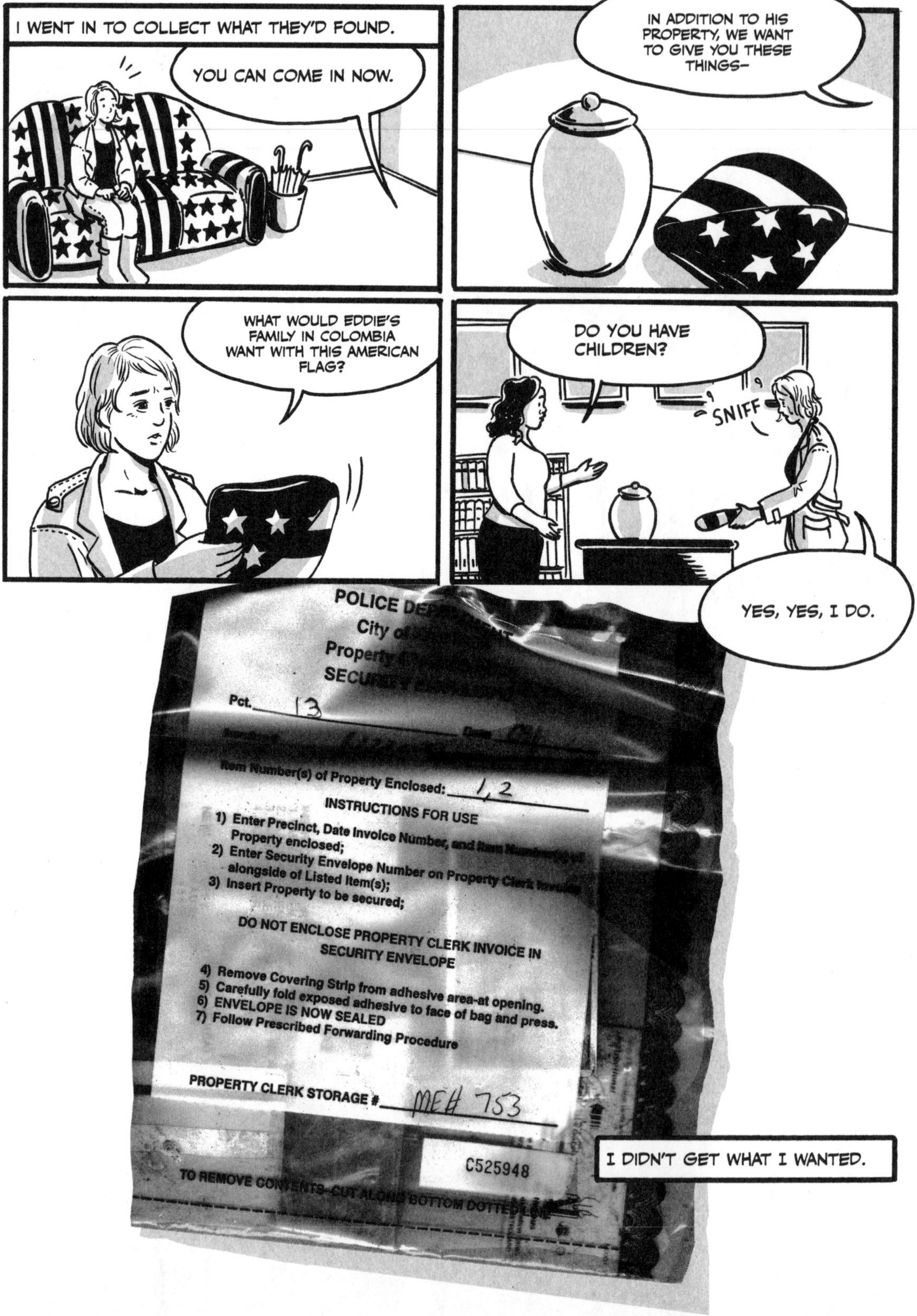
I WENT IN TO COLLECT WHAT THEY'D FOUND.
YOU CAN COME IN NOW.
IN ADDITION TO HIS PROPERTY, WE WANT TO GIVE YOU THESE THINGS–
WHAT WOULD EDDIE'S FAMILY IN COLOMBIA WANT WITH THIS AMERICAN FLAG?
DO YOU HAVE CHILDREN?
SNIFF
YES, YES, I DO.
Pct. 13
of Property Enclosed: 1,2
INSTRUCTIONS FOR USE
1) Enter Precinct, Date Invoice Number, and
Property enclosed;
2) Enter Security Envelope Number on Property Clerk
alongside of Listed Item(s);
3) Insert Property to be secured;
DO NOT ENCLOSE PROPERTY CLERK INVOICE IN SECURITY ENVELOPE
4) Remove Covering Strip from adhesive area-at opening.
5) Carefully fold exposed adhesive to face of bag and press.
6) ENVELOPE IS NOW SEALED
7) Follow Prescribed Forwarding Procedure
PROPERTY CLERK STORAGE # MEH 753
C525948
I DIDN'T GET WHAT I WANTED.

Chapter Fourteen

MAY 2002

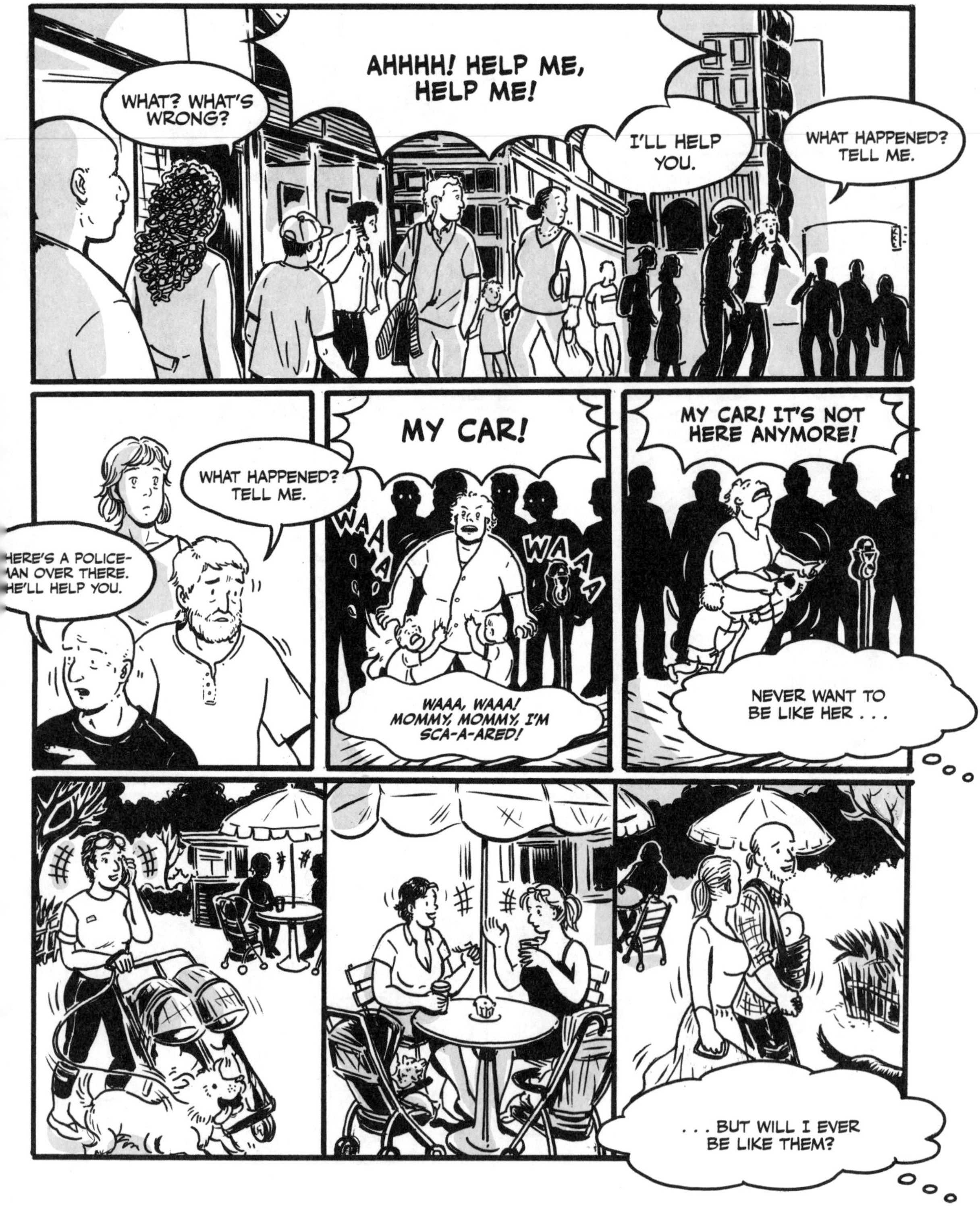
WHAT? WHAT'S WRONG?
AHHHH! HELP ME, HELP ME!
I'LL HELP YOU.
WHAT HAPPENED? TELL ME.
WHAT HAPPENED? TELL ME.
HERE'S A POLICE-MAN OVER THERE. HE'LL HELP YOU.
MY CAR!
WAAAA
WAAAA
WAAA, WAAA! MOMMY, MOMMY, I'M SCA-A-ARED!
MY CAR! IT'S NOT HERE ANYMORE!
NEVER WANT TO BE LIKE HER . . .
. . . BUT WILL I EVER BE LIKE THEM?

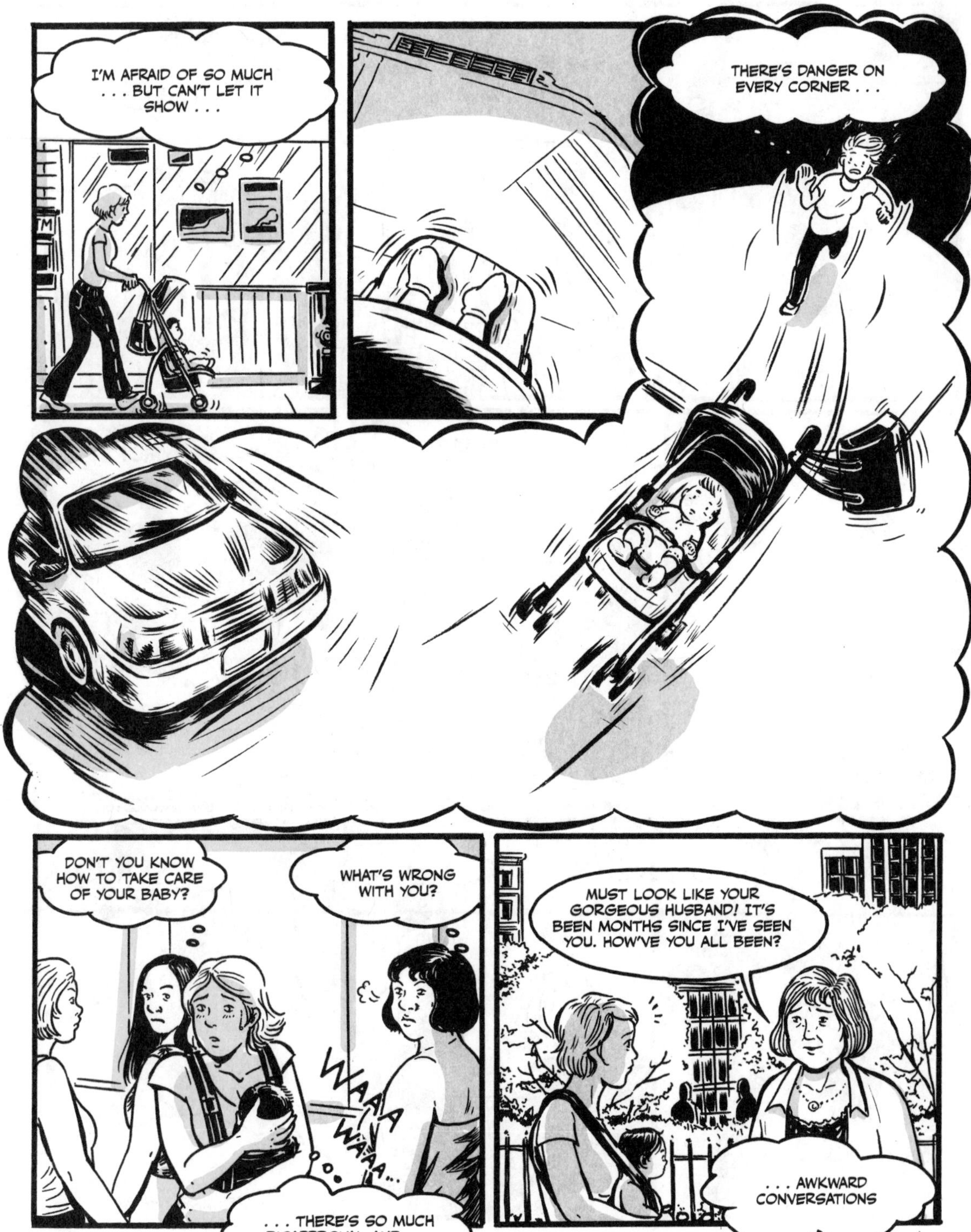

I'M AFRAID OF SO MUCH . . . BUT CAN'T LET IT SHOW . . .
THERE'S DANGER ON EVERY CORNER . . .
DON'T YOU KNOW HOW TO TAKE CARE OF YOUR BABY?
WHAT'S WRONG WITH YOU?
WAAAA WAAAA...
. . . THERE'S SO MUCH DISAPPROVAL AND . . .
MUST LOOK LIKE YOUR GORGEOUS HUSBAND! IT'S BEEN MONTHS SINCE I'VE SEEN YOU. HOW'VE YOU ALL BEEN?
. . . AWKWARD CONVERSATIONS

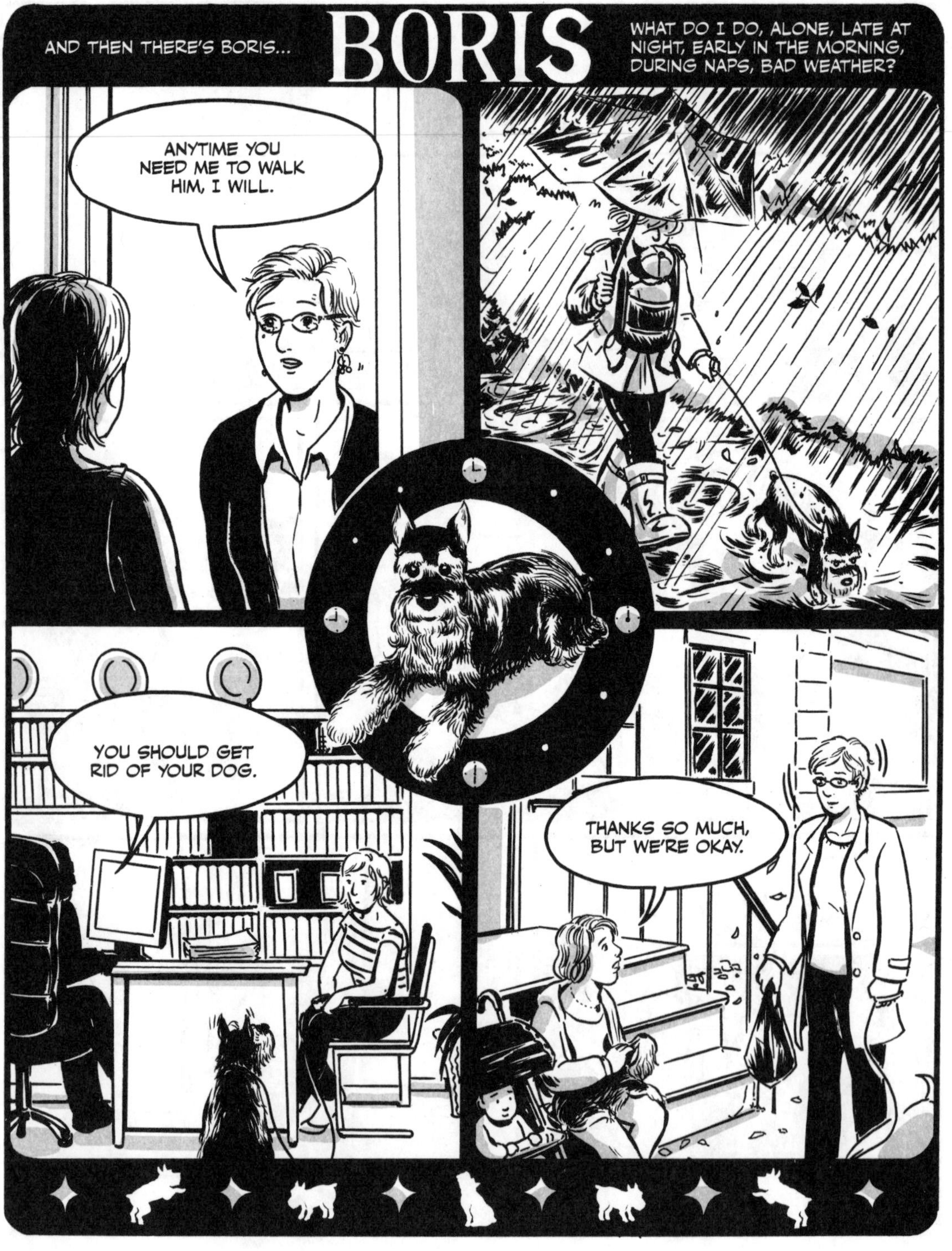
AND THEN THERE'S BORIS...
BORIS
WHAT DO I DO, ALONE, LATE AT NIGHT, EARLY IN THE MORNING, DURING NAPS, BAD WEATHER?
ANYTIME YOU NEED ME TO WALK HIM, I WILL.
YOU SHOULD GET RID OF YOUR DOG.
THANKS SO MUCH, BUT WE'RE OKAY.

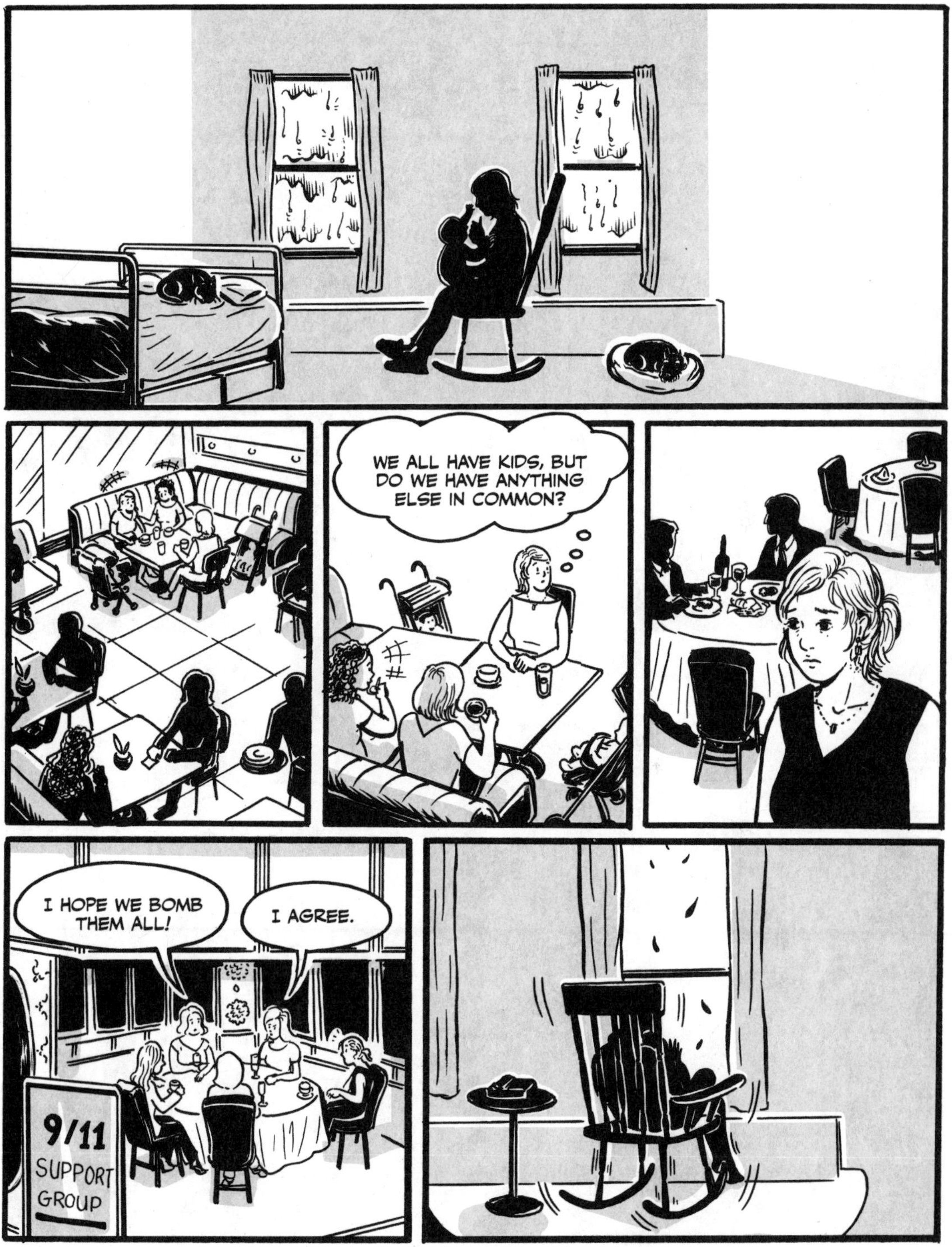
WE ALL HAVE KIDS, BUT DO WE HAVE ANYTHING ELSE IN COMMON?
I HOPE WE BOMB THEM ALL!
I AGREE.
9/11 SUPPORT GROUP

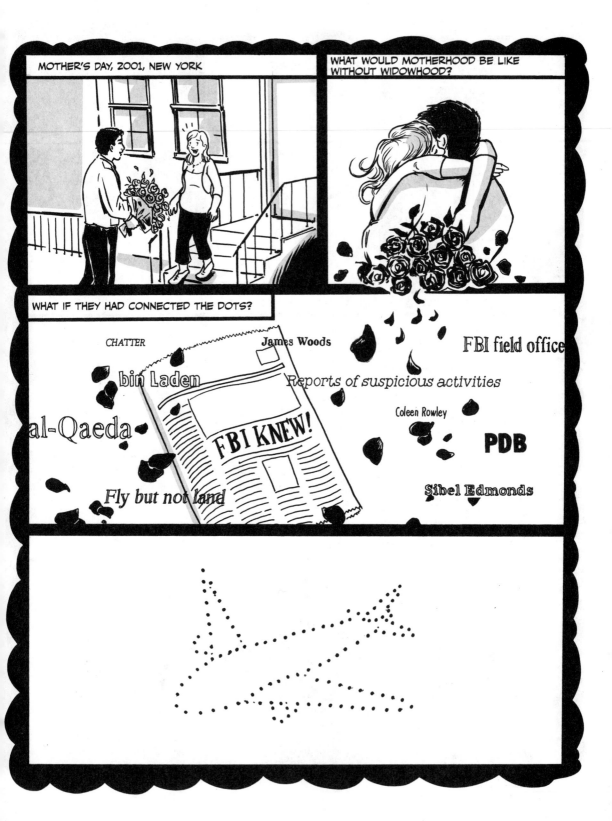

MOTHER'S DAY, 2001, NEW YORK

WHAT WOULD MOTHERHOOD BE LIKE WITHOUT WIDOWHOOD?

WHAT IF THEY HAD CONNECTED THE DOTS?

CHATTER

James Woods

FBI field office

bin Laden

Reports of suspicious activities

al-Qaeda

Coleen Rowley

PDB

FBI KNEW!

Fly but not land

Sibel Edmonds

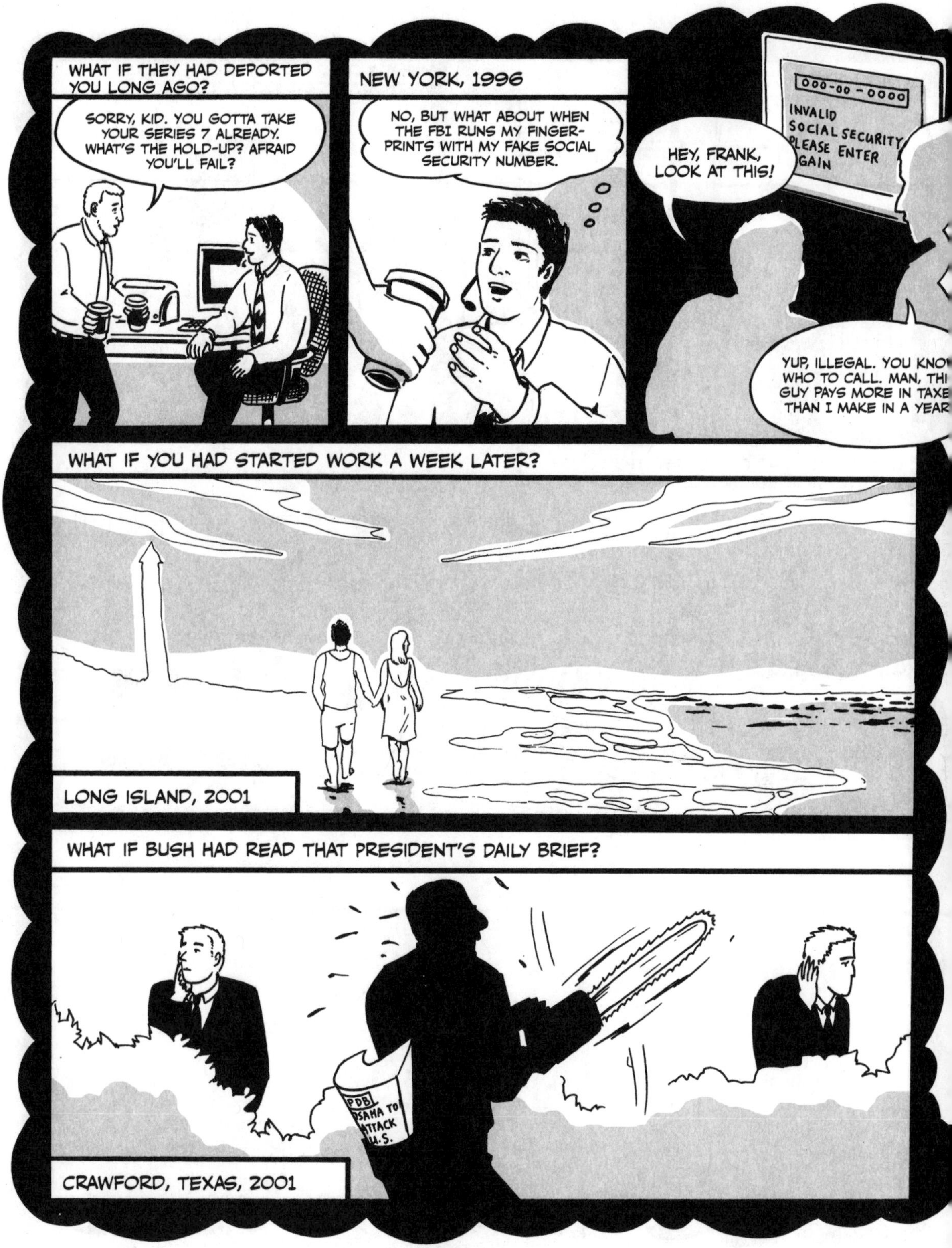
WHAT IF THEY HAD DEPORTED YOU LONG AGO?
SORRY, KID. YOU GOTTA TAKE YOUR SERIES 7 ALREADY. WHAT'S THE HOLD-UP? AFRAID YOU'LL FAIL?
NEW YORK, 1996
NO, BUT WHAT ABOUT WHEN THE FBI RUNS MY FINGER-PRINTS WITH MY FAKE SOCIAL SECURITY NUMBER.
000-00-0000
INVALID SOCIAL SECURITY PLEASE ENTER AGAIN
HEY, FRANK, LOOK AT THIS!
YUP, ILLEGAL. YOU KNO WHO TO CALL. MAN, THI GUY PAYS MORE IN TAXE THAN I MAKE IN A YEAR
WHAT IF YOU HAD STARTED WORK A WEEK LATER?
LONG ISLAND, 2001
WHAT IF BUSH HAD READ THAT PRESIDENT'S DAILY BRIEF?
PDB OSAMA TO ATTACK U.S.
CRAWFORD, TEXAS, 2001

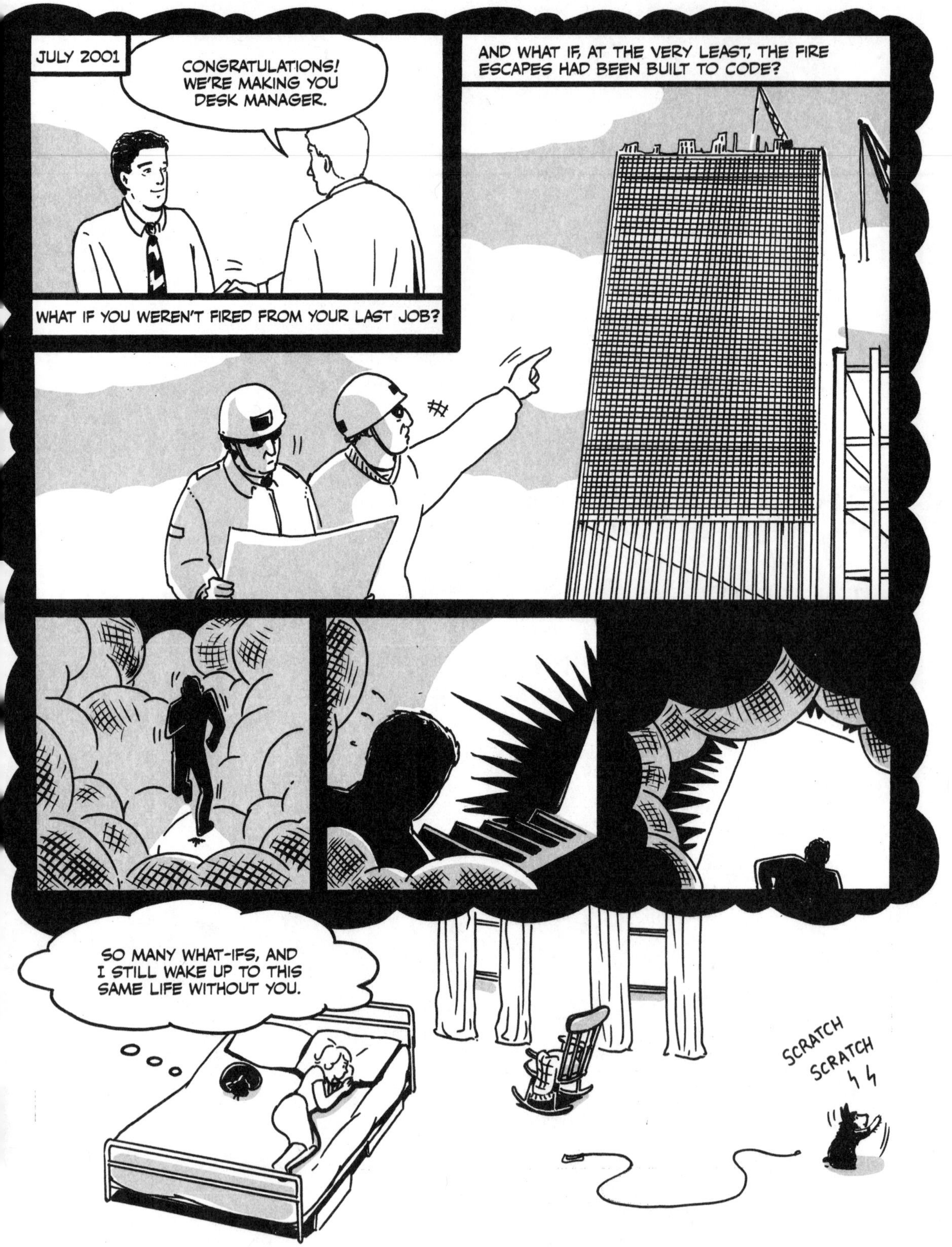
JULY 2001
CONGRATULATIONS! WE'RE MAKING YOU DESK MANAGER.
WHAT IF YOU WEREN'T FIRED FROM YOUR LAST JOB?
AND WHAT IF, AT THE VERY LEAST, THE FIRE ESCAPES HAD BEEN BUILT TO CODE?
SO MANY WHAT-IFS, AND I STILL WAKE UP TO THIS SAME LIFE WITHOUT YOU.
SCRATCH
SCRATCH

Chapter Fifteen

June 2002

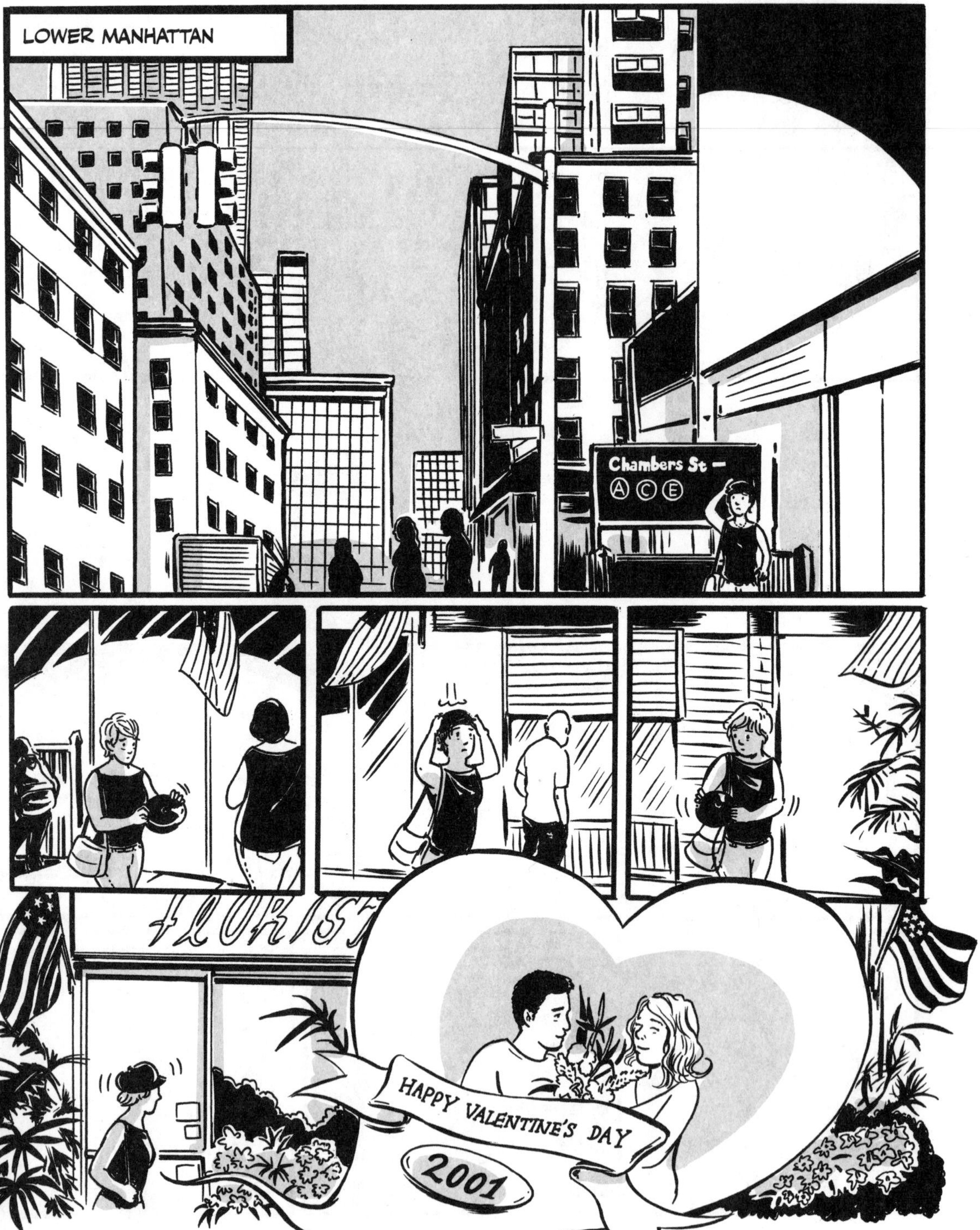
LOWER MANHATTAN
Chambers St
A C E
FLORIST
HAPPY VALENTINE'S DAY
2001

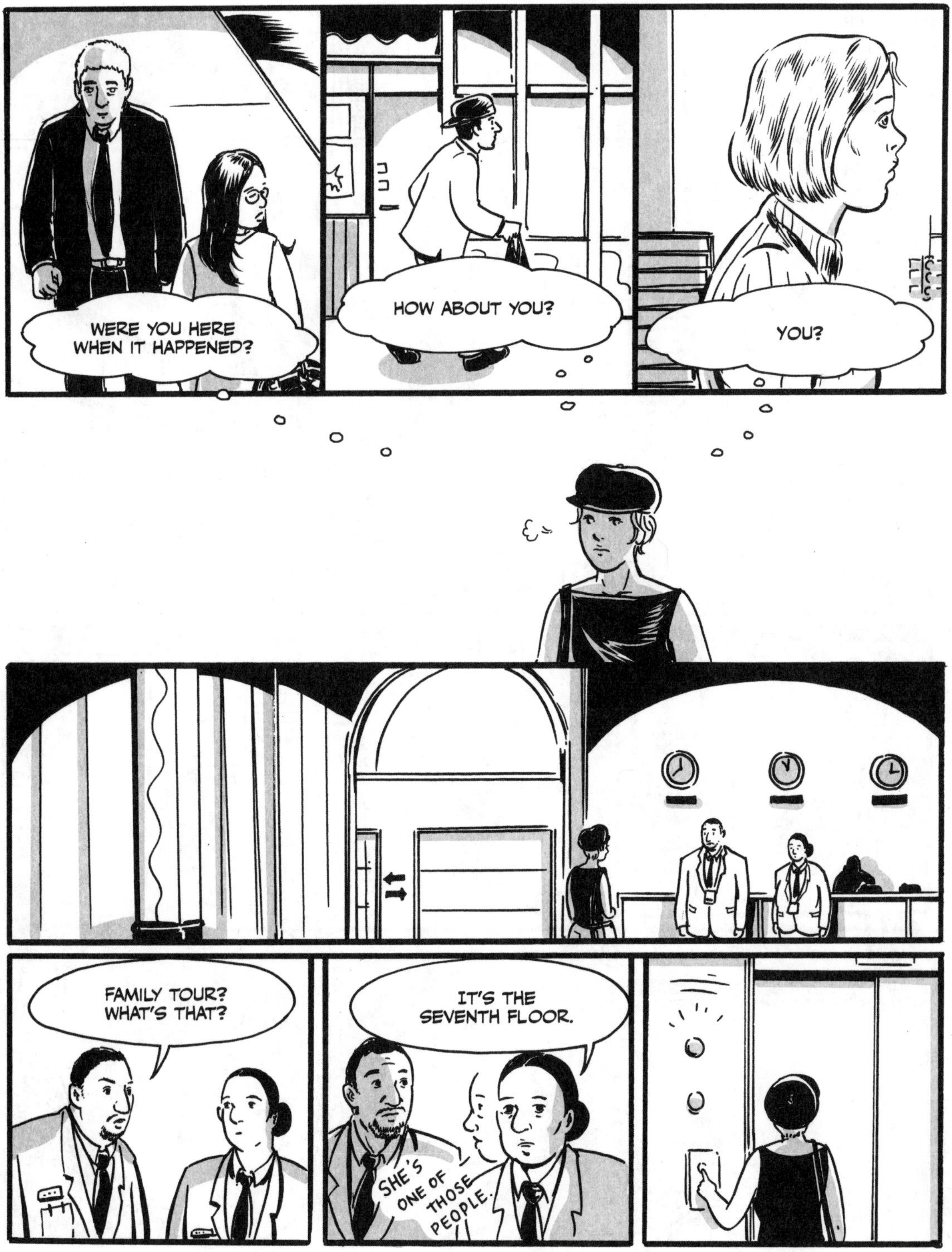
WERE YOU HERE WHEN IT HAPPENED?
HOW ABOUT YOU?
YOU?
FAMILY TOUR? WHAT'S THAT?
IT'S THE SEVENTH FLOOR.
SHE'S ONE OF THOSE PEOPLE.

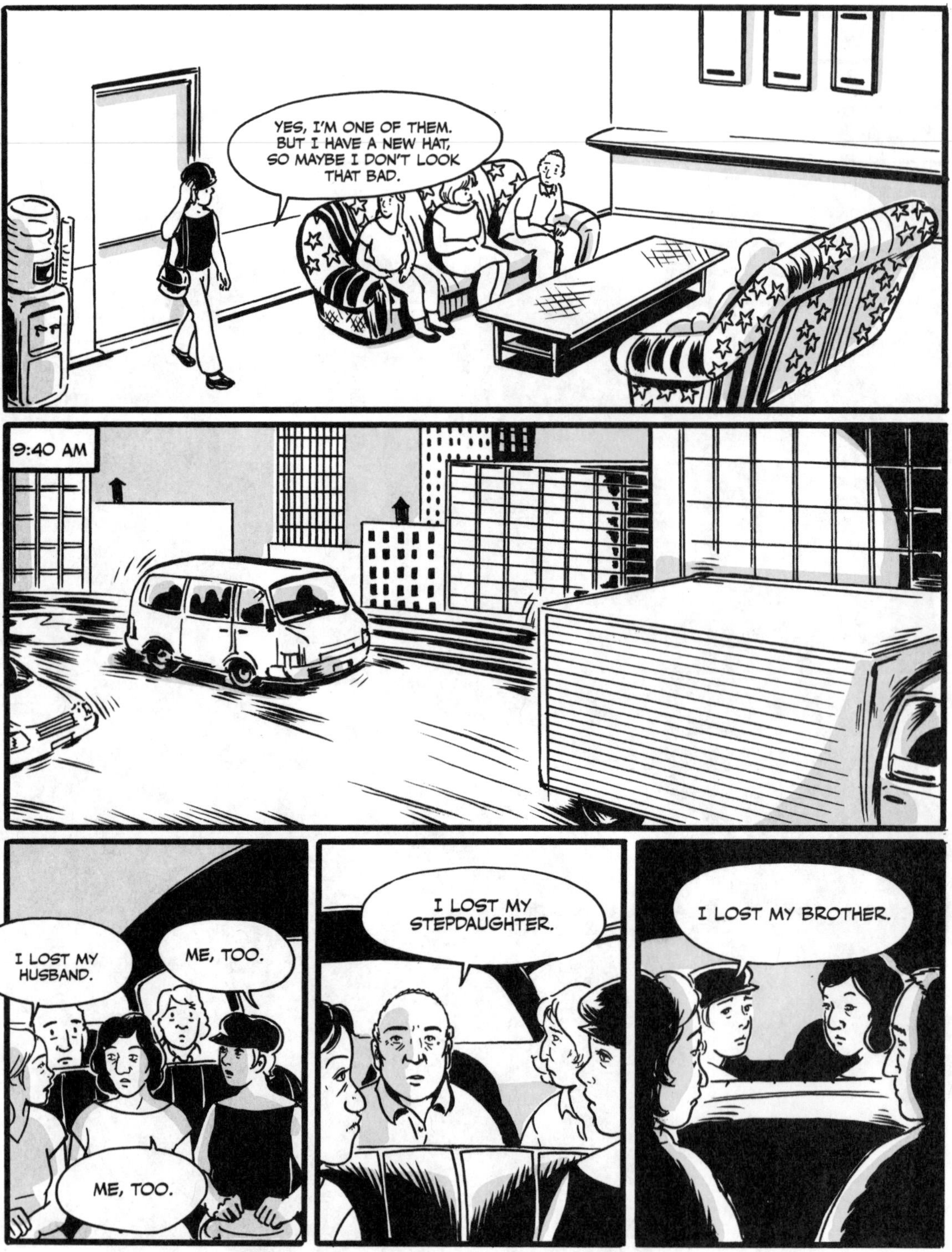
YES, I'M ONE OF THEM. BUT I HAVE A NEW HAT, SO MAYBE I DON'T LOOK THAT BAD.
9:40 AM
I LOST MY HUSBAND.
ME, TOO.
ME, TOO.
I LOST MY STEPDAUGHTER.
I LOST MY BROTHER.

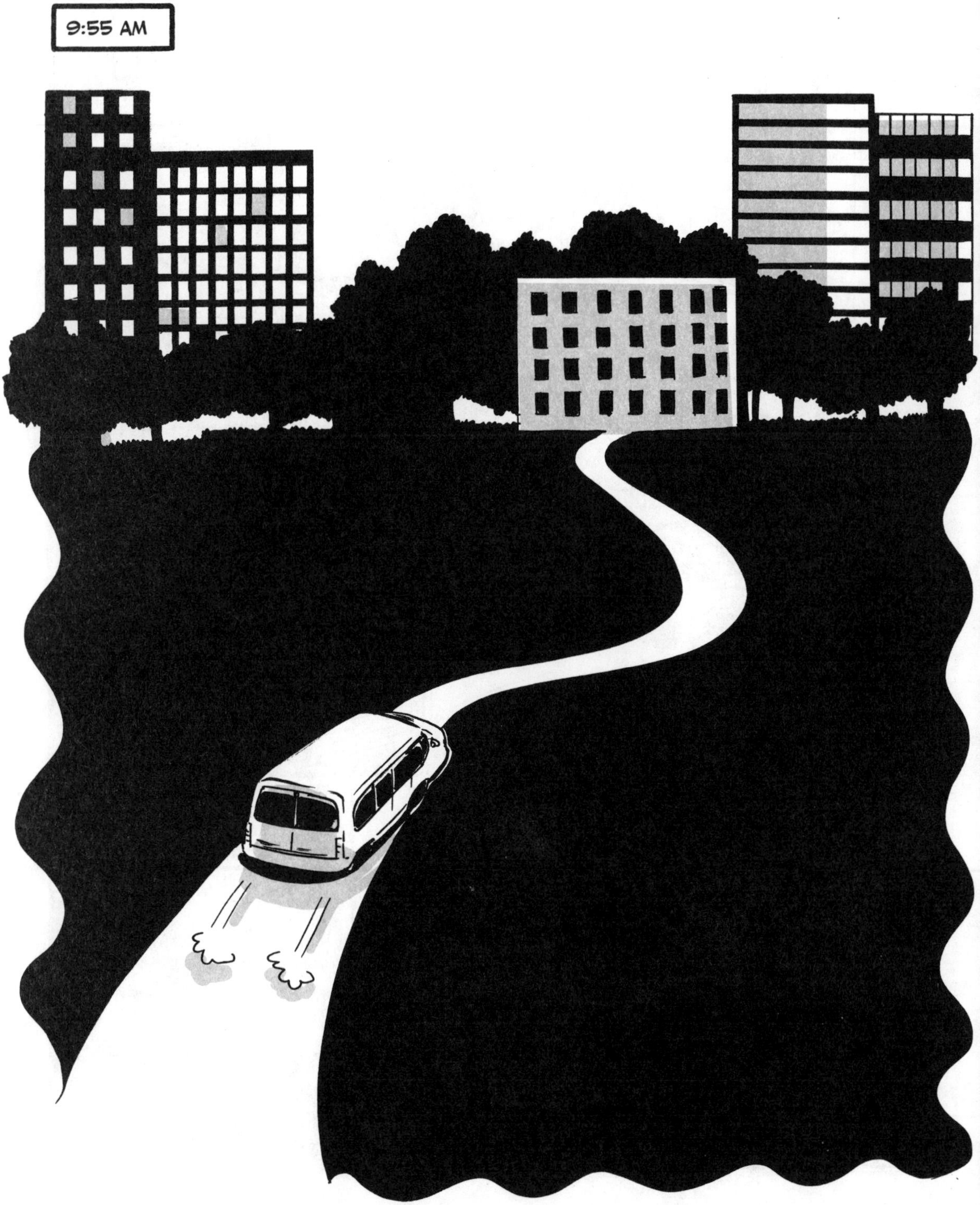
9:55 AM

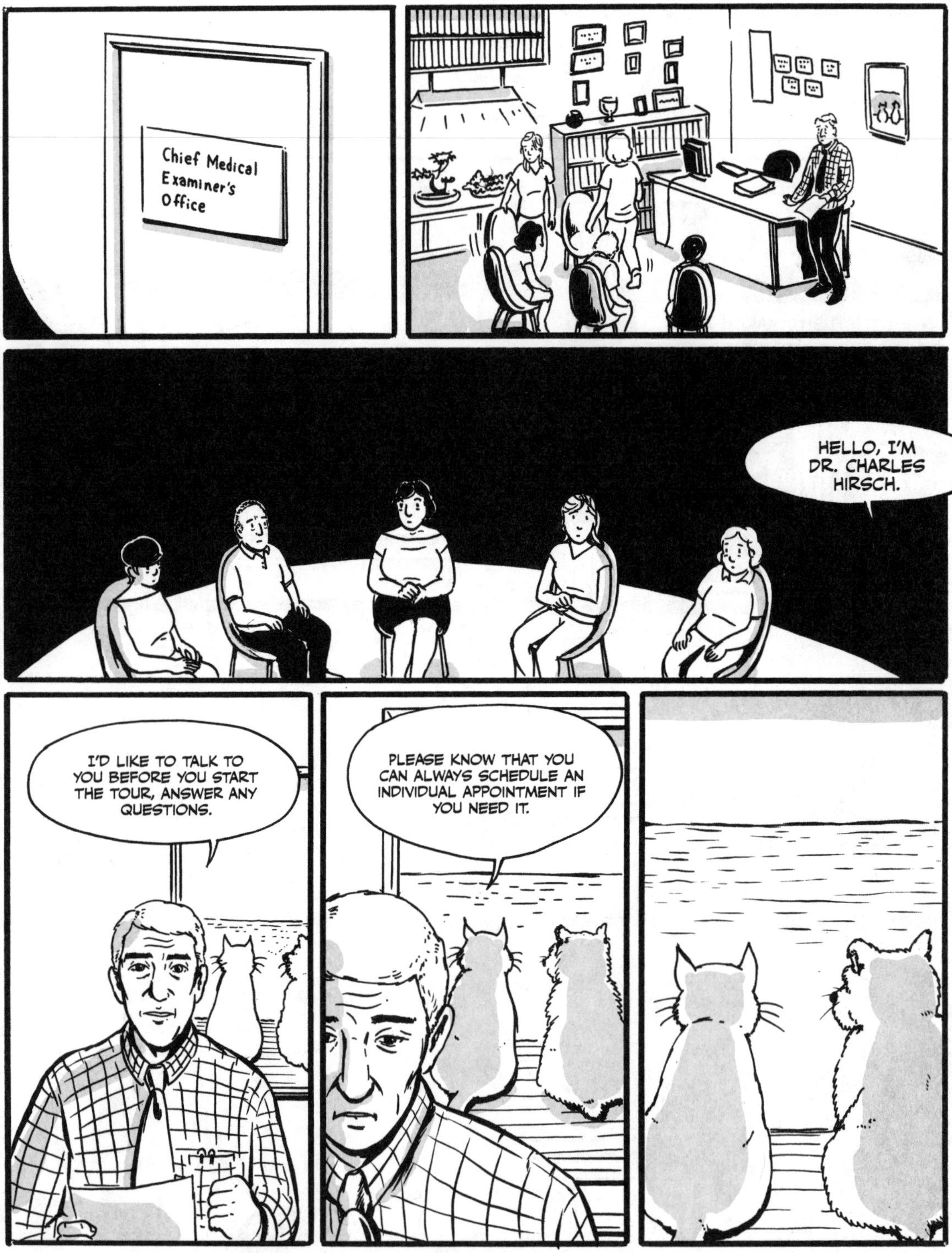
Chief Medical Examiner's Office
HELLO, I'M DR. CHARLES HIRSCH.
I'D LIKE TO TALK TO YOU BEFORE YOU START THE TOUR, ANSWER ANY QUESTIONS.
PLEASE KNOW THAT YOU CAN ALWAYS SCHEDULE AN INDIVIDUAL APPOINTMENT IF YOU NEED IT.

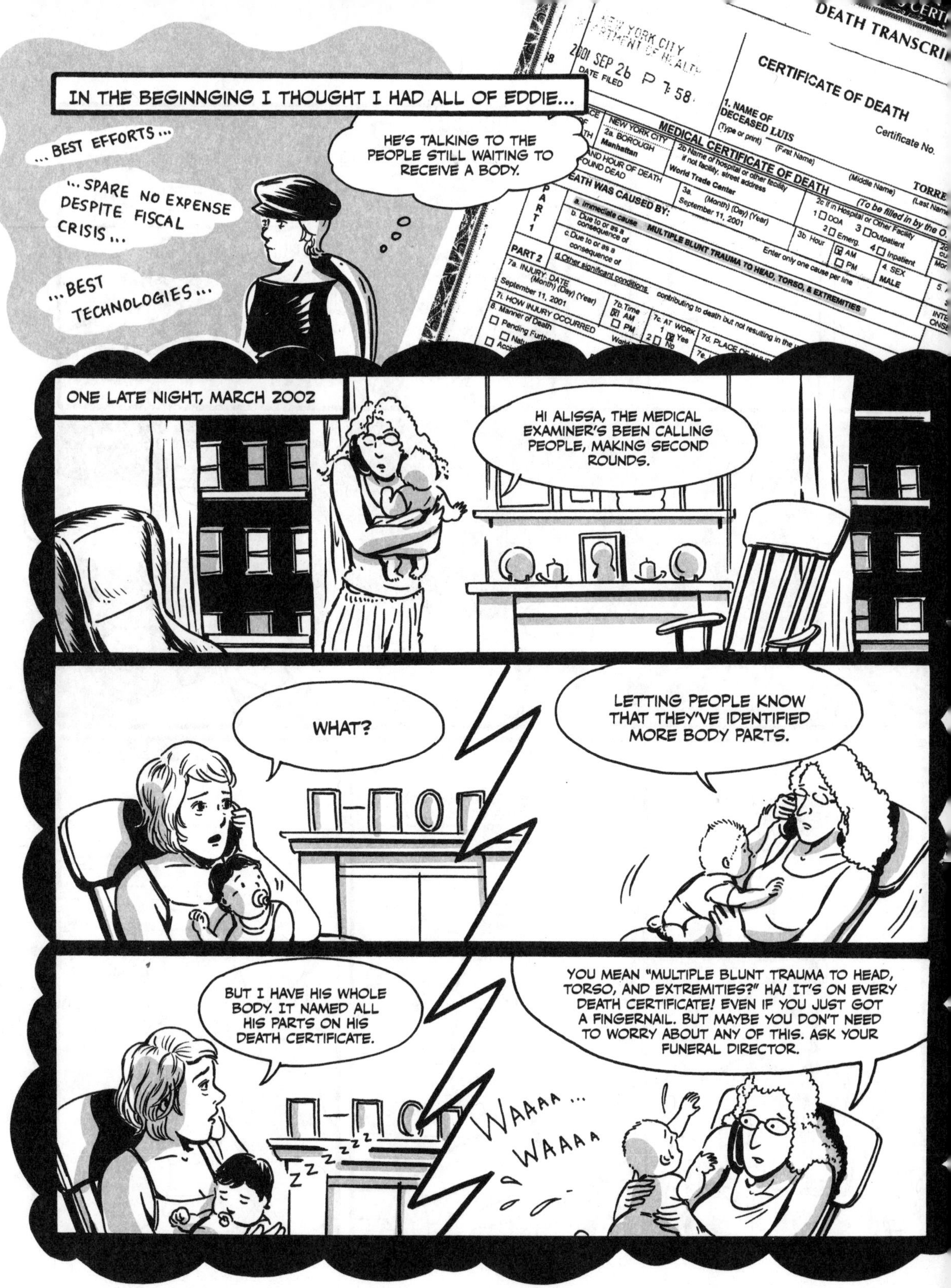

IN THE BEGINNGING I THOUGHT I HAD ALL OF EDDIE...
...BEST EFFORTS...
...SPARE NO EXPENSE DESPITE FISCAL CRISIS...
...BEST TECHNOLOGIES...
HE'S TALKING TO THE PEOPLE STILL WAITING TO RECEIVE A BODY.
2001 SEP 26 P 7:58
DATE FILED
CERTIFICATE OF DEATH
1. NAME OF DECEASED LUIS
MEDICAL CERTIFICATE OF DEATH
Manhattan
World Trade Center
September 11, 2001
MULTIPLE BLUNT TRAUMA TO HEAD, TORSO, & EXTREMITIES
MALE
ONE LATE NIGHT, MARCH 2002
HI ALISSA, THE MEDICAL EXAMINER'S BEEN CALLING PEOPLE, MAKING SECOND ROUNDS.
WHAT?
LETTING PEOPLE KNOW THAT THEY'VE IDENTIFIED MORE BODY PARTS.
BUT I HAVE HIS WHOLE BODY. IT NAMED ALL HIS PARTS ON HIS DEATH CERTIFICATE.
YOU MEAN "MULTIPLE BLUNT TRAUMA TO HEAD, TORSO, AND EXTREMITIES?" HA! IT'S ON EVERY DEATH CERTIFICATE! EVEN IF YOU JUST GOT A FINGERNAIL. BUT MAYBE YOU DON'T NEED TO WORRY ABOUT ANY OF THIS. ASK YOUR FUNERAL DIRECTOR.
WAAAA... WAAAA

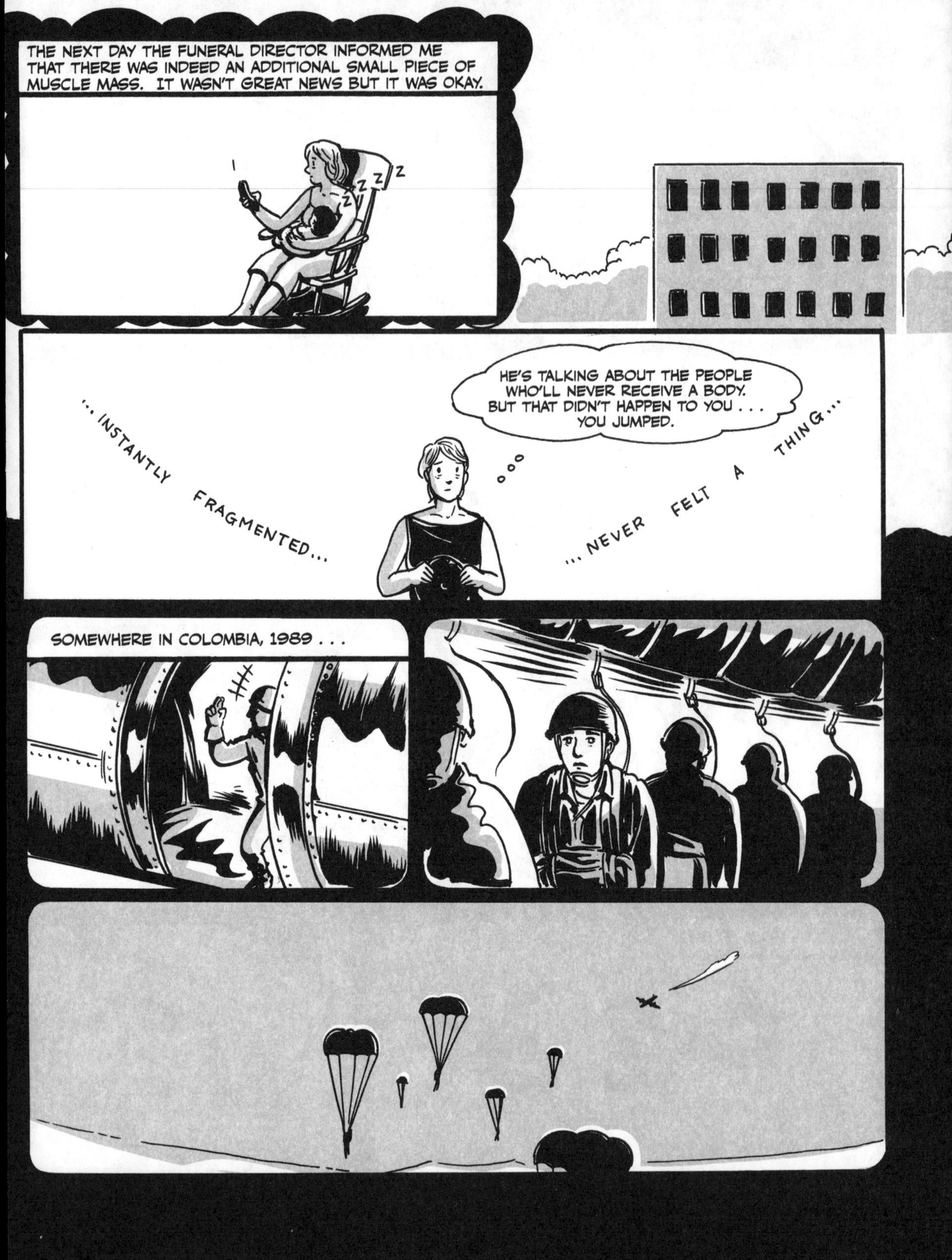
THE NEXT DAY THE FUNERAL DIRECTOR INFORMED ME THAT THERE WAS INDEED AN ADDITIONAL SMALL PIECE OF MUSCLE MASS. IT WASN'T GREAT NEWS BUT IT WAS OKAY.
Z Z Z Z
...INSTANTLY FRAGMENTED...
HE'S TALKING ABOUT THE PEOPLE WHO'LL NEVER RECEIVE A BODY. BUT THAT DIDN'T HAPPEN TO YOU . . . YOU JUMPED.
...NEVER FELT A THING...
SOMEWHERE IN COLOMBIA, 1989 . . .

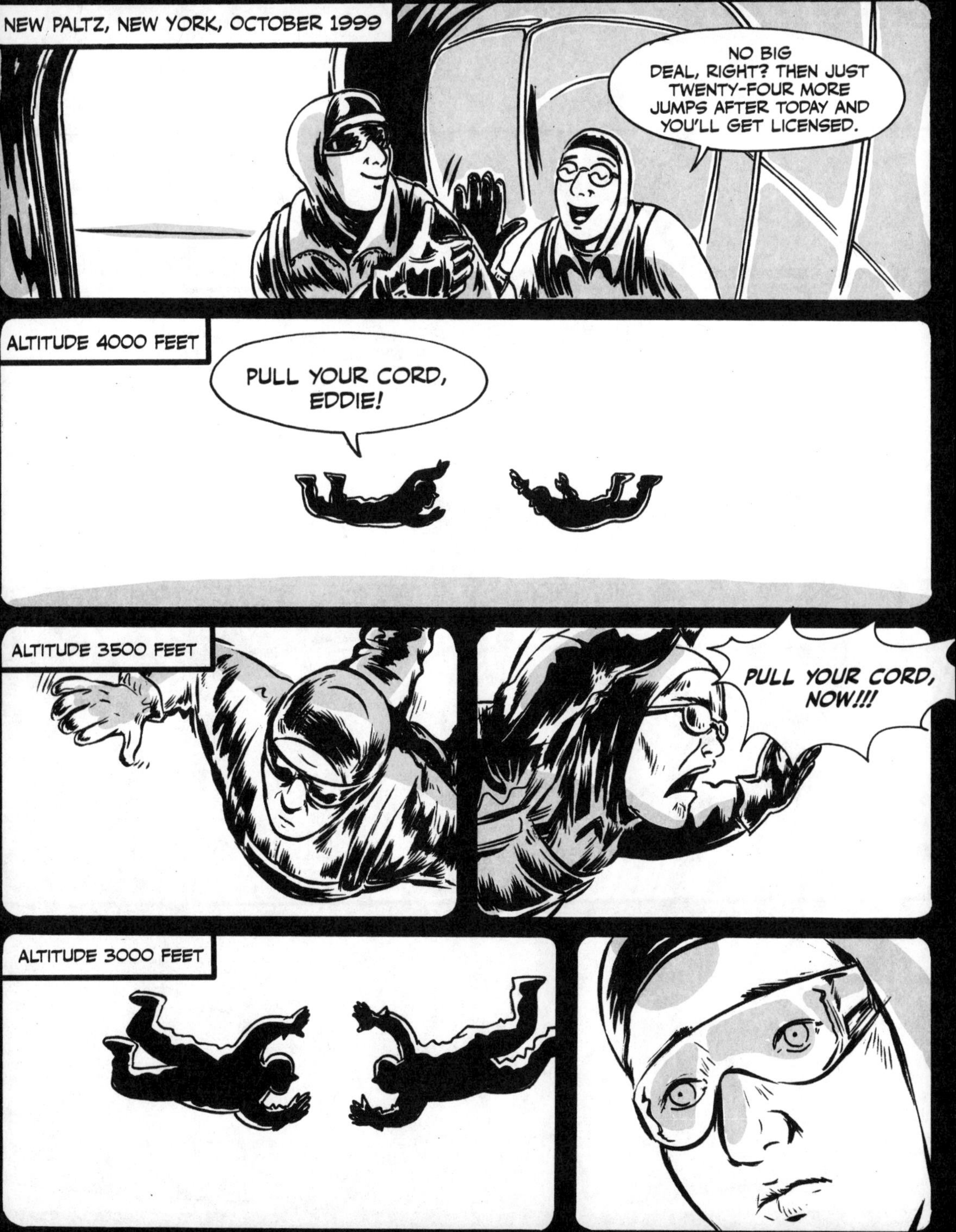
NEW PALTZ, NEW YORK, OCTOBER 1999
NO BIG DEAL, RIGHT? THEN JUST TWENTY-FOUR MORE JUMPS AFTER TODAY AND YOU'LL GET LICENSED.
ALTITUDE 4000 FEET
PULL YOUR CORD, EDDIE!
ALTITUDE 3500 FEET
PULL YOUR CORD, NOW!!!
ALTITUDE 3000 FEET

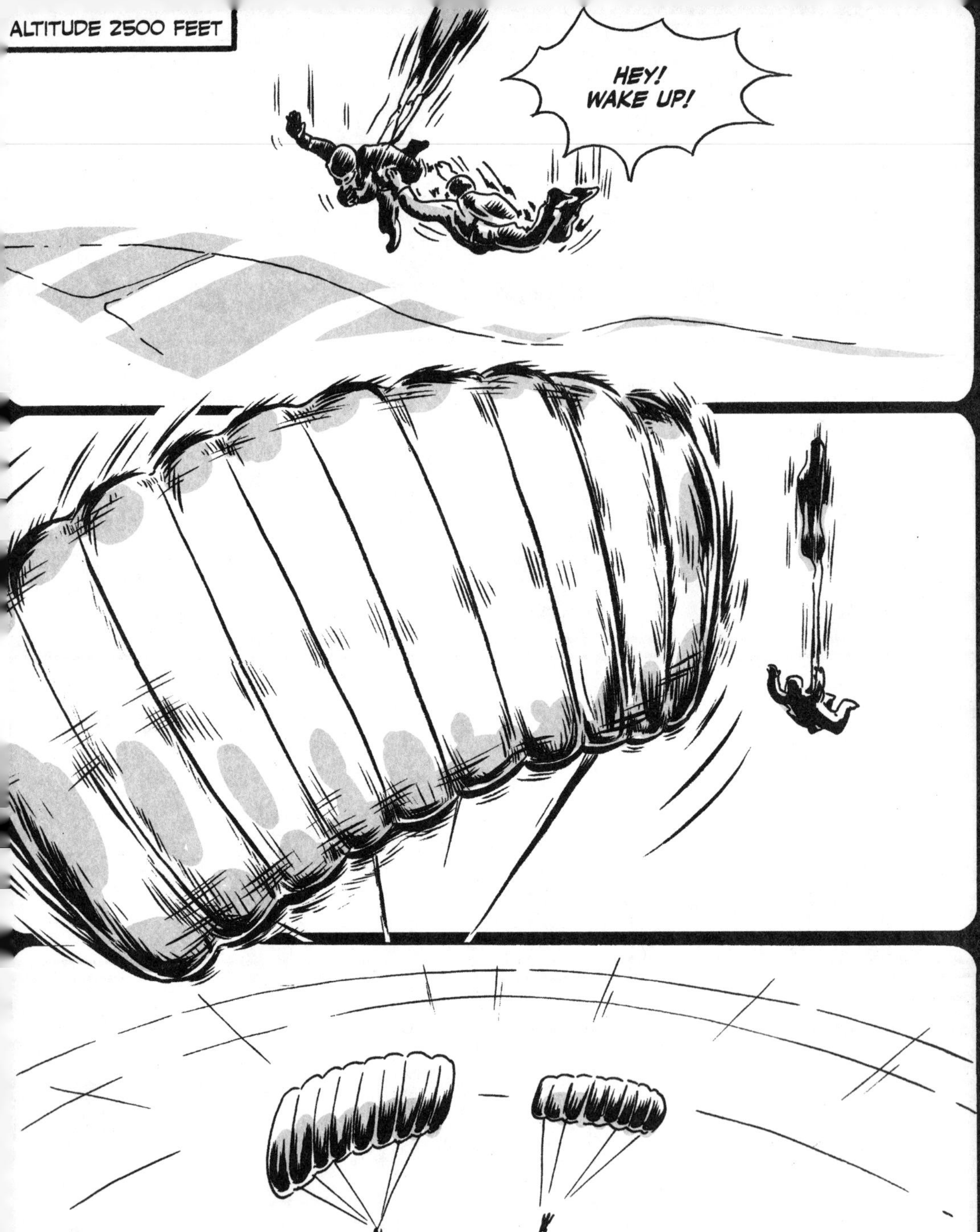
ALTITUDE 2500 FEET
HEY! WAKE UP!

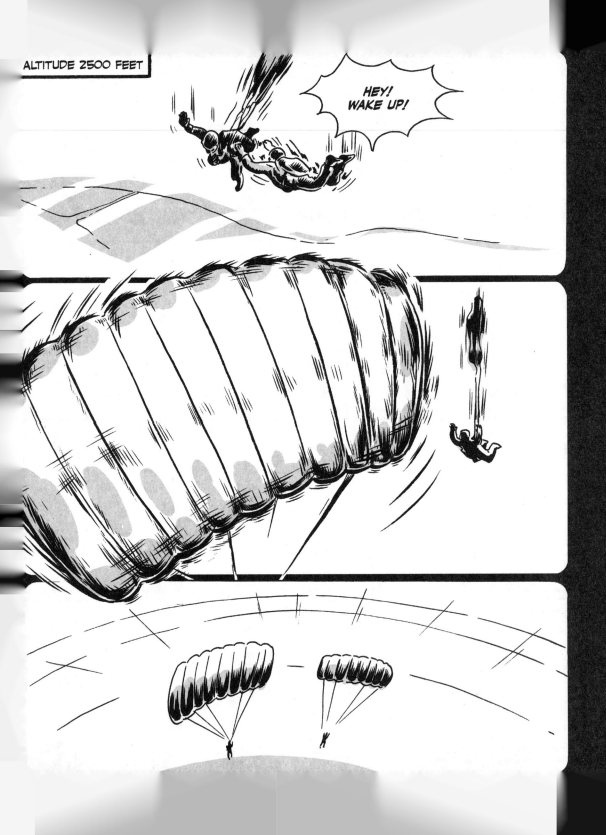

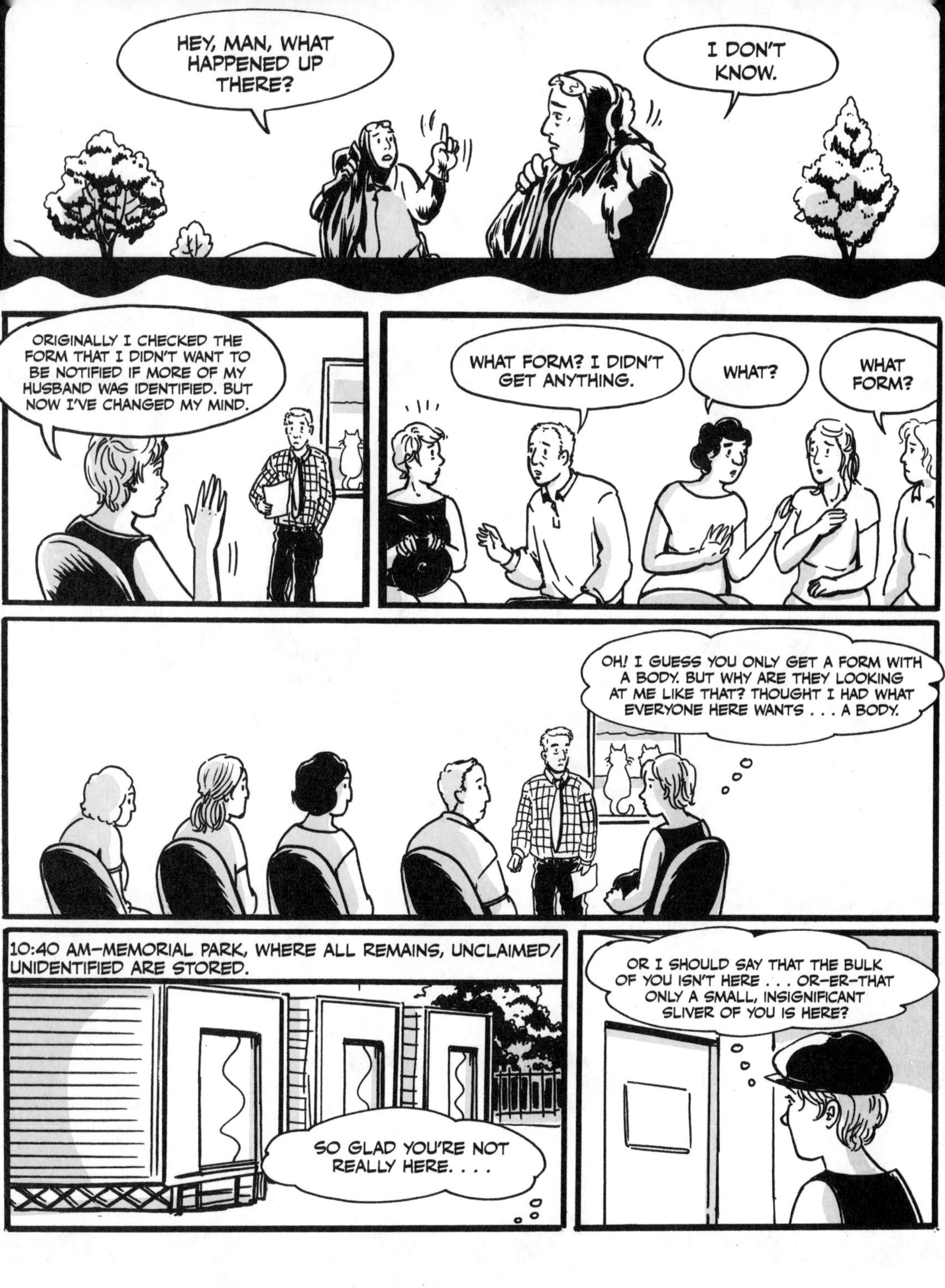
HEY, MAN, WHAT HAPPENED UP THERE?
I DON'T KNOW.
ORIGINALLY I CHECKED THE FORM THAT I DIDN'T WANT TO BE NOTIFIED IF MORE OF MY HUSBAND WAS IDENTIFIED. BUT NOW I'VE CHANGED MY MIND.
WHAT FORM? I DIDN'T GET ANYTHING.
WHAT?
WHAT FORM?
OH! I GUESS YOU ONLY GET A FORM WITH A BODY. BUT WHY ARE THEY LOOKING AT ME LIKE THAT? THOUGHT I HAD WHAT EVERYONE HERE WANTS . . . A BODY.
10:40 AM—MEMORIAL PARK, WHERE ALL REMAINS, UNCLAIMED/UNIDENTIFIED ARE STORED.
SO GLAD YOU'RE NOT REALLY HERE. . . .
OR I SHOULD SAY THAT THE BULK OF YOU ISN'T HERE . . . OR—ER—THAT ONLY A SMALL, INSIGNIFICANT SLIVER OF YOU IS HERE?

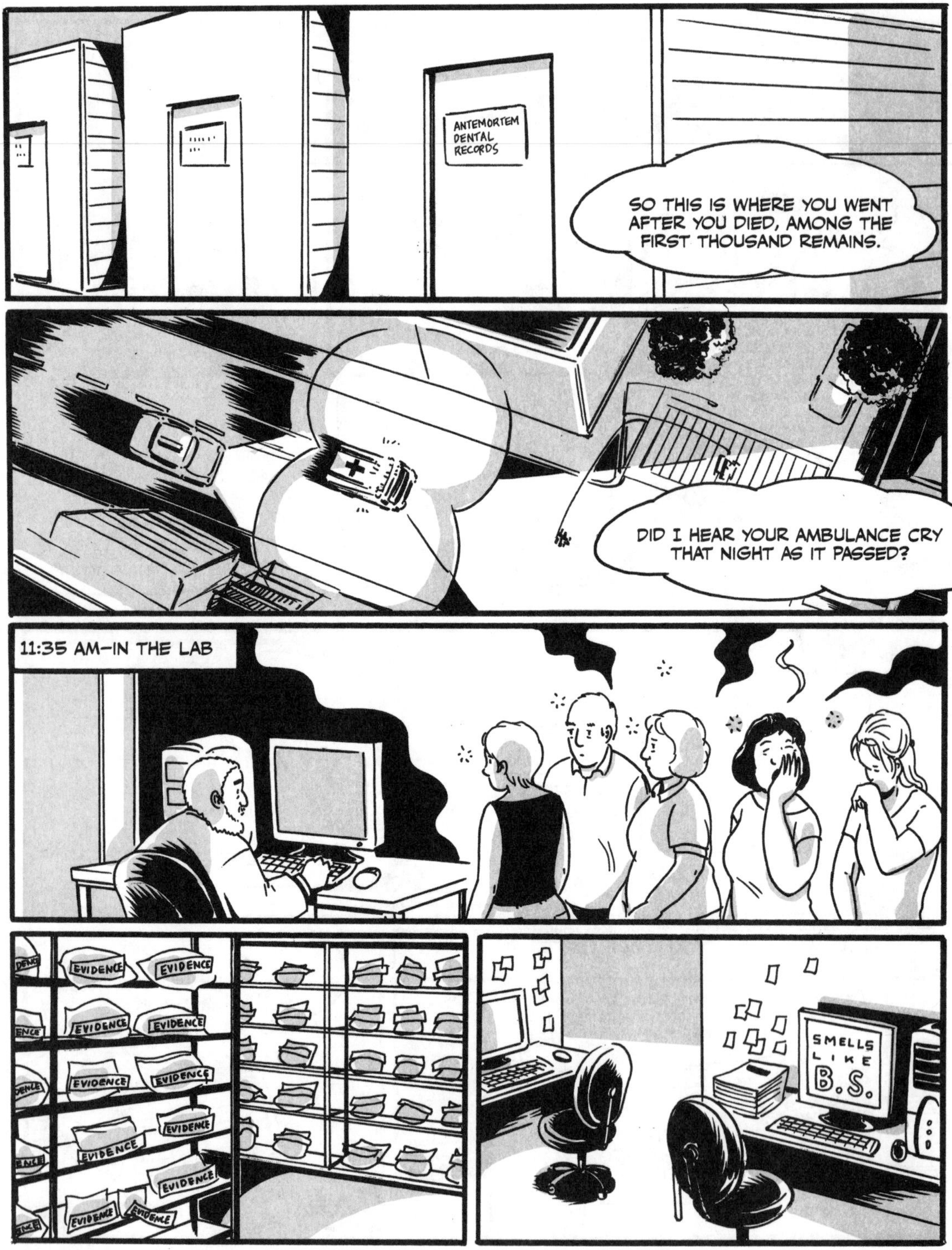
ANTEMORTEM DENTAL RECORDS
SO THIS IS WHERE YOU WENT AFTER YOU DIED, AMONG THE FIRST THOUSAND REMAINS.
DID I HEAR YOUR AMBULANCE CRY THAT NIGHT AS IT PASSED?
11:35 AM—IN THE LAB
EVIDENCE
SMELLS LIKE B.S.

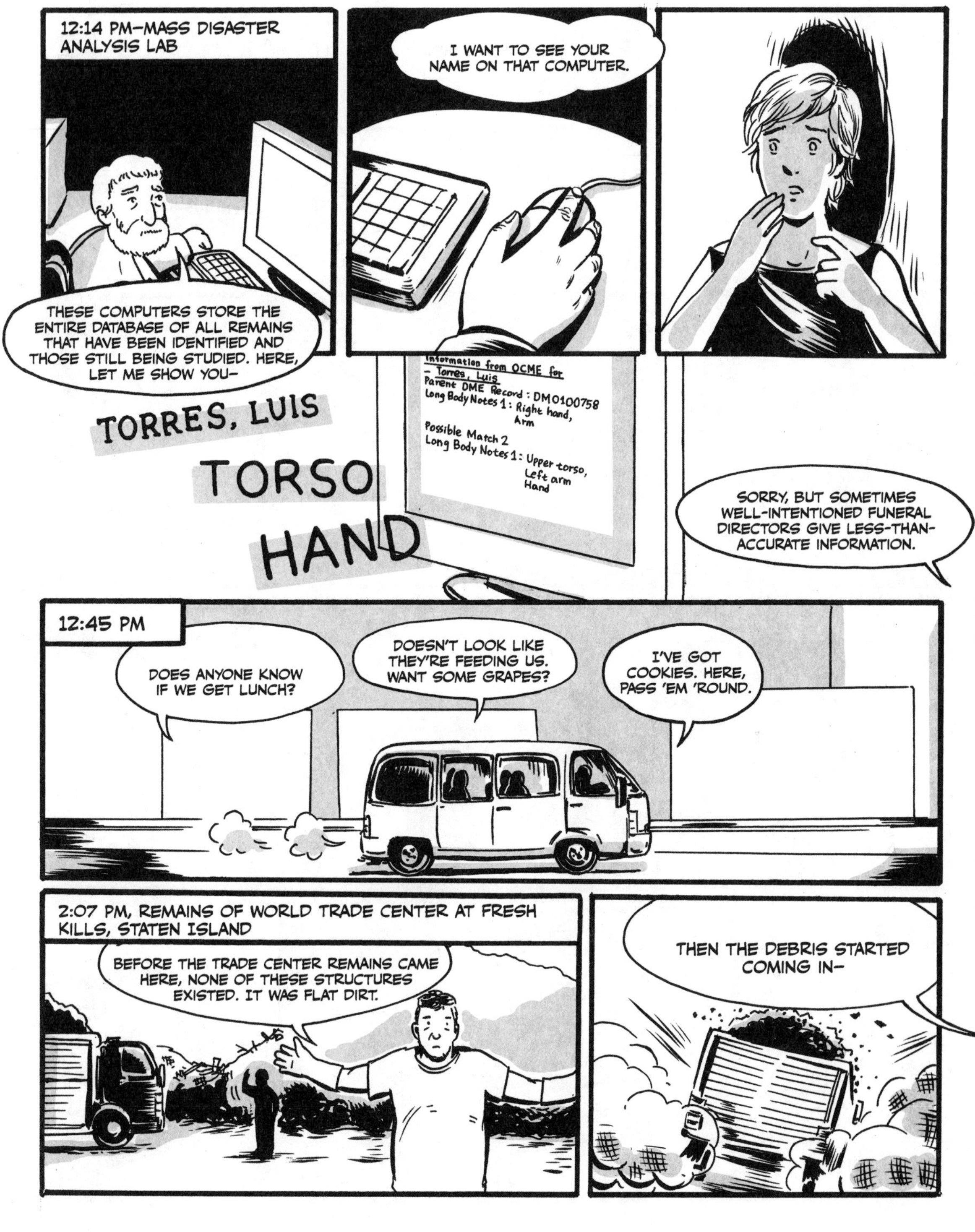
12:14 PM—MASS DISASTER ANALYSIS LAB
THESE COMPUTERS STORE THE ENTIRE DATABASE OF ALL REMAINS THAT HAVE BEEN IDENTIFIED AND THOSE STILL BEING STUDIED. HERE, LET ME SHOW YOU—
I WANT TO SEE YOUR NAME ON THAT COMPUTER.
Information from OCME for
- Torres, Luis
Parent DME Record: DM0100758
Long Body Notes 1: Right hand, Arm
Possible Match 2
Long Body Notes 1: Upper torso, Left arm Hand
TORRES, LUIS
TORSO
HAND
SORRY, BUT SOMETIMES WELL-INTENTIONED FUNERAL DIRECTORS GIVE LESS-THAN-ACCURATE INFORMATION.
12:45 PM
DOES ANYONE KNOW IF WE GET LUNCH?
DOESN'T LOOK LIKE THEY'RE FEEDING US. WANT SOME GRAPES?
I'VE GOT COOKIES. HERE, PASS 'EM 'ROUND.
2:07 PM, REMAINS OF WORLD TRADE CENTER AT FRESH KILLS, STATEN ISLAND
BEFORE THE TRADE CENTER REMAINS CAME HERE, NONE OF THESE STRUCTURES EXISTED. IT WAS FLAT DIRT.
THEN THE DEBRIS STARTED COMING IN—

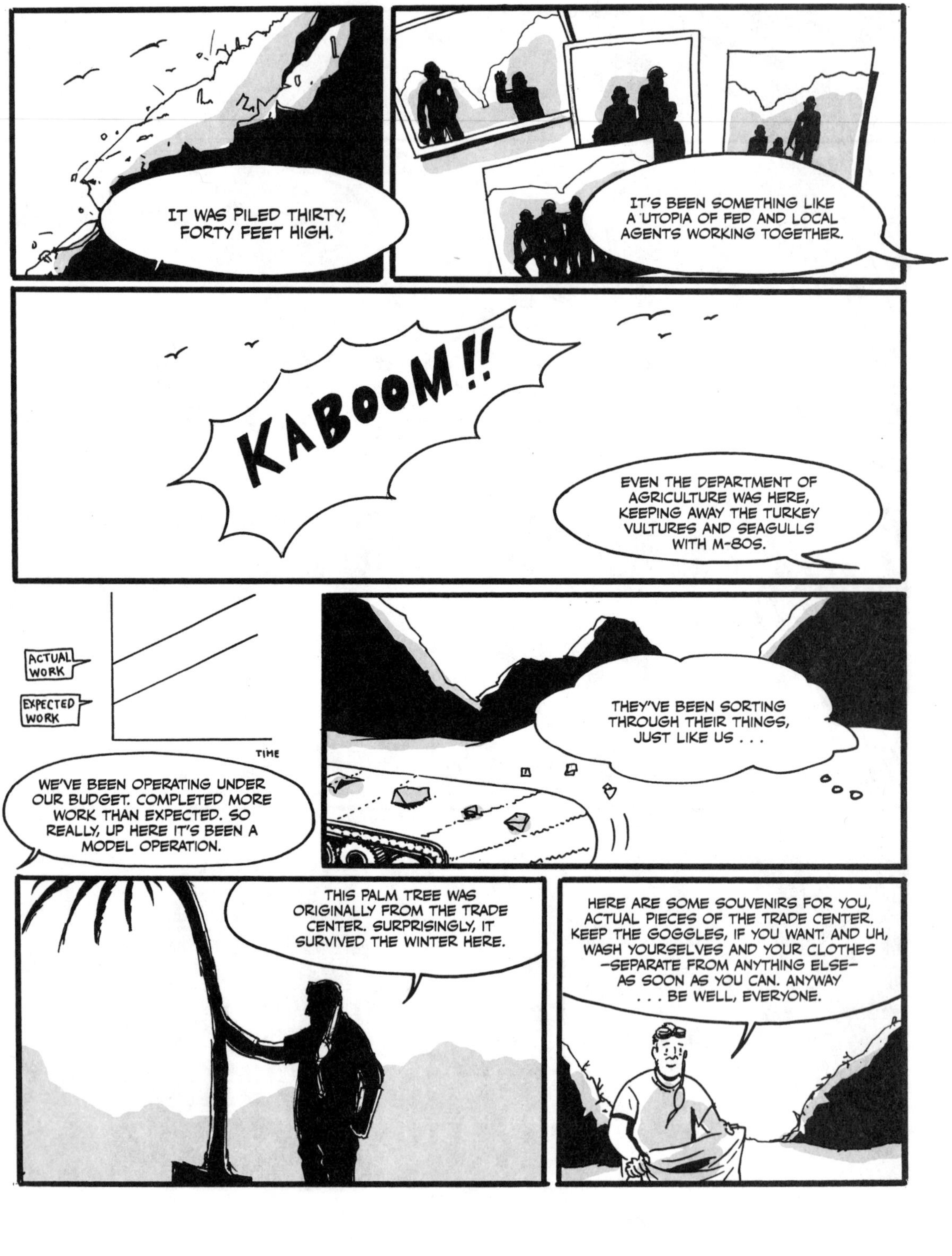
IT WAS PILED THIRTY, FORTY FEET HIGH.
IT'S BEEN SOMETHING LIKE A UTOPIA OF FED AND LOCAL AGENTS WORKING TOGETHER.
KABOOM!!
EVEN THE DEPARTMENT OF AGRICULTURE WAS HERE, KEEPING AWAY THE TURKEY VULTURES AND SEAGULLS WITH M-80S.
ACTUAL WORK
EXPECTED WORK
TIME
WE'VE BEEN OPERATING UNDER OUR BUDGET. COMPLETED MORE WORK THAN EXPECTED. SO REALLY, UP HERE IT'S BEEN A MODEL OPERATION.
THEY'VE BEEN SORTING THROUGH THEIR THINGS, JUST LIKE US . . .
THIS PALM TREE WAS ORIGINALLY FROM THE TRADE CENTER. SURPRISINGLY, IT SURVIVED THE WINTER HERE.
HERE ARE SOME SOUVENIRS FOR YOU, ACTUAL PIECES OF THE TRADE CENTER. KEEP THE GOGGLES, IF YOU WANT. AND UH, WASH YOURSELVES AND YOUR CLOTHES —SEPARATE FROM ANYTHING ELSE— AS SOON AS YOU CAN. ANYWAY . . . BE WELL, EVERYONE.

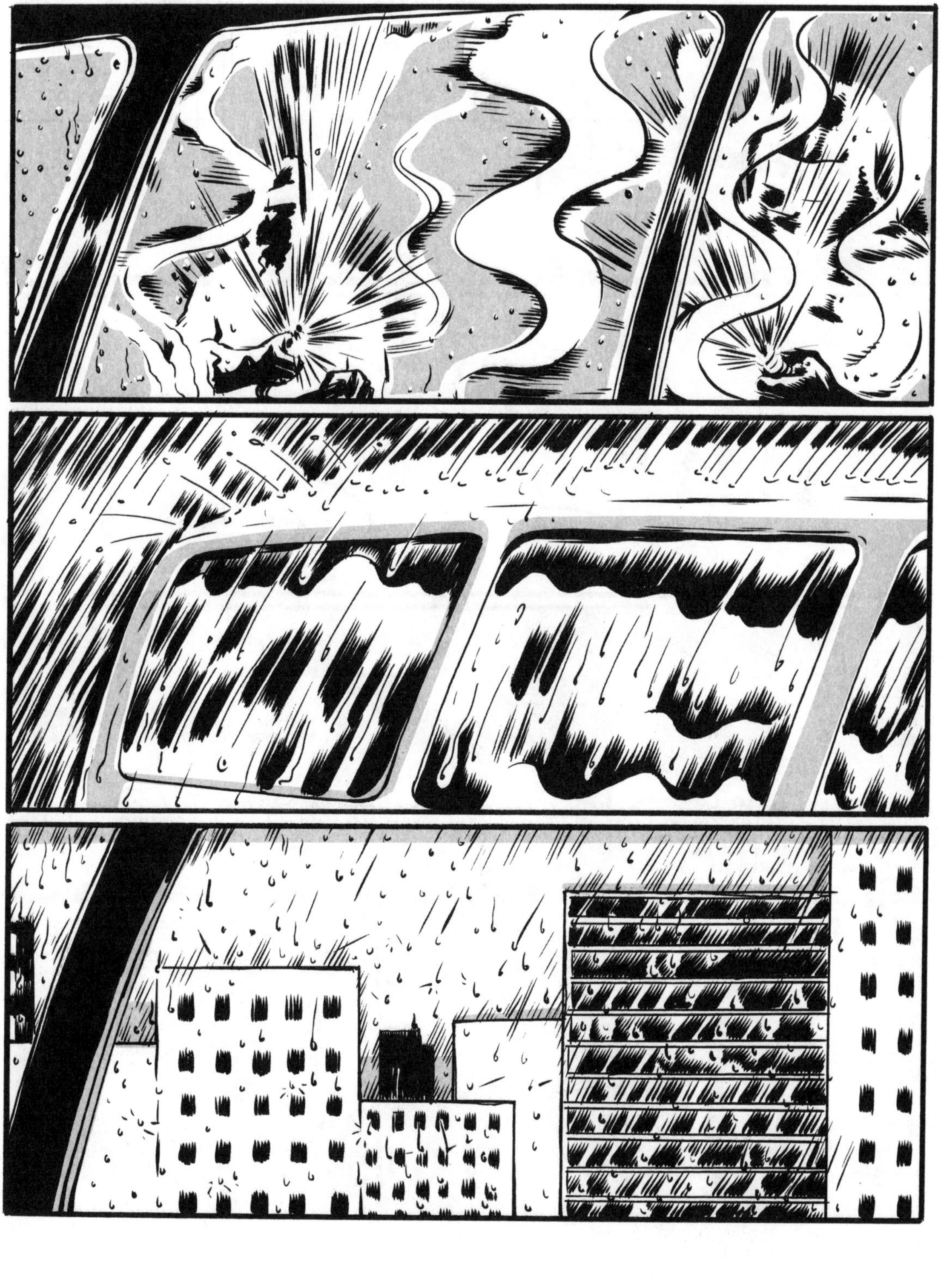

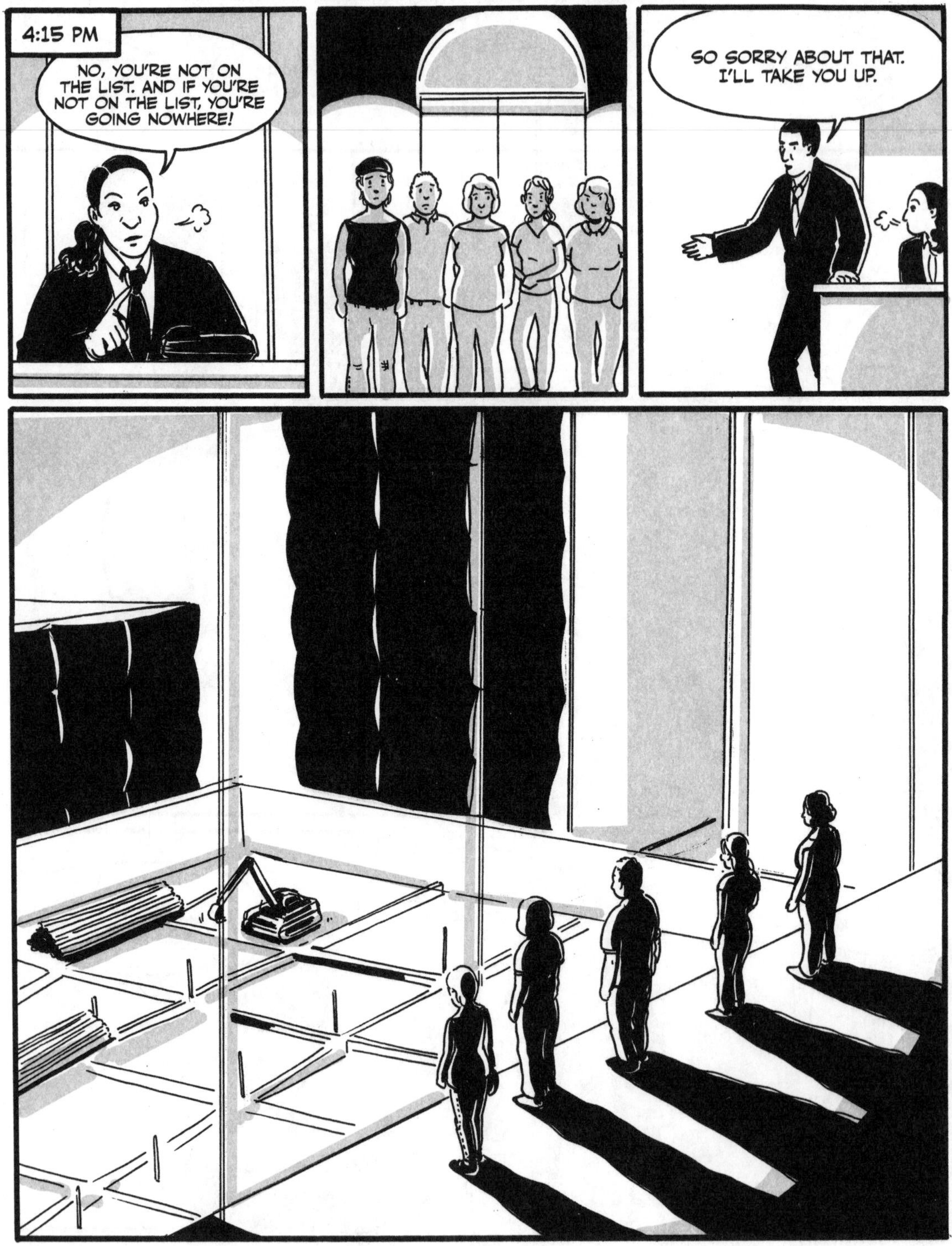
4:15 PM
NO, YOU'RE NOT ON THE LIST. AND IF YOU'RE NOT ON THE LIST, YOU'RE GOING NOWHERE!
SO SORRY ABOUT THAT. I'LL TAKE YOU UP.

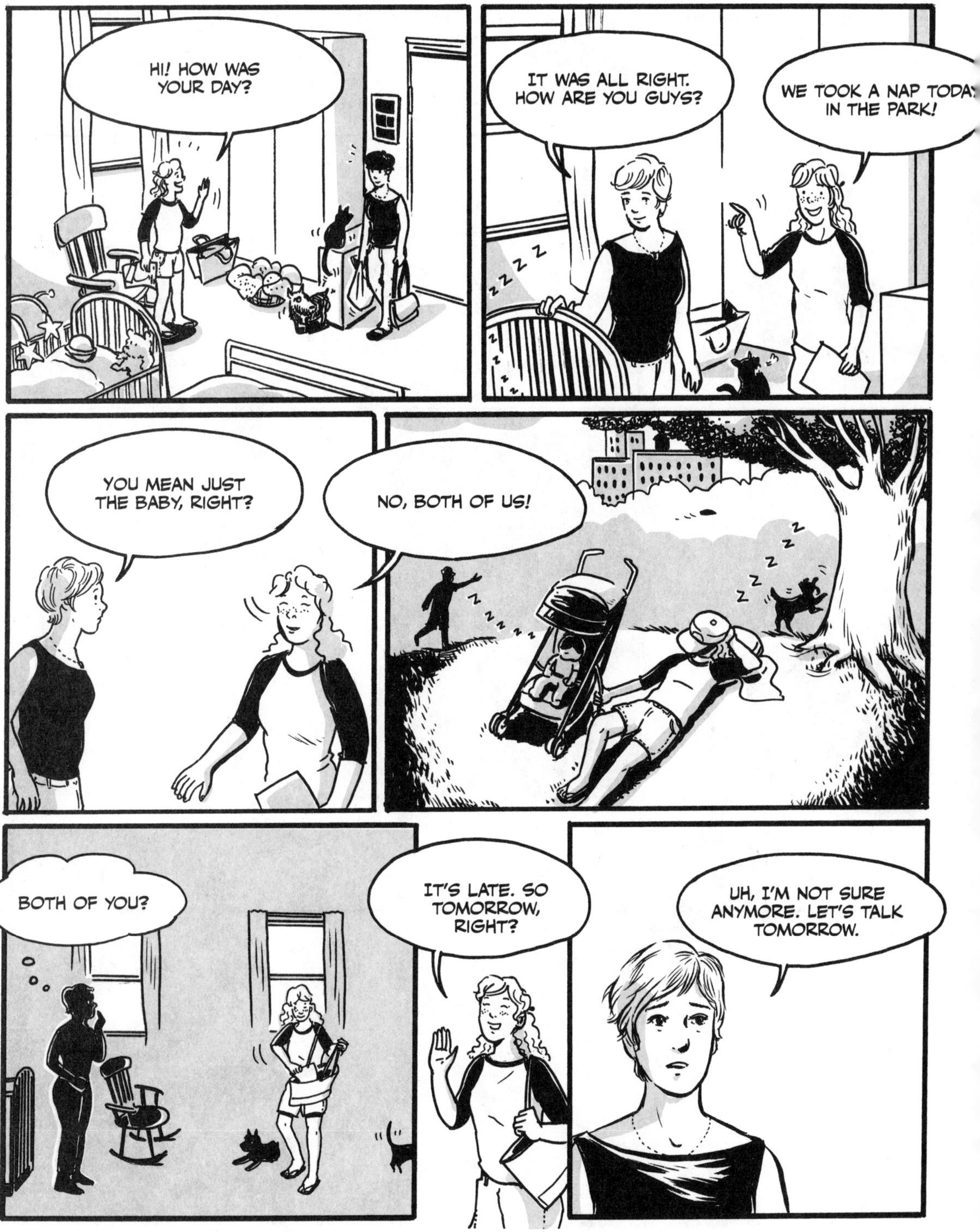
HI! HOW WAS YOUR DAY?
IT WAS ALL RIGHT. HOW ARE YOU GUYS?
WE TOOK A NAP TODAY IN THE PARK!
YOU MEAN JUST THE BABY, RIGHT?
NO, BOTH OF US!
BOTH OF YOU?
IT'S LATE. SO TOMORROW, RIGHT?
UH, I'M NOT SURE ANYMORE. LET'S TALK TOMORROW.

Chapter Sixteen

July 2002

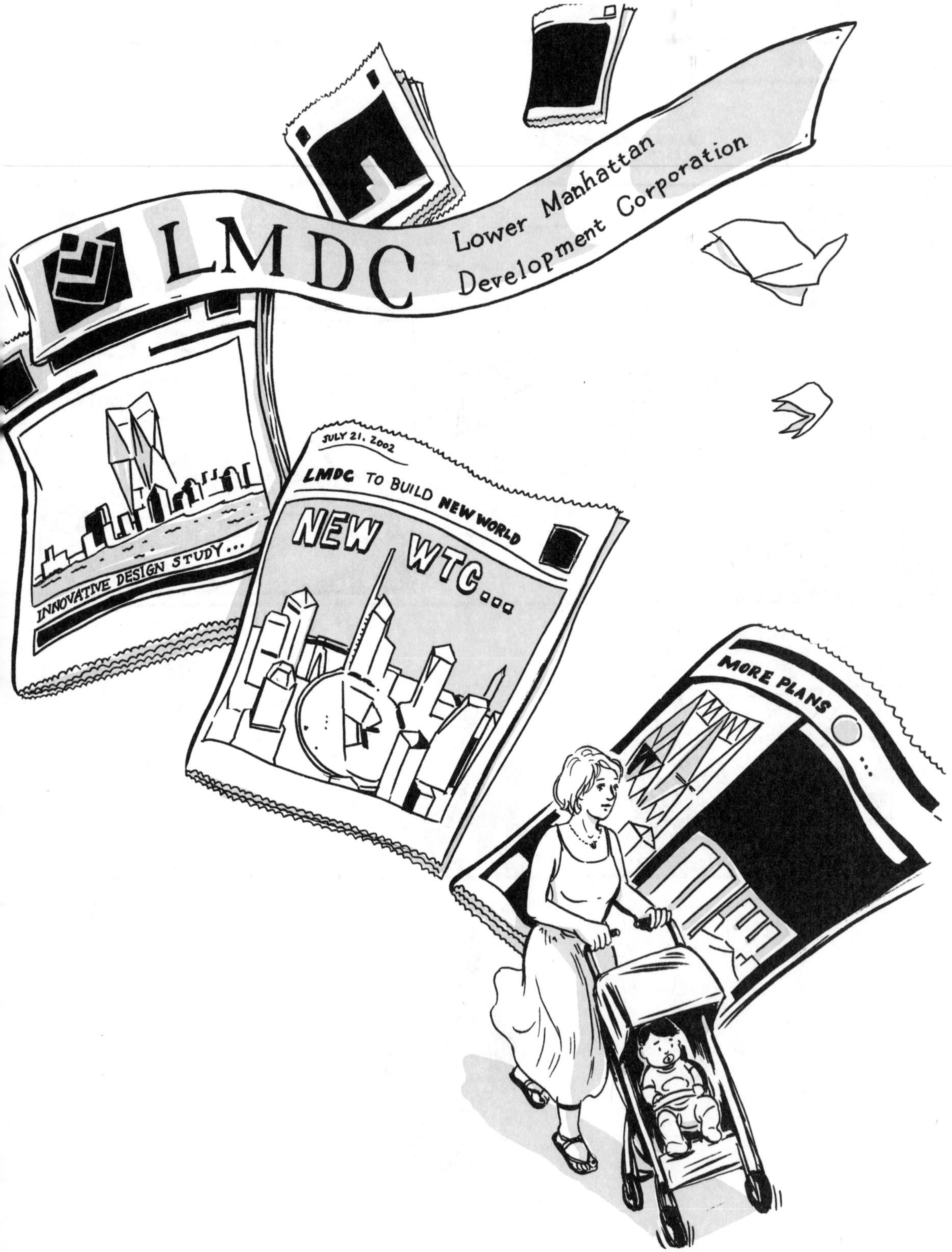
LMDC
Lower Manhattan Development Corporation
INNOVATIVE DESIGN STUDY...
JULY 21, 2002
LMDC TO BUILD NEW WORLD
NEW WTC...
MORE PLANS

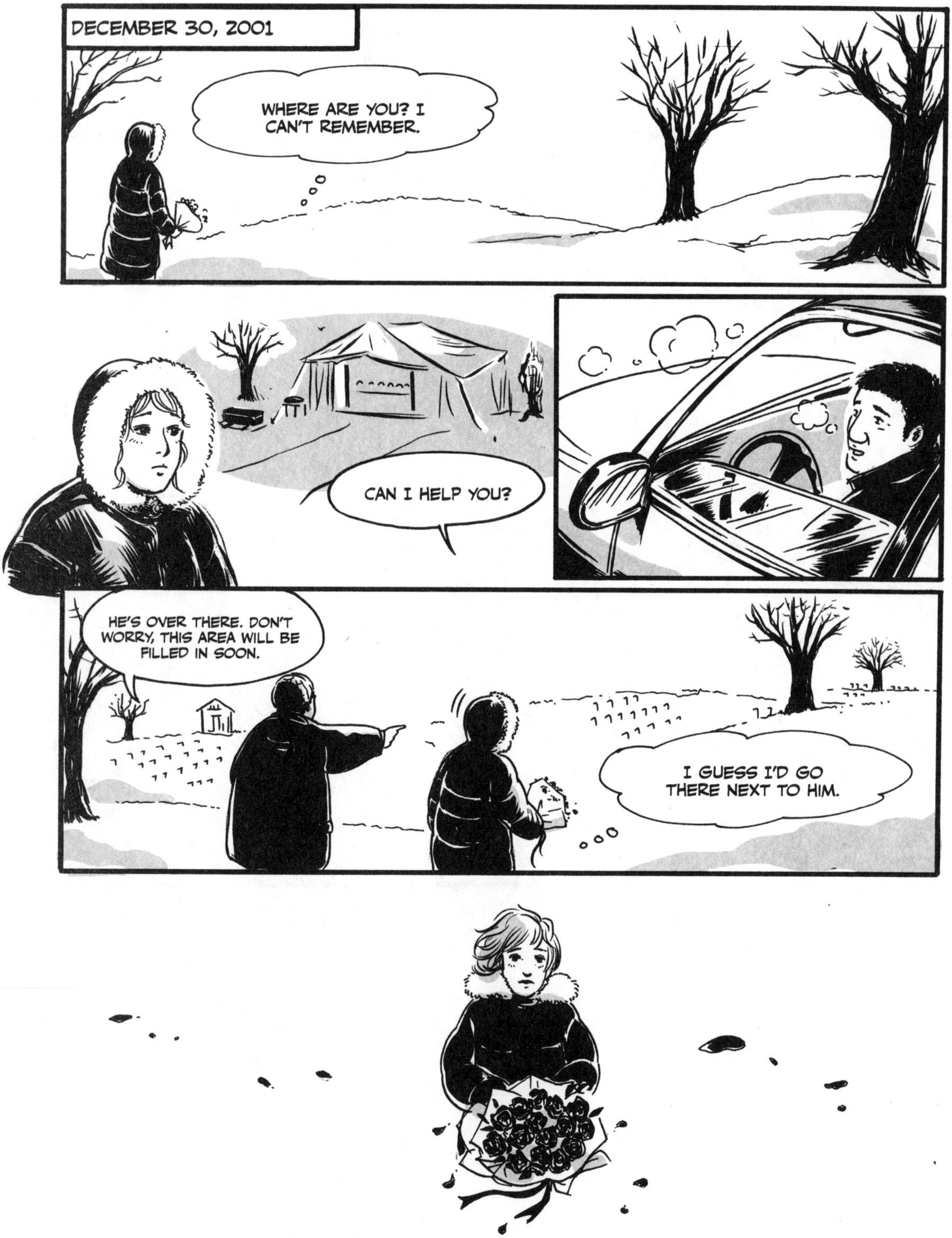
DECEMBER 30, 2001
WHERE ARE YOU? I CAN'T REMEMBER.
CAN I HELP YOU?
HE'S OVER THERE. DON'T WORRY, THIS AREA WILL BE FILLED IN SOON.
I GUESS I'D GO THERE NEXT TO HIM.

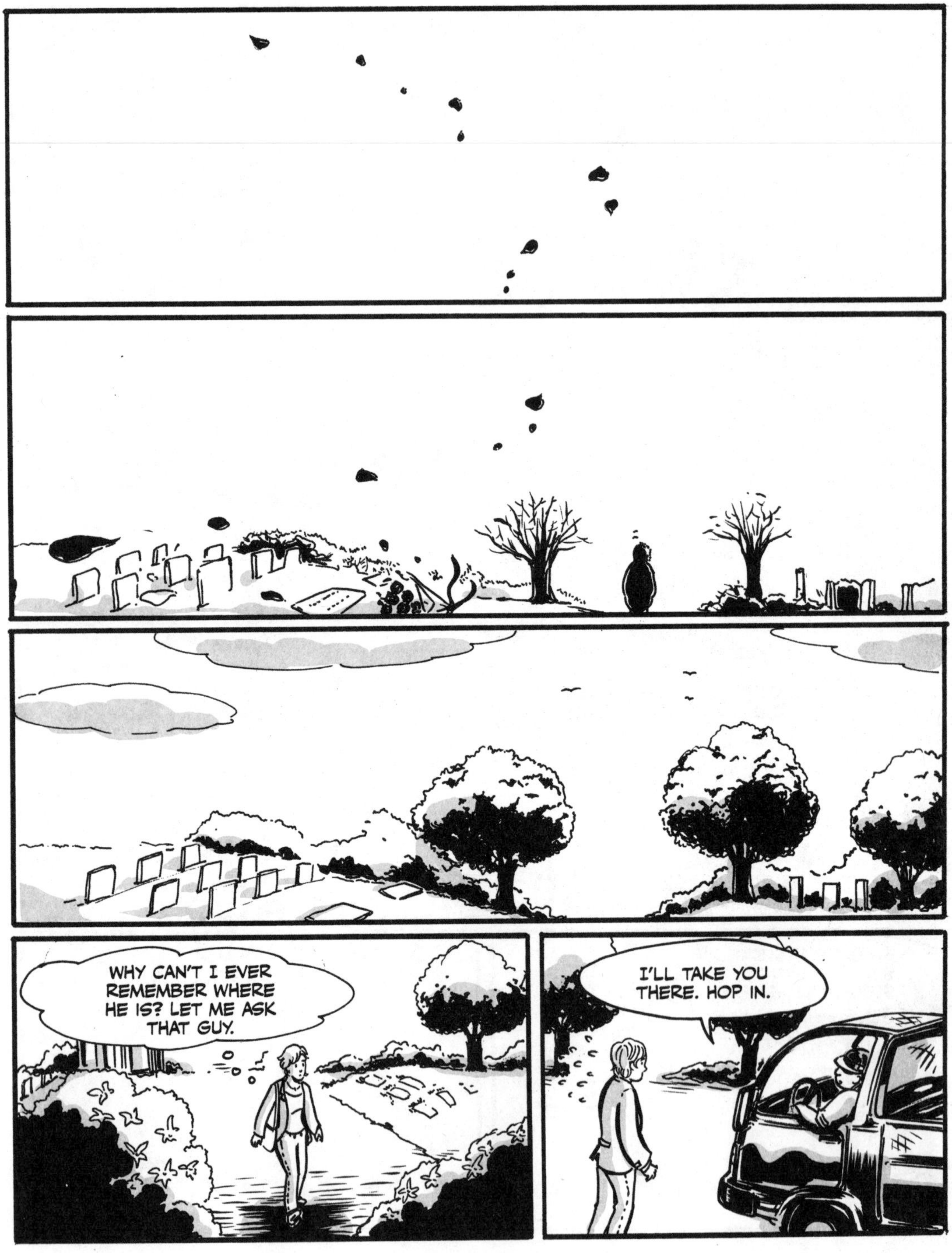
WHY CAN'T I EVER REMEMBER WHERE HE IS? LET ME ASK THAT GUY.
I'LL TAKE YOU THERE. HOP IN.

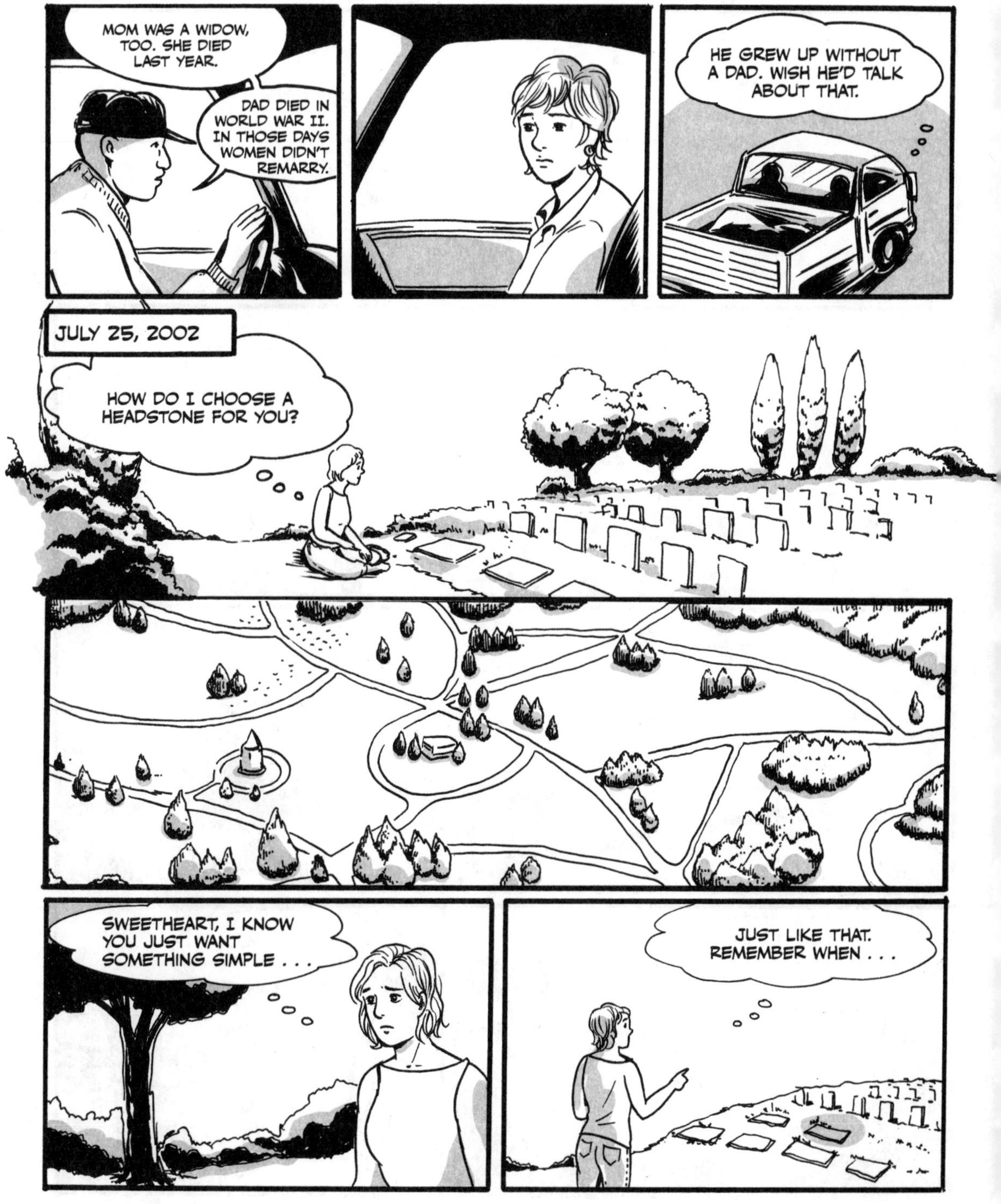
MOM WAS A WIDOW, TOO. SHE DIED LAST YEAR.
DAD DIED IN WORLD WAR II. IN THOSE DAYS WOMEN DIDN'T REMARRY.
HE GREW UP WITHOUT A DAD. WISH HE'D TALK ABOUT THAT.
JULY 25, 2002
HOW DO I CHOOSE A HEADSTONE FOR YOU?
SWEETHEART, I KNOW YOU JUST WANT SOMETHING SIMPLE . . .
JUST LIKE THAT. REMEMBER WHEN . . .

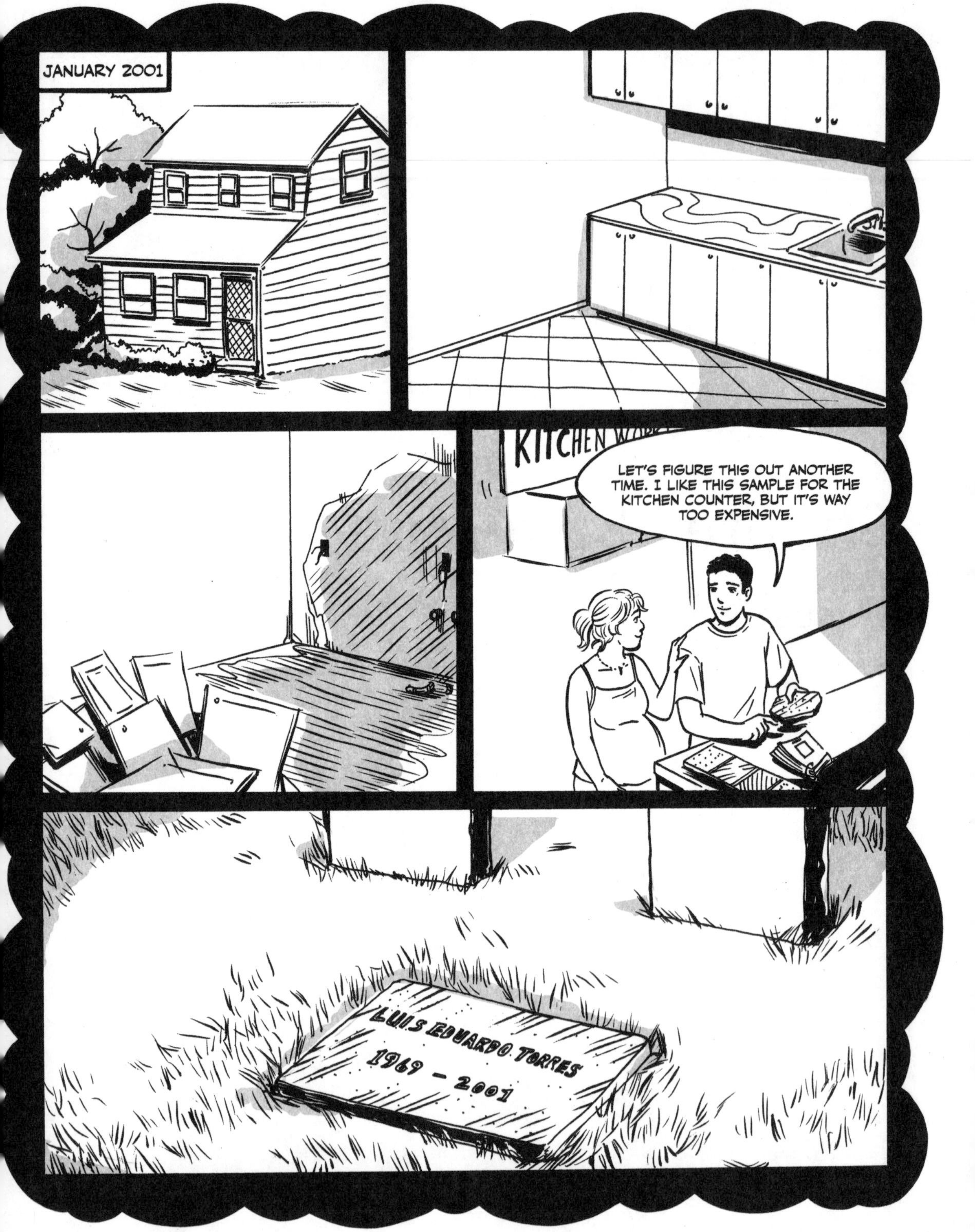

JANUARY 2001
KITCHEN
LET'S FIGURE THIS OUT ANOTHER TIME. I LIKE THIS SAMPLE FOR THE KITCHEN COUNTER, BUT IT'S WAY TOO EXPENSIVE.
LUIS EDUARDO TORRES
1969 - 2001

Chapter Seventeen

August 2002

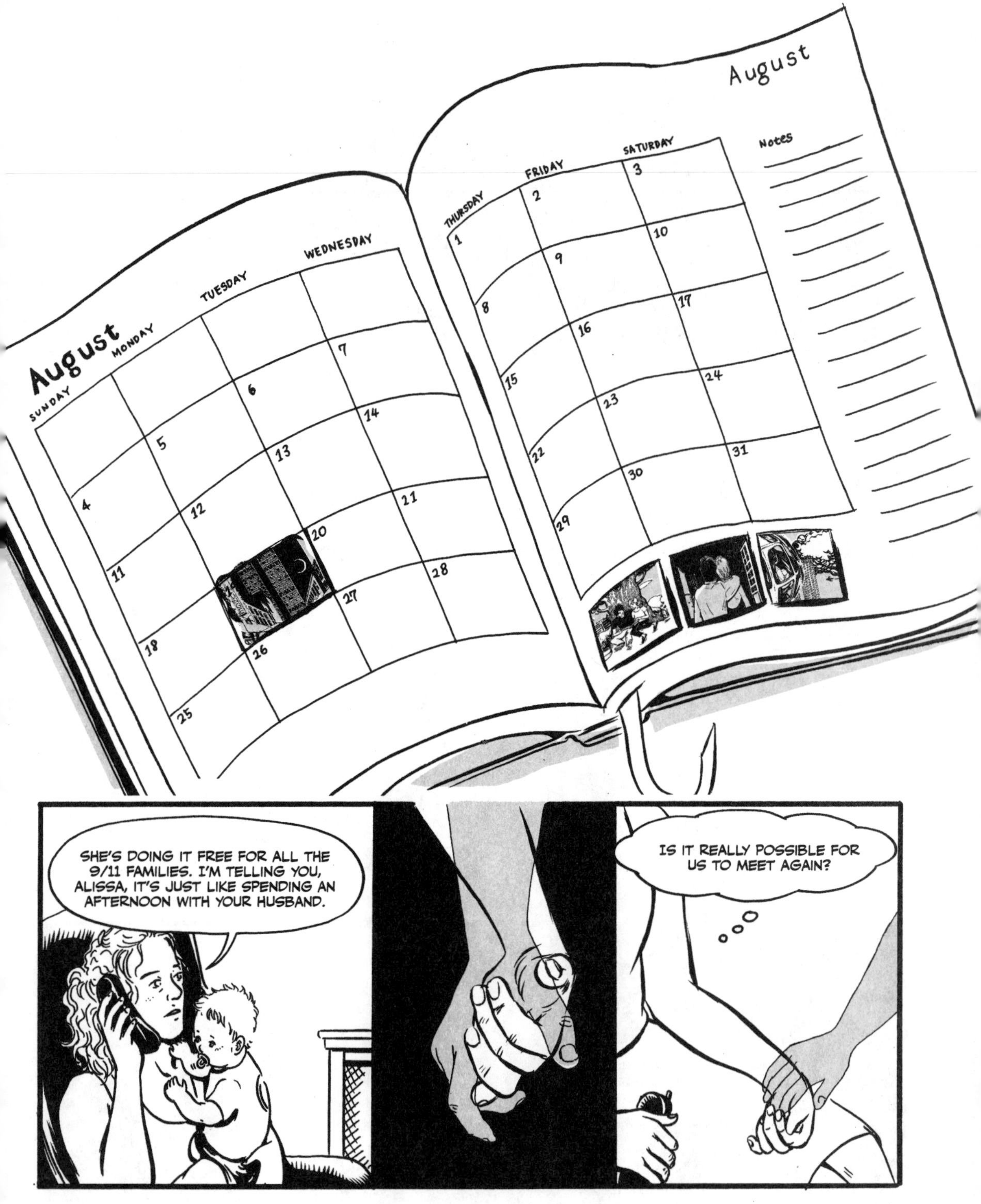
August
SUNDAY
MONDAY
TUESDAY
WEDNESDAY
THURSDAY
FRIDAY
SATURDAY
August
Notes
SHE'S DOING IT FREE FOR ALL THE 9/11 FAMILIES. I'M TELLING YOU, ALISSA, IT'S JUST LIKE SPENDING AN AFTERNOON WITH YOUR HUSBAND.
IS IT REALLY POSSIBLE FOR US TO MEET AGAIN?

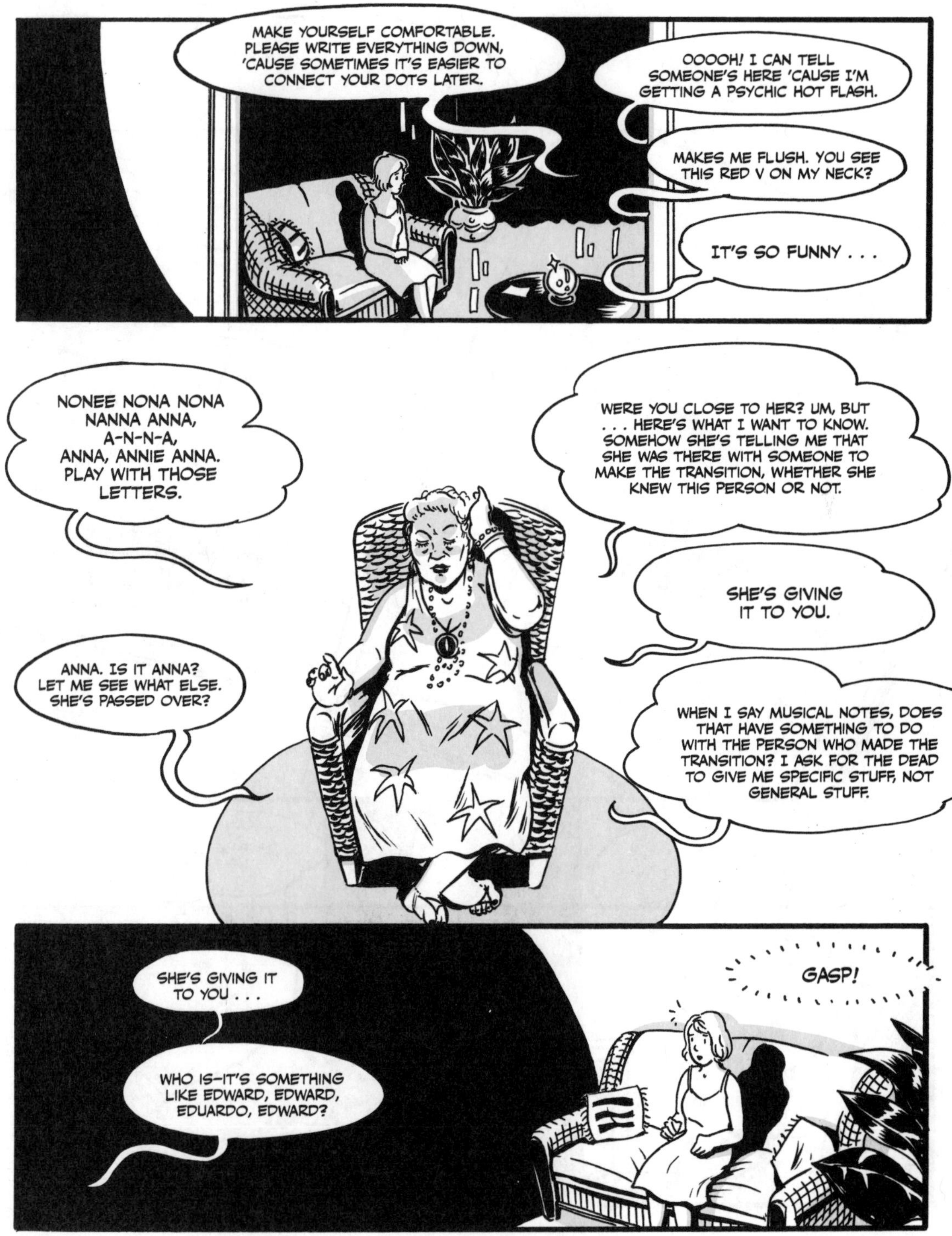
MAKE YOURSELF COMFORTABLE. PLEASE WRITE EVERYTHING DOWN, 'CAUSE SOMETIMES IT'S EASIER TO CONNECT YOUR DOTS LATER.
OOOOH! I CAN TELL SOMEONE'S HERE 'CAUSE I'M GETTING A PSYCHIC HOT FLASH.
MAKES ME FLUSH. YOU SEE THIS RED V ON MY NECK?
IT'S SO FUNNY . . .
NONEE NONA NONA NANNA ANNA, A-N-N-A, ANNA, ANNIE ANNA. PLAY WITH THOSE LETTERS.
ANNA. IS IT ANNA? LET ME SEE WHAT ELSE. SHE'S PASSED OVER?
WERE YOU CLOSE TO HER? UM, BUT . . . HERE'S WHAT I WANT TO KNOW. SOMEHOW SHE'S TELLING ME THAT SHE WAS THERE WITH SOMEONE TO MAKE THE TRANSITION, WHETHER SHE KNEW THIS PERSON OR NOT.
SHE'S GIVING IT TO YOU.
WHEN I SAY MUSICAL NOTES, DOES THAT HAVE SOMETHING TO DO WITH THE PERSON WHO MADE THE TRANSITION? I ASK FOR THE DEAD TO GIVE ME SPECIFIC STUFF, NOT GENERAL STUFF.
SHE'S GIVING IT TO YOU . . .
WHO IS-IT'S SOMETHING LIKE EDWARD, EDWARD, EDUARDO, EDWARD?
GASP!

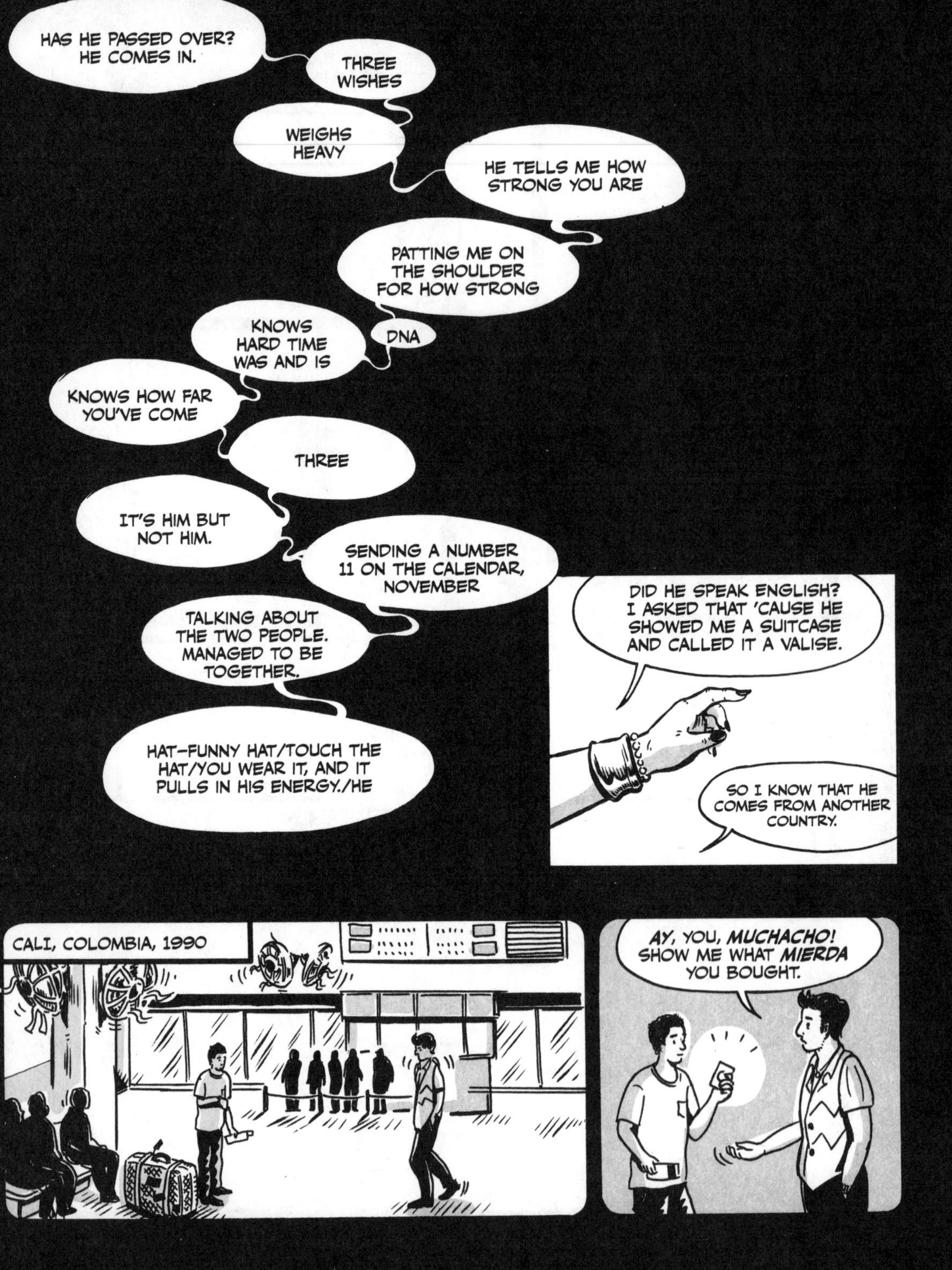
HAS HE PASSED OVER? HE COMES IN.
THREE WISHES
WEIGHS HEAVY
HE TELLS ME HOW STRONG YOU ARE
PATTING ME ON THE SHOULDER FOR HOW STRONG
KNOWS HARD TIME WAS AND IS
DNA
KNOWS HOW FAR YOU'VE COME
THREE
IT'S HIM BUT NOT HIM.
SENDING A NUMBER 11 ON THE CALENDAR, NOVEMBER
TALKING ABOUT THE TWO PEOPLE. MANAGED TO BE TOGETHER.
HAT–FUNNY HAT/TOUCH THE HAT/YOU WEAR IT, AND IT PULLS IN HIS ENERGY./HE
DID HE SPEAK ENGLISH? I ASKED THAT 'CAUSE HE SHOWED ME A SUITCASE AND CALLED IT A VALISE.
SO I KNOW THAT HE COMES FROM ANOTHER COUNTRY.
CALI, COLOMBIA, 1990
AY, YOU, *MUCHACHO*! SHOW ME WHAT *MIERDA* YOU BOUGHT.

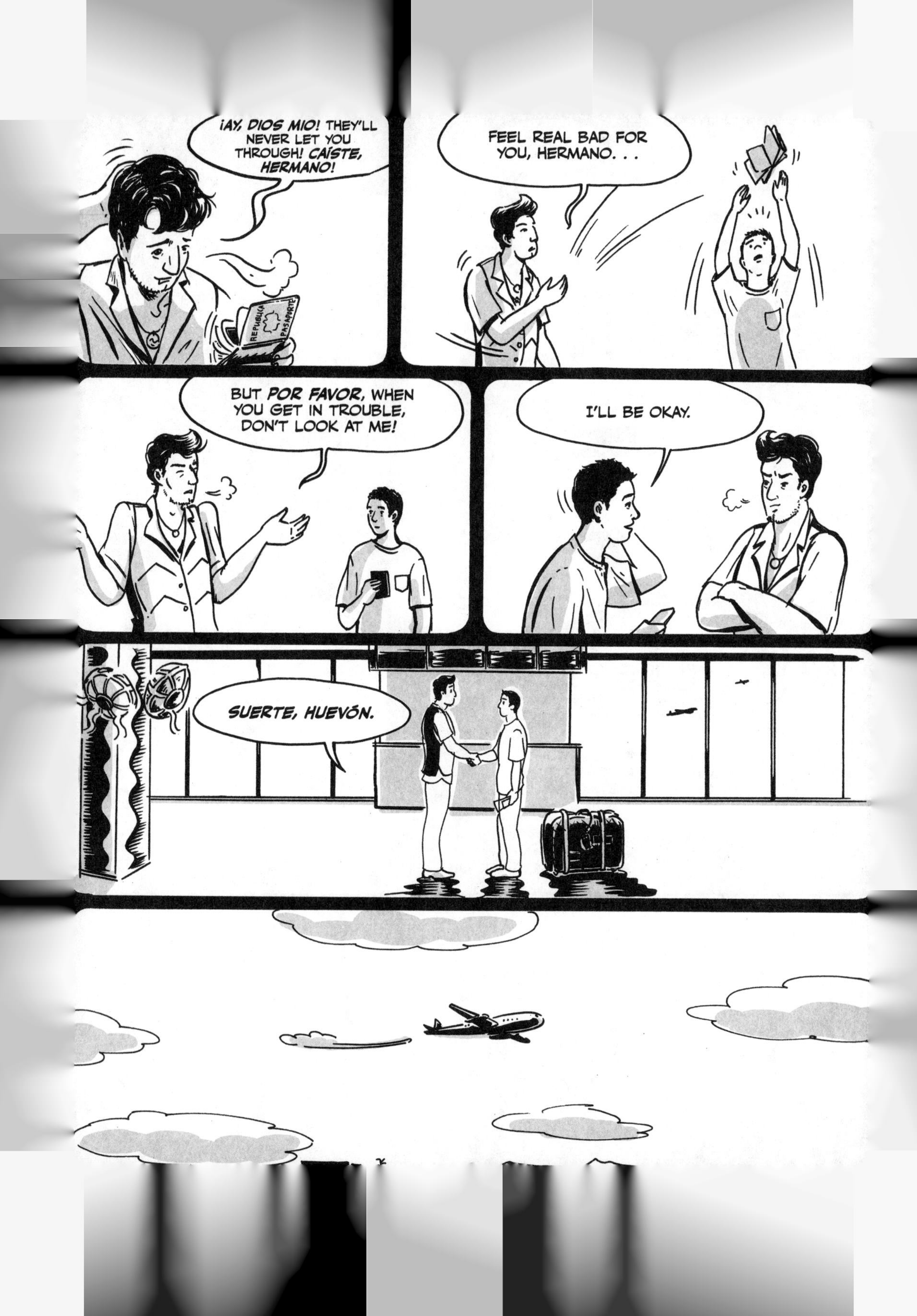

¡AY, DIOS MIO! THEY'LL NEVER LET YOU THROUGH! CAÍSTE, HERMANO!
REPUBLICA PASAPORTE
FEEL REAL BAD FOR YOU, HERMANO. . .
BUT POR FAVOR, WHEN YOU GET IN TROUBLE, DON'T LOOK AT ME!
I'LL BE OKAY.
SUERTE, HUEVÓN.

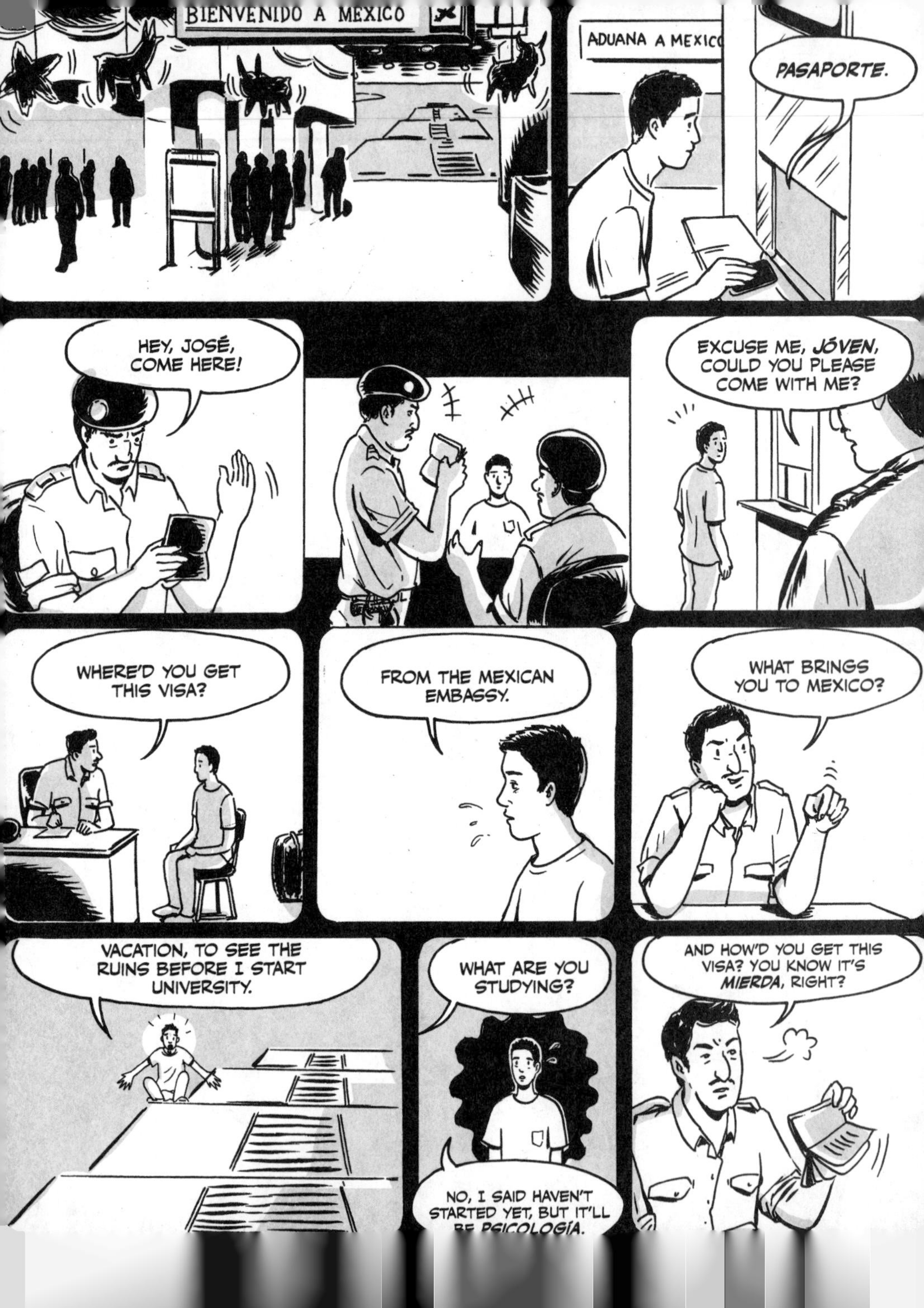
BIENVENIDO A MEXICO
ADUANA A MEXICO
PASAPORTE.
HEY, JOSÉ, COME HERE!
EXCUSE ME, JÓVEN, COULD YOU PLEASE COME WITH ME?
WHERE'D YOU GET THIS VISA?
FROM THE MEXICAN EMBASSY.
WHAT BRINGS YOU TO MEXICO?
VACATION, TO SEE THE RUINS BEFORE I START UNIVERSITY.
WHAT ARE YOU STUDYING?
NO, I SAID HAVEN'T STARTED YET, BUT IT'LL BE PSICOLOGÍA.
AND HOW'D YOU GET THIS VISA? YOU KNOW IT'S MIERDA, RIGHT?

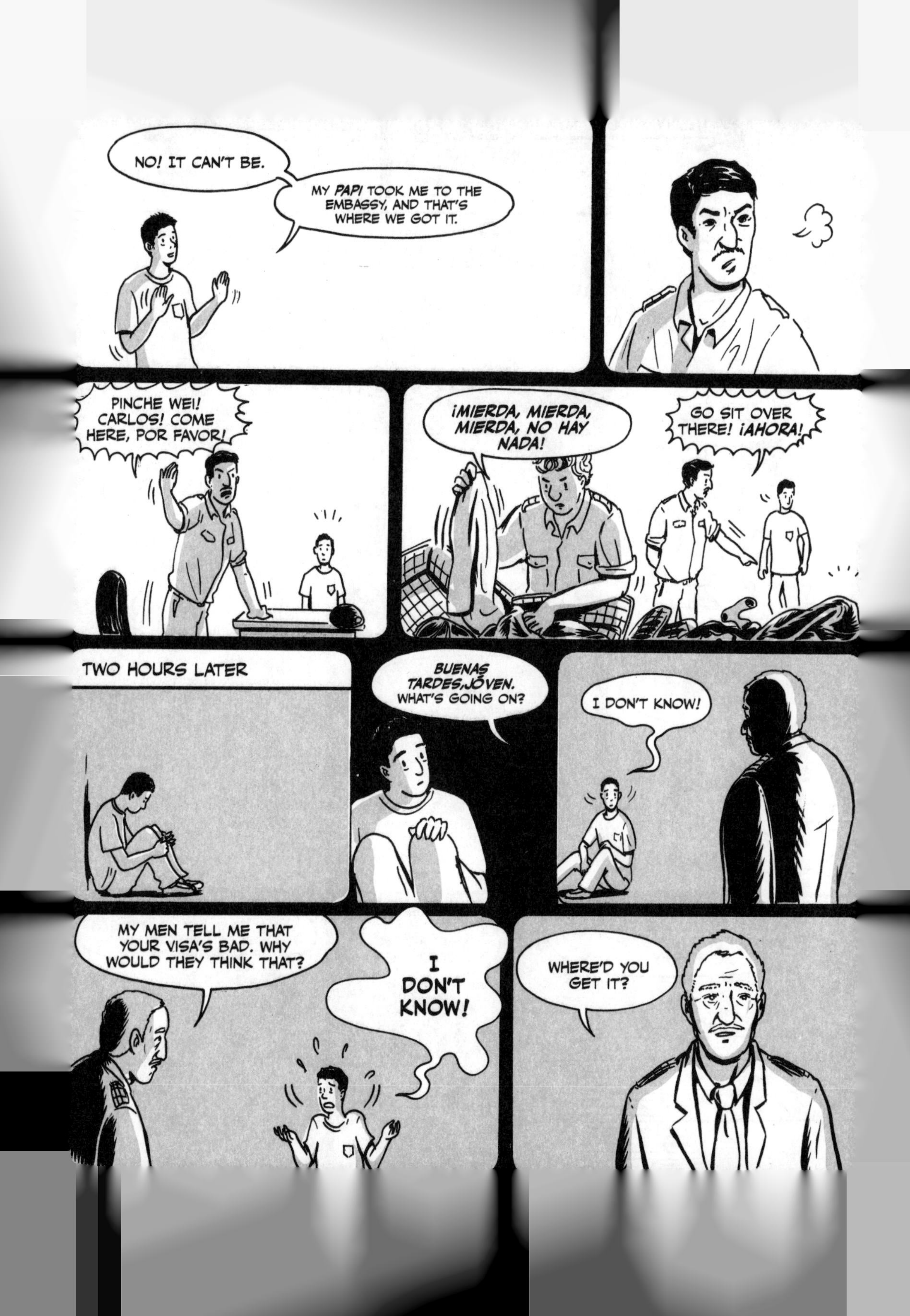
NO! IT CAN'T BE.
MY *PAPI* TOOK ME TO THE EMBASSY, AND THAT'S WHERE WE GOT IT.
PINCHE WEI! CARLOS! COME HERE, POR FAVOR!
¡MIERDA, MIERDA, MIERDA, NO HAY NADA!
GO SIT OVER THERE! ¡AHORA!
TWO HOURS LATER
BUENAS TARDES,JÓVEN. WHAT'S GOING ON?
I DON'T KNOW!
MY MEN TELL ME THAT YOUR VISA'S BAD. WHY WOULD THEY THINK THAT?
I DON'T KNOW!
WHERE'D YOU GET IT?

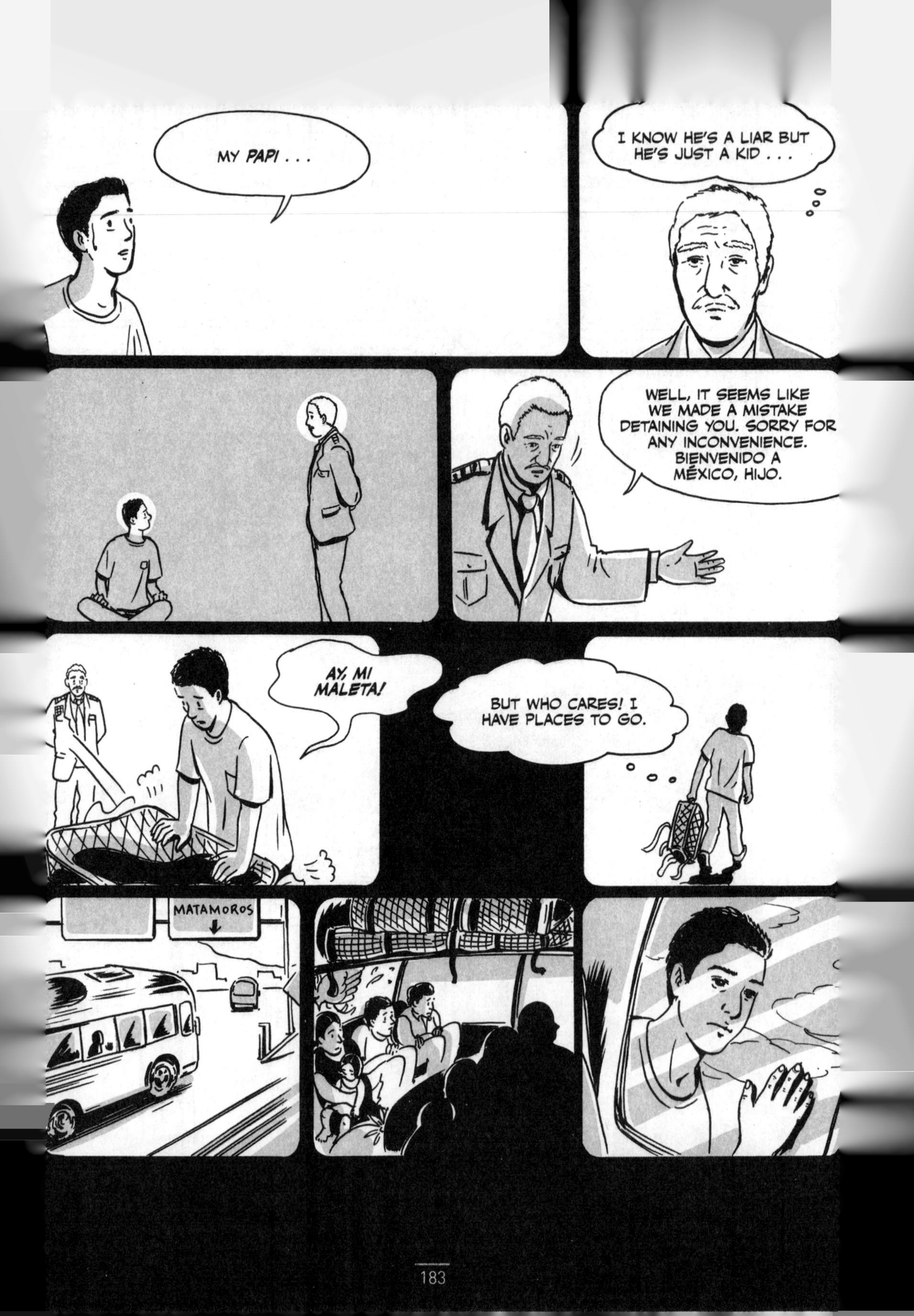

MY *PAPI* . . .
I KNOW HE'S A LIAR BUT HE'S JUST A KID . . .
WELL, IT SEEMS LIKE WE MADE A MISTAKE DETAINING YOU. SORRY FOR ANY INCONVENIENCE. BIENVENIDO A MÉXICO, HIJO.
AY, MI MALETA!
BUT WHO CARES! I HAVE PLACES TO GO.
MATAMOROS

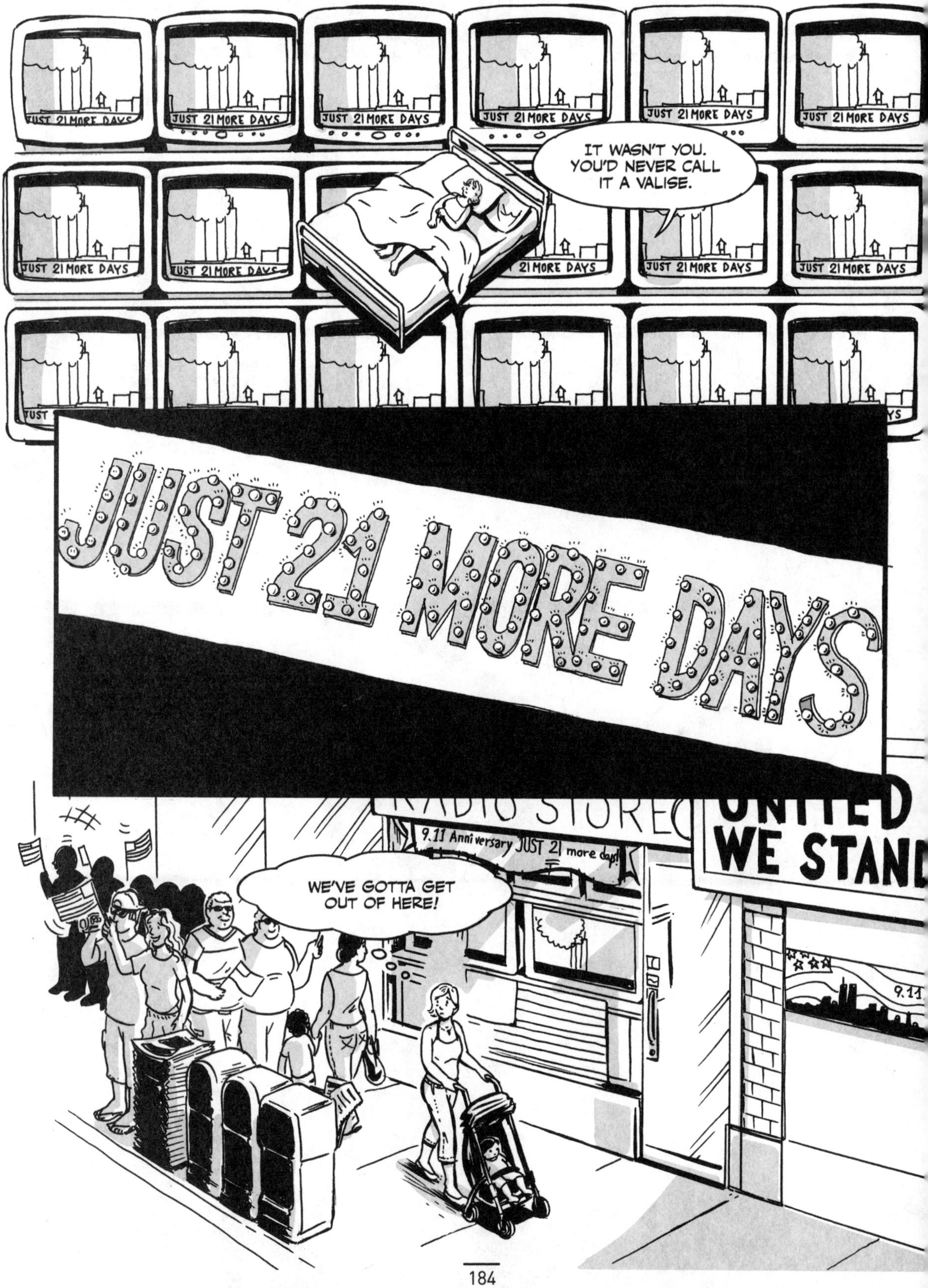
JUST 21 MORE DAYS
IT WASN'T YOU. YOU'D NEVER CALL IT A VALISE.
JUST 21 MORE DAYS
9.11 Anniversary JUST 21 more days!
WE STAND
WE'VE GOTTA GET OUT OF HERE!

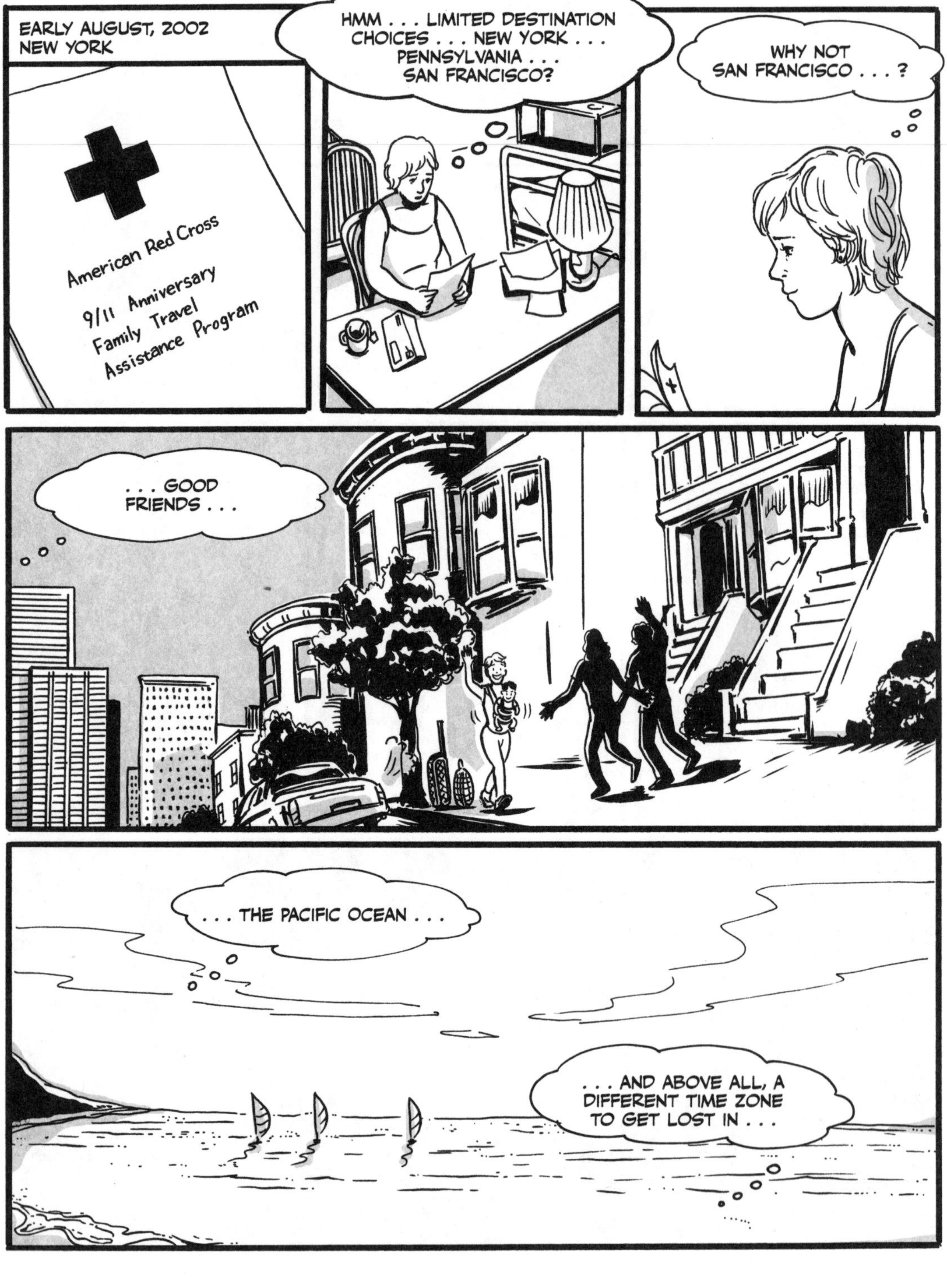
EARLY AUGUST, 2002
NEW YORK
American Red Cross
9/11 Anniversary
Family Travel
Assistance Program
HMM . . . LIMITED DESTINATION CHOICES . . . NEW YORK . . . PENNSYLVANIA . . . SAN FRANCISCO?
WHY NOT SAN FRANCISCO . . . ?
. . . GOOD FRIENDS . . .
. . . THE PACIFIC OCEAN . . .
. . . AND ABOVE ALL, A DIFFERENT TIME ZONE TO GET LOST IN . . .

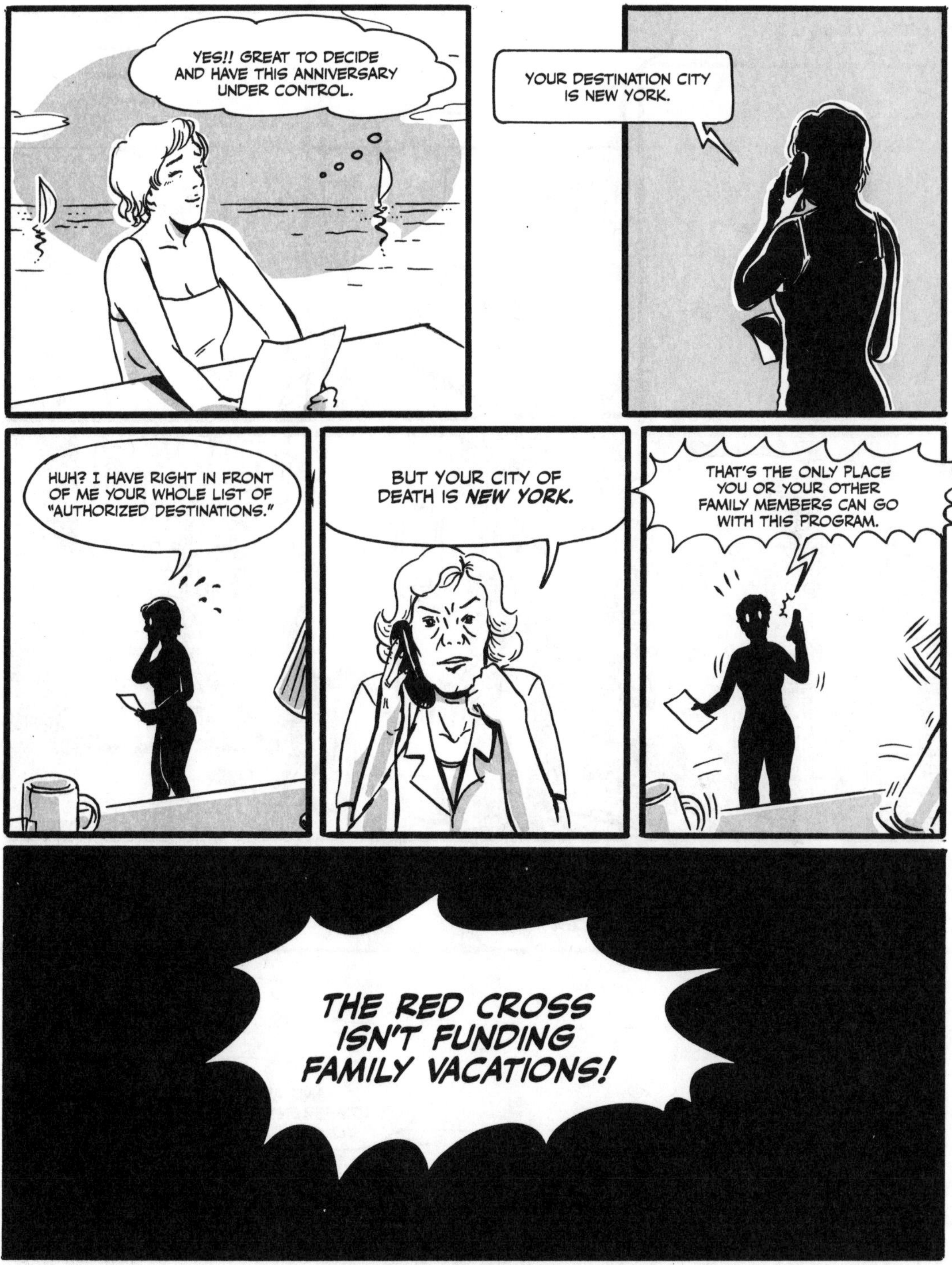
YES!! GREAT TO DECIDE AND HAVE THIS ANNIVERSARY UNDER CONTROL.
YOUR DESTINATION CITY IS NEW YORK.
HUH? I HAVE RIGHT IN FRONT OF ME YOUR WHOLE LIST OF "AUTHORIZED DESTINATIONS."
BUT YOUR CITY OF DEATH IS *NEW YORK.*
THAT'S THE ONLY PLACE YOU OR YOUR OTHER FAMILY MEMBERS CAN GO WITH THIS PROGRAM.
THE RED CROSS ISN'T FUNDING FAMILY VACATIONS!

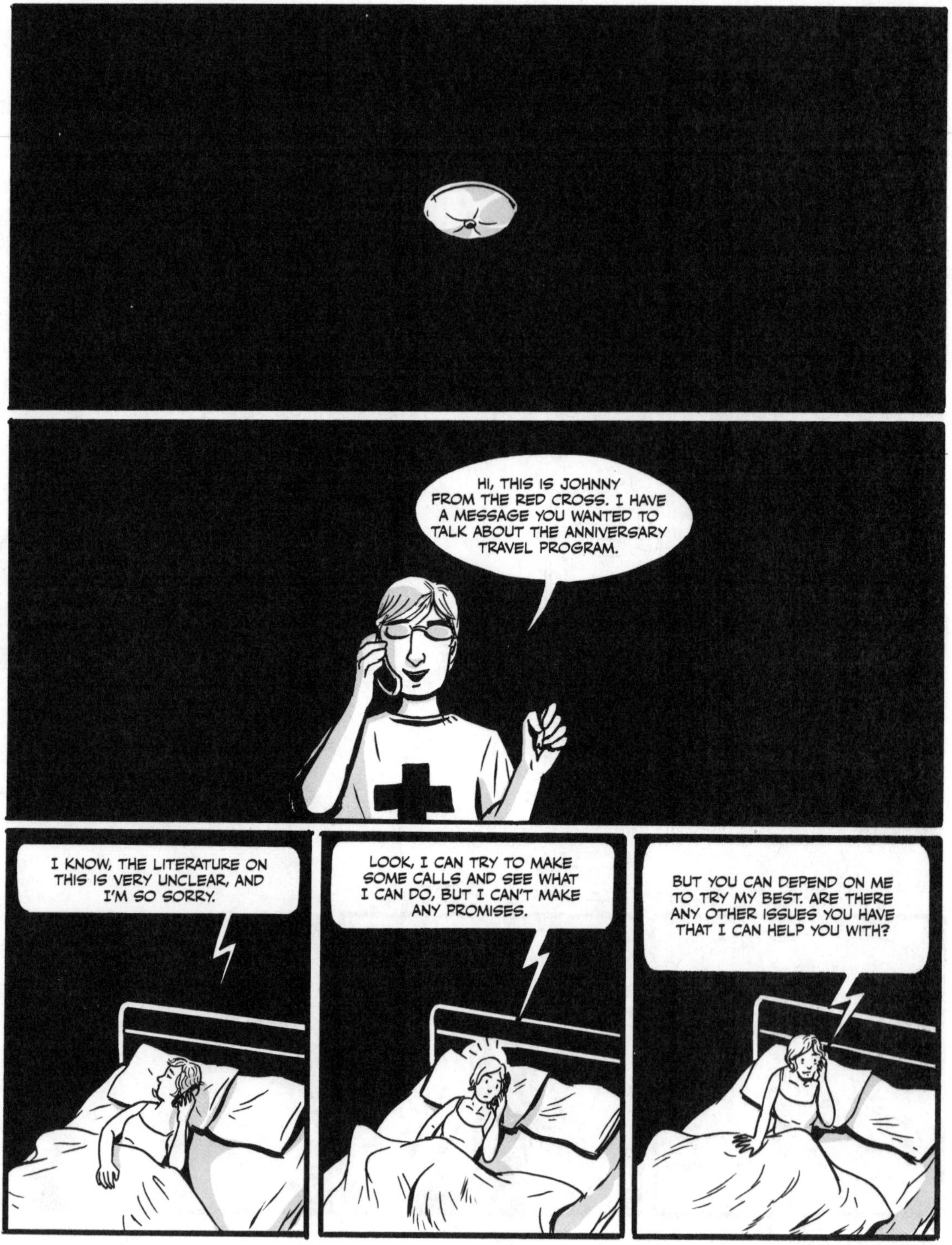
HI, THIS IS JOHNNY FROM THE RED CROSS. I HAVE A MESSAGE YOU WANTED TO TALK ABOUT THE ANNIVERSARY TRAVEL PROGRAM.
I KNOW, THE LITERATURE ON THIS IS VERY UNCLEAR, AND I'M SO SORRY.
LOOK, I CAN TRY TO MAKE SOME CALLS AND SEE WHAT I CAN DO, BUT I CAN'T MAKE ANY PROMISES.
BUT YOU CAN DEPEND ON ME TO TRY MY BEST. ARE THERE ANY OTHER ISSUES YOU HAVE THAT I CAN HELP YOU WITH?

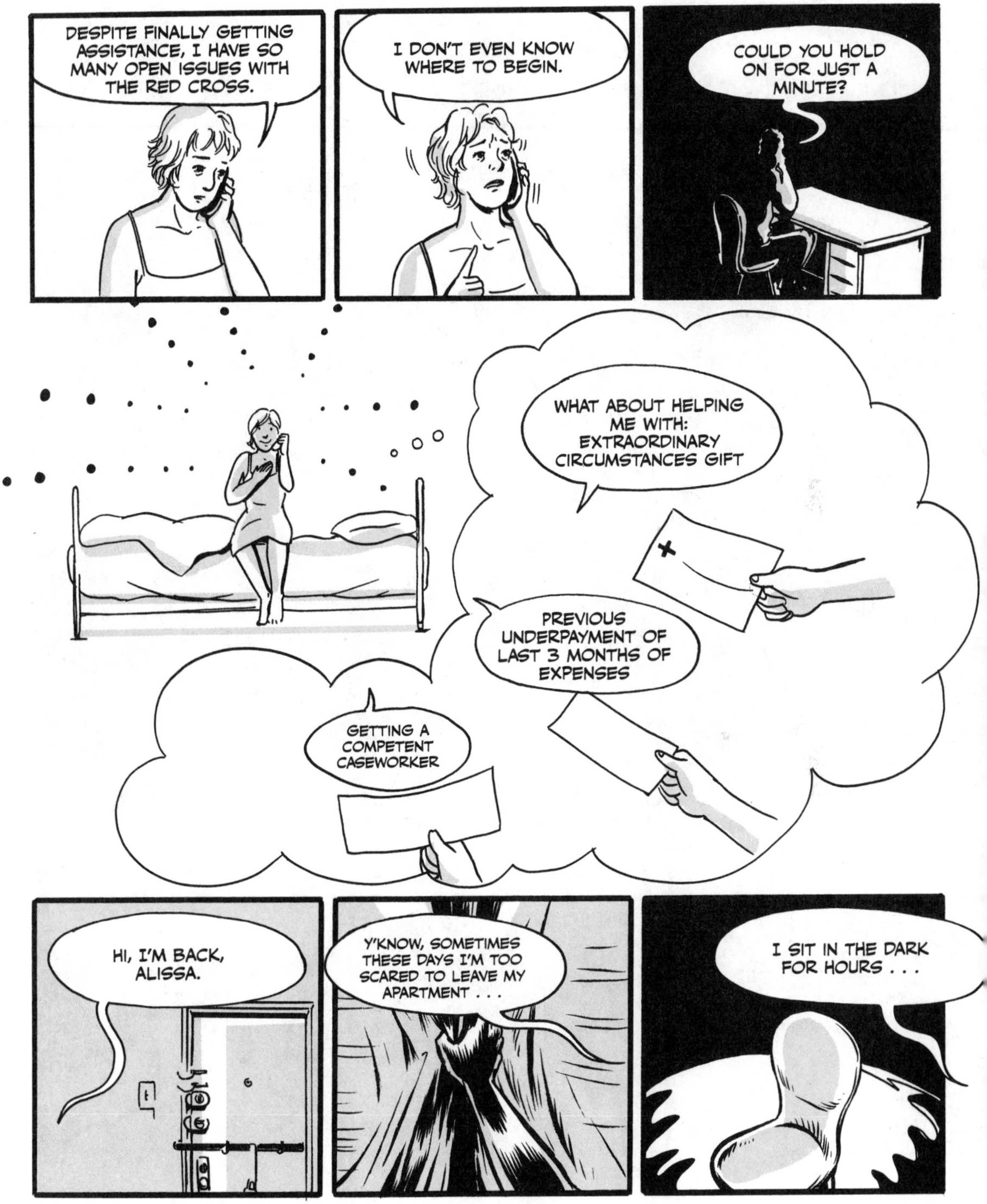
DESPITE FINALLY GETTING ASSISTANCE, I HAVE SO MANY OPEN ISSUES WITH THE RED CROSS.
I DON'T EVEN KNOW WHERE TO BEGIN.
COULD YOU HOLD ON FOR JUST A MINUTE?
WHAT ABOUT HELPING ME WITH: EXTRAORDINARY CIRCUMSTANCES GIFT
PREVIOUS UNDERPAYMENT OF LAST 3 MONTHS OF EXPENSES
GETTING A COMPETENT CASEWORKER
HI, I'M BACK, ALISSA.
Y'KNOW, SOMETIMES THESE DAYS I'M TOO SCARED TO LEAVE MY APARTMENT . . .
I SIT IN THE DARK FOR HOURS . . .

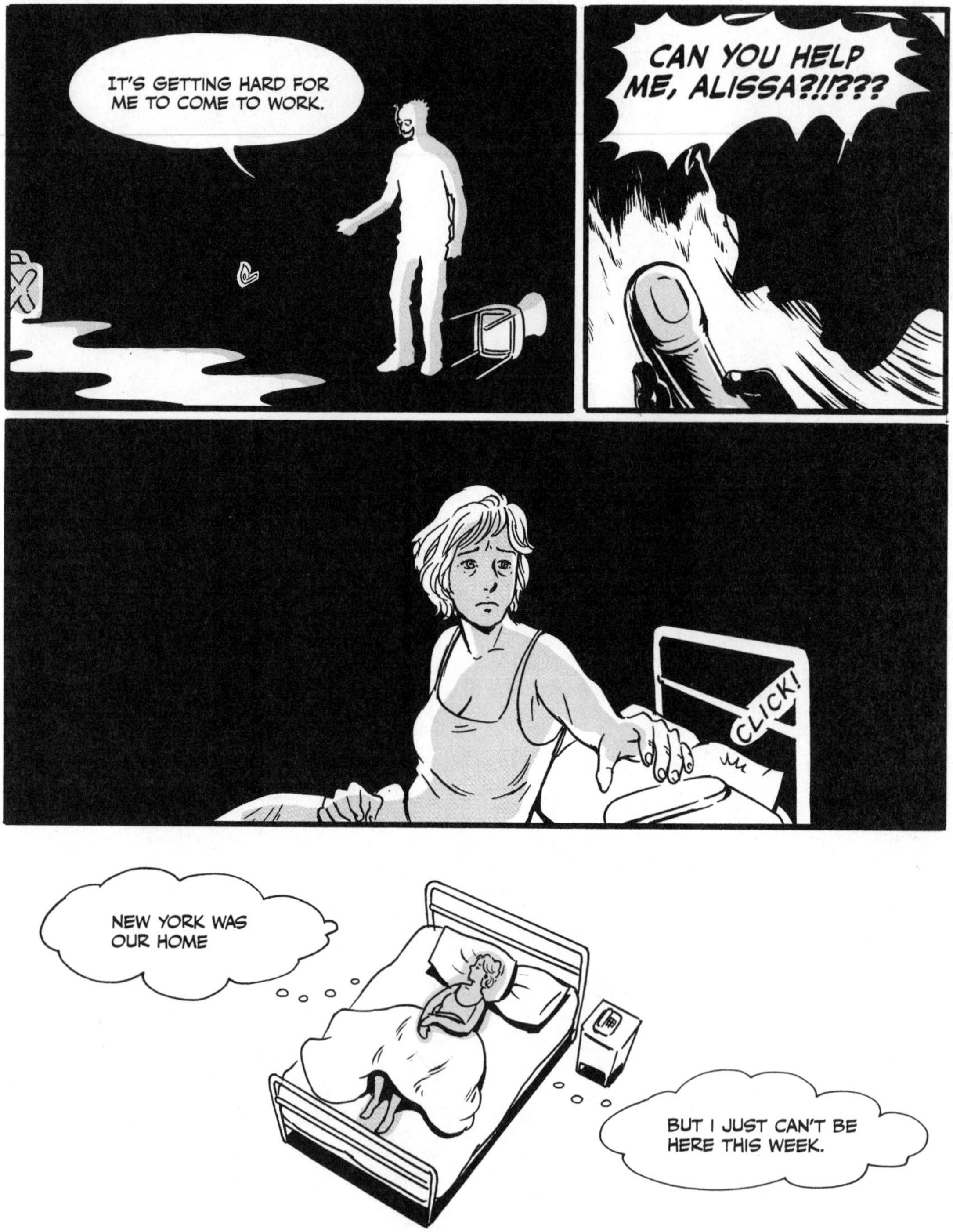
IT'S GETTING HARD FOR ME TO COME TO WORK.
CAN YOU HELP ME, ALISSA?!!???
CLICK!
NEW YORK WAS OUR HOME
BUT I JUST CAN'T BE HERE THIS WEEK.

Chapter Eighteen

SEPTEMBER 2002
THE ANNIVERSARY

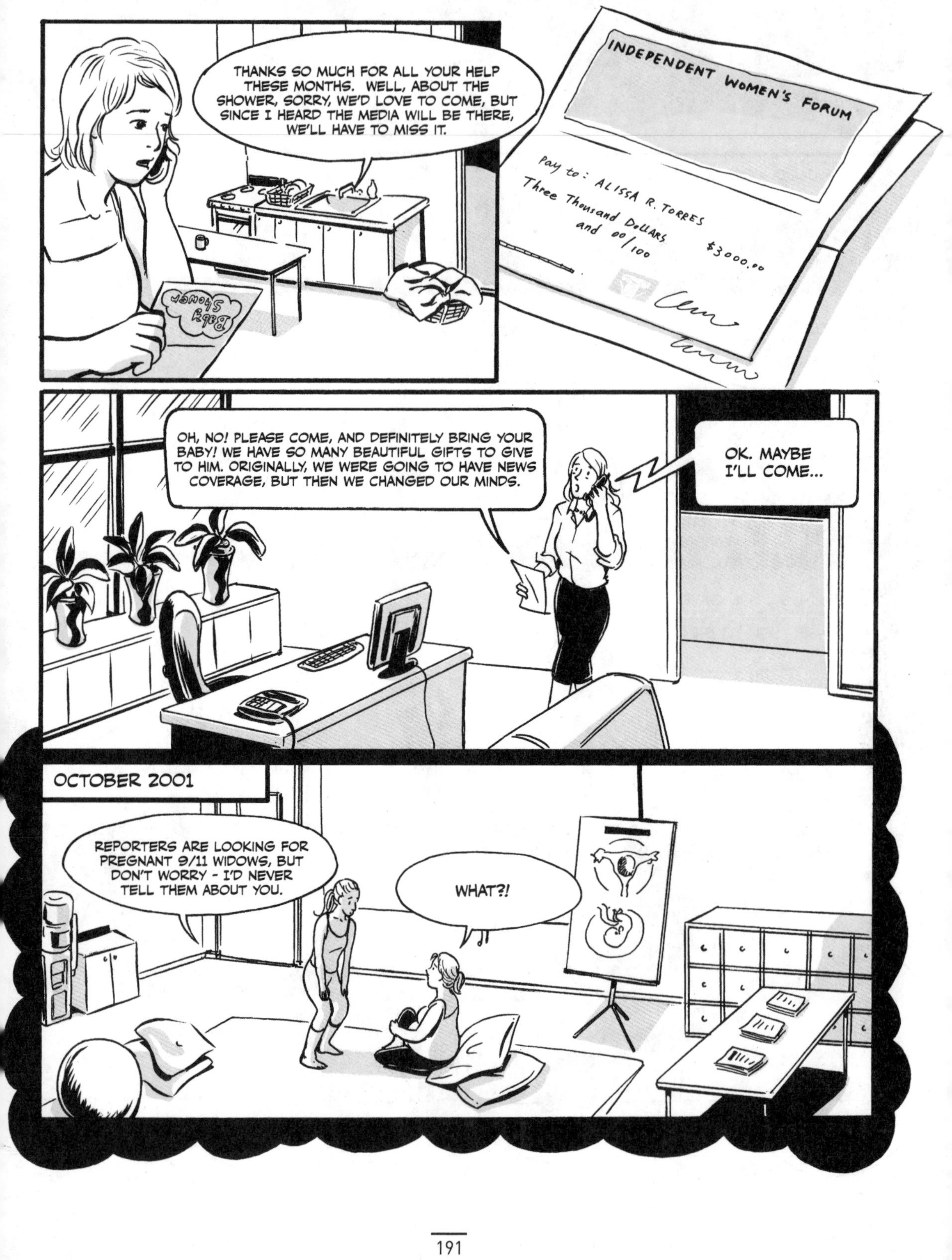
THANKS SO MUCH FOR ALL YOUR HELP THESE MONTHS. WELL, ABOUT THE SHOWER, SORRY, WE'D LOVE TO COME, BUT SINCE I HEARD THE MEDIA WILL BE THERE, WE'LL HAVE TO MISS IT.
INDEPENDENT WOMEN'S FORUM
Pay to: ALISSA R. TORRES
Three Thousand Dollars and 00/100
$3000.00
OH, NO! PLEASE COME, AND DEFINITELY BRING YOUR BABY! WE HAVE SO MANY BEAUTIFUL GIFTS TO GIVE TO HIM. ORIGINALLY, WE WERE GOING TO HAVE NEWS COVERAGE, BUT THEN WE CHANGED OUR MINDS.
OK. MAYBE I'LL COME...
OCTOBER 2001
REPORTERS ARE LOOKING FOR PREGNANT 9/11 WIDOWS, BUT DON'T WORRY - I'D NEVER TELL THEM ABOUT YOU.
WHAT?!

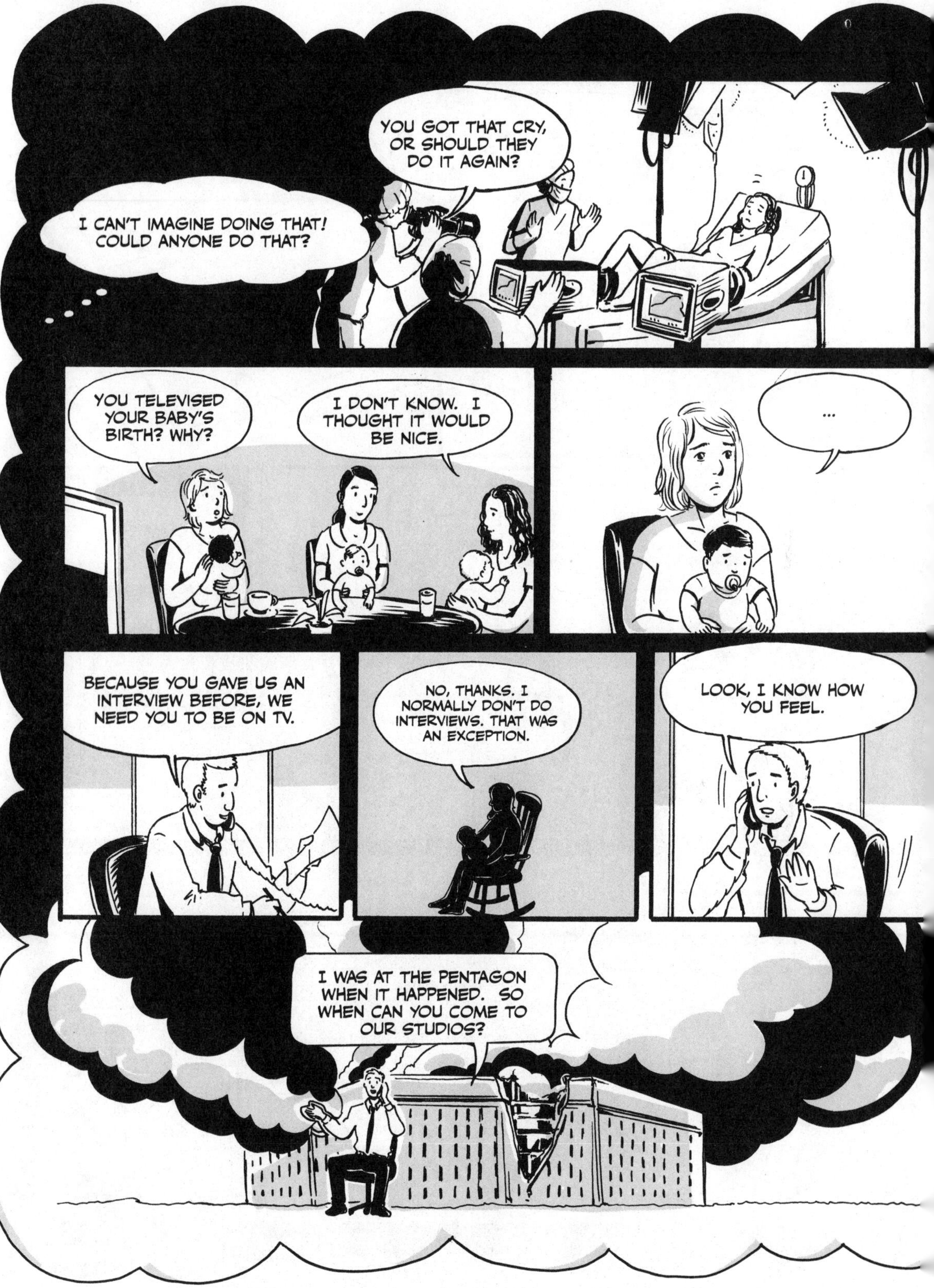
I CAN'T IMAGINE DOING THAT! COULD ANYONE DO THAT?
YOU GOT THAT CRY, OR SHOULD THEY DO IT AGAIN?
YOU TELEVISED YOUR BABY'S BIRTH? WHY?
I DON'T KNOW. I THOUGHT IT WOULD BE NICE.
...
BECAUSE YOU GAVE US AN INTERVIEW BEFORE, WE NEED YOU TO BE ON TV.
NO, THANKS. I NORMALLY DON'T DO INTERVIEWS. THAT WAS AN EXCEPTION.
LOOK, I KNOW HOW YOU FEEL.
I WAS AT THE PENTAGON WHEN IT HAPPENED. SO WHEN CAN YOU COME TO OUR STUDIOS?

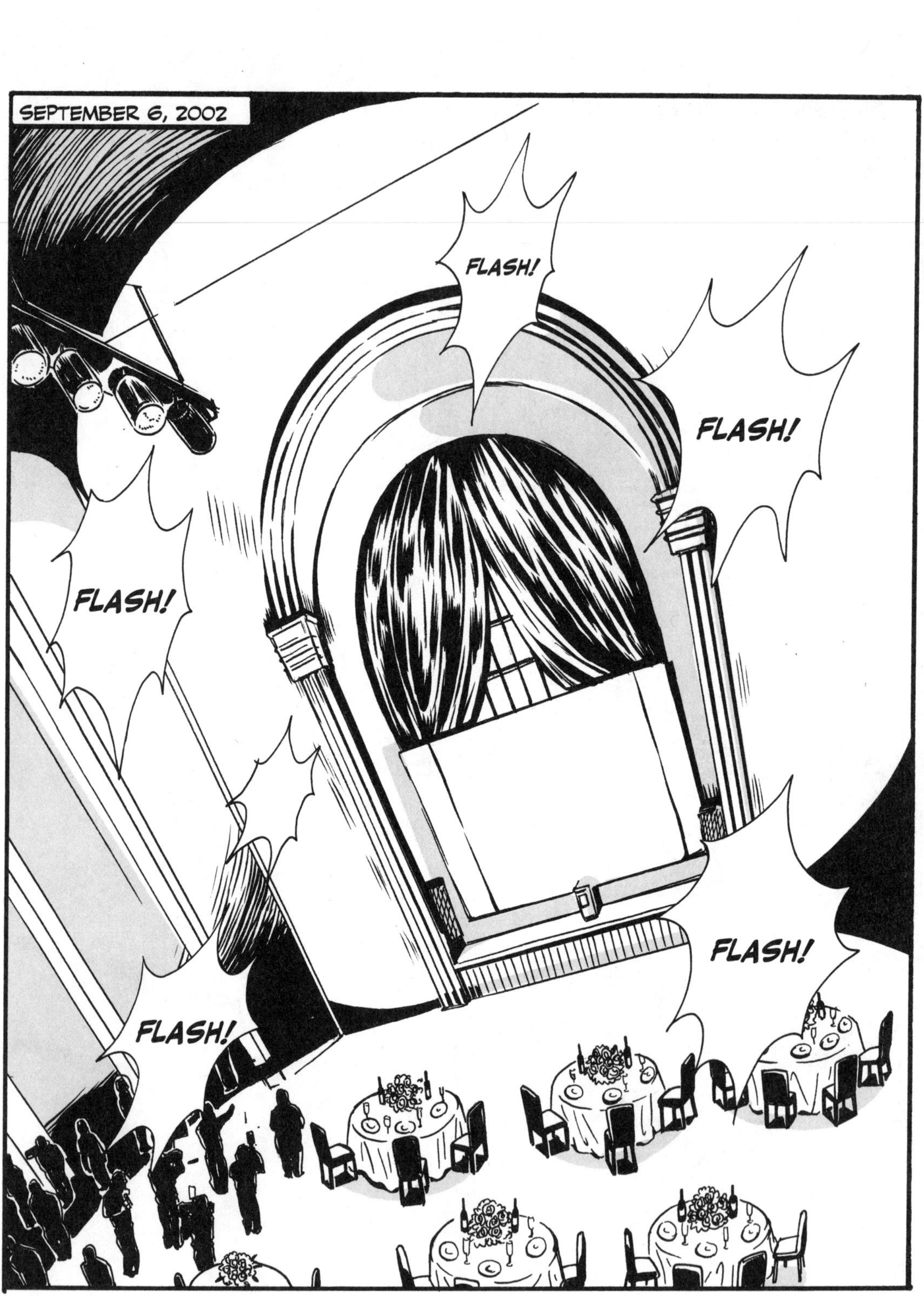
SEPTEMBER 6, 2002
FLASH!
FLASH!
FLASH!
FLASH!
FLASH!

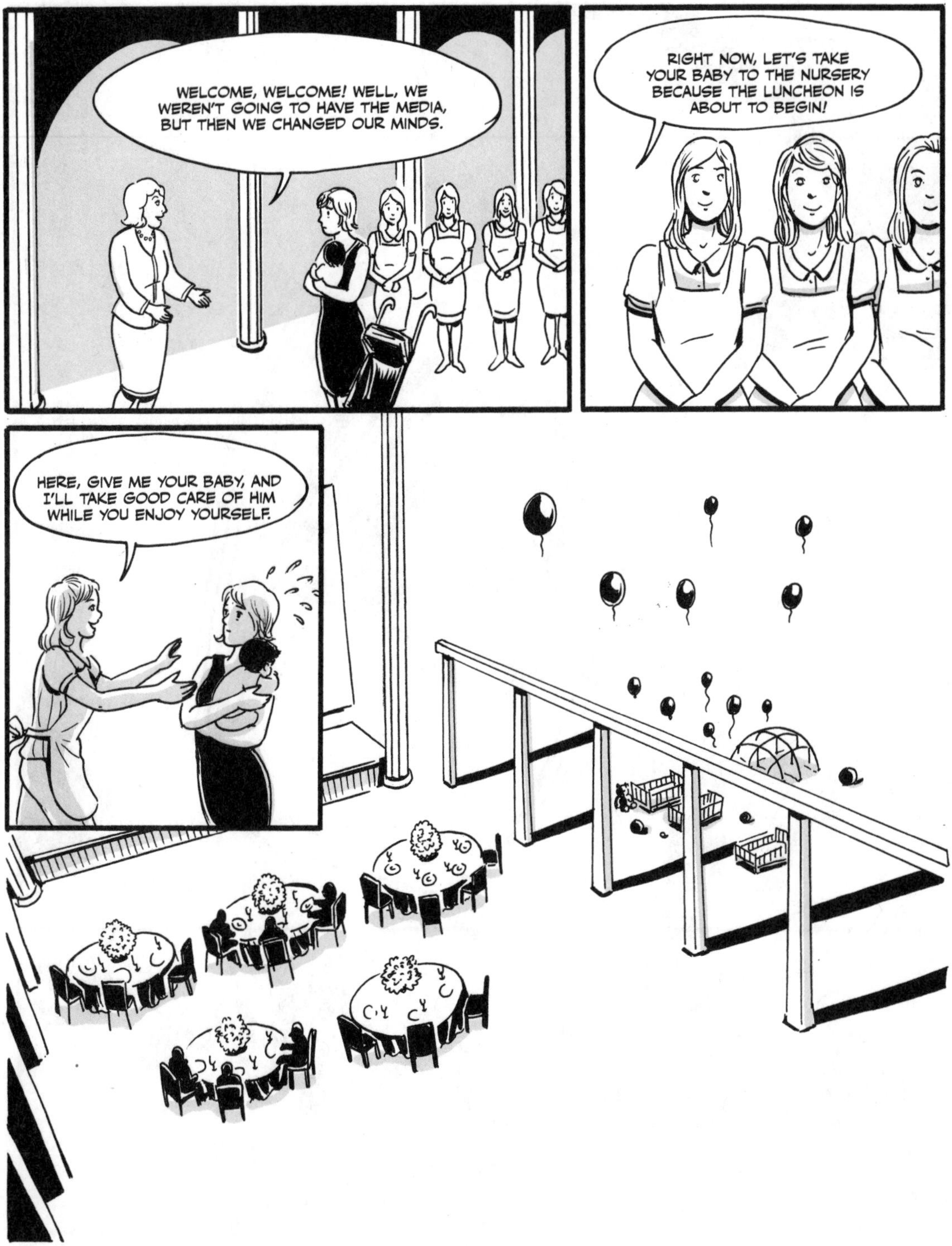
WELCOME, WELCOME! WELL, WE WEREN'T GOING TO HAVE THE MEDIA, BUT THEN WE CHANGED OUR MINDS.
RIGHT NOW, LET'S TAKE YOUR BABY TO THE NURSERY BECAUSE THE LUNCHEON IS ABOUT TO BEGIN!
HERE, GIVE ME YOUR BABY, AND I'LL TAKE GOOD CARE OF HIM WHILE YOU ENJOY YOURSELF.

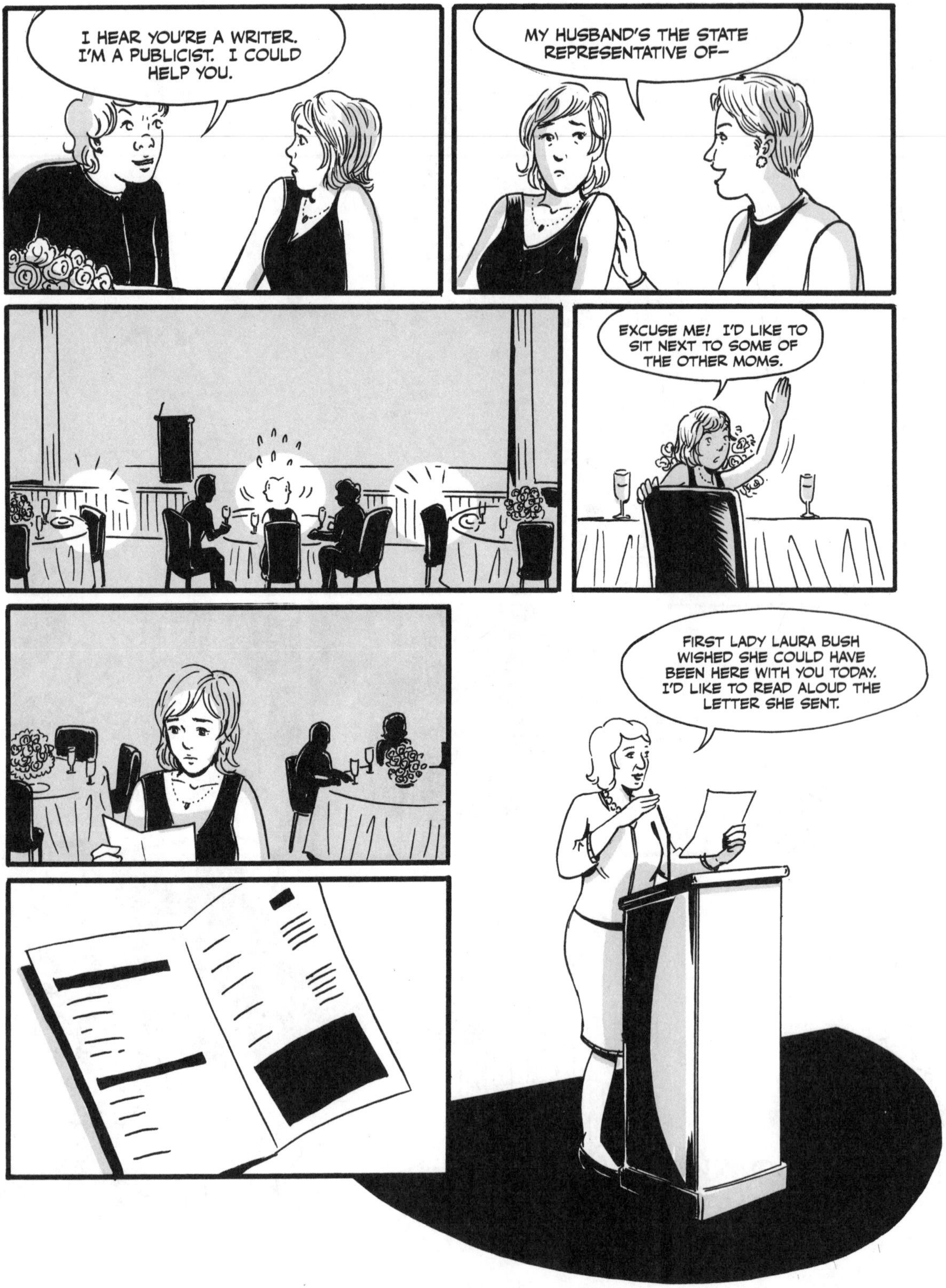
I HEAR YOU'RE A WRITER. I'M A PUBLICIST. I COULD HELP YOU.
MY HUSBAND'S THE STATE REPRESENTATIVE OF–
EXCUSE ME! I'D LIKE TO SIT NEXT TO SOME OF THE OTHER MOMS.
FIRST LADY LAURA BUSH WISHED SHE COULD HAVE BEEN HERE WITH YOU TODAY. I'D LIKE TO READ ALOUD THE LETTER SHE SENT.

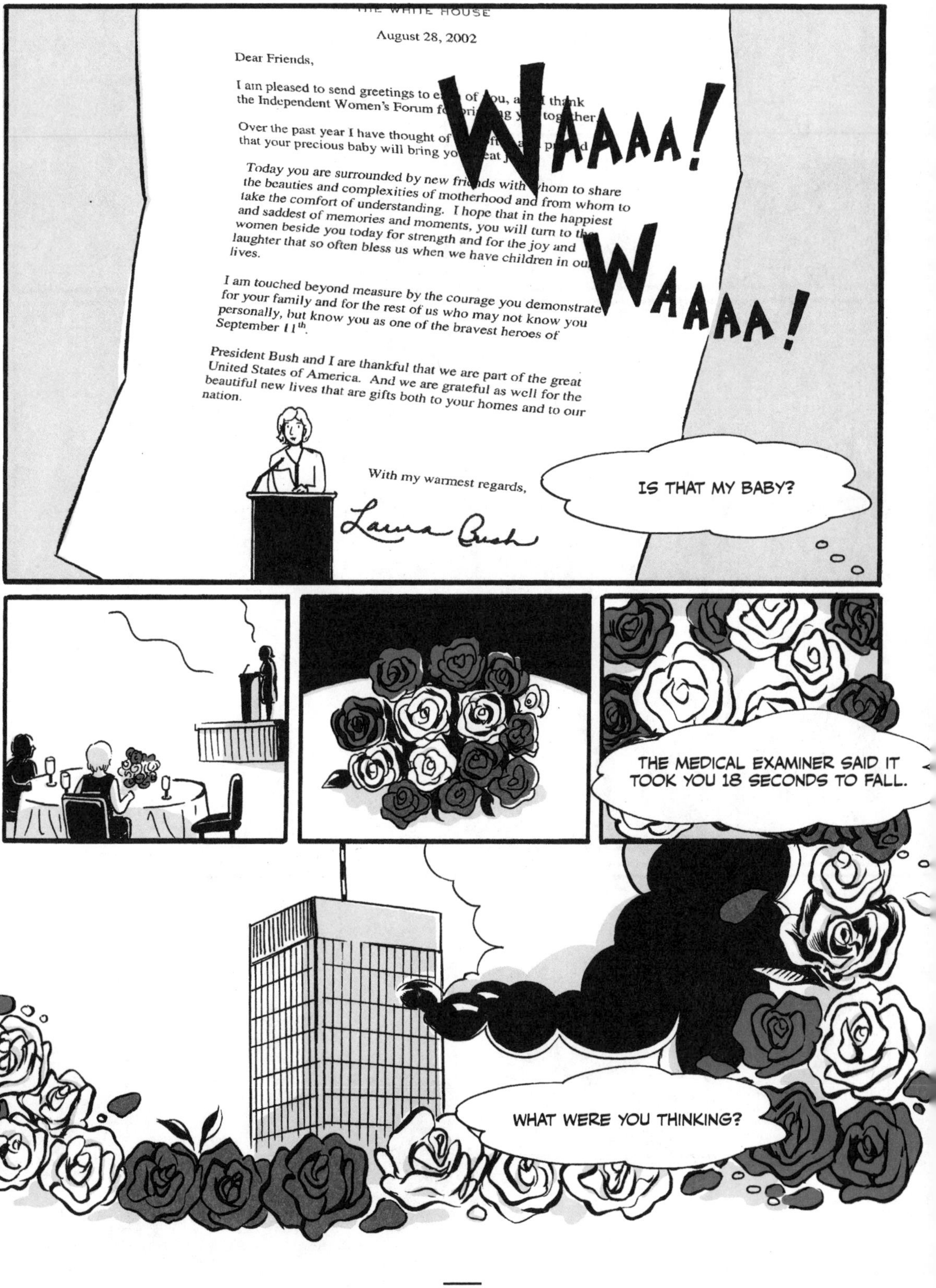
THE WHITE HOUSE
August 28, 2002
Dear Friends,
I am pleased to send greetings to e... of ...ou, a... I thank the Independent Women's Forum fo... bri...g y... tog...her.
Over the past year I have thought of ...ft... p...d that your precious baby will bring yo... ...eat j...
Today you are surrounded by new frie...nds with ...hom to share the beauties and complexities of motherhood and from whom to take the comfort of understanding. I hope that in the happiest and saddest of memories and moments, you will turn to th... women beside you today for strength and for the joy and laughter that so often bless us when we have children in ou... lives.
I am touched beyond measure by the courage you demonstrate for your family and for the rest of us who may not know you personally, but know you as one of the bravest heroes of September 11th.
President Bush and I are thankful that we are part of the great United States of America. And we are grateful as well for the beautiful new lives that are gifts both to your homes and to our nation.
With my warmest regards,
Laura Bush
WAAAA!
WAAAA!
IS THAT MY BABY?
THE MEDICAL EXAMINER SAID IT TOOK YOU 18 SECONDS TO FALL.
WHAT WERE YOU THINKING?

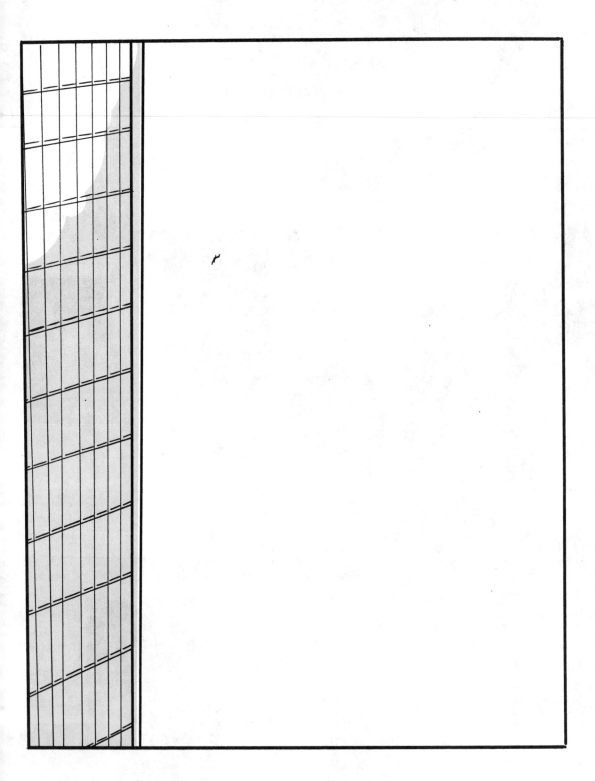

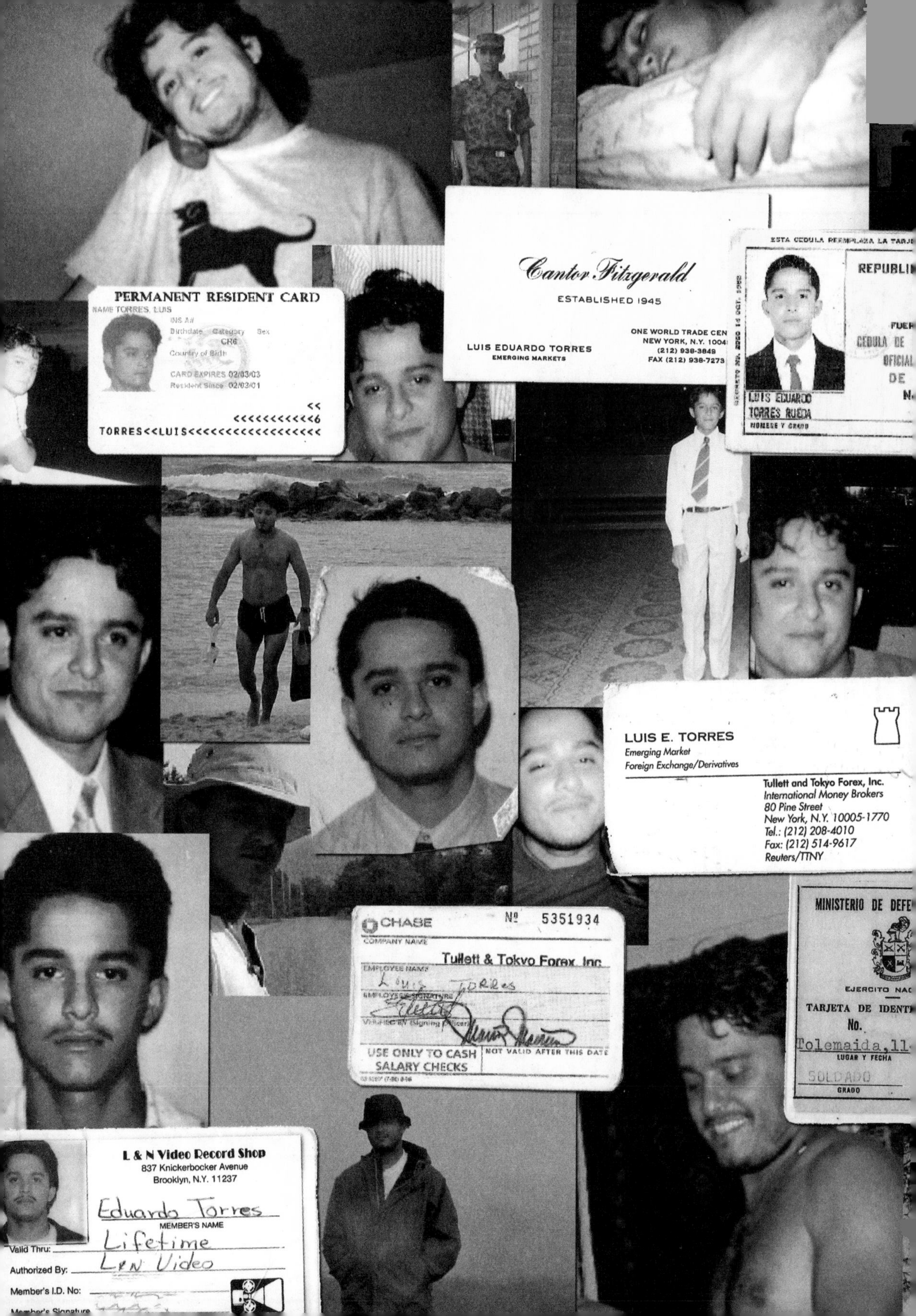
PERMANENT RESIDENT CARD
CARD EXPIRES 02/03/03
Resident Since 02/03/01
TORRES<<LUIS<<<<<<<<<<<<<<<<<<<<<
Cantor Fitzgerald
ESTABLISHED 1945
LUIS EDUARDO TORRES
EMERGING MARKETS
(212) 938-3849
FAX (212) 938-7273
REPUBLI
LUIS EDUARDO
TORRES RUEDA
LUIS E. TORRES
Emerging Market
Foreign Exchange/Derivatives
Tullett and Tokyo Forex, Inc.
International Money Brokers
80 Pine Street
New York, N.Y. 10005-1770
Tel.: (212) 208-4010
Fax: (212) 514-9617
Reuters/TTNY
CHASE
Nº 5351934
COMPANY NAME
Tullett & Tokyo Forex, Inc
EMPLOYEE NAME
USE ONLY TO CASH
SALARY CHECKS
NOT VALID AFTER THIS DATE
MINISTERIO DE DEFE
EJERCITO NAC
TARJETA DE IDENT
No.
Tolemaida,11
LUGAR Y FECHA
SOLDADO
GRADO
L & N Video Record Shop
837 Knickerbocker Avenue
Brooklyn, N.Y. 11237
Eduardo Torres
MEMBER'S NAME
Valid Thru: Lifetime
Authorized By: L&N Video
Member's I.D. No:

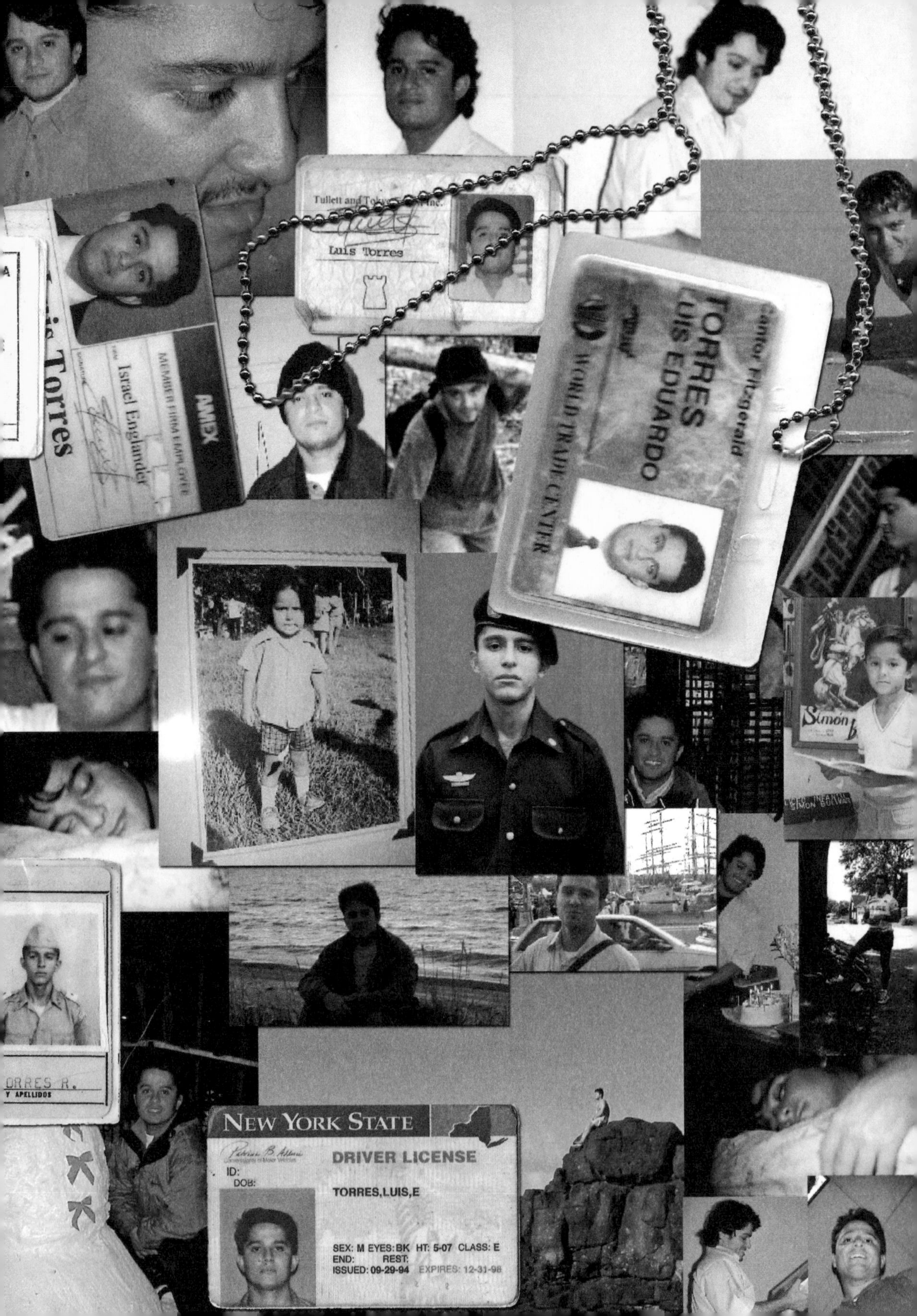
Luis Torres
Cantor Fitzgerald
TORRES
LUIS EDUARDO
WORLD TRADE CENTER
AMEX
MEMBER FIRM EMPLOYEE
Israel Englander
Torres
Y APELLIDOS
Simón
NEW YORK STATE
DRIVER LICENSE
ID:
DOB:
TORRES,LUIS,E
SEX: M EYES:BK HT: 5-07 CLASS: E
END: REST:
ISSUED: 09-29-94 EXPIRES: 12-31-98

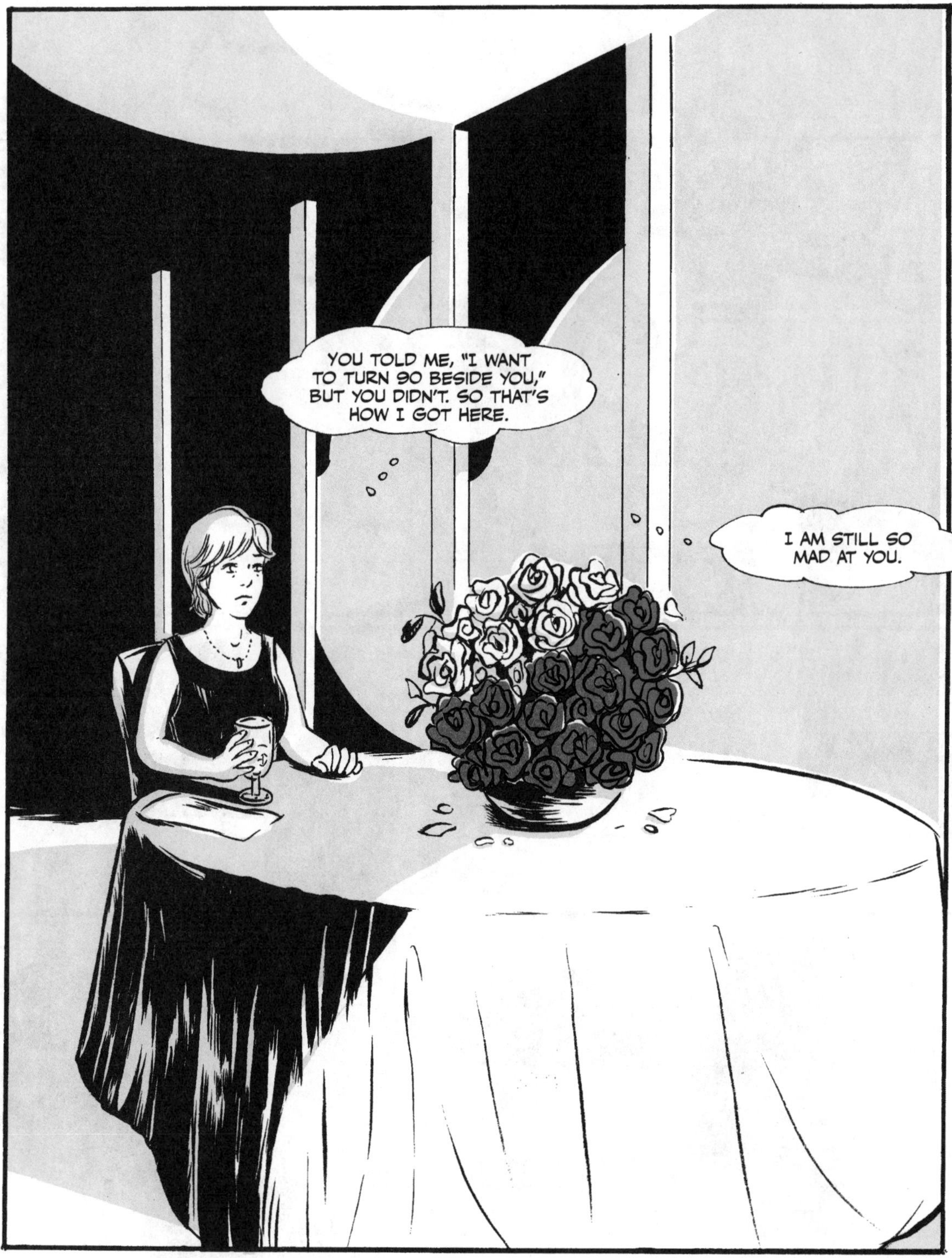
YOU TOLD ME, "I WANT TO TURN 90 BESIDE YOU," BUT YOU DIDN'T. SO THAT'S HOW I GOT HERE.
I AM STILL SO MAD AT YOU.

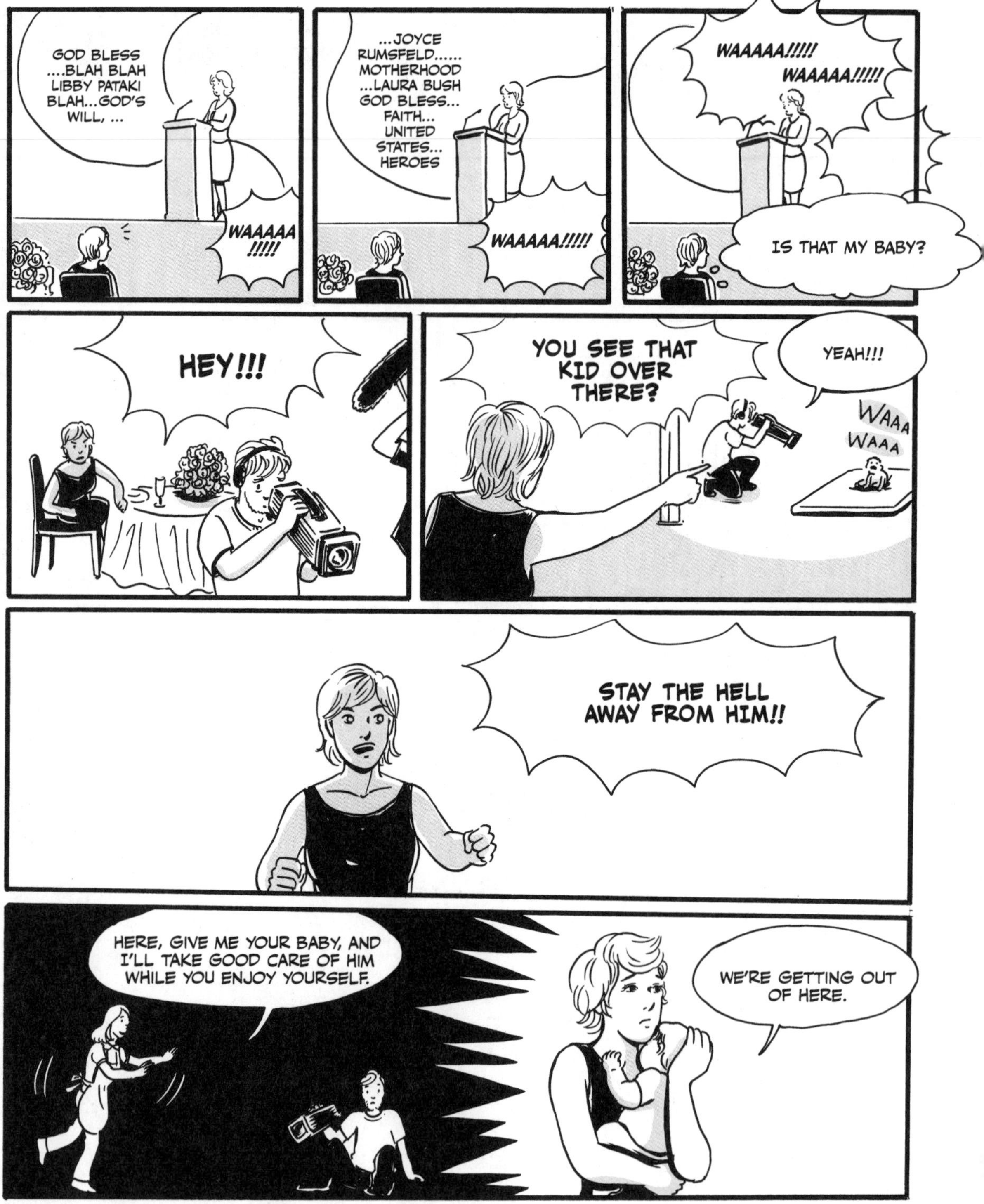
GOD BLESS ....BLAH BLAH LIBBY PATAKI BLAH...GOD'S WILL, ...
WAAAAA !!!!!
...JOYCE RUMSFELD...... MOTHERHOOD ...LAURA BUSH GOD BLESS... FAITH... UNITED STATES... HEROES
WAAAAA!!!!!
WAAAAA!!!!!
WAAAAA!!!!!
IS THAT MY BABY?
HEY!!!
YOU SEE THAT KID OVER THERE?
YEAH!!!
WAAA
WAAA
STAY THE HELL AWAY FROM HIM!!
HERE, GIVE ME YOUR BABY, AND I'LL TAKE GOOD CARE OF HIM WHILE YOU ENJOY YOURSELF.
WE'RE GETTING OUT OF HERE.

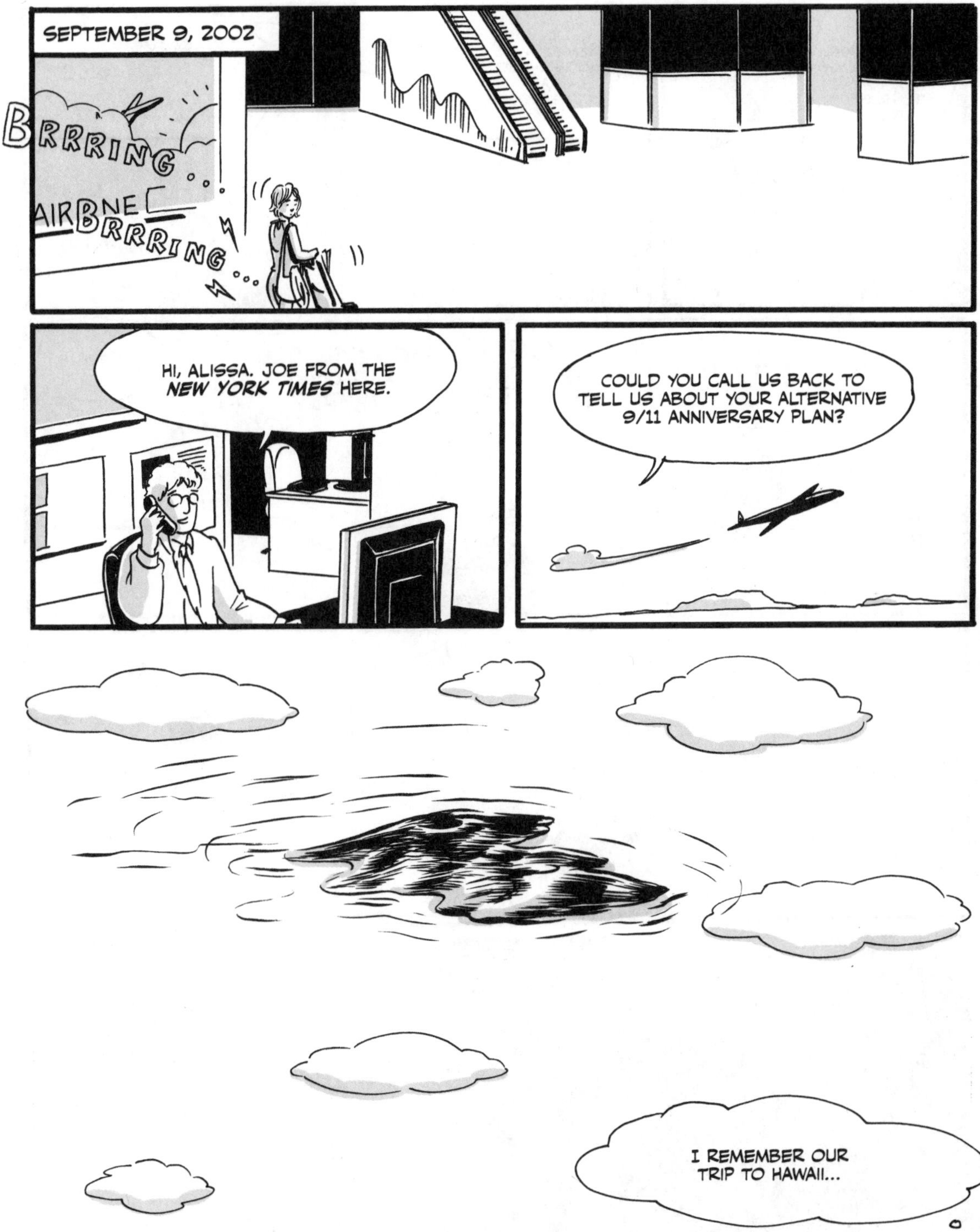
SEPTEMBER 9, 2002
BRRRING...
BRRRRING...
HI, ALISSA. JOE FROM THE *NEW YORK TIMES* HERE.
COULD YOU CALL US BACK TO TELL US ABOUT YOUR ALTERNATIVE 9/11 ANNIVERSARY PLAN?
I REMEMBER OUR TRIP TO HAWAII...

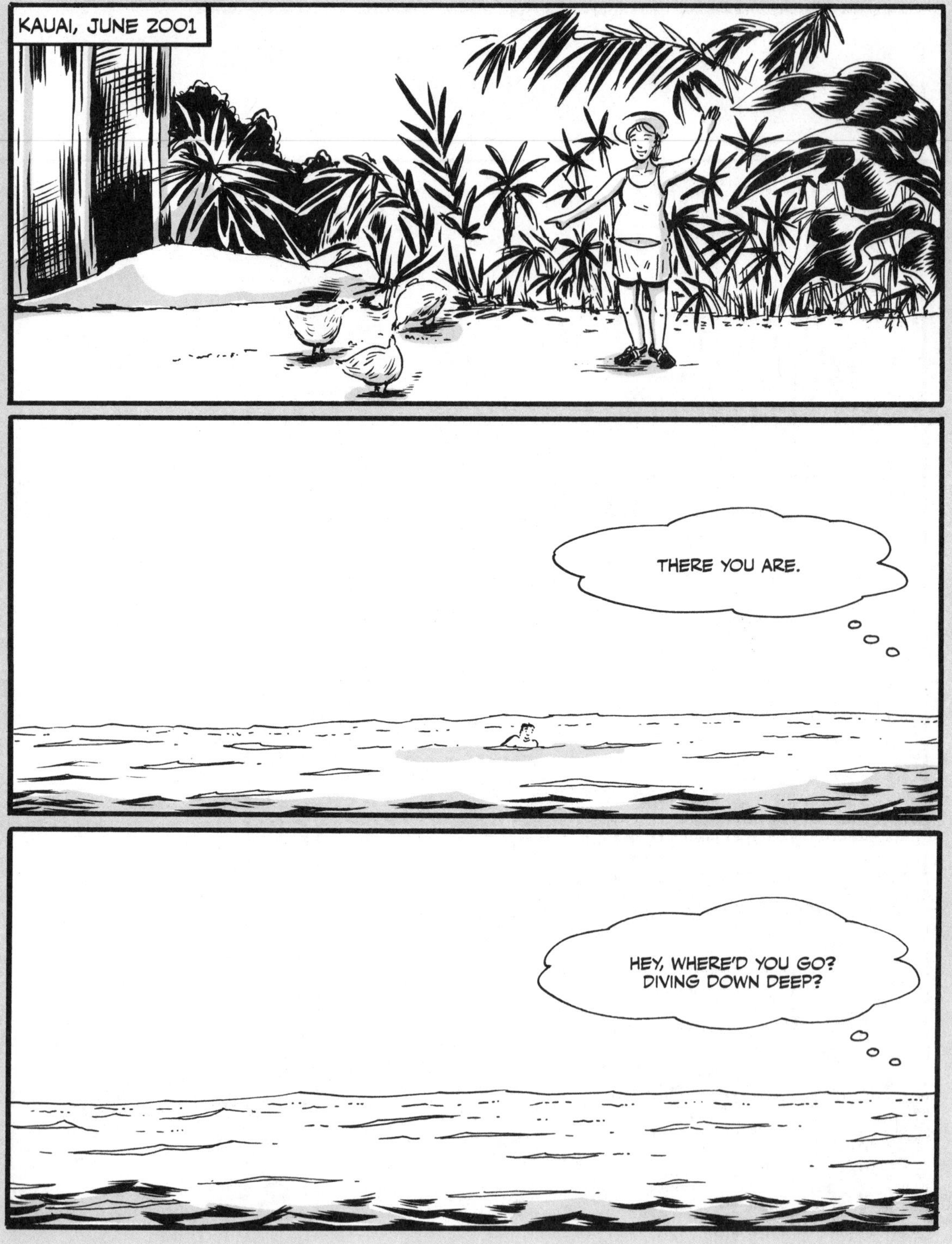
KAUAI, JUNE 2001
THERE YOU ARE.
HEY, WHERE'D YOU GO? DIVING DOWN DEEP?

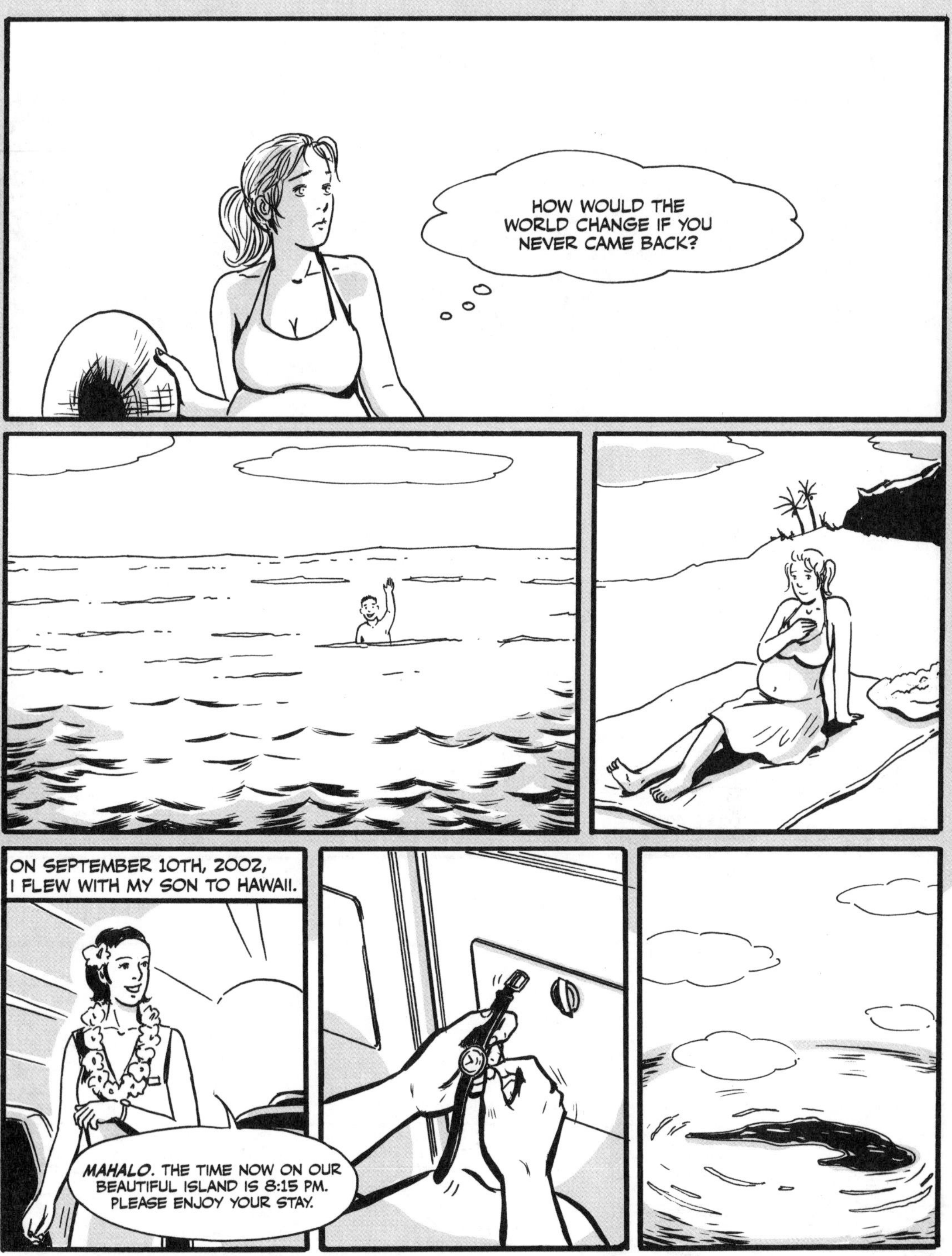
HOW WOULD THE WORLD CHANGE IF YOU NEVER CAME BACK?
ON SEPTEMBER 10TH, 2002, I FLEW WITH MY SON TO HAWAII.
MAHALO. THE TIME NOW ON OUR BEAUTIFUL ISLAND IS 8:15 PM. PLEASE ENJOY YOUR STAY.

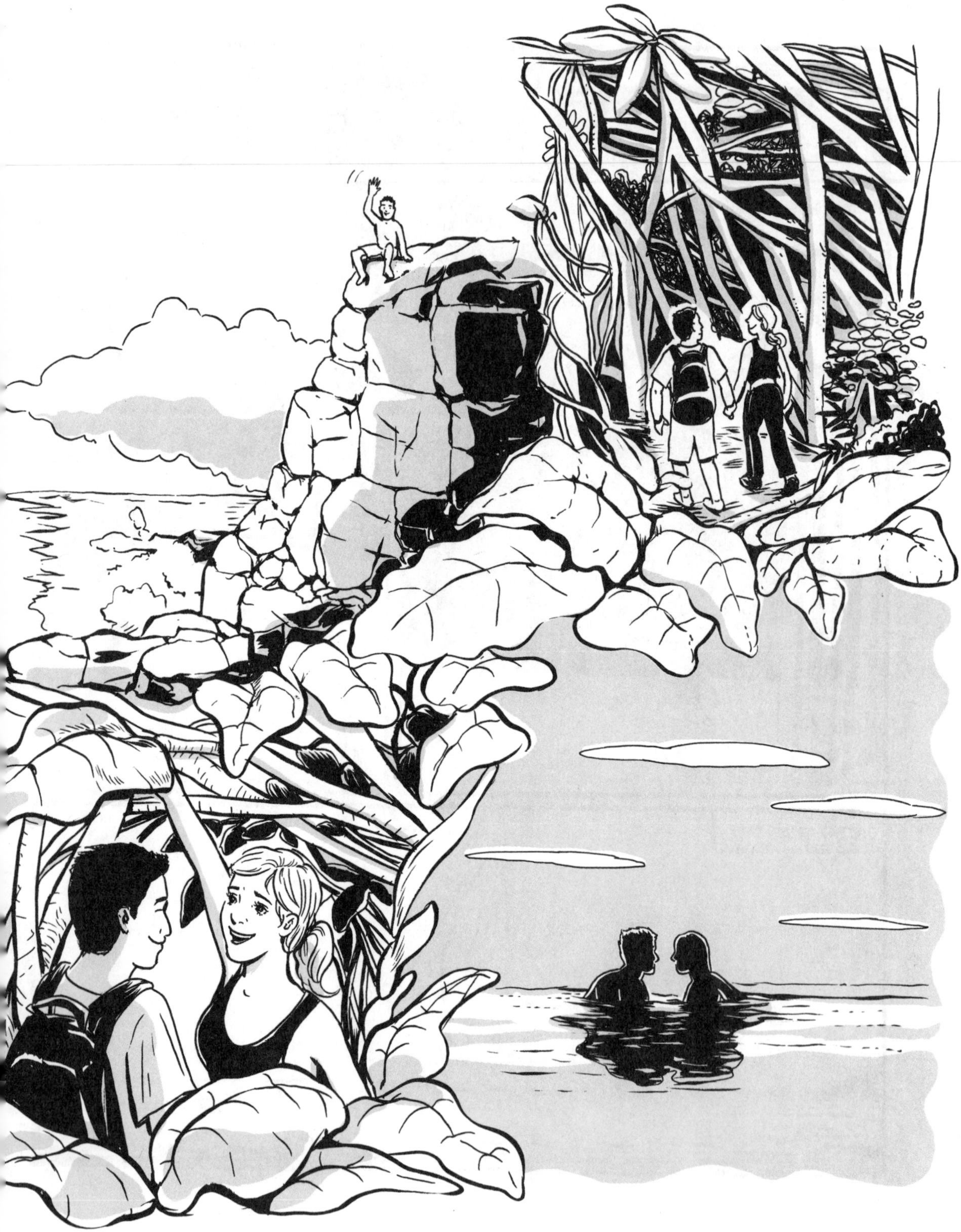

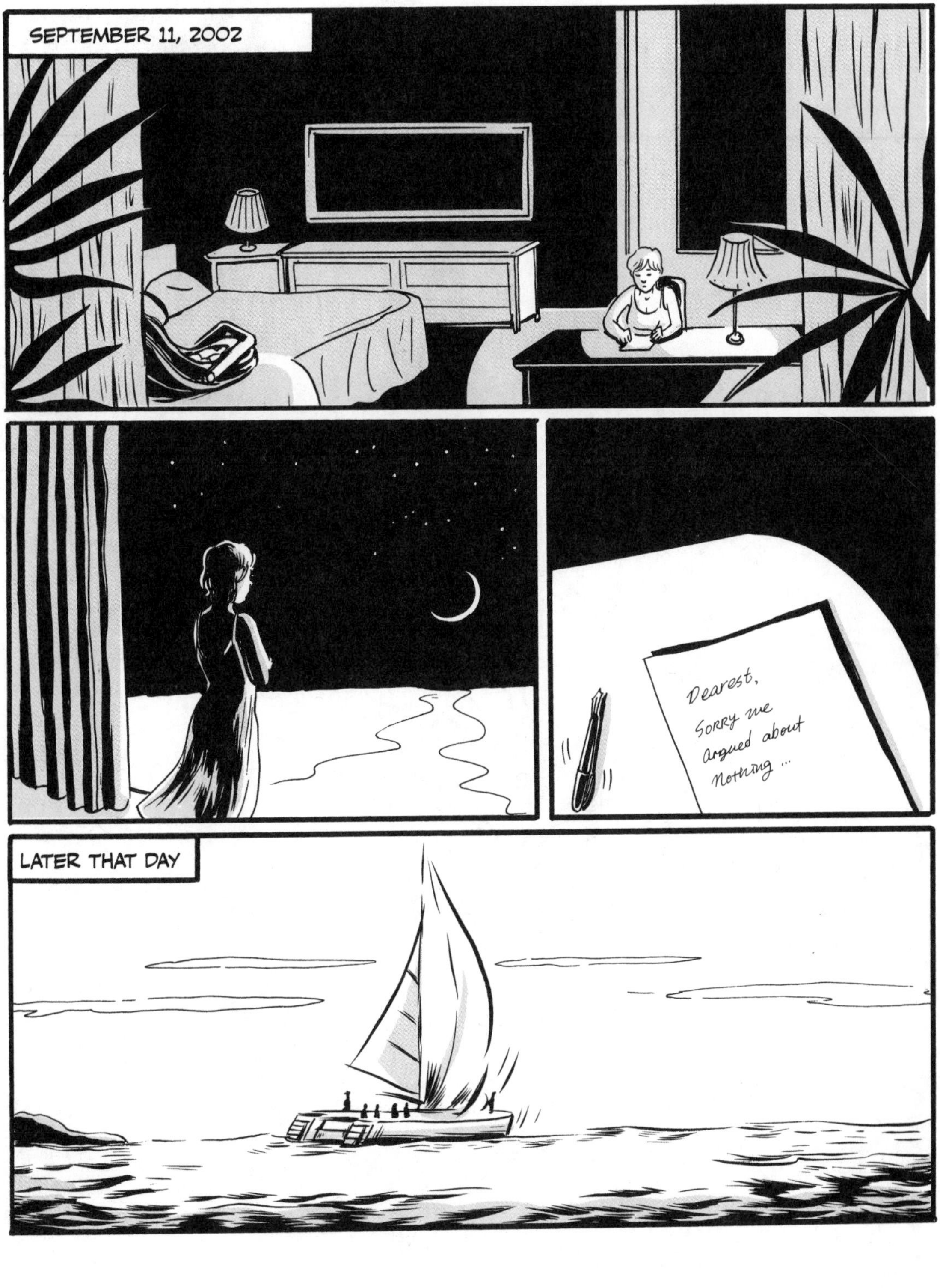
SEPTEMBER 11, 2002
Dearest,
Sorry we argued about nothing ...
LATER THAT DAY

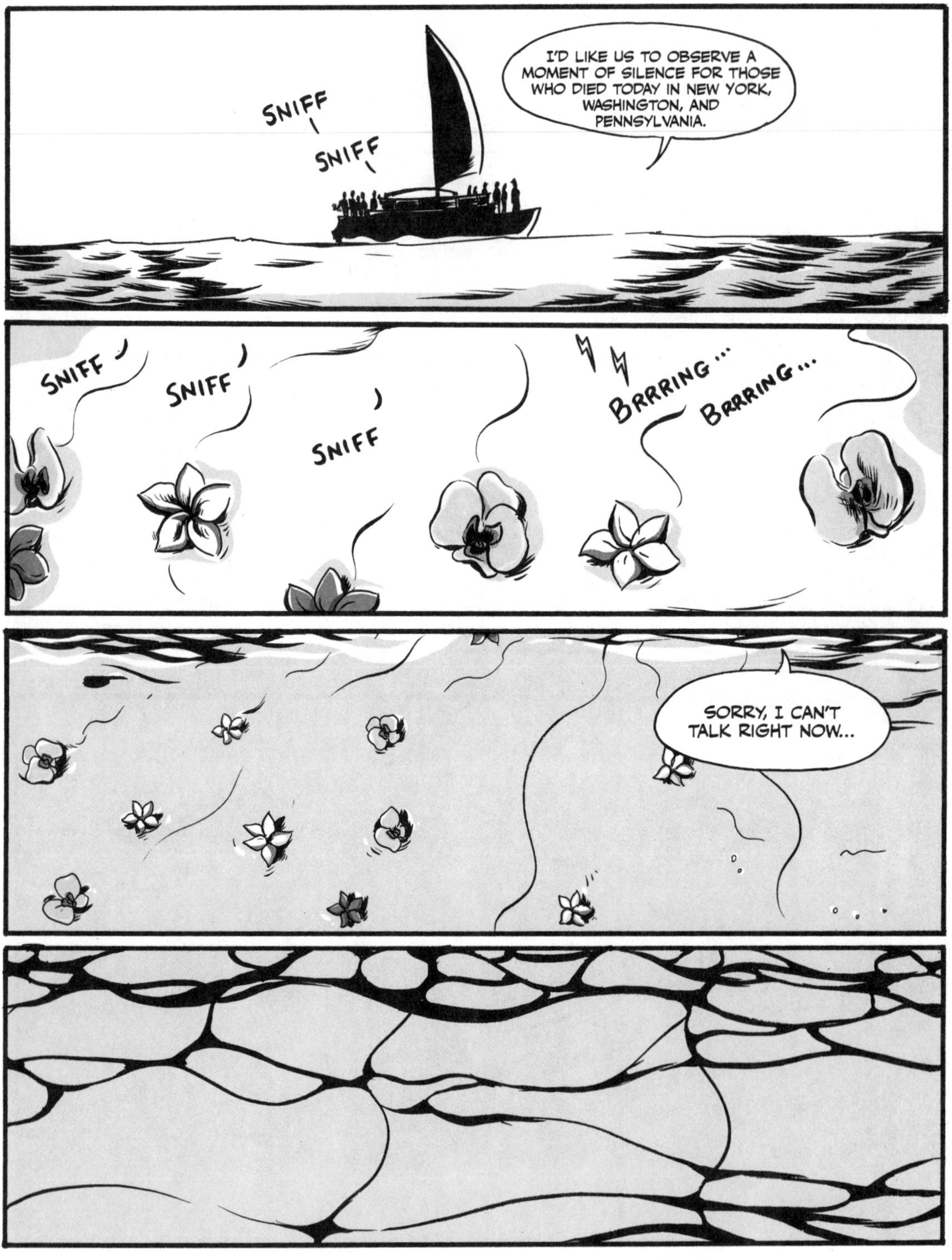
I'D LIKE US TO OBSERVE A MOMENT OF SILENCE FOR THOSE WHO DIED TODAY IN NEW YORK, WASHINGTON, AND PENNSYLVANIA.
SNIFF
SNIFF
SNIFF
SNIFF
SNIFF
BRRRING...
BRRRING...
SORRY, I CAN'T TALK RIGHT NOW...

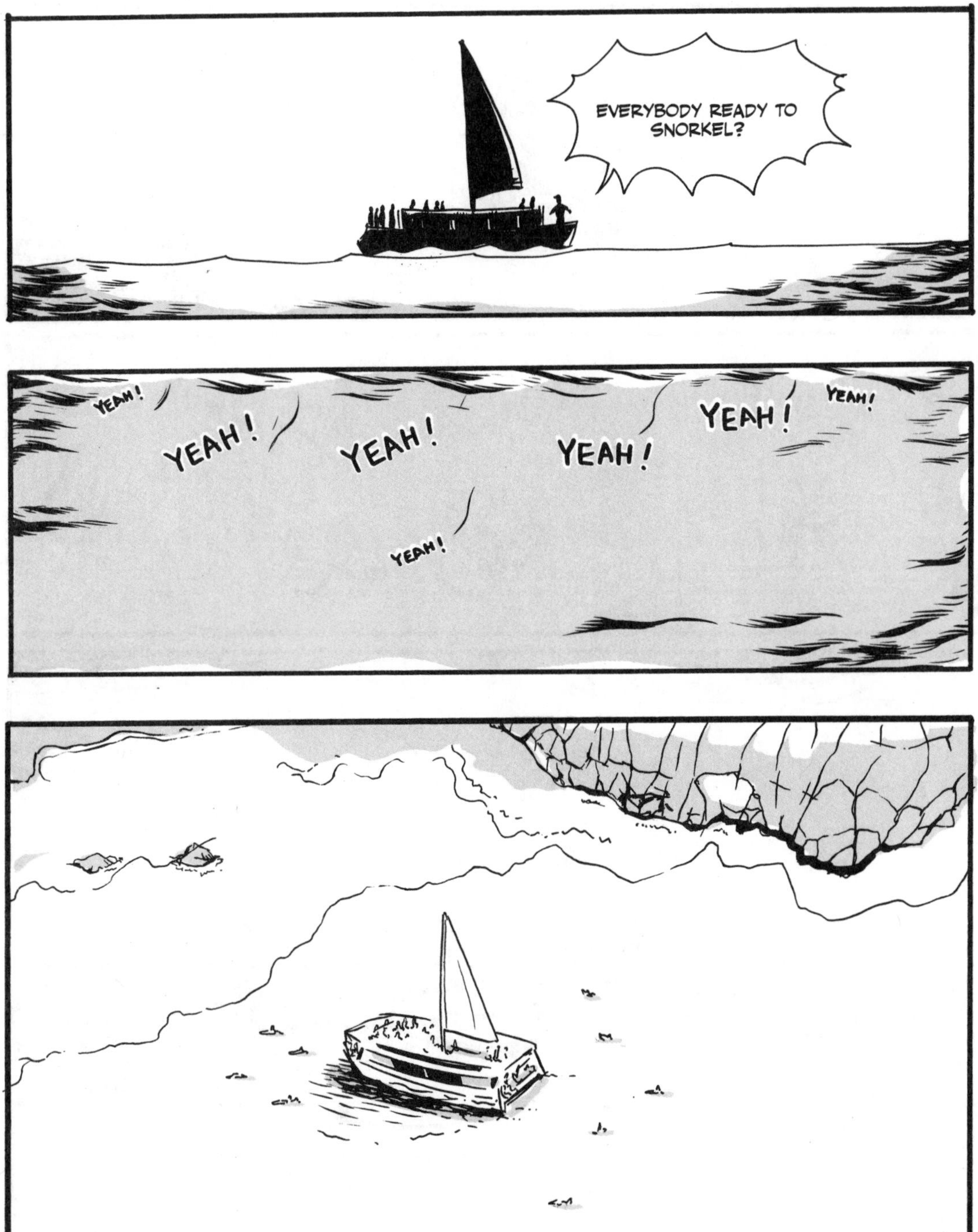
EVERYBODY READY TO SNORKEL?
YEAH!
YEAH!
YEAH!
YEAH!
YEAH!
YEAH!
YEAH!

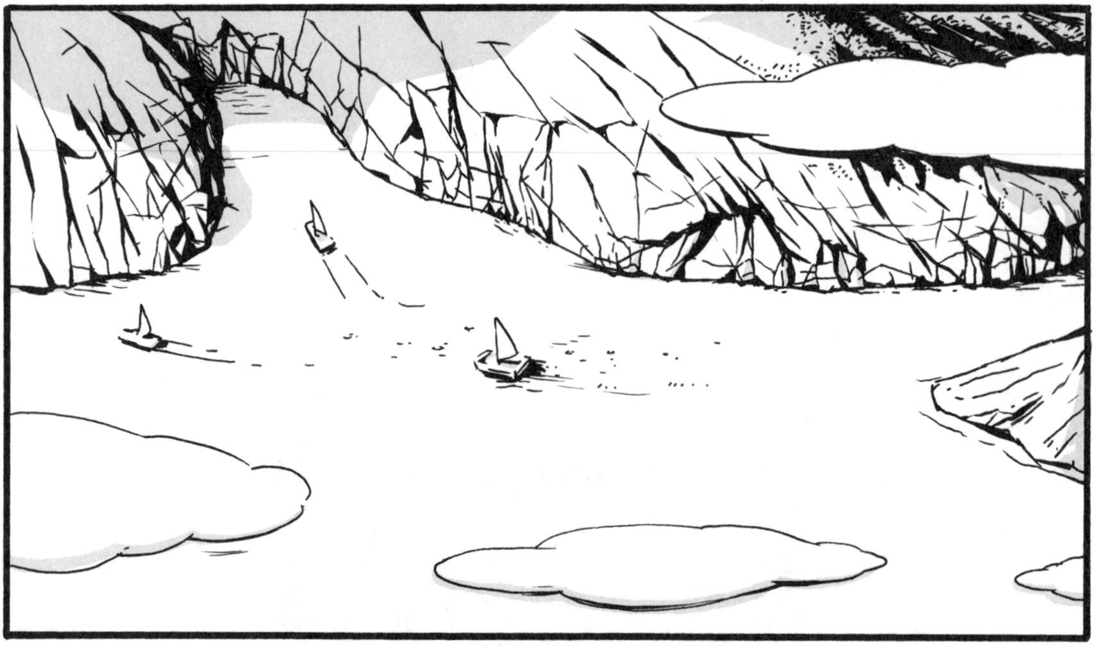

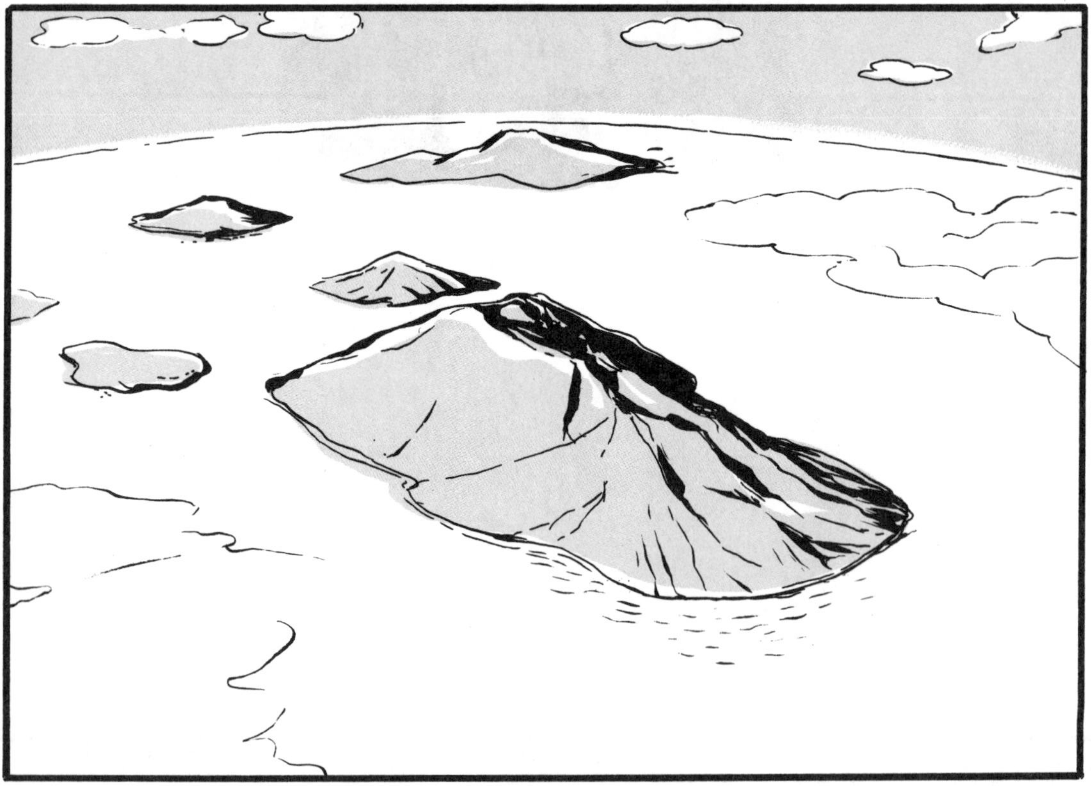

ALTHOUGH I WAS SO CONFUSED BY WHO I WAS AND HOW I WAS SUPPOSED TO BE, I KNEW SO FIERCELY THAT I WAS ALIVE, TOGETHER WITH MY SON, AND THAT IT WAS A BEAUTIFUL DAY.

ACKNOWLEDGMENTS

Seven years after a tragedy that affected us all, I look back and appreciate all the kindness and generosity that was bestowed upon us. It allowed me to create this book; it enabled us to survive and thrive.

I especially want to thank:

Eddie Torres whose life, love, and death inspired this book. Joshua Torres, our son, who gave me the most compelling reason to remember and write down everything that happened, and whose long naps gave me the time to write most of this book. My mom, Rita Rosenberg, for all her love and efforts, Maricela and her family for so much, and Lucelley, Kevin, and Nicholas for their strength despite all their heartbreak.

Carla Fine, author of *No Time to Say Goodbye* and *Touched by Suicide,* became my first mentor in widowhood and writing. Stacy Morrison, editor in chief of *Redbook Magazine,* became my second mentor and role model; she helped me connect with the publishing world and gave me the courage to deal with the marketplace and the media.

Theresa Wheeler, who was there for me at all the most important times.

I also want to thank the following people whose support meant so much; even the smallest of their gestures brightened innumerable dark days:

Boris, Kaya, Lula Ray, Leyla Ebtehadj, James Esguerra and his family, Estee Lipenholtz, Yulia Krieger, Janice Sloane, Bonnie Hannibal, my volunteer doula, the woman who gave me private Lamaze classes at Beth Israel Hospital, Anne Sloane, Marilyn, George and Stephen Sage, the woman from Texas who bought Josh pajamas, a grandmother in New Hampshire who bought Josh a savings bond with pennies she saved, a Japanese monk who fasted for donations, Peter Klausner, Maureen Vincie, Arlene Katz, Linda Anderson, Diane Perchinski, Audrea Buxbaum, Kathleen Troy, Phil Fierro, dairy farmers who sold a cow to donate to a 9/11 charity, William Pass, Kernan Huttick, Jane Wood, Kathy Kinsella and Chris, Vinicius Navarro, Michael Shafran, Stuart Rosenberg and Gena Lustig Rosenberg, Maria Theresa Rueda de Torres, Ellen Wallach, Rachel Hyman, Amy Lee and the DFTA Training and Quality Assurance units, my Chelsea neighbors, Lynae Darbes, Terri Decker, Howard, Allison and Edie Lutnick, the woman from Social Security, the handyman who bought Josh really cool sneakers, Virginia Springer, Jeff and Arlene Angard, Michael and Linda McLachlan, Kelley Wolff, Astrid, John who planted a sunflower on 22nd Street, Juan Hiraldo, Michael McMillan, William, Felicia Smith Kleiner, J. K. Rowling for Harry Potter, and so many other writers who communicated with me so much through their books, Tibor Drimmer, Suzette Rayford, Yukako Hayashi and her friends, Jimmy Koga, Devra and Robert Miller, Music Together, Sara Buff, Tara Thorne, Frances Montes, Anthony Depalma, Jennifer Sweeney, Anrea Berne, Doug Farwell, Dena Mermelstein, Patrick and Allison, Father Michael Lapsley, Calvin Luther Martin, Eve Small, Xhana, Fifa, Helen Kraus, Shelley Messing, Cassandra Cook, Assurbanipal Babilla, El Gates, S. H. Jarvis, the Hawaiian people who bought me the necklace and sent it with a special care package, Glenn Raucher, Juan Guttierez, Nabil Ashour, Colleen Kelly, Rita Lazar, Adele Welty, Bari Zahn, Rabbi Norman Patz, the 9/11 community, and all the people everywhere who gave, and especially those who gave with their hearts.

And finally, I want to thank the following people for making this book happen:

Sungyoon Choi for her creativity, hard work, and endurance; Judy Hansen for having faith in this book from the start and never letting it go; N. Christopher Couch for so much smarts and insights as well as the patience to listen to my frustrations; Chris Schluep, the best editor a writer could hope for; Chris and Lydie Raschka for giving me advice and encouragement in the home stretch; Erich Schoeneweiss, Penny Haynes, Sue Moe, Kate Blum, April Flores, and the many people at Villard/Random House who were a part of this book; Denis Kitchen, Sabrina Jones, Frank Curtis, Fahimeh Gooran,and Nahid Mozaffari for their Farsi translations; and David Chelsea.

About the Author

ALISSA TORRES lives in New York with her son and dog.

About the Illustrator

SUNGYOON CHOI is a graduate of the School of Visual Arts in New York City and has produced short comics as well as illustrations for *The New York Times.*